P9-CRO-631

THE NEW WEBSTER'S COMPUTER TERMS

Prepared by
Charles J. Sippl

LEXICON PUBLICATIONS, INC.

A

"hello" program, A program that can be designated individually for each user or account and made nonabortable. The hello program can ask the user for further identification and automatically log him or her off if the correct response is not input.

(FX) fixed area, A specific area on magnetic disk where data files (or computer programs) may be stored and protected.

A except B gate, Same as gate, A and not B (see gates).

A or not B gate, See gates.

a/d and d/a chips, Circuits for conversion of an analog signal to digital signals and back again (digital to analog).

abend, A procedure to halt a computer program, usually because of a program error or system fault, before the job has been completed. Stands for abnormal end.

abend, An abnormal ending of a program due to illegal operations or inappropriate requests of the operating system.

abort, To stop the running of a program on a computer when something goes wrong that cannot be corrected at that time.

abort timer, communications, A device that monitors dial-up modems for receipt of data traffic. After a call is established, if data is not received after a preset time, the abort timer disconnects (hangs up) the call.

absolute address, Refers to the character or group of characters indicating location in storage which the central processing unit (CPU) can interpret directly.

absolute address, An address that is the actual location in computer storage of a particular piece of data.

absolute coding, Program coding in which the instructions to the computer are written in machine language, i.e., understood directly by the computer without translation.

absolute error, The magnitude (size) of an error, disregarding whether it is a plus or minus error; or, if the error is in a vector, disregarding the direction of the error.

absolute instruction, A computer instruction used in absolute coding (see absolute coding).

absolute joystick, A joystick which provides a one-to-one correspondence between all of its various positions and all the points on the display screen with which it is used.

absolute value, The value of a number irrespective of its sign.

absorbency, A property of paper pertaining to the distribution of fibers (optical character recognition term).

abstract, (1) A short form or summary of a document. (2) To shorten or summarize a document.

abstract symbol, A symbol whose shape is not indicative of its meaning.

abstracting, automatic, Searching for the criteria by which human beings judge what should be abstracted from a document, as programmed.

a-bus, A primary internal source-bus in the ALU of some types of microcomputers.

ac, (1) alternating current, (2) automatic computer, or (3) analog computer.

ac dump, The intentional, accidental, or conditional removal of all alternating current power from a system or component.

acc, An abbreviation for accumulator.

acceleration time, The time between the interpretation of instructions to read or write and the transfer of information to or from storage (same as start time).

acceleration time, Refers to the time passing between the interpretation of a read or write instruction from the CPU to a peripheral device and the actual moment when the data transfer begins. Acceleration time is also called start time.

acceptable quality level (AQL) test, See AQL test.

acceptance test, A test used to demonstrate the capabilities and workability of a new computer system.

access, A procedure to retrieve information from or store information in a computer memory device.

access, The process of obtaining data from or placing data into storage.

access arm, A mechanical device that positions the reading and writing mechanism on a storage unit (on disk drives).

access device, sequential, A memory device, such as magnetic tape, in which data items can be reached only in sequence.

access, direct, The ability to read or write information at any location within a storage device in a constant amount of time.

access, immediate, The ability to obtain data from or place data into a storage device or register directly, without serial delay due to other units.

access, instantaneous, Getting and putting data from and into a storage device in a relatively short period of time.

access method, The method used to transfer data into or out of the memory of a computer by a program.

access, multiple, The capability of a system to send or receive (input and output) from many locations.

access, parallel, Simultaneous access to all bits in a storage location comprising a character or word (same as simultaneous access).

access, random, A method of accessing data from a storage device that is not dependent on the last access of data.

access, simultaneous, See access, parallel.

access time, Refers to the amount of time required from the instant that the CPU asks for data from a peripheral storage device until that data is transferred to it.

access time, The time between when information is called for and when it is completely accessed.

access, zero, Relates to the ability to obtain data in such a relatively short period of time that it seems like no time at all.

access-coding, minimal, Refers to a technique of coding to minimize the time used to transfer words from auxiliary storage to main storage.

accessibility, The convenience of a physical location (contrasted with availability, which relates to time available for use of the system).

accessory, An added feature designed to increase the function or add to the capacity of equipment without altering the basic function of the equipment.

account reconciliation, Preparation of a numerically sequenced list of cleared checks developed by the magnetic ink character recognition (MICR) data processing system used by banks.

accounting checks, Accuracy control methods, such as the use of control totals, cross totals, and hash totals.

accounting function, The system of keeping track of machine usage and recording it.

accounting machine, A machine that reads information from cards and that produces lists and totals on forms or continuous paper (see tabulating equipment).

accounting machine, electrical (EAM), Punched card equipment, such as sorters, collators, accounting machines, etc. (see tabulating equipment).

accumulator, A special memory location within the CPU used to perform arithmetic operations. Typically data is brought from memory into the accumulator, operated on, and moved back into a memory location.

accumulator (acc), A part of the logical-arithmetic unit of a computer used in logical and arithmetic operations (see register).

accumulator register, Part of the arithmetic unit in which the results of an operation remains, and into which numbers are brought to and from storage.

accumulator shift instruction, A computer instruction that causes the contents of an accumulator register to shift to the left or right.

accuracy, Freedom from error, as related to programs, operations, machine capability, and data.

accuracy calibration, The limit of error in the finite degree to which a device can be measured.

accuracy, conformity, A concept that includes simple and combined conformity errors.

accuracy control characters, A specific character used to indicate whether the data is in error, is to be disregarded, or can or cannot be represented on a particular device.

accuracy control system, A system of error detection and control.

acetate base, A transparent cellulose backing on magnetic tapes.

ACIA, See asynchronous communications interface adapter.

ACK, Signal for affirmative acknowledgement, as used in transmission to indicate that a previous transmission (block) has been accepted by the received. ACK signifies that the receiver is ready to accept the next block of transmission.

acknowledgement character, A character sent back to a sending station by a receiving station indicating that what was just sent was received (communications).

acknowledgment (ACK), A character or group of characters generated at a receiving device to indicate to the sending device that information has been received correctly.

ACM, See Association for Computing Machinery.

acoustic coupler, A communication device between a remote terminal and the computer by means of a telephone handset and telephone lines. The handset is placed in the acoustic coupler which converts data into a sequence of tones which are then transmitted over telephone lines.

acoustic coupler, A device with a speaker that mates with the telephone's transmitter, which also has a microphone that mates with the telephone's transmitter. To send data to the computer, the terminal operator dials the computer's number and nests the telephone into the coupler's cups.

acoustic modem, A device of the modulator-demodulator type that converts electrical signals to telephone tones and back again.

acoustical treatment, Changes made to floors, ceilings, and other surfaces of a computer center to keep the noise level down.

acquisition and control system, data, The system is designed to handle a wide variety of real-time applications, process control, and high-speed data acquisition.

acquisition, data, Operations consisting of data collection, data reduction, and digital test control applications in scientific/engineering environments. Also in remote business operations (manufacturing plants and retail outlets, warehouses, sales offices, etc.).

acronym, A word formed from the first letter or letters of the words in a name, term, or phrase; e.g., Fortran for FORmula TRANslation and Cobol from COmmon Business-Oriented Language.

action, control, The correction made for a deviation or error by a controller.

action, rate, A type of action in which the rate of correction is made proportional to how fast the condition is going awry.

action, spot, A spot on the face of a cathode ray tube (CRT) that stores a digit and holds a charge.

active element, A circuit or device that receives energy from a source other than the main input signal.

active file, A file to which entries or references are made on a current basis.

active master file, A master file containing relatively active terms.

activity, A term indicating the changes to or reference to an active file (see active file).

activity ratio, The ratio of the number of records that have activity to the total number of records in that file (see active file).

actual address, The real, designed address of a location built into a computer by the manufacturer.

actual coding, Program coding in which the instructions to the computer are written in machine language, i.e., understood directly by the computer, without translation (same as absolute coding).

actual decimal point, A decimal point that is printed as an actual character or, if in computer storage, requires a position of storage.

actual time, Performance of computing during the time an event is taking place.

actuating signal, A specific pulse in the control circuitry of computers.

ACU, See automatic calling unit.

ADA A high-level computer, U.S. government-sponsored programming language designed for real-time applications and for control of simultaneous performance of several operations.

ada language, Department of Defense (DOD), A relatively new language that gives preference to full English, words and has 62 reserved"words." It was especially designed as a military service language.

ADAPSO, See Association of Data Processing Service Organizations.

ADAPSO, Association of Data Processing Service Organizations, an association of U.S. and Canadian data processing service organizations.

ADAPT, A compiler system and a program for the numerical control of tools. It is designed to produce tapes to drive numerically controlled machine tools.

adapter, channel, A device that permits the connection between various data channels of differing equipment (communications).

adapter, communication line (CLAT), A semiautomatic device used to link buffer units with remote teletype units.

adapter, data, The data adapter is a special processor which converts the input data or output information to or from the internal codes used by the computer.

adapter, Dataphone, A brand name of a communications line adapter. Transceivers, transmitters, and receivers are Dataphone adapters or components of digital-plotting communication systems.

adapter, on-line, A device that permits a high-speed computer-memory-to-computer-memory linkage (connection).

adapter, transmission, A device that connects remote and local devices to data adapters (communications).

adapter unit, data, This device can be attached to either a selector channel or a multiplexor channel to greatly expand the input/output capabilities of the system (communications).

adapting, The ability of a system to change how it works, based on its environment.

adc, See analog-to-digital converter.

add, Boolean, A logical add (Boolean algebra); see add, logical.

add, false, A logic add (Boolean), as opposed to an arithmetic add.

add, logical, In Boolean algebra, combining two numbers in a logical sense to produce a result, as opposed to adding them in an arithmetic add.

add operation, A computer instruction to add.

add time, Refers to the time required for a computer to perform an addition, exclusive of time required to obtain quantities from storage and put sum back into storage.

add time, The time needed to perform an addition in a computer (see add-subtract time).

adder, A device that forms a sum as an output from two or more inputs.

adder, analog, A specific amplifier (analog computer) with output voltage that is the weighted sum of the input voltages.

addition, The function of combining quantities according to specific machine (computer) design and rules (data processing).

addition, destructive, The sum replaces the augend (the value of the augend is lost) in the execution of an add instruction in the computer (see augend).

addition item, An item to be added to a file in a designated place.

addition, record, A new record in a master file being updated, or a new record added to a file without moving or erasing any record in the file.

addition, serial, Addition in which pairs of digits of the two numbers are added starting in the right-most position of each.

addition table, An area or computer storage area that contains a table of numbers to be used during the table-scan concept of addition.

addition, zero access, Adding a number to another number in a computer where the resulting sum ends up in place of the second number.

add-on memories, On some systems, any combination of memories in any mix of types and speeds can be used with the LSI microprocessor.

address, (1) A label, name, or number identifying where information is stored in a computer. (2) The operand portion of a computer instruction.

address (noun), Each location in computer memory is identified by an address, which allows the computer to find the location of a specific data item (or instruction).

address (verb), To call up data from or place it into a memory location.

address, absolute, An address that is the actual location in computer storage of a particular piece of data.

address, actual, The real, designed address of a location built into a computer by the manufacturer.

address, arithmetic, Specific locations used for the results of computations.

address, base, A given address from which a final address is derived by combination with a relative address.

address, base, A number that is an address in a computer instruction and that serves as a reference point for other addresses appearing in the computer program.

address, bus, Often a unidirectional bus over which digital transmission appears to identify either a particular memory location or a particular input/output device.

address comparator, A device used for verifying that the correct address is being read. A comparison is made between the address being read and the address specified to be read.

address computation, A calculation that creates or changes the address portion of a computer instruction.

address conversion, The translation of the relative or symbolic addresses into absolute addresses either by computer or manually (see absolute address).

address, direct, One which specifies the exact storage location of an operand.

address, direct, An address in a computer instruction that indicates where the location of the operand is without any other references (synonymous with first-level address).

address, double, A computer instruction that contains an operation and that specifies the location of an operand and the result of the operation.

address, dummy, An artificial address used to show an example to someone.

address, effective, The address of the memory location that is actually accessed during execution of an instruction that requires memory access.

address, effective, The address actually used in execution of a computer instruction. It may be different from the address in the instruction in storage in that it is modified in some way prior to execution of the instruction.

address, external device (ED), This address specifies which external device the computer instruction is referring to.

address, first-level, An address in a computer instruction that indicates where the location of the operand is without any other references (synonymous with direct address).

address format, The particular arrangement, layout, or organization of the address portion of a computer instruction.

address format, The arrangement of the address parts of a computer instruction.

address, four, A computer instruction having four addresses.

address, four-plus-one, A computer instruction containing four operand addresses and one control address.

address generation, The production of numbers or symbols by means of a computer instruction; the symbols are then used to form an address.

address, immediate, A computer instruction address that is used as data by the instruction of which it is a part (synonymous with zero-level address).

address, indexed, An address in a computer instruction that is modified by the contents of an index register.

address, indirect, An address in computer instruction that refers to another address to be actually used.

address, instruction, The location (address) where an instruction is in computer storage.

address, machine, The actual address used by the computer in executing an instruction.

address modification, An operation which causes an address to be altered.

address modification, The process of changing an address in a computer instruction during the running of the computer program containing the instruction.

address, multiple, A type of instruction that specifies two or more addresses of various locations or units.

address operand, The location in storage of a part of a computer instruction; the element to be operated on or entered into an operation.

address part, The part of a computer instruction that defines the address of a register or storage location.

address register, A register in a computer where an address is stored.

address, relative, An address that is altered to an absolute address at the time the program is run on the computer.

address, single, A code that specifies a single station that is to receive traffic.

address size, The number of positions in a computer instruction used to hold an address.

address, specific, An address that indicates the exact storage location (related to absolute code).

address switches, manual, External control switches used by an operator to select a storage address.

address, symbolic, A label assigned to identify a particular element, function, or variable. Helpful to programmers in identifying fields of data: e.g., net pay might be called NETPAY, or total cost might be TOTCST, etc.

address, synthetic, an address generated by instructions in the computer program using the addresses.

address, variable, An address that is modified before it is used each time.

address, zero-level, A computer instruction address that is used as data by the instruction of which it is a part (synonymous with immediate address).

addressability, Addressability refers to the capability of a unit of memory to be addressed.

addressable register, A specifically located device in storage represented by particular storage location numbers.

addressed location, specific, In random access devices, an address that may be directly accessed without a sequential search.

addressed memory, Memory sections that contain each individual register.

addressing, The method used to address memory locations, e.g., direct, indirect, indexed.

addressing, direct, An instruction addressing mode in which the memory reference specifies a memory location that contains the data to be operated on.

addressing, direct, A method for specifically citing an operand in a computer instruction by the operand's location in storage.

addressing, fixed position, Storing or recording small units of information without disturbing adjacent information (magnetic tape).

addressing, implied, The addressing method used in certain computers in which instructions having a zero address instruction format refer automatically to the location following that effected by the last instruction executed.

addressing, indirect, (1) A method of addressing that points to the address of the address to be used. (2) Any level of addressing other than first-level or direct addressing.

addressing modes, microprocessor, Some standard addressing modes include direct, immediate, and indirect, but many processors offer other modes.

addressing, relative, Using addresses that are modified at the time the program is run on the computer. At that time the addresses are changed to absolute addresses.

addressing, specific, Same as absolute addressing.

addressing system, The method used in labeling storage locations in various computer system storage devices such as main storage, disk storage, and drum storage.

add-subtract time, The time needed to perform an addition or subtraction in a computer. It does not include the time required to get the quantities from storage and put the results back into storage.

ADI, American Documentation Institute.

ADIS, An abbreviation for automatic data interchange system, developed by Teletype Corporation.

adjacency, (1) The spacing between two consecutive printed characters. (2) The condition in which two consecutive characters are closer than the specified distance.

adjacent channel, A channel that has a frequency band adjacent to that of the reference channel.

adjacent channel interference, Such interference occurs when two modulated carrier channels are placed too close together in frequency.

adjacent channel selectivity, The ability to reject signals or channels adjacent to the desired signals.

adjoint (adjoint system), A method of computation used in the study of systems with time-varying coefficients.

administrative data processing, The business data processing functions, such as recording, classifying, and summarizing transactions usually of a financial nature.

administrative terminal system (ATS), A time-sharing software system developed by IBM.

ADP, See automatic data processing.

ADPE, An abbreviation for automatic data processing equipment.

ADPS, An abbreviation for automatic data processing system.

advance item, A technique to group records for operating successively on different records in memory.

AED, The abbreviation for automated engineering design system.

AFIPS, American Federation of Information Processing Societies.

AGC, See automatic gain control.

agenda, An ordered list of the major operations of a procedure for a solution or computer run (this usage corresponds somewhat to the "agenda" for a meeting).

AIB, An abbreviation for American Institute of Banking.

alarm, audible, A sound signal used to indicate a malfunction or error condition in a computer program.

alarm-repeated transmission, An alarm that can be heard after three successive failures to transmit or receive a transmission line.

ALD, See analog line driver.

alertor, An alarm device that "watches" the person who watches the machine. If there is no movement from the person in a certain length of time, the alarm sounds.

algebra, Boolean, A type of algebra names after George Boole (uses binary logic, i.e., the logical operations OR, AND, NOT, etc.).

algebra, switching, Boolean algebra, applied to switching circuits, etc.

algebraic expression, Statements made of symbols and signs following mathematical syntax and rules.

algebraic language, a language using symbols and letters to express various mathematical relationships.

algebraic-oriented language, An incorrect name for ALGOL.

ALGOL, A computer language developed by an international committee in the 1960s. ALGOL stands for ALGOrithmic Language.

ALGOL, An acronym for ALGOrithmic Language, a data processing language.

algorithm, A sequence of instructions that tell how to solve a particular problem.

algorithm, A fixed step-by-step procedure used to accomplish a given result.

algorithm, scheduling, A set of mathematical rules included in the scheduling routine of an executive program (in an operating system).

algorithm translation, Using a specific computational method to translate one language to another.

algorithmic, The process of using algorithms.

algorithmic language, A language used to solve problems using algorithms.

algorithmic routine, A type of program or routine that works toward solution of a problem in a distinct method as opposed to trial-and-error methods.

alias, A name for something that is not the real name but the name of something of the same nature or type, a slang term such as red tape, GIGO, etc.

alignment, The process of adjusting components of a system for proper interrelationship, often applied to the synchronization of components in a system.

allocate, To assign actual storage locations to program routines and subroutines.

allocation, The assignment of blocks of data to specified storage locations.

allocation and loading program, A program that links together relocatable binary elements for execution or future use.

allocation, dynamic storage, A method of assigning storage areas for subroutines to the first storage available. The effect is to optimize storage use.

allocation, resource, The process of determining the best use of men, machine, material, money, space, and other resources in a project or to accomplish some goal. A computer program may be used to accomplish this.

allocation, storage, A method of reserving blocks of storage for certain information.

all-purpose computer, A computer that has a combination of characteristics that is more than usually thought of for a general-purpose vs. special-purpose computer.

alpha, (1) The first letter of the Greek alphabet, and thus a symbol representing "first." (2) An abbreviation for alphanumeric. (3) A feature of representation of data in alphabetical characters in contract to numerical.

alphabet , A character set excluding numbers.

alphabetic, Using the letters of the alphabet and special characters of period,, comma, asterisk, and others.

alphabetic code, A system of alphabetic abbreviations used in data processing (contrasted with numeric code).

alphabetic string, A sequence of letters of an alphabet; a character string.

alphabetic word, A word that consists only of letters.

alphabetic-numeric, The character set that includes the letters of the alphabet, numbers, and other symbols.

alphameric, The contraction of "alphanumeric" or "alphabetic-numeric."

alphameric characters, A generic term for numbers, letters, and special characters.

alphameric code, A system of coding using alphameric characters.

alphanumeric, 1 A contraction of alphabetic-numeric. 2 Refers to a character set that contains both letters and numerals, and usually special characters.

alphanumeric, Same as alphabetic-numeric.

alphanumeric instruction, A computer instruction that can be used as well with numeric or alphabetic data.

alphanumerical, A coding system using alphameric characters.

alter mode, A mode of operation of a computer that permits altering to take place.

alteration gate, Same as gate OR (see gates).

altering, An operation for changing, adding, or deleting information in a computer.

alternate optima, Different solutions to the same optimization problem.

alternate routine, Assignment of a secondary communications path that is used when the primary path is not available.

alternation, tape, Selection of first one tape unit then another to allow a computer operator to put on and remove tapes during processing.

alternative denial gate, Same as gate, NAND (see gates).

ALU, See arithmetic and logical unit.

AM, See amplitude modulation.

AMA, (1) American Management Association, (2) American Medical Association.

ambient, The surrounding medium.

ambient conditions, The conditions of the surrounding medium (pressure, etc.).

ambiguity, Having more than one meaning.

American National Standards Institute (ANSI), Formerly ASA and USASI, an organization that develops and publishes industrial standards (see American Standards Association and United States of America Standards Institute). ANSI is a nonprofit, nongovernmental organization that serves as the national clearinghouse and coordinating body for the voluntary standards in the United States as regards computers and information processing.

American Standard Code for Information Interchange (ASCII), A standard coding method for computer representation of numbers, letters, etc.

American Standards Association (ASA), Formerly United States of America Standards Institute (USASI), now American National Standards Institute (ANSI). An association responsible for the establishment of American standards. Specific subgroups are responsible for the data processing industry standards.

ammeter, An instrument used to measure electric current in amperes (amps).

amortization, A financial term that, when used in a computer context, usually refers to the periodic allocation or charge of the costs of computer equipment over its useful life.

ampere, A unit of electrical current or rate of flow of electrons. One volt across one ohm (of resistance) causes a current flow of one ampere.

amphibolous, Ambiguity, uncertainty, doubtfulness.

amphibology, An ambiguous phrase.

amplification, 1 The strengthening or gain of a weak signal. Contrasts with attenuation. 2 The ratio between the output signal power and the input signal power of a device.

amplifier, A device capable of putting out an enlargement of the wave form of electric current, voltage, or power that is the input.

amplifier, buffer, An amplifier that has been designed to isolate a preceding circuit from a following circuit.

amplifier, differentiating, A specific amplifier in analog computers.

amplifier, high gain, A special voltage amplifier used in analog computers.

amplifier, power, A circuit that amplifies both voltage and current.

amplifier, see-saw, Same as sign-reversing amplifier.

amplifier, sign-reversing, An amplifier whose output and input voltage are equal in magnitude but opposite in sign.

amplifier, video, An electronic circuit that strengthens electronic signals sent through it within a certain amplitude/frequency range.

amplify, To utilize an input of voltage, current, or power so as to obtain an output of greater magnitude through the relay action of a transducer.

amplitude, The strength of a signal. Amplitude and time are the two parameters of any signal.

amplitude, The maximum numerical value of a periodically varying quantity, e.g., an alternating current, a radio wave, etc.

amplitude modulation (AM), A method of conveying information through a carrier signal by modifying the carrier signal's amplitude. The most common use of AM is in radio broadcasting, although it is also used in data communications.

amplitude modulation (am), A form of modulation where the amplitude of the carrier varies as the amplitude of the original signal.

amplitude, pulse, The maximum instantaneous value of a pulse.

analog, Pertaining to data in the form of continuously variable physical quantities. Contrasts with DIGITAL.

analog, The representation of numerical values by means of physical variables (contrasted with digital).

analog adder, A specific amplifier (analog computer) with output voltage that is the weighted sum of the input voltages.

analog channel, A type of channel on which data transmitted can take any value within the limits of the channel.

analog comparator, A device that performs range checking on digital values developed by an analog/digital converter.

analog computer, A computer that uses physical quantities - such as voltage, current, or resistance - to represent numerical quantities to solve operational problems.

analog computer (ac), A type of analog computer (see analog computer).

analog device, a device that represents numbers as physical quantities; e.g., by lengths as in a slide rule, or by voltage currents as in an analog computer.

analog digital analog converter system, This is a system that performs fast, real-time data conversions between analog and digital computers.

analog divider, Made up of two analog units to perform analog division.

analog input expander, A unit that permits an analog input system to be configured around the data adapter unit.

analog integration, a process performed in an analog computer by means of an operational amplifier with a capacitor instead of a resistor in the feedback loop.

analog interrupt mode, An analog computer's being in the "hold" mode, also called the "freeze" or "interrupt" mode. All computing is stopped, and the values of the variables are frozen (held where they are).

analog line driver (ALD), A device in an analog computer (a power amplifier).

analog multiplexor/R, A device used to provide low-level differential switching of analog input signals. High-level signals can also be handled.

analog multiplexor/S (HLSE), A solid-state, high-level, single-ended (HLSE) multiplexor.

analog multiplier, An analog device that develops an analog product (result of multiplying).

analog network, An arrangement of circuits representing physical values to express mathematical relationships through electric or electronic means.

analog output, large scale integration (LSI), As opposed to digital output, the amplitude is continuously proportionate to the stimulus, the proportionality being limited by the resolution of the device. Some chips or single circuits are microminiaturized, but they combine these linear and digital functions for converters and codecs (coder decoders).

analog representation, A representation having discrete values but continuously variable.

analog scaling, The process of restricting the variable in an analog computer so as not to exceed the prescribed limits of the machine.

analog start control, A push button to start a problem on an analog device.

analog stop control, This control ends processing in an analog device and permits the final values to be read.

analog-to-digital conversion, The process of converting analog signals from a voltage level to digital information using an analog digital converter (adc).

analog-to-digital converter (adc), The device that changes electrical analog voltages into digital values for acceptance in a digital processor's memory.

analysis, The study of problems using systematic procedures breaking down the complex entity into constituent parts and examining their relationship, the ultimate goal being the construction of an algorithm for computer solution.

analysis, The process of examining a problem and its elements using a defined procedure.

analysis area, An area of main storage in which data that is required to monitor or debug programs is written.

analysis block, A block of computer storage in which testing or statistical data is stored.

analysis, contour, A reading technique in optical character recognition (OCR) used for handwritten material because of the nonstandardized appearance of the input.

analysis, dynamic, The study of effects on controlled variables in a control system with disturbance inputs.

analysis, file, A study of data file characteristics.

analysis, logic, The analysis used to determine what specific steps are required to produce the desired computer output.

analysis mode, A mode of computer operation in which program testing data or statistical data may be automatically recorded.

analysis, network load, A listing of characteristics such as volumes of documents, frequency of processing, and a special time requirement in a station-to-station message sending environment.

analysis, numerical, The study of methods that may be used to obtain solutions to mathematical problems and of the potential errors in such solutions.

analysis, operations, The scientific approach to solving operational problems (such as linear programming, PERT, statistical theory, etc.).

analysis, procedure, An analysis of a business activity to determine precisely what must be accomplished and how.

analysis, sensitivity, An analysis of the results of tests or trials of values to determine the response, interdependence, etc. of the values.

analysis, statistical, A technique that uses mathematical means and computer capability to handle a wide variety of business and scientific problems when large amounts of data must be evaluated and analyzed.

analysis, stroke, A method of analysis used in character recognition.

analysis, systems, The study of an activity, procedure, method, or any such element to determine what should be accomplished and how.

analysis, variance, A statistical estimate of probabilities (by comparing variances).

analyst, A person who is skilled and trained to define and analyze problems and design solutions that may be implemented by a computer.

analyst, computer applications, A job classification of employees who give software oriented technical sales support to salespersons of computer equipment.

analyst, programmer, A person who is skilled in computer programming and problem definition and solution.

analyst, systems, A person who defines a problem in data processing terms and may indicate to programmers the directions for specific data processing solutions.

analyst, systems, A person who designs information handling systems which will be implemented in part on a computer.

analytic relationship, The relationship that exists between concepts and their corresponding terms, by their definition and inherent scope of meaning.

analytical engine, A general-purpose computer conceived by Charles Babbage in 1833.

analytical graphics, Usually concerns business graphics which are intended for use as analytical decision-making tools as opposed to graphics suitable for presentations to clients.

analytical statistics, Used to draw statistical inferences about characteristics of a ''universe'' of data from a sample.

analyzer, A computer routine used to analyze a computer program by summarizing instruction references to storage and tracing sequences of branches.

analyzer, differential, A computer used to solve many types of differential equations (usually an analog computer).

analyzer, digital differential (DDA), A specific incremental differential analyzer, generally electronic (see analyzer, differential).

analyzer, network, An analog device that is used to simulate electrical networks.

ancillary equipment, Same as peripheral equipment.

AND, A Boolean algebra operator that gives a value of true only when both variables connected by the AND are true.

AND gate, See gates.

AND NOT gate, Same as A and not B gate or B and not A gate (see gates).

angstrom, A unit of wavelength.

annex memory, Same as buffer.

annex storage, Same as associative storage.

annotation, A note added by way of comment or explanation.

annunciator, An electrically controlled signaling apparatus for indicating which of the connecting lines is calling.

ANSI, See American National Standards Institute.

answer back, voice (VAB), A prerecorded voice response to a telephone-type terminal that is linked to a computer.

antenna, A metallic device used for radiating or receiving radio waves.

anticipatory staging, The moving of blocks of storage between disk and main memory in anticipation of their potential need by running programs.

anticoincidence gate, Same as gate, exclusive OR (see gates).

AP, See attached processor.

aperture, An opening or open space; refers to a type of card.

aperture card, A card with an opening containing microfilm.

APL, See automatic programming language.

append, A procedure to add something to the end of something else. For example, when data is added to the end of an existing file, the file is said to have been appended.

appliance computer, Those types of systems that can be attached or embedded within various appliances for control purposes; or those systems that control a variety of automatic functions usually to operate home-oriented or special environmental tasks.

application, The system or problem to which a computer solution is applied.

application, business, Data processing applications such as inventory, sales, purchasing, payroll, etc. (contrasted with scientific applications).

application, computer, A problem or job to be solved or accomplished on a computer.

application, inquiry, A computer application that involves the interrogation of stored information.

application notes, A particular form of documentation endemic to the semiconductor industry that refers to engineering detail or changes or problems of design of microcomputers or their component parts.

application package, A set of computer programs and/or subroutines used to solve problems in a particular application.

application, real-time, Access of computer information in a real-time environment.

application, scientific, A computer application or solution to a scientific problem (as opposed to commercial or business applications).

application, slave, A computer application in which two computers perform the same functions at the same time and if any malfunction occurs in one computer, the other (the slave) takes over.

application, stand-by, An application in which two or more computers are used in one system and, as in the case of an inquiry system, all are available for immediate activation and action in case of failure of one of them.

applications study, The process of determining the methods and procedures for using a computer to solve specific problems.

approach, An arrangement of events to accomplish a goal (same as method).

approach, brute force, To try to undertake with existing equipment a mass of problems that don't use precise computation or logical manipulation.

approach, heuristic, a trial-and-error method of problem solving.

approach, systems, Solving a problem from the "big picture" vantage point, not solving a bunch of little problems and then trying to put them all together.

APT, See automatic programming tool.

APT III, An extended version of APT.

AQL (acceptable quality level test), The level is usually of some percentage, say 1%. If more than 1% of various parts fail, the entire lot fails to meet the acceptable quality level and is rejected.

arbitrary access, Equal access time to all computer memory locations.

area, In data processing, a part of computer storage set aside for specific purposes.

area, analysis, An area of main storage in which data that is required to monitor or debug programs are written.

area, common storage, A specified common area in computer storage referenced by Fortran and other programs.

area, constant, An area of main storage set aside for the storage of a value that remains constant ("constant" means doesn't change).

area, contact, The surface in common between two (electrical) conductors, a connector and conductor, or two connectors across which electricity flows.

area, fixed (FX), A specific area on magnetic disk where data files (or computer programs) may be stored and protected.

area, input, A specified section of computer storage reserved for receiving data that comes into the computer.

area, input/output, A specified section of computer storage reserved for data that comes into the computer or goes out of the computer (to and from input/output devices).

area, instruction, A part of computer storage where program instructions are stored.

area masks, weighted, A set of characters (in character recognition) that theoretically render all input specimens unique, regardless of size or style.

area, output, A specified section of computer storage reserved for data that goes out of a computer (to a printer, tape drivers, or other devices).

area search, A term used in information retrieval to describe examination of a collection of data and selection of those items that pertain to one group, such as a class or category.

area, storage, A specific location or locations used for defined purposes, such as input/output area, constant area, or an area containing a program, etc.

area, temporary storage, An area of computer memory used for intermediate states of computation (sometimes called "scratch-pad" memory).

area, user, An area of magnetic disk storage containing user programs and subroutines, contrasted with reserved areas containing compilers, etc.

argument, As in the argument of a function, e.g. f (x) or sin (x), where x is the argument.

arithmetic address, Relates to specific locations used for the results of computations.

arithmetic and logic unit (ALU), The CPU chip in microprocessors that actually executes the operations requested by an input command. In all computers some combination of arithmetic and/or logic operation execution is required. The arithmetic and logic unit performs this function.

arithmetic check, Verifying an arithmetic calculation, e.g., multiplying 4 x 2 to check the operation 2 x 4.

arithmetic, double precision, Uses two computer words of memory to represent one number, when a single word won't provide enough accuracy in arithmetic calculations.

arithmetic expression, An expression made up of data names, numbers, and symbols, such as: AMT + 3 or TOTAL :- AVG.

arithmetic instruction, A computer instruction to add, subtract, multiply, divide, take the square root of, etc.

arithmetic, internal, The arithmetic calculations performed by the arithmetic unit (in the CPU) of a computer.

arithmetic logic unit (ALU), That part of the CPU which performs arithmetic operations. The ALU is composed of circuitry which is able to do binary arithmetic and Boolean logic operations.

arithmetic, multiprecision, A form of computer arithmetic in which two or more computer words may be used to represent each number.

arithmetic operation, A computer operation of ordinary arithmetic operations performed on numbers (contrasted with logical operation).

arithmetic, parallel, Arithmetic operations in a computer where all digits of a number are operated on simultaneously (contracted with arithmetic, serial).

arithmetic register, The particular register in a computer that holds operands for certain operations, e.g., it may hold the multiplier for multiplication.

arithmetic relation, A relation which consists of two arithmetic expressions separated by a relational operator, such as $\langle , \rangle$.

arithmetic section, See arithmetic unit and ALU.

arithmetic, serial, Arithmetic operations in a computer where each digit of a number is operated on one at a time (contrasted with arithmetic, parallel).

arithmetic shift, Shifting the digits of a number to the left or right (in a unit of the computer); has the effect of multiplying or dividing the number (e.g., multiplying or dividing by 10 for each place shifted in a decimal number).

arithmetical operation, A computer operation performed following arithmetic rules, i.e., the operands are the addend and augend, the result is the sum.

arm, access, A mechanical device that positions the reading and writing mechanism on a storage unit (on disk drives).

armed state, The state of an interrupt level in which it can accept and "remember" an input signal.

ARPANET, A large packet-switched communications network developed by the Department of Defense in 1969 that continues to serve as a model for networks of this type.

ARQ, See automatic request for repetition.

array, An arrangement of data in computer storage such as a row of data or data columns and rows, e.g., a table of numbers.

array, data, An arrangement of data on magnetic tape, punched cards, computer storage, etc.

array, indexed, An array of data items in which the individual items can be accessed by use of a subscript or index. An indexed array is also called a subscripted array, subscripted list, or indexed list.

array processor, An especially fast processor (computer) that reduces the time to do strings of iterative arithmetic such as matrix and signal processing operations, using in effect coprocessors.

arrows, cursor, The keys on a keyboard that are marked with arrows and control the movement of the cursor without explicitly typing characters. The direction of the arrows on the keys indicate in which direction the cursor will move.

art-assembly system, A shorthand English language computer programming system developed by Univac.

articulation, As it relates to communications, the percentage of spoken phonemes (see phoneme) that can be correctly understood by a listener.

artificial cognition, The ability of a machine to optically sense a character and determine what character it is by comparing it to a set of characters and selected the one nearest in shape.

artificial intelligence, An area of study in the field of computer science. Artificial intelligence is concerned with the development of computers able to engage in human-like thought processes such as learning, reasoning, and self-correction.

artificial intelligence, (1) The concept that machines can be improved to assume some capabilities normally thought to be like human intelligence such as learning, adapting, self correction, etc. (2) The extension of human intelligence through the use of computers, as in times past physical power was extended through the use of mechanical tools. (3) In a restricted sense, the study of techniques to use computers more effectively by improved programming techniques.

artificial language, A programming language whose rules and syntax were explicitly developed before it was used. For example, PASCAL and COBOL are both artificial languages.

artificial language, A computer language that has been designed for ease of communication in a particular area (application), but that is not natural to that area (contrasted with a natural language that has come about through long usage).

artificial perception, Same as artificial cognition.

ARU, See audio response unit.

ASA, See American Standards Association.

ASA, See American Standards Association.

ascending sort, Placing data records in order, where each record has a higher (or equal) number (or letter) such as a set of data records in Social Security number order, where each record has a higher number than the one before it.

ASCII, American Standard Code for Information Interchange, in which binary numbers represent alphanumeric symbols.

ASCII, See American Standard Code for Information Interchange.

ASIS, American Society for Information Science.

ASLIB, Association of Special Libraries and Information Bureaus.

ASP, See attached support processor.

aspect card, A card used for the accession numbers of documents in an information retrieval system.

aspect indexing, A method of indexing by use of two or more terms so that all information relating to an items may be found.

aspect ratio, The proportions of the TV picture area; the aspect ratio of television is four units of width to every three units of height. This is expressed as a 3 x 4 or 3:4 aspect ratio.

ASR, See automatic send-receive set.

assemble, The process of translating a computer program (in an assembly language) from the symbolic form that the programmer has written to the machine language (computer's own language).

assembler, A program which takes the mnemonic form of the computer's language and converts it into binary object code for execution.

assembler, A computer program that translates the symbolic coding that a programmer wrote into machine language (that the computer "understands").

assembler, macro, An assembler that brings high-level language features to assembly language programming. They translate a single multi-argument source line into a sequence of machine instructions.

assembler program, Same as assembler.

assembler, symbolic, An assembler that lets the programmer write computer instructions in a symbolic language.

assembly, The process of translation of computer programs that is accomplished by an assembler.

assembly, connector, The combination of an electrical plug inserted into a mated receptacle.

assembly control statements, Special statements (instructions) written by a programmer and used in the assembly process by the assembly program.

assembly language, A computer programming language in which one assembly language statement translates into one machine computer language instruction; as contrasted with high-level language in which one language statement usually translates into many machine language instructions.

assembly language, development system, A specific assembly language of various CPU chips that is designed to minimize the number of different instruction mnemonics or operation codes.

assembly language listing, A computer-printed listing of the computer program that was processed by an assembler.

assembly language output, Same as assembly language listing.

assembly language processor, An assembler with greater capability (more sophisticated) than an ordinary assembler.

assembly line balancing, A computer program designed to aid people in production control management in determining the most efficient operation in an assembly line type of production.

assembly list, A computer-printed listing of a computer program that was processed by an assembler.

assembly program, Same as assembler.

assembly routine, Same as assembler.

assembly system, An assembly language and its assembler.

assembly unit, A device that associates and joins several parts of a computer program.

assignment, facilities executive, The assignment of computer memory and facilities in a computer program.

Association for Computing Machinery (ACM), An organization composed of people devoted to the advancement of the science and art of computer technology.

association indexing, A study of word usage following two approaches.

associative memory, A high-speed search of computer memory based on the content rather than computer addresses.

associative storage, A storage system in which computer storage locations are identified by their contents.

associative storage registers, Registers that are identified not by their name or position but by content.

assumed decimal point, A place in a computer stored number where the decimal point is assumed to be.

astatic, Not stable or steady.

asterisk protection , Printing asterisks (*) in front of a dollar amount (as on paychecks).

asymmetry, A characteristic of anything lacking symmetry.

asynchronous, A characteristic of a computer pertaining to lack of time coincidence of operations (contrasted with synchronous).

asynchronous communications interface adapter (ACIA), A device to provide the data formatting and control to interface serial asynchronous data communications information to bus organized systems.

asynchronous computer, A computer that starts operations based on the previous operation or availability of parts of the computer.

asynchronous data transmission, A method of data transmission dependent on the condition of the transmitting line at that time.

asynchronous device, A unit that has an operating speed not related to anything it's connected to.

asynchronous machine, Machine that has operating speeds not fixed to a specific frequency of the system.

asynchronous operation, A method of computer processing in which one operation is completed before the next operation starts.

asynchronous output (transmission), A method of transmission of data in which timing is not critical.

asyndetic, A characteristic meaning conjunctions and connectives are not used - e.g., catalogs, programs, etc., - without cross-reference.

atom, In data processing, an operator or operand in a computer instruction.

atomic symbols, In data processing, a string of letters or numbers starting with a letter.

attached processor (AP), A processor added to the main central processor, often sharing its channels and memory.

attached support processor (ASP), Using multiple computers (usually two that are connected) to increase the efficiency of processing many jobs of short duration.

attention device, An attention-getting method for displays on a computer display terminal (such as a CRT).

attenuate, To reduce the amplitude (height of the wave) in an electrical signal.

attenuation, Reduction of an electrical signal measured in units, decibels, or percentages.

attenuation, echo, The rates of transmitted electrical power at an output terminal to the amount reflected back to the same terminal.

attenuation, signal, The reduction in the strength of electrical signals.

attribute, A characteristic that sets something apart from others. In computer data such things as location, length, and type of data.

audible alarm, A sound signal used to indicate a malfunction or error condition in a computer program.

audio, Sound frequencies that can be heard by the human ear.

audio cassette record interface, A device that allows virtually unlimited memory storage for data or software. Operates by modulating audio frequencies in the record mode. Demodulates recorded data in playback mode.

audio response, Verbal reply to inquiries (may be prerecorded responses in a time-shared on-line system).

audio system, Type of equipment that can store and process data from (recorded or transmitted) voice.

audio tape storage unit, A unit capable of storing computer programs and/or data on ordinary audio cassette tape using audio tones to represent binary data.

audio-response unit (ARU), A device that can connect a computer system to a telephone to provide voice response to inquiries made.

audit, The operations developed to check the validity and accuracy of data in a data processing environment.

audit, in-depth, A very detailed audit (see audit) of a single transaction.

audit programming, Use of a computer program as an auditing tool.

audit trail, A system for tracing the flow of data through a computer or business system.

audit trail, A traceable path or record of transactions which may be used to check back through.

auditing, The process of performing an audit.

audo-indexed addressing, An addressing mode that results in the contents of an index register being automatically altered by some specified amount each time such an instruction is actually executed.

augend, A number to which another number (addend) is added to get a sum.

augment, To increase a quantity to bring it to its full value.

augmentation, The process of augmenting.

augmenter, The quantity added to another to augment it (bring it to its full value).

auto bypass, A process that enables continuous operation of downstream terminals when another terminal in the daisy chain is powered down.

auto restart, A condition such that when power returns after an interruption and the auto restart was armed by the power fail interrupt program, this feature restarts the CPU at the point of program interruption, avoiding loss of instructions or data.

autoabstract, The information selected from a larger body of information through the use of automatic or machine methods.

autobalance, A mechanism made of gears, used to perform (mathematical) differentiation.

autochart, Often refers to a type of documentor used for the automatic production and maintenance of charts, principally flowcharts.

autocode, A method used by a computer to develop a machine-coded computer program.

autocoder, An IBM computer programming language.

auto-index, An index prepared by data processing procedures.

auto-man, A type of switch that may be set on automatic or manual.

automata theory, A theory that relates the study of application of automatic devices to various behaviorist concepts and theories.

automated management, All kinds of management accomplished with the aid of data processing equipment.

automated production management, Management of production planning, scheduling, design, control, etc., using data processing equipment.

automated teller machine (ATM), Equipment such as cash dispensers, customer balance reporters, and bank machines with other capabilities.

automath, A computer program that translates mathematical notation into computer instructions (Honeywell).

automatic, Processors and systems designed to function without human intervention.

automatic abstracting, Searching for the criteria by which human beings judge what should be abstracted from a document, as programmed.

automatic branch exchange, private, A dial exchange that provides private telephone service within a company and also connection to the public telephone network.

automatic calling unit (ACU), A dialing device that permits a machine (business) to automatically dial calls over a communication network.

automatic carriage, A device on a computer printer that moves the paper under computer control.

automatic check, the checking devices built into a computer (built-in check).

automatic check-out systems, Tests applied to each component and subsystem of aircraft, missiles, weapons, etc., to evaluate the overall system operation.

automatic code, A code that allows a computer to translate a symbolic language into the computer's language.

automatic computer, A computer capable of performing long series of operations without human intervention

automatic control, Control achieved by electronic devices that automatically regulate processes and other events.

automatic control panel, A panel of lights and switches used by a computer operator.

automatic crosstell, Transmission of air surveillance information in the American Air Defense System.

automatic data processing (ADP), Data processing performed on electrical and electronic equipment.

automatic data processing equipment, A machine or group of machines (containing electronic circuitry) used for data processing.

automatic data processing system, The whole of procedures, processes, personnel, and automatic data processing equipment.

automatic dialing unit, A modem or device capable of automatically generating dialed digits for a call.

automatic dictionary, The component of computer language translating that provides a word-for-word substitution from one language to another.

automatic electronic data-switching center, A communications center design for relaying information by automatic electronic means.

automatic error correction, A technique used to correct transmission errors automatically.

automatic error detection, A characteristic in a computer program that permits detection of its own errors.

automatic exchange, A communication exchange with no intervention by operators (people).

automatic gain control (AGC), An electronic circuit that adjusts the incoming signal to a predetermined level; an automatic volume control usually denotes an audio function while ALC (automatic level control) denotes the parallel video function.

automatic interrupt, An automatic computer program controlled interruption of operation that causes a branch to a specified computer storage location.

automatic loader, A loader program implemented in a special ROM (read-only memory) that allows loading of binary tapes or the first record or sector of a mass storage device. A type of bootstrap loader plus a binary loader.

automatic message, Incoming communications messages are automatically directed to a selected outgoing circuit based on the content of the message.

automatic message-switching center, A center in which messages are automatically routed based on their content.

automatic plotting, The drawing of a graph under computer direction (control).

automatic program interrupt, The progress of a computer program is interrupted to do ''first things first'' when a priority operation arises.

automatic program interruption and time-sharing, The automatic interrupt feature that provides maximum time-sharing and efficiency in operation.

automatic programming, Techniques such as compiling and assembling computer programs.

automatic programming language (APL), A programming language developed by Iverson with an unusually extensive set of operators and data structures; uses mathematical notation.

automatic programming, mnemonic, A computer programing system that allows for mnemonic expression.

automatic programming tool (APT), A computer program used for numerically controlled machine tools such as cloth cutters and drafting machines (Univac).

automatic recovery program, A computer program that enables a computer system to keep functioning when a piece of equipment has failed.

automatic request for repetition (ARQ), A system using an error detection code that automatically initiates a request for retransmission.

automatic routine, A computer program routine that is used only when certain conditions occur.

automatic segmentation and control, A method used to fit computer programs into computer memory by fitting different segments in at different times.

automatic send-receive set (ASR), A communications device that is a combination teletypewriter, transmitter, and receiver.

automatic stop, An automatic stopping of computer operation when an error is detected by computer checking devices.

automatic switchover, In case of a stand-by machine, the capability to switch over to it when the other machine is faulty.

automatic tape transmitter, Same as automatic tape reader, it reads, feeds, holds, etc., reels of tape.

automatic teaching, Computerized instruction that involves an interplay between the student and the computer.

automatic test equipment (ATE), Devices such as in-circuit testers that are capable of efficiently testing printed circuit boards containing a wide variety of LSI and microprocessor devices.

automatic transaction recorder, Computer routines in which information about transactions are recorded.

automaton, A machine that has been designed to simulate the operations of living things.

automonitor, A computer program used to instruct a computer to make a record of its information handling operations.

automotive computer, Many types often combine keyboard, display, and other components to display fuel management system features. Some units monitor speed, distance, fuel flow, time, battery voltage, several temperatures, fuel consumption, fuel remaining, and other activities.

autonomous devices, A computer system in which no device (unit) is dependent upon another for its timing.

autoplotter, A system used in computer programming to plot graphs, histograms, etc., under computer control.

autopolling, In communications, a party-line device that provides for automatic transmission from station to station, as predetermined.

auxiliary console, An operator console other than the main console (see console).

auxiliary data, Data that is associated with other data, but that is not a part of it, such as comment data, back-up data, etc.

auxiliary equipment, Various devices or units used with a computer such as data processing card sorters, card punches, etc.

auxiliary operation, An operation performed by equipment not under constant control of the central processing unit of a computer.

auxiliary routine, A special computer program routine used to assist in the operation of the computer and in debugging other routines.

auxiliary storage, The storage devices other than main storage of a computer, such as magnetic tape, magnetic disk, etc.

availability, The percentage of time that a piece of data processing equipment is operating correctly.

available machine time, The time that the computer is available for use and operating correctly.

available time, The time that a device may be used or is used.

AVC, See automatic volume control.

average calculating operation, A typical calculating operation (in a computer) longer than an addition and shorter than a multiplication.

average effectiveness level, A percentage figure used to measure computer availability.

average operation time, The average time to perform one add, one multiply, and one divide.

average, weighted, An average in which some values are valued more heavily than others.

awaiting repair time, The time between reporting a problem and the beginning of repair operations.

awareness, network, The condition in which the central processor of a computer is aware of the states of the network.

B

B and not A gate , (See gates).

B ignore A gate, See gates.

B ignore A negative gate, See gates.

B implies A gate, See gates.

B or not A gate, See gates.

Babbage, Charles (1792-1871), The man who conceived the analytical engine in 1833 (the forerunner of today's general purpose computer).

background, In data processing, a section of computer storage used for background processing.

background noise, Extra bits or words that must be ignored or removed from the data at the time the data is used. Errors introduced into the system, especially one or more characteristics of any entity such as voltage, current, and data. Loosely, any disturbance tending to interfere with operations.

background processing, Work the computer handles when work of a higher priority doesn't require parts of the computer's resources.

background program, A computer program that is of a lower priority than another program (foreground program) and has to wait its turn to use the computer.

background reflectance, The ability of a surface to reflect; a characteristic of the surface upon which optical characters are printed for recognition.

backing storage, The storage devices other than main storage (same as auxiliary storage).

backspace, To move backwards instead of forwards, as with the print mechanism on a typewriter or printer, or the cursor on a CRT screen. To backspace a file is to move towards the beginning of the data.

back-up, A generalized term, may refer to a copy of some data that may be used if needed, an alternate method to be used if necessary, another computer system available if needed, etc.

back-up copy, A protection procedure to avoid the destruction of original data or processed information. A copy is often preserved, usually on a different medium.

back-up, manual, A manual method of processing that may be used if the computer isn't available.

back-up system, A system that uses several sophisticated error detection and correction techniques in spotting and correcting equipment.

backward read, A feature that some magnetic tape units have that permits the transfer of data to computer storage while moving the tape in the reverse direction.

badge reader, A device that reads information (such as employee number) from a badge-like card and enters the data into a computer.

balanced circuits, An electrical circuit (with balanced voltage).

balanced error, A range of error that may be the same amount in either a plus or minus direction.

balanced line, An electrical line with balanced voltage.

balanced sorting, A technique used in sorting programs to merge strings of sequenced data.

ballistics, The science of motion of projectiles in flight.

band, 1 A range of frequencies between two defined limits. 2 A group of recording tracks on a magnetic drum.

band, (1) A range of frequency. (2) A recording area on magnetic drum or tape.

band, clear, In optical character recognition, an area that must be kept free of unrelated printing.

band, dead, A range of values in which the incoming signal can be altered without changing the outgoing response.

band, frequency, The range of frequencies.

band, guard, Any unused frequency band (to guard against interference).

band-elimination filter, A filter that has a single attenuation band (see attenuation).

bandpass, The difference in cycles per second between the limiting frequencies of a band.

bandpass filter, A filter that has a single transmission band.

bandwidth, The difference in frequency between the highest and lowest frequency in a band.

bandwidth, nominal, The maximum band of frequencies assigned to a given channel.

bandwidth, RF, The frequency difference between the highest and lowest frequencies of a radio frequency (RF) signal.

bank, An assemblage of fixed contacts used to establish electric connections.

bank, data, A collection of data that is accessible by a computer.

bank on-line teller system, A system of bank teller computer consoles linked to a central computer.

BANKPAC, A group of generalized computer programs used to serve the data processing needs of banks.

banner word, The first word in a data file record.

bar code, Coding of consumer or other products through use of printing of packages or labels using combinations of bars of varying thicknesses to represent characters and numerals; the most popular in the United States is the UPC or universal product code accepted by most grocery and many other retail stores.

bar code (optical) scanner, An optical scanning device that can read bar codes on documents.

bar, cross, A type of automatic telephone-switching system using movable switches mounted on bars.

bar, fixed type, A type bar on a data processing printer that cannot be removed by an operator (contrasted with interchangeable type bar).

bar, interchangeable type, A type bar on a data processing printer that can be removed by the operator to change the alphabet available to a print position.

bar printer, A data processing printer whose characters are positioned along a type bar.

bar, type, A long narrow bar that holds the type (set of characters) used on a bar printer.

barrel, A cylindrical part of an electrical contact that accepts an electrical conductor.

barrier layer, An electrical layer at the contact surface between a metal and a semiconductor or between two metals.

base, The radix of a number system, i.e., the decimal system has a base of ten; the binary system has a base of two.

base, A quantity used to define a system of representing numbers. In the decimal system, the base is 10; in the binary system, the base is 2.

base, acetate, A transparent cellulose backing on magnetic tapes.

base address, A number that is an address in a computer instruction that serves as a reference point for other addresses that appear in the computer program.

base, data, The set of data accessible to a computer.

base number, Same as radix (the number of characters available for use in a numbering system).

base point, Used to separate the whole part of a number from its fractional part (e.g., a decimal point).

base register, A register in a computer whose contents are used to modify a computer instruction prior to its execution.

base, time, A designed and controlled function of time by which some process is controlled or measured.

baseband, 1 The frequency band occupied by the aggregate of the transmitted signals before they have modulated a carrier. 2 A signal in the frequency band of (1).

baseband, A frequency band used for the transmission of picture and synchronization signals in television and some telephone systems.

BASIC, One of the easiest computer languages to learn; popular with beginners and small computer users.

Basic, See Beginner's All Purpose Symbolic Instruction Code.

basic code, Computer code using absolute addresses and operation codes (synonymous with specific code and one-level code).

basic coding, Computer instructions written in the computer's own language (machine language); same as absolute coding.

basic linkage, A linkage (interconnection of computer routines, programs, etc.) which follows the same set of rules each time it is used.

basic operating system (BOS), One of many operating systems (see operating system).

batch, A group of all instructions or data relevant to a program or a group of similar programs that is retained in batches for processing in a single run.

batch, A group of documents to be processed as a group at one time.

batch data processing, Computer processing of a group of related items generally gathered until there is enough to process.

batch processing, A technique used where items are collected into groups prior to processing on a computer.

batch processing interrupt, A feature of a real-time system where the computer's batch processing program may be interrupted to permit handling of a real-time transaction.

batch processing, real-time, A real-time system that is designed to automatically allow batch processing to take place as facilities in the computer are freed.

batch, remote, A method of entering jobs into the computer from a remote terminal.

batch, total, A total accumulated by adding certain quantities from each record in a batch of data records.

battery, station, The electric power source used for signaling at a station.

baud, A unit of measurement of serial data transmission which is usually taken to represent bits per second.

baud, A unit of measurement of signalling speed (generally bits per second as a measure of data flow).

baud rate, A transmission rate that is in effect synchronous with signal events - usually bits per second.

Baudot code, The standard five-channel teletypewriter code.

Bayesian statistics, A type of statistics that uses estimates of probability distribution in order to incorporate new data using Bayes' equation.

bay, patch, A concentrated assembly of electrical tie points.

b-bus, A second source-bus to the ALU in many two- or three-bus microcomputers.

BCD, See binary coded decimal.

BCD, binary-coded decimal, Refers to a decimal notation in which the individual decimal digits are each represented by a group of four binary digits.

BCO, See binary coded octal.

BCS, British Computer Society.

beam, holding, A beam of electrons in a cathode ray tube (CRT) used to keep holding the picture on the screen.

beam storage, Storage units that use one or more beams of electron or lights (cathode ray tube, CRT storage) (see CRT).

beat, Same as word-time which is the time required for a computer word to pass a given point electronically.

beginning file label, A label in the beginning of a file that describes the contents of the file (on magnetic tape and disk, etc.).

beginning tape label, A description of the contents of the tape located at the beginning of the tape.

beginning-of-tape (BOT) cartridge, The point to which the cartridge tape is rewound.

beginning-of-tape marker, A reflective spot on the magnetic tape at the beginning of the tape reel.

behavioral simulation, Simulation of psychological and/or sociological behavior of individuals and groups.

bell character, A control character that activates a signal, thus calling for attention by humans for intervention.

belled mouth, A widened entrance to the barrel of an electrical connector.

benchmark, A test that measures the speed, accuracy, or other operational parameters of computer equipment. The performance of a computer system is tested by using special programs known as benchmark programs.

benchmark, A point of reference used to judge something compared to a standard.

benchmark problem, A problem used to evaluate the performance of computers (compared to each other).

benchmark routine, A set of problems (may be computer programs) that aid in judging the performance of equipment (data processing).

benchmarking, Any of several techniques for evaluating different computer systems by running the same job on each and comparing the time required for completion.

BFO, An abbreviation for beat-frequency oscillator.

bias, A measure of the amount of imbalance of a set of measurements, an unbalanced error.

bias check, Varying equipment operating conditions (e.g., voltage, frequency) in order to locate defectiveness of parts, a computer maintenance procedure.

bias test, high-low, A type of bias testing (see bias testing).

biased data, A distribution of data records in a file that is being sorted (affects sorting time).

bibliography, A list of documents by subject or author, an annotated catalog of documents.

bidirectional flow, Flow that can go in either direction.

bidirectional operation, An operation in which reading, writing, or searching of stored information may be done in either direction.

bifurcated contact, A contact used in printed-circuit connectors (in digital computers).

bifurcation, Separating or branching into two parts (such as a bifurcated contact that is slotted lengthwise to provide additional points of contact).

billibit, One-thousand-million (or one billion) binary digits; same as kilomegabit.

billicycle, One billion cycles, same as kilomegacycle.

billing, cycle, Using a time basis for repeated billing (e.g., four weeks).

billing system, post, A system in which the customer bills (invoices) are sent after the order has been shipped.

billisecond, One billionth of a second, same as nanosecond.

BIM, See beginning-of-information marker.

binary, A number system that uses only two digits: 0 and 1. Binary numbers are basic for use by computers, since many electrical devices have two distinct states: on and off.

binary, (1) A numbering system based on 2s rather than 10s (as in the decimal system). Only the digits 1 and 0 are used. (2) A characteristic in which there are two possible alternatives.

binary arithmetic, The arithmetic of the number system which uses only two digits: 0 and 1.

binary Boolean operation, A specific type of Boolean operation in which there are two operands, and the result depends on both of them.

binary card, A standard data processing card with data punched in binary form (by columns or rows).

binary cell, A cell of one binary digit; a one-bit register or position.

binary chain, A series of binary circuits arranged so each circuit affects the condition of the circuit that follows it.

binary code, Any code using only two distinguishable code elements or states, representing the binary digits 1 and 0.

binary code, A coding system using binary digits (0 and 1).

binary code, dense, A code in which all possible combinations are used.

binary coded character, A decimal digit or alphabetic character, etc.; represented by a predetermined combination of binary digits (pattern of 0s and 1s).

binary coded decimal (BCD), A numerical representation in which decimal digits are represented by binary numerals.

binary coded decimal notation, A method of representation of decimal numbers by using a four-digit binary number.

binary coded decimal number, A number consisting of successive groups of four binary digits (e.g., 0110, 1001, 1010).

binary coded decimal representation (BCD), A system of representation of decimal numbers in which each decimal digit is represented by four binary digits.

binary coded digit, One set of binary numbers representing a decimal digit.

binary coded octal (BCO), A numerical representation in which octal digits are represented by binary numerals.

binary counter, (1) A counter that counts using the binary number system. (2) A counter that can assume one or two stable states.

binary density, The amount of binary information that can be stored per unit area on a magnetic storage medium such as tape or disk.

binary digit (bit), May be a 0 or a 1, the digits used in the binary numbering system.

binary digits, equivalent, The number of binary digit places required to express a number written in another number system's notation.

binary dump, A dump recorded in binary representation, instead of the more commonly used hexadecimal representation.

binary element, An element of data that may assume one of two possible states (e.g., plus or minus).

binary logic, Digital logic elements that operate in two states (such as, on and off, 1 and 0, high and low, etc.).

binary mode, A mode in which operations use the binary number system, allowing use of 1 and 0 only.

binary notation, A numeration system in which only two symbols are allowed, such as 0 and 1.

binary number, A number composed of a combination of the digits 0 and 1, used in the base 2 numbering system (binary numbering system).

binary numeral, A set of digits that represents a quantity written in binary form (all 1s and 0s).

binary one, One of the two possible binary digits that has the value of unity assigned to it (the other digit being binary zero).

binary operation, A particular operation that depends on strict adherence to Boolean algebra rules (logic operations).

binary point, The arithmetic point that separates the whole from the fractional part in a binary number (similar to decimal point in a decimal number).

binary, row, The representation of binary data on punched data processing cards across the rows (as opposed to binary, column).

binary search, A method of searching for an element in a table or sequential file by successively halving the table (file) to narrow down the location of the element.

binary signaling, A mode in communications in which information is represented by the presence or absence, or by plus or minus variations.

binary, straight, Binary representation of binary numbers.

binary synchronous communications (BCS), A widely used protocol in the communications industry developed by IBM, also known as BYSYNC regarding transmission between batch and other video display terminals.

binary synchronous communications (BSC), A full-duplex line protocol for communications that is being superseded by high-level data link control (HDLC).

binary unit, A bit (binary digit).

binary variable, A variable that can assume either one of two values.

binary zero, One of the two binary digits (0 and 1) that represents the lack of magnitude (the off condition of on/off).

biconditional gate, Same as gate, exclusive-NOR (see gates).

biometrics, Measurement and system evaluation (using statistical means) of biological systems and characteristics.

bionics, The study of phenomena of living organisms and application of the knowledge gained to develop operating hardware, techniques, and methods useful to mankind.

biosensor, A mechanism for detecting and transmitting biological data from an organism in a way that permits processing, display, or storage of results.

bipolar, A type of electric signal in which a logical "true" is opposite a logical "false" in polarity (as opposed to unipolar).

bipolar chip slice, Often a CPU chip with speed advantages of discrete logic and all the processor-oriented advantages of modular CPU buildup, e.g., using several 2-bit, 4-bit, or other size "slices."

bipolar chips, Various microcomputer systems make use of bipolar chips to develop signal levels that are compatible with standard industry bipolar parts. Bipolar chip technology provides faster parts than some other technologies.

bipolar device technology, An alternative to the side-by-side MOSFET is a layered structure. Such structures are referred to as bipolar devices; they resolve, to some extent, both deficiencies of n- and p-channel MOS.

biquinary, A number system representation in two parts, a binary portion and a quinary portion.

biquinary code, A two-part code in which each decimal digit is represented by the sum of a binary part and a quinary part.

bird, whirley, The slang term for magnetic disk pack equipment.

bi-stable, The capability of assuming either of two stable states, thus of storing one bit of information.

bistable, Capability of assuming one of two stable states.

bistable multivibrator, A circuit capable of assuming either one of two stable states (same as flip-flop).

bistable trigger circuit, A circuit capable of assuming either one of two stable states (same as flip-flop).

bit, Short for 'binary digit.' Bits are represented in computers by two-state devices, such as flip-flops or magnetic spots. A bit is the smallest unit of information which can be held on a computer.

bit (binary digit), May be a 0 or a 1, the digits used in the binary numbering system.

bit, check, A binary check digit (often a parity bit).

bit density, A measure of bits recorded per unit of length (e.g., bits per inch, bpi).

bit, guard, A bit contained in a computer word (or group of words) to indicate that the contents of memory cannot be altered (used in file protection).

bit, information, Bits that are genuine databits, not check bits or other kinds (in data communications).

bit instructions, Bit instructions often test, set, or reset any bit in memory and are valuable for setting flags and for monitoring and controlling on/off functions, such as switches, relays, valves, and indicators.

bit, link, A special one-bit register in a computer (see bit).

bit location, A storage position on a record capable of storing one bit (see bit).

bit mapped display, high resolution, A display technique which uses a single memory location within the computer to control a particular dot of light on the screen, thus significantly increasing the clarity and definition of graphic images on the screen.

bit parallel, A specific method of simultaneous movement or transmission of all bits in a continuous set (stream) of bits over separate wires.

bit, parity, A bit that is appended to a byte in order to make the total number of bits either even (even parity) or odd (odd parity).

bit, parity, Parity can be even or add; if a bit pattern has an odd number of bits in an even parity machine, the parity bit will be "turned on" (set to one) and vice versa. This method is used to permit internal checking in data transfer (see bit).

bit pattern, The possible combination of bits used to represent data (number of possible patterns) (see bit).

bit position, A location of a binary digit in space or time.

bit rate, The rate at which binary coded signals are signalled or transmitted in a specified length of time.

bit rate, (1) The speed at which bits are transmitted; (2) the rate at which bits pass a given point on a communications line (see bit).

bit rate devices, Devices that provide the reference frequencies required by serial interfaces (TTY, UART, cassette, modem) and that also furnish adjustment-free crystal stability with easily changed, multiple frequencies.

bit, serial by, A characteristic of data handling in equipment, handled a bit at a time, one after the other.

bit, sign, A binary digit (0 or 1) set to represent minus or plus.

bit significance, A bit in an instruction that indicates that the instruction is of a certain type.

bit site, The location of a bit of information on magnetic tape, disk, etc.

bit slice microprocessor, Represents a class of semiconductor devices used in constructing microcomputers. Bit-slice circuits are being produced in Schotky-TTL form by many companies. Some chips are 2 bits wide, others are 4 bits wide and wider.

bit, start, A bit used in asynchronous transmission to signal the beginning of transmission of a group of data bits, such as a character. Start bits enable the receiver to tell where a new group of data starts.

bit, stop, A bit used in asynchronous transmission to signal the end of transmission of a group of data bits, such as those making up a character. Having a stop bit at the end of each group of data bits improves readability.

bit, stop, Often the last element of a character designed for asynchronous serial that defines the character space immediately to the left of the most significant character in accumulator storage.

bit stream, Refers to a string of bits transmitted over a communication line. there are no separations between the groups of characters.

bit stream, Bits being transmitted over a circuit one after the other in a stream (communications) (see bit).

bit stream transmission, A method of transmission using a bit stream and timing intervals (see bit stream).

bit string, A one-dimensional array of bits (all in a row) (see array).

bit, zone, Special bits in character bit patterns; in punched cards, the top three rows of punches (they become zone bit parts when in computer storage).

bits per inch (BPI), Used for measuring density of data on a recording medium.

bits, service, Not information bits or check bits, but other types such as indicators of conditions (see bit)

black box, A slang or general term for describing almost any type of electronic device built for a special purpose, or which causes a system to function in a non-standard fashion. Also, any electronic or mechanical device which performs specified functions but whose inner workings are unknown to the user.

black box, A slang term, that refers to electronic devices associated with computers.

blank, A condition or signal usually represented by no magnetics in a given character location on a tape. Sometimes used as a control character.

blank, (1) No characters recorded, (2) a code (bit pattern) representing a blank.

blank character, "Prints" as a space (blank).

blank column detection, A feature of blank column and double sensing on some data processing machines (obsolete items).

blank instruction, A computer instruction that tells the computer to do nothing but go on to the next instruction (the purpose is to hold a place for another instruction to replace it later).

blank medium, Blank forms, unpunched paper tape, blank magnetic tape.

blank paper tape coil, Paper tape that has no information recorded on it yet.

blank, switching, The range of values that a signal can be altered without changing the outgoing response (synonymous with dead space, dead zone, and similar to neutral zone).

blanking signal, The pulses added to the video signal to indicate that the signal from the beam to the target area should be cut off, since the beam is in fly-back.

blank-transmission test, Checking for blanks in a data field.

blast, To release areas of storage for other use (no longer needed by the currently operating computer program).

block chaining, A procedure used to associate two blocks of computer storage with each other.

bleed, Spreading of ink beyond the edges of a printed character (optical character recognition).

blinking characteristics, Used for drawing the operator's attention to errors caught by the system and to areas of the video screen that require attention; the split-second on/off of characters, the cursor, or other symbols.

block, Refers to a sequence of characters or bytes which are grouped together to be treated as a complete unit of information. Typically, blocks consist of a fixed number of bytes called the block length. Data blocks are used extensively in data communications and when storing information on tape or disk.

block, A group of words or characters considered as a unit (in computer processing).

block, analysis, A block of computer storage in which testing or statistical data are stored.

block, control, A specific storage area containing control information for processing tasks, functions, etc.

block, data control, A control block used with access routines to provide information needed to receive and store data.

block, data set control (DSCB), A standard control block needed to manipulate the data set in a direct access device.

block diagram, A graphic representation of operations; a planning and design chart that shows paths of information flow.

block gap, The space (distance) between blocks of data on magnetic storage media (same as interblock gap).

block, input, Synonymous with input area.

block length, Refers to a measure of the length of a block generally expressed by the number of characters within that block. Also called block size.

block length, Expressed in total number of records, words, etc., contained in a block (see block).

block loading, A technique in which sections of programs are loaded into adjacent sections in main memory.

block, output, Synonymous with output area.

block parity system, A system of using parity bits to detect errors in data transfer of a whole block (see parity).

block record, Same as physical record (contrasted with logical record).

block, register, The set of 16 general registers (some computers) (see register).

block sequencing, A procedure that ensures that the data arrives in the proper sequence and that no blocks are lost or duplicated.

block sort, A method of sorting (sorting first on the most major position to separate the data into several groups to be further sorted).

block, stand-by, A block of storage that is set aside or reserved.

block storage, A section of computer storage considered as a single element.

block structure, A technique of blocking program segments for storage purposes

block, table, A subset of a table of data or computer instructions.

block transfer, Moving a whole block of data from one place to another (in computer storage).

block, variable, A data design in which the number of characters or records in data blocks may vary.

blockette, A subdivision of a group of consecutive computer words.

blocking factor, The number of records per block (see blocking).

blocking, The combining of two or more records into blocks (see block).

blockmark, An indicator mark in storage that indicates the end of a data block.

board, An electrical panel used in data processing machine that is hand-wired by the user; also known as plug board, panel, or wire board.

board, control, A removable panel in unit record equipment

board, plotting, That surface of a plotting machine on which the curves, graphs, charts, etc. are displayed.

board, plug, A control panel or wiring panel inserted into a data processing machine to control its functions (see board).

board, test, Switchboard equipment with testing apparatus (telephone).

board tester diagnostics, A quality that determines the long-term productivity of a digital board tester, the effectiveness of a tester depends on its ability to detect and isolate failures to the precise fault.

board, wiring, Same as a control panel.

book, A large segment of computer memory.

book message, A message that is sent to two or more destinations (communications).

book, run, Contains the information necessary to operate the computer while running specific programs.

bookkeeping operation, The bookkeeping (keeping track of what's happening) in the computer; operations that don't directly contribute to the solution of the problem.

Boolean, An algebra developed by George Boole (logical operations as opposed to arithmetic operations).

Boolean algebra, Refers to the specific study of operations carried out on variables that can have only two values: 1 (true) and 0 (false); developed by George Boole, a 19th century mathematician, as principles of mathematical logic.

Boolean algebra, A type of algebra named after George Boole (uses binary, logic, i.e., the logical operations OR, AND, NOT, etc.).

Boolean logic, Logic used in applications of information retrieval and circuit-switching designs.

Boolean variable, A two-valued variable, such as true or false, on or off, etc.

boost, To increase the power output of an operational amplifier by circuit modification (electricity).

bootleg program, A routine used to start the reading of a computer program (into the computer) by means of its own action.

bootstrap, A common technique used to start the reading of computer programs into the computer.

bootstrap loader, A computer subroutine built usually into the hardware to initiate reading of another computer subroutine.

bootstrap routine, tape, In some systems, used to "bootstrap" programs from magnetic tape (see bootstrap).

BOP messages, bit-oriented protocols (BOPs) are more straightforward and universal than many others. These are transmitted in frames, and all messages adhere to one standard frame format.

border-punched card, Same as margin-punched card.

bore, The inside diameter of the hub (center) on a magnetic tape reel.

borrow, An arithmetically negative carry used in (computer) internal arithmetic (concept similar to how we "borrow" when subtracting numbers).

BOS, See basic operating system.

bottom-up method, A (computer) compiling technique (reverse of top-down method) (see compiling).

bound, An upper or lower limit that a value can be.

boundary interface, A boundary point at which different elements of the system are linked together or between a human and a computer system. For instance, the interface between the user and the system might be the VDU keyboard.

boundary, page, The (computer) address of the first unit (byte or word) in a page of memory (see page of memory).

boundary register, In a multi-programmer system, a special register to designate the upper and lower addresses of each user's memory block.

box, In a flowchart, represents an element treated as a unit.

box, black, A slang term referring to electronic devices associated with computers.

box, connection, An electrical panel found in punched card machines.

box, decision, Used in flowcharting to indicate a choice between one or more paths (see flowchart).

box, stunt, A device to perform functions such as carriage return, line feed, etc., in a teleprinter.

box, universal button, A coined term for a set of push buttons whose functions are determined by the computer program.

BPI, See bits per inch.

bpi, bits per inch, Unit used to measure the recording density of magnetic tape.

bps, Bits per second. A measurement used to measure the speed of data transmission.

BPS, See basic programming support.

branch, See conditional branch.

branch, To depart from the sequential execution of computer instruction (same as transfer or jump).

branch exchange, private automatic, A dial exchange that provides private telephone service within a company and also connection to the public telephone network.

branch instruction test, A test indicated by the computer instruction testing for greater than, negative, less than, or other conditions.

branch, program, A path in a program that is selected from two or more paths by a program instruction.

branch, unconditional, A computer instruction that causes a branch to another part of the computer program (not based on a test). (Contrasted with branch, conditional.)

branching, A computer operation that involves selecting one of two or more courses of action.

branch-on indicator, Branching takes place depending on indicator settings (a conditional branch).

branch-on switch setting, A computer program instruction that may cause a branch based on a switch condition.

branch-on-zero instruction, A conditional branch instruction that tests the arithmetic accumulator for zero.

branchpoint, The point in a computer program or routine at which one of two or more choices is selected (see conditional branch for clarification).

breadboard, A term referring to a rough (or experimental) construction of a model of a process, device, etc.

break key, Forces an interrupt of incoming messages when used with half-duplex systems; holds transmission line low as long as key is depressed.

break, sequence (sorting), A point between strings in sorting (see strings).

break, string, The point in a string at which no more records with higher (or lower in descending strings) belong on the string.

breakpoint, conditional, A breakpoint at which the routine can be continued if the right conditions exist (see breakpoint).

breakpoint instruction, An instruction that may cause branching to a supervisory routine (or a type of conditional branch).

breakpoint, program, The point in a program at which the program stops running. Breakpoints are set by a programmer to check for errors in the program.

bridge, central office, A device used to combine several (telephone) lines from several offices (supplied by the telephone company).

bridge tap, An undesirable, undetermined length of line attached to a communications line.

brightness, The ability of paper to reflect light (in optical character recognition).

brightness ratio, Indicates as a ratio the difference between the whitest and the blackest object in a scene; the range from brightest white to darkest black as it occurs in the scene being recorded.

broadband, See WIDEBAND.

broadband, In data transmission, the capability of handling frequencies greater than voice grade (see voice grade).

broadcast, To send the same message to all stations on a circuit at the same time (communications).

branch, conditional, A computer instruction that causes a branch based on a test of some condition (see branch).

B-rules, Artificial Intelligence, Rules in a backward production system. They are applied to goal descriptions to produce subgoal descriptions.

brute force approach, To try to undertake with existing equipment a mass of problems that don't use precise computation or logical manipulation.

BSAM, Basic sequential access method, a database system procedure.

BSC, See binary synchronous communications.

BTAM, An abbreviation for basic telecommunications access method.

bubble memories, Memories that are actually tiny cylinders of magnetization whose axes lie perpendicular to the plane of the single-crystal sheet that contains them.

bubble memory advantages, Exceed some other memory types by offering higher speed, smaller size, less weight, and lower power consumption.

bubble sort, A sorting method that exchanges a pair of numbers (replace each other), if they are out of order.

bucket, A slang term for anything that can hold something, generally a portion of storage.

buffer, A common computer device generally used for the temporary storage of data that is located between two other devices of differing speeds, e.g., output from computer (faster) will be held in a buffer before it is sent to a printer (slower).

buffer, (1) buffer storage, (2) an isolating circuit, (3) an auxiliary storage device to hold data temporarily, (4) a storage device used to compensate for differences in rates of flow of chart.

buffer, amplifier, An amplifier that has been designed to isolate a preceding circuit from a following circuit.

buffer, data, A temporary storage device used between two devices of different rates of data flow.

buffer, drum, Using magnetic drum storage as a temporary holding place for data.

buffer, ESI control, An acronym for Externally Specified Index control, this is a type of buffer control which makes it possible to handle a number of computer channels. ESI allows other transactions to run without interruption.

buffer gate, Same as gate, or (see gates).

buffer, input/output, The temporary storage area for input and output of a computer.

buffer memory register, A register used for temporary storage.

buffer, refresh, A temporary storage location which holds the screen display information as a screen image is refreshed.

buffer stocks, A level of inventory kept on hand to avoid out-of-stock conditions.

buffer storage, Any of several devices that temporarily store information during transfer; storage between devices to make up for differences in speeds.

buffer storage locations, A set of storage locations used to temporarily hold data to compensate for differences in data rates going from one device to another.

buffering, exchange, A technique for input/output buffering (see buffered computer).

bug, A fault or error in a computer program.

bug, (1) a mechanical, electrical, or electronic defect in the computer, (2) an error in a computer program, (3) a high-speed telegraph key.

bug monitors, Functions are to spot problems in system hardware and software, detail errors caused by software bugs, equipment malfunction, or line problems.

building block principle, A system that can have additional equipment to form a larger system; also called modularity.

built-in check, A provision in the computer (hardware) to verify the accuracy of data that is moved around and processed by parts of the computer.

built-in controls, Error checking devices built into data processing equipment.

bulk eraser, A device used to erase or destroy the information on a reel of tape.

bulk storage, Computer storage of a large volume but at a slower speed, such as magnetic disk (also called external or secondary storage).

bureau, service, A data processing organization that provides services to customers, i.e., they sell manpower and computer time.

burn in, A phase of component testing in which very early mortality or failures are discovered or screened out by running the circuit for a specified length of time, typically 168 hours.

burst, error, A data transmission method using designed error bits.

burst mode, A mode of communications between the computer and the input/output devices (contrasted with byte mode).

bus, An electrical route between several devices along which data flow.

bus, (1) a circuit, (2) a path over which information is transferred.

bus cycles, Generally each processor instruction requires one or more bus cycles, the first that fetches an instruction from the location addressed by the program counter, others to reference a device, and so on.

bus, data, One of three buses which make up a system bus. A data bus transfers words in the computer from one location to another. For example, a data bus is responsible for transferring words from the central processing unit (CPU) to main memory.

bus, data, Most computers communicate internally through the use of a data bus; most are bi-directional; e.g., transferring data to and from the CPU, storage, and peripheral devices.

bus error traps, Most are time-out errors or attempts to reference addresses on the bus that have made no response within a certain length of time. Many are caused by attempts to reference nonexistent memory, nonexistent peripheral devices, and so on.

bus hub, A place on a control panel for entrance and exit of pulse signals.

bus messages, Messages are transmitted to the processor via two basic routes; one method sends the message as a set of control signals on a control bus, while the other method sends the message as data on an I/O bus.

bus multiplexing, Various address and data words are multiplexed over 8- and 16-bit buses. During a programmed data transfer, the processor first asserts an address on the bus for a fixed time; the processor then executes the programmed input or output data transfer.

bus polling protocol, The bus protocol allows for a vectored interrupt by the device; device polling is not required in interrupt processing routines, producing considerable savings in time.

bus wire, A group of wires that allow memory, the CPU, and the I/O devices to exchange words.

business application, Data processing applications such as inventory, sales, purchasing, payroll, etc. (contrasted with scientific application).

business compiler, A language compiler for business-oriented programming languages, such as Cobol.

busing, daisy chain, A procedure of propagating signals along a bus; devices not requesting a daisy-chained signal respond by passing the signal on.

but lines, Parallel lines and control logic are often referred to collectively as the I/O bus; they transfer information between microprocessor and I/O devices.

button box, universal, A coined term for a set of push buttons whose functions are determined by the computer program.

button, emergency, A button on a computer to be pushed only in case of emergency (such as fire, etc.); generally is a "pull" device more recently (instead of a push button).

button, panic, A slang term that suggests a "magic" button needs to be pressed to save a panic situation.

button, start, A push button used to start operations or get ready for operation of various units of a computer system.

bypass procedure, A procedure used to get the most vital information into a main computer when a line control computer fails.

byte, The smallest group of bits which can be addressed individually. A byte usually contains eight bits. Each byte corresponds to one character of data.

byte, (1) A unit of computer storage, (2) a unit of data representation, e.g., an 8-bit byte used to represent data (an 8-bit byte fits into a byte of storage).

byte location, effective, The actual storage location (indicated in an address in a byte addressing instruction).

byte mode, An alternate mode of communications between the computer and the input/output devices (contrasted with burst mode).

byte multiplexing, A process of delegating time to input/output devices to use the channel to get information into main memory.

C

C, The name of a high-level, problem-oriented programming language. C is a highly structured language that bears a strong resemblance to PASCAL.

C, A somewhat structured and high-level language developed by Bell Laboratories to optimize run-time size and efficiency.

cable, An assembly or wrapping of electrical wires in a protective covering.

cable, coaxial, A cable of at least one transmission line of (at least) two conductors insulated from one another.

cable, connecting, A cable used to transfer electricity between two pieces of equipment.

cable, input/output, A wire(s) or bus(es), etc., used to connect input or output devices to the computer.

cable, quaded, A cable having conductors in groups of four.

cable, tape, A cable containing flat metallic ribbon conductors.

cable, TV, The system whereby images are transmitted to TV sets over coaxial cable (wire) for a fee to the customer.

CACD, An abbreviation for computer-aided circuit design.

cache memory, A buffer-type memory of high speed that is filled at medium speed from main memory, often with instructions and programs. Higher operating speeds can be achieved with those items found in cache memory; if they are not found, a new segment is loaded, stacks grow and shrink from one end.

cache memory "hit", The effectiveness is based on the percentage of time that the data to be fetched can be transferred from the high-speed cache, as opposed to lower-speed memory; if the data is found in cache, it is called a "hit."

CAD, computer-aided design, The use of a computer-based system to assist in the design of electronic circuits, machine parts for industry, and so on.

CAD/CAM, Abbreviation for computer-aided design/computer-aided manufacturing; this refers to graphics software developed to assist in design and manufacturing.

CAD/CAM, Programs that make up computer-aided design and computer-aided manufacturing systems.

CAI, An abbreviation for computer-assisted or computer-aided instruction.

CAL, See conversational algebraic language.

calculating, Computation such as multiplication, addition, substraction, etc.

calculator mode, An operating mode, available with some computer systems, which allows the terminal to be used as a desk calculator.

calibrated instrumentation, Procedures designed to ascertain, usually by comparison with a standard, the locations at which scale/chart graduations should be placed to correspond to a series of values of the quantity that the instrument is to measure.

call, To branch or transfer control to a computer program subroutine.

call instruction, A type that diverts program execution to a new area in memory (sequence of directives) and still allows eventual return to the original sequence of directives.

call word, The word that identifies a computer program subroutine.

call-directing code (CDC), A two- or three-character code used in teletypewriter systems to activate a particular machine or group of machines.

called party, The location connected to in a telephone network.

calling, selective, In communications, the selection of a station to receive transmission of a message.

calling sequence, A set of instructions used to provide linkage to and from computer program subroutines.

calling unit, automatic (ACU), A dialing device that permits a (business) machine to automatically dial calls over a communication network.

calls, subroutine, The linkage between a subroutine and a main program.

CAM, An abbreviation for content addressed memory.

CANCL status word, Indicates that the remote computing system has deleted some information.

canonical, In database systems, a regular, standard, or simplified form of an expression or scheme.

capability, stand-alone, The ability of a device to function independently from any other equipment for part or all of the time.

capacitance, A measure of ability to store an electrical charge.

capacitance, distributed, The virtual capacitance (electrical) existing between adjacent loops in a coil.

capacitive coupling, Alternating current coupling by a capacitor instead of a transformer.

capacitor, A device for storing an electric charge on two conducting plates separated by an insulating material.

capacitor, An electronic component.

capacity, The amount of information that all or part of a computer can store. For example, a 1MB computer will have a main memory capacity of 1 Megabyte of data.

capacity, Ability to hold, store, handle, or accommodate.

capacity, circuit, The number of channels that can be handled at the same time.

capacity, memory, The number of units of storage that can be used for data.

capacity, rated, A general term for the output that can continue indefinitely, in conformity with a criterion — e.g., heating, distortion of signals, or a wave form.

capacity, register, The upper and lower limits of the numbers that can be processed in a computer register.

capacity, storage, Storage capacity, or 'capacity,' refers to the amount of information a computer system or storage device (tape, disk, and so on) is capable of storing at any one time. A personal computer with a capacity of 64K will be able to store 65,536 bytes of information in its inbuilt memory.

capacity, storage, The maximum number of bits, bytes, characters, words, etc., that can be stored in a device at one time.

capacity, system, The expected throughput of a computer system.

capacity, word, The number of characters in a computer word.

caption, A heading that indicates the contents of a folder.

carbon spot, A section of carbon paper on a multipart form so that only that area is reproduced on the copy (or copies).

carbon stability, The resistance of carbon (ribbons and forms) to deterioration (during storage on the shelf especially).

card, Generally, punched card used in data processing.

card, 80-column, A standard punched card with 80 columns for data recording.

card, aperture, A card with an opening containing microfilm.

card cage, A housing for a microcomputer that is usually of rugged construction such as a 16-slot metal box with interconnections for circuits, buses, memories, and so on.

card code, The code used for data representation in punched cards.

card, CPU, CPU chips require various input signals to generate output signals often developed through the use of assorted I/O and memory devices mounted with them on a printed circuit board or card.

card deck, A set (deck) of punched cards.

card face, The side of a punched card that contains printing.

card, IBM, A data processing punched card that has become known as an "IBM card" (through common usage).

card image, An internal representation in computer storage reflecting what was in a punched card that was read.

card, logic, A functional card containing electrical components and wiring circuitry (not a punched card), several of which are in a computer.

card magnetic stripe reader, Can read mag-stripe ID or other cards coded with binary coded decimal or hexadecimal digits. A self-contained module often consists of a molded high-impact resistant, reinforced card guide used with a read head, PC board, card limit switch, and so on.

card, master, A punched card that contains information for a group of cards to follow.

card punching printer, See CPP.

card reader, A device capable of reading punched card holes.

card, transition, A specific control card in a deck of program cards.

card verifying, The process of verifying the contents of punched cards using a verifier.

cards per minute, See CPM.

caret, A symbol ( ) used to show the place of an insertion.

carriage control tape, Same as control tape.

carriage restore key, A button on a printer that returns the printer carriage to a start position.

carriage return, In a character-by-character printing mechanism, the operation that causes the next character to be printed at the left margin.

carriage space key, A push button on a computer printer that spaces the paper vertically.

carrier, A specific wave that has constant amplitude and frequency, and a phase that can be modulated by changing amplitude, frequency, or phase.

carrier, common communications, A company that furnishes communications service, such as a telephone company.

carrier, continuous, A communications carrier in which transmission is not interrupted.

carrier, data, The medium used to communicate data, i.e., "carry" data.

carrier, land line, These operate microwave radio or broadband cable links for their backbone (long-haul) network and use VG (voice grade) lines (leased or dialed) to reach local customers.

carrier noise, Residual modulation, i.e., undesired variations in frequency in a signal.

carrier, transmission, Refers to transmission in which the transmitted electric wave results from the modulation of a single-frequency wave by an information-carrying (modulating) wave.

carrier wave, The frequency of a signal with no intelligence until it is modulated by another signal of intelligence.

carriers, value-added, A relatively new class of communications common carrier, authorized to lease raw communication trunks from the transmission carriers. They augment these facilities with computerized switching, and provide enhanced or "value-added" communication services.

carry, The "carry" in an arithmetic operation such as addition.

carry flag, An indicator that signals when a register overflow or underflow condition occurs during mathematical operations with an accumulator.

carry, partial, A type of carry in an addition operation.

carry time, The time needed for a carry in an arithmetic operation.

Carterphone Decision, U.S. Supreme Court decision that allows telephone subscribers to connect their own equipment to lines owned and maintained by public utilities including privately owned telephones, switchboards, data processing equipment, and so on.

cartridge, A self-contained device, usually a magnetic recording device.

cascade control, In an automatic control system, each control unit regulates the next control unit.

cascade merging, A method of merging used in a sort program.

case shift., In telegraph receiving, the shift from letters to case numbers case or vice versa (analogous to shifting from lower case to upper case and vice versa on a typewriter).

case, test, Testing a sample of data.

cassette, A self-contained, continuous, and self-winding package of reel-to-reel blank or recorded film, videotape, or electronically embossable vinyl tape for recording of sound or other types of computer input signals.

cassette bootstrap loader, Automatically locates the top of memory and relocates itself to the top of memory, enabling program loading from memory location zero.

cassette recorder, microcomputer-based, Numerous cassette recorders are programmed to log data from any user-specified instrument in formats readable by almost any type of terminal or cassette.

cassettes, digital-tape, These cassettes consist of cartridge-enclosed, magnetically-coated tape to record and play back text. Information on a cassette is accessed serially.

catalog, A list of items arranged for easy reference.

catalog, under, A compiled list of holdings in two or more libraries.

catalog, union, A compiled list of the contents of two or more magnetic tape libraries.

catastrophic errors, When so many errors have occurred that the job is terminated.

category, A classification of a logical grouping.

category, display, The type or class of data to be visually displayed.

catena, A chain or series.

cathode, The element in a vacuum tube that emits electrons.

cathode ray tube (CRT), A television-like display device attached to a computer or used as a remote terminal.

cathode ray tube oscilloscope, See CRO

CATV, Cable or Community TV: A system with two-way capacity to conduct signals to the head end as well as away from it, providing entertainment and education programs to customers on a coaxial cable system for charged fees.

CCD, See charge coupled device.

CCITT, Comite Consultatif Internationale de Telegraphic et Telephonie, an international consultive committee that sets international communications usage standards.

CCTV, See closed-circuit TV.

CDS, An abbreviation for compatible duplex system or comprehensive display system.

cell, The storage for one unit of information, also a data element.

cell, binary, A cell of one binary digit, a one-bit register or position.

cell, data, A mass storage device which utilizes strips of magnetic tape housed in a rotating cylinder.

cell, data, The smallest unit of data (see data cell drive).

cell, magnetic, A basic storage element.

center, display, A position on a display screen.

center feed tape, Paper tape with feed holes in the center of the tape.

center, primary, A control center connecting other (telephone) toll centers.

center, sectional, A control center that connects primary centers together (a Class 2 office).

center switching, A communications center where circuit switching and message switching take place.

center, toll, A central office where toll message circuits terminate.

center, zero, A special telephone trunk switching center serving a group of primary centers.

centerline, stroke, A line used to designate the midpoint of characters in optical character recognition.

central communications controller, The controller in a communications system that handles messages.

central control unit, Same as the central processing unit (CPU) of a computer.

central office, A common facility that performs switching in a communications network.

central office exchange, Same as central office.

central processing element (CPE), Using bipolar technology and bit-slice architecture, each CPE represents a 2-bit or a 4-bit slice through the data processing section of a computer. Several CPEs, arrayed in parallel, form a processor of any desired word length.

central processing unit, See CPU.

central processing unit (CPU), The central processor of a computer system; contains main storage, arithmetic unit, registers, etc.

central processor, The part of a computer that contains arithmetic logic and control capabilities.

central scanning loop, A loop of instructions that determines what is to be performed next.

central terminal unit (CTU), A unit that supervises communications between teller consoles and the processing center.

centralized control, The control of all processing by a single unit.

centralized data processing, Processing (at one location) all data involved with a given activity.

Centrex, Telephone equipment in a central office that serves subscribers on a PABX basis.

certified tape, Magnetic tape that has been certified to have zero errors (or less than a specified number).

CFM, An abbreviation for cubic feet per minute or cathode-follower mixer.

chain, binary, A series of binary circuits arranged so each circuit affects the condition of the circuit that follows it.

chain, Markov, A model used to determine the sequence of events in which a given event is dependent on the preceding event.

chain printer, A printer that uses a chain mechanism for printing.

chained file, A procedure used to retrieve data in which each data record contains the address of another record with the same key.

chaining, A method of storing and retrieving data records.

chaining, command, The execution of several commands in a command list on one or more records.

chaining, data, The gathering of information from more than one area of memory.

chaining search, A method of search that leads one from one place to another until the record is found or to the end of the "chain."

change, control, A change in the control field — minor, major, etc.

change file, A file of transactions to be processed against (thus updating) the related master file.

change, minor control, A change in the least significant control level.

change record, A record used to change information in a master file record.

change, step, A change in a single increment from one value to another in negligible time.

change tape, A tape to be processed to update a master tape (synonymous with transaction tape).

changeable storage, Devices in which storage can be removed from the machine and put back later such as disk packs, tape reels, etc.

channel, Refers to a part of the computer that connects it with its peripheral devices. All communications between the computer and its peripherals pass through a channel.

channel, A path on which signals can be sent to carry data.

channel adapter, A device used to permit the connection between data channels of different equipment.

channel, adjacent, A channel that has a frequency band adjacent to that of the reference channel.

channel, analog, A type of channel on which data transmitted can take any value within the limits of the channel.

channel bandwidth, Channel direction is characterized by bandwidth. The greater bandwidth allows proportionately higher transmission rates — usually specified as the number of line-signal elements per second (the baud rate).

channel, communications, An electrical transmission path among two or more stations or locations.

channel controller, The controller in a multiprocessor system that allows each processor to have access to every channel in the system.

channel, data, The two-way data path between input/output devices and a computer processor.

channel, dedicated, A communications channel reserved or committed for a specific use.

channel, duplex, A channel that can provide transmission in both directions at the same time.

channel, half-duplex, A channel capable of sending and receiving signals, but only in one direction at a time (contrasted with full-duplex channel).

channel, information, The transmission equipment between two terminals (communications).

channel multiplexer, data, Allows multiple data break capability (see data break).

channel, phantom, A communications channel that has no independent conductive path.

channel, reverse, A means of sending and receiving at the same time in communications.

channel selection, input/output, Pertains to the capability of a computer to select a particular channel for use.

channel, selector, Provides a path and control between the computer and input/output devices; used with high-speed devices.

channel, simplex, A communications channel that allows transmissions in one direction only.

channel, simplex, A communications channel capable of transmission in one direction only.

channel, subvoice grade, A channel whose bandwidth is less than that of voice grade channels.

channel synchronizer, A device providing signals to control transfer of data at proper times and sequence.

channel, two-wire, A channel in which transmission is only in one direction at a time.

channel types, Simplex, half-duplex, and duplex circuits are some channel types. The names indicate only the directional capability of the channel.

channel utilization index, The ratio of the information rate (per second) to the channel capacity (per second).

channel, voice grade, A channel used for speech transmission usually with an audio frequency range of 300 to 3,400 Hertz; also used for transmission of analog and digital data.

channelize, To divide a communications circuit into several channels.

channels, paper tape, Information channels, e.g., 8-channel tape has eight channels of code positions.

character, Any symbol that can be stored and processed by a computer.

character, A symbol in a set of symbols.

character, acknowledgement, A character sent back to a sending station by a receiving station indicating what had just been sent was received (communications).

character, bell, A control character that activates a signal, which calls for attention by humans for intervention.

character boundary, An imaginary or real rectangle that is the boundary for a character in a document.

character check, tape, The parity bit in a tape character code.

character code, directing, Routine indicator(s) at the start of a message to indicate destination.

character collating sequence, The sequence formed by characters in a particular coding system. Usually special characters are lower in value than alphabetic which are in turn lower than numeric.

character, control, A character used to indicate a control function.

character crowding, The reduction of space between characters on magnetic tape.

character, delete, A character used to get rid of erroneous or undesirable characters.

character, end-of-text, A character used to indicate the end of the text in data communications transmission.

character error indication, Often indicated by a blinking character, by an intensification of a character, word, or by field or writing a message to the operator.

character fill, See fill.

character, illegal, A combination of bits (a character) accepted as invalid by a data processing machine.

character, least significant, The character in the right-most position of a field or word.

character, locking shift, A control character indicating all characters that follow should be of the shifted set of characters. (Compared somewhat in concept to the locking of the shift key on a typewriter.)

character, magnetic, A character that is imprinted with magnetic ink.

character, negative acknowledge, A communications character used for control and accuracy checking.

character, nonnumeric, Any allowable character except a numeric digit.

character, nonprinting, A character that is decoded as a blank for printing purposes.

character printer, A printer that prints a character at a time, such as a typewriter device.

character reader, A device that can read characters optically or magnetically.

character recognition, Refers to the technology of using a machine to sense, and encode into a machine language, characters which are written or printed to be read by human beings.

character recognition, Identifying or reading characters optically, magnetically, etc.

character set, The numbers, letters, and symbols associated with a given device or coding system.

character set, That set of characters used to distinguish data, may include numbers, letters, a blank, special symbols such as $, ., #, *, etc.

character, skew, A form of misregistration in character recognition.

character, space, A character designed to prevent a print.

character spacing reference line, A vertical line used to determine horizontal spacing of characters (in optical character recognition).

character, special, In a character set, a character that is neither a numeral nor a letter.

character, special, A character other than a digit or a letter, such as $, *, +, ., #, etc.

character, start of heading, A character sent by a polled terminal that indicates the beginning of addresses of stations to receive the answering message.

character, start of text, A control character used in communications to end and separate a heading and indicate beginning of message content (text).

character string, A sequence of characters in a row.

character stroke, A line segment or mark used to form characters in optical character recognition.

character style, The style (construction characteristics) of a character in optical character recognition.

character, switching control, A specific character used to control the switching of devices from on to off or vice versa.

character, sync, Transmitted to establish character synchronization in synchronous communications. When the receiving station recognizes it, the station is said to be "synchronized" with the transmitting station, and communications can begin.

character, tape, A character composed of bits across the longitudinal channels of a tape.

character transfer rate, The speed that data may be read or written, e.g., characters per second.

characteristic distortion, A fixed distortion resulting in either shortened or lengthened impulses.

characters, alphameric, A generic term for numbers, letters, and special characters.

characters, idle, Control characters used in data transmission for synchronization (communications).

characters per second, Abbreviation cps. This is the term used to describe the speed of operation of a character printer.

characters per second, The maximum number of characters per second that a terminal or device can transmit or receive in asynchronous mode.

characters, throw-away, Characters transmitted in a communications system that are used for timing purposes.

charge, A quantity of unbalanced electricity in a body, i.e., excess or deficiency of electrons, giving the body negative or positive electrification respectively.

charge coupled device (CCD) memories, A species of an analog shift register, a semiconductor device in which an applied electrical field induces potential minima for signal charge packets at storage sites, at or near the surface of the semiconductor material. It is competitive in price with disk but more reliable, easier to maintain with lower power dissipation; with simple cooling requirements, it is also small in size and light in weight.

charge, shift, The amount of money charged for extra shifts of computer use beyond the base lease price charged by the computer manufacturer.

charge, storage, The cost per unit of storage on devices such as disk, drum, or tape.

charge-coupled device (CCD), A special type of computer memory chip offering high storage density with low power consumption.

chart, detail, A flowchart done in detail, step by step.

chart, logic, Same as program flowchart, showing the logical steps used to solve a problem.

chart, process, A flowchart of the major steps of work in process, synonymous with flow-process diagram (see flowchart).

chart, run, A flowchart of one or more computer runs to show input and output.

chart, system, A flowchart of a system showing the flow of information.

chart, work distribution, A listing of duties and responsibilities of personnel related to the job under study.

chassis, The metal base on which electronic equipment is built.

check, A test of a condition.

check, arithmetic, The verification of an arithmetic calculation, e.g., multiplying 4 x 2 to check the operation 2 x 4.

check, automatic, A provision constructed in hardware for verifying the accuracy of information transmitted, manipulated, or stored by any unit or device in a computer.

check, bias, Varying equipment operating conditions (e.g., voltage, frequency) in order to locate defectiveness of parts; a computer maintenance procedure.

check bit, A binary check digit (often a parity bit).

check, built-in, A provision in the computer (hardware) to verify the accuracy of data that is moved around and processed by parts of the computer.

check character, A parity character added to a group of characters to assist in error detection-correction.

check, consistency, Methods of checking to see that a piece of data is consistent with the rules to handle it.

check, cyclic, A method of error detection which checks every nth bit, n + 1 bit, n + 2 bit, and so forth.

check, data, An error in the data read, caused by a flaw on the recording surface of a magnetic tape or disk or other such medium. This type of error cannot be corrected at that place nor can that particular portion of the recording surface be used again.

check, desk, Checking a program for errors without the aid of the computor.

check, diagnostic, A routine used to locate a malfunction in a computer.

check digit, A redundant digit (or digits) carried within a unit item of information (character, word, block, and so on) which provides information about the other digits in the unit in such a manner that an error can be spotted.

check digit, The use of one or more redundant digits used for checking purpose.

check digit sum, A digit that reflects various combinations of summing done on a number; used for checking purposes.

check digits, Digits used in processing for checking purposes.

check, hardware, Use of checking features built into computers to check for any changes in data as it's moved around in the computer system.

check indicator, A device in a computer that displays or otherwise indicates that an error has occurred in a checking operation.

check indicator instruction, A computer instruction that directs a signal device to be turned on for the purpose of calling the computer operator's attention to the instruction in use.

check light, A computer (or other machine) indicator light that is lighted when there is an error condition of some kind.

check, limit, Checking data in a computer program to see that it is within predetermined limits.

check, longitudinal, A checking process done by counting bits.

check, machine, An automatic check or a programmed check of machine functions.

check, marginal, A technique used in preventative maintenance.

check nonexistent code, Same as a validity check (see nonexistent code).

check, overflow, A test done by the computer to determine whether or not an overflow has occurred. If the overflow check reveals that an overflow has indeed occurred, an error message will be printed.

check problem, A problem used to see if a computer or program is working properly.

check, program, An automatic error check in a computer program.

check, range, Checking to see that a value falls between maximum and minimum values as defined.

check reset key, A push button on a computer used to reset some error conditions.

check, selection, An automatic check to see if the correct register, input/output device, etc., was selected.

check, sequence, (1) checking in a computer program to see that the records in a file are in order; (2) a process performed on a collator (machine) to check the order of punched cards.

check, sight, Visual verification by a person (not a machine).

check, sign, A test for change in the sign (plus or minus) of a data field.

check, sum, The checking that takes place when digits are summed.

check, summation, A checking procedure used to verify that no digits have changed since the last time they were summed.

check, system, A performance check on a system.

check total, One of many totals used for checking calculations.

check, transfer, Checking the accuracy of a data transfer.

check, transverse, An error control method based on preset rules of character formation.

check, twin, A redundancy or duplication check.

check, unallowable code, An automatic check for a nonpermissible code.

check, validity, A specific check made for the accuracy of character coding; in addition, it can be a reasonableness check on data.

checking feature, A built-in capability of some computers to automatically check its own performance (feature of the computer).

checking, internal, The features of equipment that help improve accuracy by checking for things such as hole counts, parity checks, validity checks, etc.

checking, loop, A method of checking data transmission by sending data back to the sender.

checkout, A general term to describe the process of looking for and eliminating errors.

checkout, program, The process of determining that a computer program is performing as expected for all conditions.

checkout systems, automatic, Tests applied to each component and subsystem of aircraft, missiles, weapons, etc., to evaluate the overall system operation.

checkpoint, A place in a routine where a check, or a recording of data for restart purposes, is performed.

checkpoint, A point in a machine run in which data is saved in case a restart is necessary later.

checkpoint/restart, In database management, checkpoints may be used at intervals throughout an application program to write information to permit a clean restart of the program at the checkpoint.

checks, accounting, Accuracy control methods such as the use of control totals, cross totals, and hash totals.

checks, systems, Checks made on overall systems operations (by software or hardware).

chip, A small integrated microelectronic circuit package containing many logic elements; a small piece of silicon impregnated with impurities in a pattern to form transistors, diodes, and resistors.

chip architecture, Microprocessor chips include the arithmetic logic unit (ALU), the general-purpose registers, and the control bus structure, all depending on chip pins, chip size, off-chip memory, and I/O bus structure.

chip, electronic, A tiny piece of silicon on which an integrated circuit is built, the circuits being mass-produced on circular sheets of silicon called wafers that are then cut into dozens of individual chips, often square or rectangular.

chip I/O lines, Each line on the chip can often act as either an input or output, can be dedicated to some specific purpose, can be programmable generally or on a word basis only.

chip, memory, Random access memory (RAM) chips are used primarily for variable data and scratch pad; read-only memory (ROM) chips are used primarily to store instruction sequences; programmable read-only memory (PROM) chips are used for quickly tailoring general-purpose computers. Other memory type chips fill other gaps.

chip microprocessor, Usually the so-called "computer on a chip" — i.e., an LSI (large-scale integrated) circuit, capable of performing the essential functions of a computer, all residing on a single silicon chip according to the component integration design.

chip select (cs), Some LSI chips normally have one or several chip selects, the CS line being used to select one chip among many. When selected, the chip examines the rest of its pins, in particular the address bus that specifies a location/register within the chip design.

chip, silicon, A small piece of silicon on which very complex miniaturized circuits are made by photographic and chemical processes. Silicon chips are semiconductors.

chip technology, LSI (large-scale integration) technology is used to build microprocessor chips and is centered primarily around metal oxide semiconductor (MOS) devices, often with densities that range from 500 to more than 10,000 transistors and other devices per chip. Chip size is generally from 0.15 inch square to 0.25 inch square.

choice, logical, Making the right decision from a group of alternate possibilities.

chroma demodulator, Has synchronous detectors that must pull the color information out of a phase-modulated subcarrier and combine it with brightness information to create the proper mixtures of primary colors at the video output stage.

chrominance, signal, A combination of luminance and color signals.

CICS, See customer information control system.

CICS customer information control system, A software system used by many banks to provide an interface between the operating system access methods and application programs to allow remote or local display terminal interaction with the database of customer information.

CIM, See computer input microfilm

CIM - Computer Input Microfilm, A device or system to interpret characters that use microfilm imagery rather than printing on a paper, the process involving scanning, converting representations to computer language and arranging the information in memory such as tape or disk.

cinching, Slippage between the layers of tape on a roll.

cipher, An algorithmic transformation performed on a symbol-by-symbol basis on any data.

cipher, block, This cipher method enciphers fixed-sized blocks of bits under the control of a key that is often approximately the same size as the blocks being encoded.

circuit, Complete path for an electric current.

circuit, (1) A communications link, (2) a system of electrical conductors through which electric current flows.

circuit, asynchronous, A circuit without a synchronizing clock pulse whose operation is triggered only by signal levels.

circuit, bistable, A circuit capable of assuming either one of two stable states (same as flip-flop).

circuit, bistable trigger, A circuit capable of assuming either one of two stable states (same as flip-flop).

circuit board, Printed circuit boards are used abundantly in testers to complex digital computers, offering increased economy, easier mass production, reduction of worker errors, computerized testing, miniaturization, increased complexity, increased ruggedness, and easier troubleshooting.

circuit board backplane, A printed circuit board (PCB) which contains sockets other PCBs can plug into it at right angles. Generally, a backplane does not contain electronic components.

circuit board, expansion, A printed circuit board (PCB) that adds additional capabilities and functions to a computer's hardware. The expansion board plugs into a slot inside the computer and is generally accessed by referencing the address assigned to the slot.

circuit breaker, A device designed to open electric circuits under abnormal operating conditions, e.g., excessive current, heat, high ambient radiation level, and so on. Also called constant breaker.

circuit, bus, Usually a group of circuits that provide a communication path between two or more devices, such as between a central processor, memory, and peripheral equipment.

circuit capacity, 1 The number of communications channels that can be derived from a given circuit at the same time. 2 The information capacity, measured in bits per second, of a circuit.

circuit capacity, The number of channels that can be handled at the same time.

circuit card, A printed-circuit board containing electronic components.

circuit, computer, Often fall into the following categories: storage circuits, triggering circuits, gating circuits, inverting circuits, and timing circuits; others may be power amplifiers, indicators, output devices, and so on.

circuit, data telephone, A telephone circuit capable of transmitting digital data.

circuit, dedicated, A communications circuit reserved or committed for a specific use.

circuit, differentiating, A circuit whose output function is proportional to a derivative.

circuit, digital, An on/off switch-like circuit; should be called a binary circuit.

circuit, discrete component, A circuit of individual transistors, resistors, etc., as contrasted with integrated circuit.

circuit, etched, Refers to integrated circuits and their construction.

circuit grade, The information carrying capability in speed or type of signal (communications).

circuit, integrated, See INTEGRATED CIRCUIT.

circuit, integrated (IC), One of many hundreds of types often containing gates, flip-flops that are etched on single crystals, ceramics, or other semiconductor materials and designed to use geometric etching and conductive ink or chemical deposition techniques all within a hermetically sealed chip.

circuit, logic, One of many types of switching circuits such as AND, OR, etc., that perform logic functions.

circuit, logical, A type of switching circuit such as AND, OR, and other Boolean logic operations gates.

Circuit, monolithic integrated, One of several logic circuits that are etched on chips of material (see integrated circuit).

circuit, multipoint, A circuit that interconnects several that must communicate on a time-shared basis.

circuit, multitone, Two or more channels being used at the same time in the same direction for transmitting a signal between two points.

circuit, nanosecond, A circuit with a pulse rise or fall time measured in billionths of seconds.

circuit, neutral, A teletypewriter circuit with current in only one direction.

circuit, party line, A multistation net on a single circuit.

circuit, printed, A circuit in which resistors, capacitors, diodes, transistors, and other circuit elements are mounted on cards and interconnected by conductor deposits. The cards are treated with a light-sensitive emulsion: The exposed fixing areas are retained, while acid baths eat away those portions that are designed to be destroyed. The base is usually a copper-clad card.

circuit reliability, The percentage of time a circuit meets operational standards.

circuit, send-request, A circuit in which signals are originated to select whether to send or receive data (in half-duplex service).

circuit, short, When an abnormal connection of relatively low resistance between two points of a circuit, the result is a flow of excess (often damaging) current between these points.

circuit, single, A circuit capable of nonsimultaneous two-way communication.

circuit switch, A switching system that completes a circuit from sender to receiver (in communications).

circuit switching, Same as line switching.

circuit, synchronous, A circuit whose operation is controlled by a synchronizing clock pulse.

circuit, tank, A component of a mercury acoustic delay line.

circuit tester, Device or system employing a digital processor and storage media to supply programmed test instructions, translate product error data, and perform arithmetic and other computations.

circuit, transmitted data, A circuit that carries signals originated by the data terminal equipment; not required for receive-only service.

circuit, tributary, A circuit that connects as a drop or drops to a switching center.

circuit, trunk, A circuit that connects two data switching centers.

circuit, way operated, A circuit shared by three or more stations (party line).

circuitry, solid-state, The solid-state components in computers.

circuits, balanced, An electrical circuit (with balanced voltage).

circuits, control, Those circuits relating to computer execution of instructions.

circuits, discrete, Electronic circuits built from separately manufactured components (contrasted with integrated circuit).

circuits, instruction control, The circuit used to control the carrying out of instructions in the proper sequence.

circuits, printed, Resistors, capacitors, diodes, transistors, etc., that are mounted on cards (used in computer circuits).

circuits, sealed, Very tiny circuits that are sealed in place.

circuits, storage, Flip-flops (see flip-flop).

circuits, sweep, The circuits that guide the movement of a beam in a tube.

circuits, sync, Circuits in radar and television that control the movements of the scope beam.

circuits, timing, Circuits used to control time delay or duration.

circular shift, A shift in which positions shifted out of one end of a word or register fill in from the other end (in a circular way).

circulating register, A specific kind of computer register used for shift instructions.

circulating storage, Devices that store information in a pattern of pulses that are sensed, amplified, reshaped, and reinserted into the device.

circumscribe, To limit, to bound, to enclose.

citation, index, A reference list of documents that are mentioned or quoted in a text.

CIU, See computer interface unit.

CIU (Computer Interface Unit), A device used to match and connect a CPU (central processing unit) to peripheral devices.

cladding, The transparent medium which surrounds the core of an optic fiber.

cladding, fiberoptics, The low refractive index material that surrounds the core of the fiber and protects against surface contaminant scattering; often a glass material but in plastic-clad silica fibers. The plastic cladding also may service as the coating.

class, A group, often a subdivision of a category.

class name, phase, Nonterminal nodes in formal language theory.

classification, An arrangement of data in groups.

classify, To arrange data into groups according to some criteria.

CLAT, See communication line adapter.

CLAT, See adapter, communication line.

clear, To erase the contents of a storage device by replacing the contents with blanks or zeros.

clear, To erase or return to zeros, such as a storage area or register.

clear band, In optical character recognition an area that must be kept free of unrelated printing.

CLK, An abbreviation for clock.

clock, A circuit that generates a series of evenly spaced pulses. A computer with a faster clock rate is able to perform more operations per second.

clock (clk), A timekeeping, synchronizing or pulse counting device in a computer system.

clock, control, An electronic clock in a computer.

clock, day, An electronic clock used in real-time processing (in a computer).

clock, digital, A clock having output signals in digital representation.

clock, externally generated, Often the on-chip oscillator can be disabled and the timing generator can be driven by a clock comprising (a) single-phase true and complement inputs and (b) instruction execution and input/output timing (in microcycles).

clock, frequency, The frequency of periodic pulses that schedules the operation of a computer (see synchronous).

clock, master, The electronic source timing signals in a computer.

clock pulse, Any pulse used for timing purposes.

clock pulse generator, A unit that generates pulses for timing purposes in a computer.

clock rate, The time rate that a clock emits pulses (in a computer).

clock, real-time, A register and circuitry combination that automatically maintains time in conventional time units for use in program execution and event initiation.

clock signal, A clock pulse used to control timing of various functions.

clock stretching, selective, A technique capable of resolving digital timing differences among system components and obtaining the maximum performance out of each component.

clock, synchronous, A clock frequency used to control the timing in a computer.

clock system, Often a microprocessor timing system that relies on a clock system, used to cycle the computer through the various states required during operation.

clock time (real-time), The use of a built-in clock in a real-time system for timing purposes.

clock, time of day, A clock that records hours, minutes, and seconds (over a 24-hour period) in the central processor of a computer.

clock track, Same as a timing track; containing pulses developing a clock signal to aid in reading data.

closed entry contact, A female contact designed to prevent entry of pins larger than specified size.

closed loop, A technique, system, or device involving feedback of data for control or checking purposes.

closed loop system, A system in which a computer controls a process without human intervention.

closed shop, A computer installation that is run only by specified personnel; it's "hands-off" for everyone else (contrasted with open shop).

closed subroutine, A computer program subroutine that is stored separately and linked into various computer programs as needed.

closed-circuit signaling, A type of signaling in which the signal is initiated by increasing or decreasing the current.

closed-circuit TV (CCTV), Closed-circuit tv cameras and monitors to provide increased control, more efficient operation, and greater security by using fewer people than previously. Users can observe and control several locations simultaneously due to alarms and keyboards, usually computer-controlled.

CLT, See communication line terminal.

clutch cycle, The time between operations of a clutch driven device.

CML, See current mode logic.

CML, Current mode logic, a technology used in the construction of some major computers, particularly some IBM types.

CMOS, See complementary metal oxide semiconductor.

CMOS - Complementary Metal Oxide Semiconductor, A family of integrated circuits whose output structure consists of an N-type MOS-

FET and a P-type MOSFET in series that offers low power and low voltage in operation. (FET = Field Effect Transistor.)

CNC, Computer Numerical Control represents the direct use of computers in automated machinery and process control.

coalesce, To combine two or more files into one.

COAM equipment, Stands for customer owned and maintained communication equipment, such as terminals.

coating thickness, The thickness of tape coatings.

coaxial cable, A cable of at least one transmission line of two conductors insulated from one another.

COBOL, Common Business Oriented Language. Most widely used programming language in large commercial data processing systems.

Codabar code, A type of bar code read by wand scanners, designed by Monarch Marking System, Inc., for use in discount and variety stores where POS (point-of-sale) systems are installed. Also used in libraries, medical institutions, industrial control, photographic processes, and other industries.

CODASYL, Conference on Data Systems Languages. An organization for computer users.

CODASYL, Conference on Data Systems Languages, organized by the Department of Defense.

code, The specific form in which information is entered into a computer (e.g., binary, ASCII, hexadecimal). Also, code is often used to refer to the instructions contained in a computer program. For example, 'How many lines of code does this program use?'

code, (1) a system of symbols for representing data or instructions; (2) to write a computer program.

code, absolute, Program code using absolute (actual) addresses and operators.

code, alphabetic, A system of alphabetic abbreviations used in data processing (contrasted with numeric code).

code, alphameric, A system of coding using alphameric characters.

code, basic, Computer code using absolute addresses and operation codes (synonymous with specific code and one-level code).

code, binary, A coding system using binary digits (0 and 1).

code, biquinary, A two-part code in which each decimal digit is represented by the sum of a binary part and a quinary part.

code, card, The code used for data representation in punched cards.

code check, unallowable, An automatic check for a nonpermissible code.

code, command, Same as operation code, i.e., the portion of a computer instruction that specifies the operation to be performed.

code, computer, (1) The system of coding used for data in a computer, (2) the set of instruction codes that may be used for a computer.

code conversion, Changing from one coding structure to another.

code conversion, data, Translating alphameric data into computer representation of data; usually done by the computer.

code, cyclic, A special type of binary code.

code, data, Sets of characters structured to represent data items of a data element, i.e., a coding method.

code, dense binary, A code in which all possible combinations are used.

code, dictionary, An alphabetical arrangement of words and terms and their meanings.

code, directing character, Routine indicator(s) at the start of a message to indicate destination.

code, EBCDIC, Extended binary coded decimal interchange code, a standard code used in data processing.

code, error detecting, A code in which errors produce a forbidden code combination.

code, external device (ED), An address code of an external device that specifies which operation is to be performed.

code, false, A character that is not accepted as a valid combination of bits by a machine (computer).

code, forbidden, A representation of data that has no accepted equivalent.

code, hamming, An error correction code.

code holes, Data holes as opposed to feedholes in perforated tape.

code, Hollerith, An alphanumeric punched card code (not used widely), named after its inventor, Dr. Herman Hollerith.

code, identifying, A code in data processing punched cards or perforated tape to identify the contents or their origin.

code, illegal, A character or symbol that seems to be proper but is not a true element of a defined alphabet.

code, instruction, The set of symbols (and their definitions) that are intelligible to a given computer.

code, internal, The data representation structure of a computer; e.g., in most systems a byte is 8 bits, a half-word is 3 bytes, etc. The internal code is an 8-bit character.

Code, International, The system in radio telegraph in which combinations of dots and dashes stand for letters of the alphabet.

code, interpreter, An interim code that must be translated to computer coding before use.

code line, One computer instruction written by a programmer on one line.

code, line-feed, A code that causes page teleprinters (and others) to move the platen up one line.

code, M out of N, A form of binary code in which M of the N digits are always in the same state.

code, machine, (1) The symbols or numbers assigned to parts of a machine; (2) same as operation code.

code, macro, A coding method that permits single words to generate many computer instructions during translation.

code, MICR, The code used in magnetic ink character recognition, developed by the American Bankers Association.

code, mnemonic, Code that assists people in remembering what things stand for such as ACC for accumulator, NET for net pay, etc.

code, mnemonic operation, A computer operation code, as something easy to remember, such as A for add, S for subtract, etc.

code, morse, A system of dot-dash signals for communications. Not used for data communications.

code, nonexistent, A combination of bits that is not acceptable as a valid combination.

code, numeric, A code scheme using only numbers.

code, object, The code produced by a compiler or assembler (after translation from source code) in computer programming.

code, one-level, Computer code using absolute addresses and operation codes (synonymous with specific code and basic code).

code, operation, The symbol (code) that tells the computer which operation to perform.

code, optimized, A computer program's compiled code that contains no inefficiencies or unnecessary instructions. Optimized code is the best solution to a problem.

code, optimum, A computer code that is especially efficient.

code, pulse, A code made up of patterns of pulses.

code, reflected, A binary code that only changes by one bit going from one number to the next.

code, relative, Computer program code written with addresses relative to an arbitrarily selected position.

code, self-checking, A coding system used to detect errors in transfer of data (checks for loss or gain of bits).

code, self-complementing, A specific machine language in which the code of the complement of a digit is the complement of the code of the digit.

code, self-demarcating, Same as code, self-demarking.

code, self-demarking, (1) A code in which symbols are arranged to avoid the generation of false combinations by two successive codes; (2) same as error-detecting code.

code set, A group of coded information; a coding structure.

code, sites, Positions where data can be represented, such as punching positions.

code, skip, A code used to tell the machine to skip certain fields in memory.

code, specific, Computer code using absolute addresses and operation codes (synonymous with basic code and one-level code).

code, stop, A code read in the reader of tape-operated equipment that stops the reader and suspends operation.

code, straight-line, Computer program code in which coding is repeated instead of using programmed loops.

code, symbol, A code used to identify equipment in a records inventory.

code, symbolic, Computer program coding in symbolic (source) language.

code, teletype, A standard 5-channel code used in the telegraphy industry.

code, ternary, A code in which only three states are considered.

code, unit distance, A code in which the signal distance between consecutive words is one.

code, unitary, A code of one digit that is repeated a varying number of times to represent elements of the code.

code value, A value of any of the elements in a code set.

codec, A microelectronic coder-decoder that provides the essential translation between analog voice signals and the digital pulse-code modulation representation used in most computers and advanced PABX phone equipment as well as short-haul telecommunications carrier gear.

coded stop, A stop instruction in a computer program.

coder, Slang term for programmer.

coder, A person who writes computer instruction codes.

coder-decoder chip, Converts voice to digital form and back in PCM (pulse-code modulation) and other modulation systems, abbreviated codec.

codes, function, Codes used to operate machine functions such as (printer) carriage return, skip, tabulate, etc.

coding, Coding is the process of writing program instructions.

coding, The act of writing code for computer instructions.

coding, absolute, Programming coding in which the instructions to the computer are written in machine language, i.e., understood directly by the computer without translation.

coding, fixed form, Every part of computer instruction coding has to be in a certain field as contrasted with free form coding.

coding, in-line, A portion of computer program coding in the main path of a routine (program).

coding, machine, Writing code in the computer's own language (machine language).

coding, minimal access, A technique of coding that minimizes the time used to transfer words from auxiliary storage to main storage.

coding scheme, A particular system of coding.

coding sheet, A printed form used by programmers to write programs on. Generally one instruction per one line of coding.

coding, specific, A method of computer instruction coding using specific or absolute addresses.

coding, straight-line, Computer programming in which coding is repeated instead of using programmed loops.

coding, symbolic, Used to write computer instructions in other than machine language.

coding tools, Some basic types of coding tools are assemblers, editors, loaders, compilers, interpreters, microprogramming, macrocodes, and others.

coefficient, A number used to multiply another number.

coefficient, scale, Same as scale factor (a multiplier).

coefficient unit, constant multiplier, Same as scalar.

coercive force, intrinsic, A characteristic of magnetizing field strength in magnetic tape.

cognition, artificial, The ability of a machine to optically sense a character and determine which character it is by comparing it to a set of characters and selecting the one nearest in shape.

cognition, machine, A type of artificial learning by a machine, i.e., perception and interpretation based on previous experience.

COGO, An acronym for coordinated geometry; a higher-level language used in civil engineering.

coil, blank paper tape, Paper tape that has no information recorded on it yet.

coil, focusing, The coil in a writing tube that guides electrons in the beam.

coil, tape, A coil of paper tape as contrasted with a reel of magnetic tape.

coldstart, A method of resetting the computer. The contents of memory are erased, and the computer is started up again 'cold.'

collate, To merge two or more ordered sets of data or cards in order to produce one or more ordered sets which still reflect the original ordering relations.

collate, To merge two or more sets of data that are in the same order (sequence).

collating sequence, The order of a set of characters designed for a particular machine; used in comparing for high, low, equal.

collating, sequential, Combining two ordered sets of data into one and maintaining the order (sequence).

collating, sorting, A sort using continuous merging until the sequence is developed.

collation sequence, The acceptable order of characters for a given computer.

collator, A device used to collate or merge sets or decks of cards or other units into a sequence.

collator, A machine used to match, merge, sequence check, etc., decks of punched cards.

collection, data, The act of getting data and bringing it to a point for processing.

collection stations, data, Devices on production floors used to collect employee payroll data and other information.

collection system, data, A system using manufacturing information from inplant data collection stations.

color bars, Industry standards designed to adjust color TV and computer terminal equipment to match levels and phasing in common use.

column, A vertical arrangement of characters, bits, or other expressions. Contrasts with row.

column, A vertical set of positions in a punched card; a set of characters in an array (vertical).

column, card, One vertical line that contains punching positions in a card.

column, comment, Usually column 1 on punched cards which is reserved for comments.

column vector, The elements of a single column of a matrix are the components of a vector.

COM, See computer output microfilm (microform).

COM, computer output microfilm, Film produced by converting computer-generated signals into readable characters at high speeds. A small piece of film can contain many pages of information in a reduced form. This can be magnified and read using a device known as a COM reader.

combination, forbidden, A code character set or symbol that seems to be the proper element but isn't (judged to be mistaken).

combination operation, The performance of two or more operations at the same time and as a unit.

combiner, A functional block that groups several inputs to form a single output.

command, Generally, an instruction to a program or software system telling it to perform some action or to cause the execution of a certain program. For example, a print command causes the contents of a file to be printed.

command, An operation, or more specifically, a pulse signal or code to start, stop, or continue an operation.

command chaining, The execution of several commands in a command list on one or more records.

command code, The same as operation code, i.e., the portion of a computer instruction that specifies the operation to be performed.

command control program, A computer program that handles all user console commands sent to the system.

command decoder, The computer program that pre-processes commands from a user console.

command list, A sequence of steps generated by the CPU (central processing unit) for the performance of an input/output operation.

command macros, Often required for the program being executed, these reside in memory and include processing instructions such as multiply, divide, and process magnetic cards, minimizing memory requirements for specific applications.

command mode, The time when no program is active for a given terminal (in time sharing).

command, operator, An instruction issued by a computer operator to the control program in a computer.

command, transfer, A computer instruction that changes control from one place in a program to another.

commands, system, Commands made by a user to the executive program, e.g., to save a program or data files.

comment, Specifically, a statement in a computer program that is not acted on by the computer, but that gives information to clarify the purpose of a set of instructions. Informative comments can be extremely valuable if, for example, another programmer has to amend the program at a later date.

comment, An expression that identifies or explains an operation.

common business oriented language, The Cobol programming language, the most widely used business (applications) programming language.

common communications carrier, A company that furnishes communications service such as a telephone company.

common connector, The plug and wire completing a circuit in a wiring board.

common control unit, A unit that coordinates the flow of data between the data devices and the communication facility.

common field, A field of data that is accessible to two or more computer program routines.

common hardware, Hardware such as plugs, sockets, etc., that are commonly used.

common language, (1) A technique that makes all information intelligible to the units of a data processing system, (2) a language in machine-sensible form that is common to a group of computers, (3) a single code used by devices that are manufactured by different companies.

common machine language, A machine-sensible representation that is common to a group of machines.

common software, Computer programs and routines that are in a language common to many computers and users.

common storage, Storage that is used to hold intermediate data that can be maintained between programs.

common storage area, A specified common area in computer storage referenced by Fortran and other programs.

communicating word processor, Special desktop computers that have been combined with copiers and communications capabilities. Also, optical fiber networks to allow desk-to-desk intra- and inter-company communications in seconds per page.

communication, The process of transmitting information from one place (person, device) to another.

communication channel, A path used for transmission of data.

communication, data, The transmission of data from one location to another in a communications system.

communication, intercomputer, Data is transmitted from one computer to another computer.

communication lights, Lights on the keyboard that indicate power on, punch on, low tape supply, etc., on some computers.

communication line terminal (CLT), Input and output device used when data is transmitted to or from the central processor using a communications line.

communication link, Generally, consists of the hardware and software used to provide the means for two devices, such as a computer and a terminal, to be connected so they can transmit data.

communication link, The physical connection between one location and another used for data transmission.

communication message accounting, A system, maintained by a switching device, which records statistical data concerning the messages it handles; e.g., number of messages to and from each station, message lengths, queue lengths, and so on.

communication, radio, Any communication using radio waves.

Communication Satellite Corporation (COMSAT), Represented by more than 85 members of the INTELSAT Organization to provide technical and operational services for the global satellite communications system under a management contract with INTELSAT, headquartered in Washington, D.C.

communication subsystem control, Control by function words that activate control lines.

communication switching unit, A unit that allows any two processors to share a group of communication lines.

communication theory, A branch of mathematics dealing with the properties of transmitted messages.

communication-line adapter (CLAT), A semiautomatic device used to link buffer units with remote teletype lines.

communications, Refers to the means of conveying information of any kind from one person or place to another.

communications control unit, data, The unit that scans the central terminal unit buffers for messages and transfers them to the central processor.

communications, controller central, The controller in a communications system that handles messages.

communications, data-adapter unit, This device is attached to either a selector channel or a multiplexer channel to greatly expand the input/output capabilities of the system.

communications, electrical, Communications using material with relatively low electrical resistance (such as copper wire).

communications, electromagnetic, Communications in which the electromagnetic conductor is space, e.g., radio, television, radar.

communications handshaking, The exchange of predetermined signals when a connection is established between two communicating devices.

communications, input, (1) Current voltage or power applied to a circuit or device; (2) the terminals where (1) is done.

communications lag, The time between the sending of data and the response of the receiving device.

communications linkage, Common carrier equipment providing high speed communications facilities for data transmission.

communications, message switching, time sharing, A message handling system used in large reservation systems for airlines and hotels.

communications signal, A group of waves that travel on a transmission channel to a receiver.

communications software, The sets of computer program routines used in interrupt processing, message queuing, error control, etc.

communications system, A computer system and associated equipment to handle on-line real-time applications.

communications system, data, Usually a real-time system of data communication between a computer and remote terminals.

communications trunk, A telephone line between two central offices.

community automatic exchange (CAX), A small telephone office serving a community.

commutation switch, A device used to execute repetitive sequential switching.

commutator pulse, Special pulse used to mark, clock, or control a binary digit position in a computer word.

compaction, The process of rearranging data on a disk so as to clear large areas of free storage space. As data is constantly being written and erased from a disk, especially during heavy processing, it tends to get scattered (fragmented) into small portions called extents. As this occurs, the search, retrieval, and storage processes are slowed down, which reduces the overall efficiency of the program. Frequently, a special compaction routine resolves this by locating, reassembling, and consolidating the fragmented extents. Compacting is sometimes referred to as compressing.

compaction, data, Techniques used to reduce space, cost, time, etc., in the storage and transmission of data.

compaction, incremental, A method used in data compaction in which various increments are added to an initial value.

compandor, A device used on a telephone channel to improve performance.

companion keyboard, An auxiliary keyboard that is usually located remotely (away) from the main unit.

company, telephone, Any common carrier providing public telephone service.

comparand, A word or number used for comparison to another word or number.

comparator, A device used to compare two pieces of information, two signals, etc.

compare, (1) To determine which of two quantities is higher, lower, or if they are equal; (2) to determine the relationship of a value to zero.

compare facility, The ability of a computer to execute instructions based on the outcome of various combinations.

comparing unit, A device used to compare information in cards or pulses or signals.

comparison indicators, Indicators that are set after a compare instruction, i.e., high, low, equal. (See indicator.)

comparison, logical, Comparing two elements to see if they are the same or different.

comparison of pairs sorting, A method of sorting in which two records are compared and exchange positions if they are out of order.

compatibility, The quality or ability of data or instructions to be usable on different kinds of computers or equipment.

compatibility, equipment, The ability of equipment to accept and process data and/or programs prepared by another piece of equipment.

compatibility, firmware, Also called microprogramming it provides hardware-like matching and usability of programs as implemented in many small computer systems.

compatibility, systems, The compatibility electrically, logically, and mechanically of the devices in a system.

compatibility test, Tests run on a system to check the acceptability of hardware and software.

compatible, A characteristic of a device or program that makes it acceptable to another device or machine.

compatible hardware, Equipment that can be used on several different systems (compatible from one system to another).

compatible operating system, See CAS.

compatible software, Programming language or programs that can be used on more than one computer system.

compendium, An abbreviated summary of a subject.

compensator, level, A device in the receiving equipment of a telegraph circuit.

compilation, program, The process of compiling (translating) a high-level computer programming language into machine language.

compilation time, The time that a source language computer program is compiled.

compile, To produce a machine language computer program from a source language program.

compile, programming, To produce a machine-language routine from a routine written in high-level language.

compiler, A computer program that takes as input a program written in a high-level programming language and puts it into a form known as machine language which can be understood and acted on by the computer.

compiler, A computer program used to translate other computer programs (in a high-level language) into machine language.

compiler diagnostics, A listing of programming errors detected in program compiling.

compiler generator, A generating computer program that constructs another computer program that can be used to translate computer programs for another computer.

compiler, incremental, Used in time sharing, each computer program statement is "compiled" as it is entered into the computer (in other cases all statements are read and then compiled together).

compiler, interactive, A compiler that translates each statement entered on a terminal into machine language as soon as it is entered.

compiler, maybe, A macro-generator used primarily by systems programmers.

compiler, syntax directed, A compiler based on syntactic relationships of the character string.

compiler system, Fortran, The two elements of a source language computer program and a compiler that translates the program into machine language.

compiling computer, The computer used for program compilation (may not be the same computer on which the program is executed).

complement, A number resulting from following specific rules to process another number.

complement, true, The complement for a given notation system, e.g., the binary true complement is the twos complement.

complement, twos, A value obtained by subtracting a number from the base number.

complement, zero, A complementing method.

complementary MOS (CMOS), A technology of chip manufacture design that offers advantages in lower power, less exposure to leakage-current variation and use with very low power batteries.

complementer, A device used to reverse a signal or condition to its opposite or alternate.

complete operation, An operation that obtains an instruction, processes, and returns the results to (computer) storage.

complete routine, A routine that doesn't need modification before being used.

complex, equipment, Any large mixture or group of computing equipment used for a large scale specific purpose (missile tracking, etc.)

complex number, The combination of a real number and an imaginary number.

component, An element or basic part of a whole.

component, computer, Any part of a computer such as a resistor, amplifier, etc.

component, solid-state, Components such as transistors, diodes, ferrite cores, etc., in computers and other equipment.

components, electronic, These are wires, transistors, diodes, resistors, capacitors, inductors, and so on.

components, passive, The components that play a static role in circuits and systems.

components, system, The collection of hardware and software organized to achieve operational objectives.

composite card, A multipurpose data processing punched card.

composite video signal, The signal that consists of a picture signal, blanking pulses, and sync pulses in a CRT (cathode ray tube).

composition, Preparation of a copy in a layout that is to be duplicated.

composition, file, Filing records within a computer storage unit.

compound, A combination of things; as contrasted with simple.

compound logical element, Computer circuitry that provides an output from many inputs.

compress, To condense data, with any of a variety of methods, so that it occupies less storage space.

compress, The process of reducing things such as signals, duration, bandwidth, etc.

compression, data, The elimination of all blanks, unnecessary fields, and redundant data from various records, in order to reduce the amount of storage space needed to contain them.

compression, data, Methods used to reduce the size of data elements by coding them, etc.

compression, zero, The process that eliminates the storage of leading zeros in a number.

compressor, An electronic device used to compress the volume range of a signal.

comptometer, A trade name for a specific calculator (key driven).

computation, address, A calculation that creates or changes the address portion of a computer instruction.

computational stability, The reliability and validity of a computational process.

compute limited, A situation in which the computation time is the delaying factor in receiving output.

compute mode, Also called operate mode as contrasted with hold mold.

computer, Any device capable of accepting information, applying prescribed processes to the information, and supplying the results of these processes.

computer, A machine capable of accepting information, processing it, and providing the results of the processes.

computer aided design (CAD), The capability of a computer to be used for automated industrial, statistical, biological, etc., design through visual devices.

computer aided instruction (CAI), An educational situation in which the computer is used to aid the student's instruction.

computer, all-purpose, A computer that has a combination of characteristics that is more than usually thought of for a general purpose and not a special purpose computer.

computer, analog, A computer in which the input is of a continuous nature and that measures continuously as opposed to a digital computer which counts discretely.

computer analyst, A person who determines the overall functions to be performed by a computer system and determines the major tasks the system will carry out.

computer application, A problem or job to be solved or accomplished on a computer.

computer applications analyst, A job classification of employees who give software oriented technical sales support to salesmen of computer equipment.

computer architecture, The interconnection and organization of internal circuitry in a microprocessor or computer.

computer, asynchronous, One in which each operation starts as a result of a signal generated by the completion of the previous operation or by the availability of the equipment required for the next operation.

computer, asynchronous, A computer that starts operations based on the previous operation or availability of parts of the computer.

computer, automatic, A computer capable of performing long series of operations without human intervention.

computer bomb, A program is said to have bombed if its output is incorrect or if it cannot execute because of syntax or logical errors.

computer broadcast (noun), Refers to a message transmitted to several or all users of a computer system. For example, the statement, 'The system will go down in 15 minutes,' would be a broadcast if it was transmitted to the users of the system.

computer broadcast (verb), Refers to transmission to all stations on a circuit, as opposed to one or a particular group of stations.

computer, buffered, A computer with a storage device to hold input and output data temporarily to match the relatively low speeds of input/output devices with the higher speed of the computer.

computer center, A complex of computer equipment, peripheral equipment, personnel, and the office space containing it all.

computer center manager, The person with responsibility for the entire computer center related activities.

computer circuits, Circuits used for storage, triggering, gating, timing, etc., in a computer.

computer code, (1) The system of coding used for data in a computer, (2) the set of instruction codes that may be used for a computer.

computer, compiling, The computer used for program compilation. It may not be the same computer that the program will be executed on.

computer component, Any part of a computer such as a resistor, amplifier, etc.

computer conferencing, From a remote terminal, the user puts in the code name for the recipient and at his or her own pace composes a message. When the message is complete, it is transmitted as a unit to the computer and held until the recipient requests transmission or until "live" conversations between two or more parties can be held.

computer configuration, The set of equipment that makes up a computer system.

computer, control, A computer controls processes by inputs and outputs of the process.

computer diagram, A functional diagram of computing elements.

computer, digital, A computer in which information is represented in discrete values as contrasted with analog computer.

computer duplex, A pair of identical computers (so one may always be available).

computer efficiency, The ratio of the number of hours of proper machine operation to the total hours of scheduled operation.

computer environment, A computer system's environment consists of those operating conditions under which it was designed to operate.

computer equation, A mathematical equation derived from a model that is more conveniently used on a computer.

computer, expandable, Generally, a computer is expandable if it can have more memory added to it or if it can have more disk drives added to it, additions that will expand the computer's storage capacity. Most home computers are expandable.

computer, first generation, Computer built in the technological era of development when the vacuum tube was the main electronic element.

computer, general-purpose, A computer designed to handle problem solving of many different types as contrasted with special-purpose computer.

computer graphics, The category includes a wide spectrum of services and equipment, such as digitizers, displays, printers, plotters, microfilm apparatus, and so on. Such systems can generally be divided into three main sections, all tied to the computer — input, editing, and output stages.

computer, host, A computer that is connected to a stored-program multiplexor, that is dependent upon it for certain vital functions.

computer, incremental, A special purpose computer such as a digital differential analyzer.

computer installation, (1) The whole computer facility itself including machines, people, etc.; (2) the process of delivering and installing (connecting and setting up) a computer system.

computer instruction, See instruction.

computer instruction set, That set of instructions that a particular computer can perform.

Computer Interface Unit (CIU), A device used to match and connect a CPU (central processing unit) to peripheral devices.

computer, keyboard, A computer that has keyboard input only.

computer language, A programming procedure in which instructions are in machine language.

computer legal, Something is legal if it is acceptable to a computer system's software rules. This includes syntax rules. If a statement or word in a program is not legal, then the program will not run. Instead, it will produce an error message.

computer literacy, Refers to knowledge of computers and how to use them to solve problems.

computer logic, The logic capabilities of a computer.

computer network, Two or more interconnected computers.

computer network components, Generally three types of facilities in addition to the host computer are required to accomplish computer networking: the user communication interface, the communications subnetwork, and facilities for the network control function.

computer, nonsequential, A computer that has the address of the next instruction contained in the prior instruction. It is the opposite of sequential computer.

computer, object, The computer that executes the object program as contrasted with source computer.

computer operation, A defined action. The action specified by a single computer instruction.

computer operation, Any of the many operations that may be performed by a computer, such as add, branch, compare, etc.

computer operator, An operator is someone who controls a computer or a computer-related device.

computer operator, The person who runs the computer.

computer oriented language, A term used for relatively low level languages, i.e., requiring a low degree of translation.

computer output, microfilm (COM), Outputting information onto microfilm.

computer, parallel, A computer in which data bits are processed at the same time (in parallel) as contrasted with serial computer.

computer program, A set of instructions used to solve a problem on a computer.

computer programming language, Any of many languages used to write instructions for a computer, e.g., Cobol, Fortran, assembly language, RPG, etc.

computer, remote, A computer at a location other than where the user is; generally connected by communications lines.

computer run, Processing a particular job on a computer, i.e., execution of a program, translation of a program, etc.

computer sales representative, The person who represents a particular computer company and sells their equipment.

computer satellite, Often refers to one used to relieve a central computer of relatively simple but time-consuming operations such as compiling, editing, and controlling input/output devices, sometimes connected remotely and independent of the main computer system.

computer science, Generally, computer science is a cognitive science. It is concerned with the design and application of computer hardware and computer software.

computer science, The field of study of computers.

computer, scientific, A computer designed for solving scientific problems; typically a minimum of input/output and a lot of internal processing capabilities are needed.

computer, second generation, Describes computers produced between about 1959 and 1964, the second era of computer technology development, in which the transistor replaced the vacuum tube.

computer, second generation, A computer using transistors instead of vacuum tubes that were sued in first generation computers; such computers as IBM 1401, Honeywell 800, RCA 501, etc. (See third generation computer for contrast.)

computer sensitive language, A programming language that is partly or wholly dependent upon the type of computer a program is executed on.

computer, sequential, A computer designed so instructions are generally followed one after the other.

computer, serial, A computer designed to handle digits sequentially as contrasted with parallel computer.

computer, slave, A second computer in a system used when the master computer fails (a duplicate system for backup).

computer, solid-state, A computer using primarily solid state electronic circuit elements.

computer, source, A computer that is used to prepared input for other computers.

computer, special purpose, A computer designed to be used to solve a specific class of problem or small range of problems.

computer storage, The storage in a data processing system that may be controlled automatically without need for human intervention.

computer, stored program, A computer that can store its own instructions as well as data.

computer, stored program, A general term referring to computers that have the capability of storing a computer program of instructions to the computer.

computer stores, Several thousand stores came into being for retail customers in the late 1970's that included franchised chains, independents, large company operations, such as the Tandy Corp. Radio Shack stores; all supplementing dealer and distributor stores and computer sales in toy and department stores.

computer supervisor, The person responsible for computer operations.

computer, switch control, A computer used to handle data transmission to and from remote terminals and computers.

computer, synchronous, A computer in which each operation is controlled by clock signals as contrasted with asynchronous computer.

computer systems, distributed, The arrangement of computers in an organization (not all at one location).

computer, target, The computer that a particular program is being translated to run on.

computer, third generation, Describes computers produced beginning in 1964, the third era of computer technology development in which integrated circuitry and miniaturization replaced transistors.

computer, third generation, Computers with micro-circuits and miniaturization of components.

computer throughput, The rate at which information can be accurately delivered when averaged over a long period of time. Also, the time required to perform an operation from the time it begins until the time it is successfully completed.

computer word, A set of 1s and 0s that is a unit of data or instructions in a computer.

computerize, A slang term meaning to implement an application of some process on computer equipment.

computerized numerical control (CNC), Numerical control systems for which a dedicated, stored program computer is used to perform some or all of the basic numerical control functions, usually related to factory automation and process control.

computers, coupled, Computers that are connected to each other for back up or other purposes.

computing machinery, Data processing equipment and systems.

computing, multiaccess, More than one identical input/output terminal attached to a system.

COMSAT, See communication satellite corporation.

COMSAT, Communications Satellite Corporation, A privately owned company, chartered by the U.S. Congress for voice and television signal communication by satellite.

concatenate, To combine two or more items, end to end, to form a larger item. For example, concatenating the string 'time' to the string 'wise' produces the string 'timewise.'

concatenated data set, A set of data formed by combining the data from several independent data sets.

concentrator, A type of multiplexer used in communications.

concept, cylinder, The concept that data on parallel tracks are available by merely switching read/write heads. It is an imaginary cylinder.

concept, total system, A system providing information in the right form, time, and place for decision making.

concurrent control system, A system that permits concurrent operation of many programs.

concurrent, input/output, A feature permitting input and output capabilities to be shared by two or more computer programs.

concurrent processing, Processing more than one program at a time on a computer.

concurrent real-time processing, Allows data to be processed while the business transaction is actually taking place; a communications oriented system.

condition, In the COBOL system, one of a set of specified values that a data item can assume.

condition, initial, The value of a variable prior to computation.

condition, wait, A circumstance in which transition into the ready state depends on occurrence of events.

conditional branch, A branch in a program that only occurs if a certain condition is met.

conditional branch, A computer instruction that causes a branch based on a test of some condition. (See branch.)

conditional breakpoint, A breakpoint at which the routine can be continued if the right conditions exist. (See breakpoint.)

conditional breakpoint instruction, A conditional branch that may cause the computer to stop and then branch when continuing.

conditional jump, Same as conditional branch.

conditional jump instruction, Same as conditional branch.

conditional transfer, Same as conditional branch.

conditions, ambient, The conditions of the surrounding medium.

conductance, The physical property of an element, device, branch, network, or system that is the factor by which the square of an instantaneous voltage must be multiplied to give the corresponding energy lost by dissipation as heat or other permanent radiation, or by loss of electromagnetic energy from a circuit.

conductor, A material in which electric current can flow easily. In order for a material to be a conductor, the electrons must only be tightly bound to their atoms.

conductor, A body of conductive material constructed so that it will carry an electric current.

confidence level, The confidence in results in statistical measurement.

configuration, Refers to the way in which a computer and peripheral equipment are connected and programmed to operate as a system.

configuration, computer, The set of equipment that makes up a computer system.

configuration, contact, An arrangement of contacts in multiple contact electrical connectors.

configuration, target, Same as the target computer.

conformity, accuracy, A concept that includes simple and combined conformity errors.

congestion theory, A mathematical theory dealing with the study of delays and losses of items in a communications system.

conjunction, Conjunction is the name given to the AND operation. A conjunction is true only if its propositions are all true.

conjunctive search, A type of search defined in terms of a logical product, that uses the AND instruction as contrasted with disjunctive search.

connect time, The time interval from the initial connection to the final breaking of a communication.

connect time, The time between sign on and sign off that a user is connected to a time shared system from a remote terminal.

connecting cable, A cable used to transfer electricity between two pieces of equipment.

connection box, An electrical panel found in punched card machines.

connection, dial-up, The use of a dial or push button telephone to initiate a telephone connection between a terminal and a computer.

connection, make, Manual connection in switching equipment or networks.

connective word, A Cobol programming language reserved term used to denote the presence of a qualifier.

connector, A symbol representing connection of lines on a flowchart of an operator connecting two parts of a logical statement.

connector, common, The plug and wire completing a circuit in a wiring board.

connector, electrical, Any of many devices used to connect conductors, join cables, etc.

connector flange, A metal or plastic projection around a connector.

connector, flowchart, A symbol used in a flowchart to show flow and connection of other symbols.

connector, frame, A metal or plastic portion which surrounds a connector.

connector, hermaphroditic, A connector having no male or female parts, but whose mating parts are identical.

connector, interchangeable, Connects from different manufacturers that can be used interchangeably.

connector, modular, An electrical connector with sections that are used like "building blocks" or modules.

connector, multiple, A flowchart connector indicating several lines of flow.

connector, socket, An electrical connector that has socket contacts and a plug connector.

connector, umbilical, Usually a hose to feed fuel or an electrical connector same as an OR gate.

connector, variable, A flow chart symbol indicating a programmed switch capability.

consecutive, Two or more events in time or elements in space that follow each other, i.e., are right next to each other.

consecutive computer, Computers that perform sequences of computation one after the other. It is the same as sequential computer.

consistency check, Methods of checking to see that a piece of data is consistent with the rules to handle it.

consistency errors, remote computing system, One of the types of syntax errors in which statements conflict with previous definitions.

consistent unit, A unit in which all input and output variables are represented in the same way such as by voltages only.

console, A series of devices, such as on a control panel, that allow people to communicate directly with a computer.

console, The portion of a computer where the operator communicates with the system. It contains display lights, operating buttons and switches, and often a typewriter/keyboard device.

console, auxiliary, An operator console other than the main console. (See console.)

console, bank teller, A device used by a bank teller to transmit and receive messages to and from the processing center.

console, control, The console of a computer system that allows the operator to control and monitor processing. (See console.)

console, control utility, A console used primarily to control utility and maintenance programs.

console, data station, In communications console (generally remote) that performs reading, printing, and data sending and receiving.

console, debugging, Using the computer console to debug or find errors in a computer program by stepping through instruction very slowly.

console devices, terminal, A console-like terminal that sends and receives input and output to and from the central computer.

console display register, A set of indicator lights on a computer console that display the bit pattern contents of registers.

console, graphic, A CRT device used as the primary control console for the system.

console keyboard, display, The keyboard (similar to a typewriter keyboard) on a display console.

console, message display, A computer console containing a symbol generator and a CRT, cathode ray tube, a television-like device.

console, monitor, typewriter, A typewriter-like console device that signals the computer operator when attention is needed. It monitors the activity of the system.

console operator, The person who operates the computer console.

console, operator's, See console.

console printer, An auxiliary printer used to give messages to the computer operator.

console typewriter, A typewriter keyboard device used for computer operator communication with the computer system.

console, visual display, A CRT, cathode ray tube, television-like device, that permits visual display of computer contents.

constant, A value written into a program instruction. The value does not change during the execution of the program.

constant, See constant figurative.

constant, propagation, A number expressed in the Greek letter Rho to indicate the effect on a wave in a transmission line propagating through it.

constant ratio code, A code with characters represented by combinations having a fixed ratio of one to zero.

constant storage, Parts of storage used to store non-varying quantities (constant data).

constant, system, A permanent location containing data used by systems programs (contained in the monitor section).

constant, time, The ratio of the inductance to resistance in an electric circuit, measured in seconds.

constant words, Descriptive data that is fixed or constant.

constant(s), Data that is not subject to change, i.e., remains constant during the running of a program, etc.

constraint, In mathematical programming, an equation or an inequality specified in a problem. This creates restrictions which limit the solution to the optimal one.

constraint, Restrictions, bounds, limits, etc.

constraint matrix, A matrix of constraint equations in linear programming.

consultant, systems, The person who provides technical assistance in systems analysis.

contact addressed memory, A memory in which storage locations are identified by their content.

contact area, The surface in common between two (electrical) conductors, a connector and conductor, or two connectors across which electricity flows.

contact, bifurcated, A contact used in printed-circuit connectors in digital computers.

contact configuration, An arrangement of contacts in multiple contact electrical connectors.

contact, dry reed, An encapsulated switch with two wires which act as contact points for a relay.

contact, electrical, The joint or touching of two halves of a connector or the point of electrical connection.

contact, engaging force, The force necessary to insert pins into sockets (electrical).

contact float, The amount of "give" or movement that a contact has within the insert hole.

contact, normally closed, Pairs of contacts on relays that open only when the relay coil is energized.

contact, normally open, Pairs of contacts on relays that close only when the relay coil is energized.

contact, pin, A contact used to mate with a socket.

contact separating force, The force necessary to remove pins from electrical sockets.

contact, smooth, A contact with a smooth profile, i.e., a flush surface.

contact, socket, A contact (female) used to mate with a pin (male) contact.

contacts, grid spaced, Rows and columns of contacts on connectors and printed circuit boards.

content addressed storage, Accessing data by the contents of storage rather than the address.

contention, In communications a condition in which two or more locations try to transmit at the same time.

contents, Contents of a storage location in a computer.

context, The words that affect the meaning of a word before or after it.

contiguous, Storage locations are said to be contiguous if they are adjacent to each other.

contiguous, Immediately following or preceding in time or space.

contingency interrupt, An interrupt caused by operator request at the keyboard, typing in a character, operator requests a program stop, etc.

continuous carrier, A communications carrier in which transmission is not interrupted.

continuous data, Data that can be ascertained continuously in time (related to analog devices).

continuous forms, Forms fed into a printer on a continuous roll. Continuous forms are perforated at regular intervals so that they may be easily separated after printing has been completed.

continuous forms, Data processing forms that are a long series of connected sheets to be printed on by a data processing printer.

continuous processing, On-line or real-time processing as contrasted to batch processing.

continuous simulation, Simulation using continuous data as opposed to discrete, such as controlling of missile flights, etc.

continuous stationery readers, Character readers of a special type that can only read certain forms such as cash register receipts.

continuous system modeling program, A digital computer program that simulates analog systems.

continuous systems diagnosis, A system in which there is a collection of diagnostic tasks which are processed when other higher priority things are not running.

continuous variable, A variable that can assume all values on continuous scale as contrasted with discrete variable.

contour analysis, A reading technique in optical character recognition used for handwritten material because of the non-standardized appearance of the input.

contrast, In optical character recognition the difference between reflectance of two areas.

control, The part of a computer that determines "how" and "what" will happen "when."

control action, The correction made for a deviation or error by a controller.

control action, derivative (rate), A control action in which the output is proportional to the rate of change in the input.

control action, high limiting, A control action in which the output never goes beyond a predetermined value.

control action, optimizing, Control actions that seek the most advantageous value and maintains it.

control action, system, That type of control action that concerns the nature of change of the output dependent on the input.

control, automatic, Control achieved by electronic devices that automatically regulate processes, etc.

control block, A specific storage area containing control information for processing tasks, functions, etc.

control block, data set (DSCB), A standard control block needed to manipulate the data set in a direct access device.

control board, A removable panel in unit record equipment.

control bus, A set of control lines or paths usually from 10 to 100, with specific functions to carry the synchronization and control information necessary to the computer system; such signals might be: interrupt, hold, acknowledge, read, write, etc.

control card, A punched card containing data or parameters for control purposes.

control carriage, The device that controls the feeding of continuous forms through a printer.

control carriage tape, A paper tape used to control printer functions such as skipping.

control, cascade, In an automatic control system, each control unit regulates the next control unit.

control, centralized, The control of all processing by a single unit.

control change, A change in the control field, minor, major, etc.

control change, major, In a report, a change of the major level as contrasted with intermediate and minor.

control change, minor, A change in the least significant control level.

control character, 1 A character whose occurrence in a particular context initiates, modifies, or stops a control operation or function. 2 A character used to initiate functions such as line feed, carriage return, etc.

control character, A character used to indicate a control function.

control character, print, A control character used to control printer feeding, spacing, etc.

control character, transmission, A control character used in routing messages in communications.

control circuits, Those circuits relating to computer execution of instructions.

control clerk, data, The person in a computer facility who checks incoming and outgoing data.

control clock, An electronic clock in a computer.

control, closed loop, See feedback control.

control, communication subsystem, Control by function words that activate control lines.

control computer, A computer that controls processes by inputs and outputs of the process.

control console, The console of a computer system that allows the operator to control and monitor processing (see console).

control counter, The computer address counter that contains the address of the next instruction to be executed.

control cycle, The cycle in a punched card machine that occurs with a control change.

control data, Data used for control functions.

control, derivative, Control in which the output is proportional to the rate of change of the input.

control desk, A desk-like console. (See console.)

control device character, A control character used to switch devices on or off.

control, direct, Control of one device by another without human intervention.

control, direct digital, Control obtained by a digital device.

control dump, monitor, A memory dump that may be specified in the job control information.

control, dynamic, The operation of a computer so that it can alter instructions as computation proceeds.

control equipment, remote, Control apparatus that works from a distance by electronic means.

control, executive system, An executive system in which control information is fed to the system on line or from remote locations.

control, feedback, A type of control in which a part of an output is fed back as input (in the system).

control field, The field in which control information is located. (See field).

control field (sorting), A data processing card that contains the parameters for a sort.

control flag, message, Flags that indicate whether the information being transmitted is a data or control-only message or whether it is the first, intermediate, or last block of a message.

control, flow, The sequence (in time) of computer instruction executions that relate to control of a computer system.

control function, An operation to control a device, e.g., the starting and stopping of a printer carriage, a rewind of tape, etc.

control group, The group of people who read, modify, evaluate, monitor, etc., program development.

control, height, The hand control on a CRT (cathode ray tube) that controls the height of the picture.

control, indirect, As contrasted with direct control, in which one computer is controlled by another without human intervention. If a human is involved, it is indirect control.

control instruction register, The computer register that contains the address of the next instruction.

control instructions, Computer instructions used for control functions.

control, job flow, Control processes including input/output transition between jobs and job segments, unit assignments, initialization when the computer is turned on, control between jobs and much more.

control, job-processing, A portion of the control (computer) program that starts job operations and performs functions necessary to go from one job to another.

CONTROL key, On some systems, a key on the keyboard whose effect is similar to the SHIFT key in that it does nothing unless it is pressed while another key is being pressed. The effect of both keys being pressed is to generate a nongraphic character which is recognized by the computer as a control code, which initiates a function of the computer or one of its peripherals.

control keys, keyboard, On many CRT terminals, control keys move and control the cursor, switch the terminal from one application to another, switch the communication disciplines (protocols), and cause the performance of other functions.

control language, executive, A set of control commands used in an executive system.

control language, linear programming, The language consisting of verbs (agendum names) and embodying the desired algorithm to be used prescribes the course of linear programming on a computer.

control, line, In communications a control that tells each terminal when to start transmitting.

control logic, The sequence of steps needed to perform a function.

control loop, A path used by control signals.

control, manual, Control of a computer function using manual switches.

control medium, Control functions in media such as punched cards, magnetic tape, etc.

control messages, Those messages used to determine who transmits, who receives, to acknowledge good and bad reception of blocks, or to abort transfer sequences. Such procedures are called "handshaking" procedures and also become part of the error recovery process.

control mode, In communications the mode of operation in which characters on a line are interpreted for control.

control number, A number used to compare results to prove accuracy of a process or problem.

control, numeric, A field of computer processing that involves control of machine tools, i.e., computer control of assembly line tools.

control, numerical, Systems using computers for control of operations of machinery.

control, operator, See console.

control, orthotronic, A correction technique used in transfer of information from magnetic tape to memory.

control panel, Generally part of an operator console, the control panel contains light indicators, switches, and buttons which are used to turn the power on and off, to control the computer system's various components, and to monitor the computer's activities.

control panel, (1) A removable board that can be wired to control operation of equipment same as plugboard. (2) Also refers to a console. (See console.)

control panel, automatic, A panel of lights and switches used by a computer operator.

control panel, maintenance, A panel of lights and switches used by repair men.

control panel, system, Consists of three sections for operator control, operator intervention, and customer engineering; panel(s) of lights and switches.

control procedure, Consists of administrative control of job schedules, workflow, computer usage records, data and program libraries, etc.

control, production, A system that provides information for management of a production line process to improve production.

control program, a computer program that prescribes the action to be taken by a system, device, computer, etc.

control program, command, A computer program that handles all user console commands sent to the system.

control, program execution, The control function involved in interrupt processing.

control program, input/output, The control of input and output operations by the supervisory (computer) program.

control program, master, The computer program that controls all phases of job set up, directs all equipment function and flow of data, directs the operator, etc.

control program, record, The computer program used for input/output processing that is file oriented rather than device oriented.

control programs, Specialized computer programs that contain routines that would otherwise need to be included in each program.

control, proportional, A control technique in which the action varies linearly as the condition being regulated varies.

control, real-time, Control of a system that operates at a speed to control events that take place right at that time.

control register, A computer register that contains the address of the next instruction; same as control counter.

control register, sequence, The computer register that keeps track of the location of the next instruction to be processed.

control relationship, The relationship between two devices that refers to which device controls the other.

control routine, A computer program routine that performs control functions

control routine, interrupt, The computer program routine that analyzes an interrupt.

control section, The portion of the central processing unit (CPU) which directs the step-by-step operation of the majority of the computing system.

control section, The part of a computer that controls the processing of instructions.

control, selection, The device that selects instructions to be executed in a computer.

control sequence, The sequence in which a program's instructions are executed. The instructions are executed one at a time and in order from first to last until or unless a branch instruction transfers control to another portion of the program.

control sequence, Determining the selection of instructions for execution, generally one after another in a row until a branch may change the flow.

control, sequential, A mode of computer operation in which instructions are executed in consecutive order (until a branch changes the flow).

control signal, feedback, The part of an output signal that is returned as an input to accomplish some effect, such as a fast response.

control signaling, supervisory, Signals that automatically actuate equipment at a remote terminal.

control signals, Generally refers to electrical signals which go to and come from the control unit in the central processing unit (CPU). These control signals direct the computer to perform a sequence of operations.

control signals, A wide variety of signals used to control the flow of information in computer systems.

control statement, job, Individual statements in the job control language (JCL) that provide information to the operating system as to how the job is to be run.

control statements, (1) The computer program statements used to control the flow of a program. (2) Statements providing control information to an assembler, compiler, etc.

control station, A switching network station directing operations such as polling, selecting, etc.

control, supervisory, The system of control used by a computer operator to supervise control of the computer system.

control system, A closed-loop system in which a computer is used to control a process.

control system, concurrent, A system that permits concurrent operation of many programs.

control system, data acquisition, A system designed to handle the acquisition of data, process control, and a variety of real-time applications.

control system, inventory, A system of inventory control.

control system, open-loop, A control system without feedback as contrasted with closed-loop.

control system, real-time, A system that processes data and makes decisions in real-time (automatic immediate control of a process).

control systems, internal, Programmed controls built-in to the system that governs the flow of computer operations.

control tape, A paper or plastic tape used to control a printer carriage.

control track, video, The specific area of a tape containing a series of synchronous pulses that control playback video timing and longitudinal tape speed.

control, traffic, A method of handling flow of something by means of a computer.

control transfer, To copy, exchange, transmit, etc., data.

control, transmission, Control units used in communication.

control unit, The part of the central processing unit (CPU) or operating system responsible for receiving instructions from a program in main memory, decoding them, and sending control signals to appropriate units in the computer in order to execute them. The control unit is a controller which directs the operation of the computer as a whole.

control unit, (1) A unit in a computer that directs the sequence of operations. (2) An auxiliary unit in or attached to a computer to control equipment such as magnetic tape units, card readers, printers, etc.

control, width, A hand control on a CRT (television-like device) that controls the width of the picture.

controlled machine tools, numerically, Computer controlled machinery in manufacturing.

controlled variable, A value or condition manipulated, regulated, or controlled by computer.

controller, A device that automatically regulates a controlled variable or system.

controller, channel, The controller in a multiprocessor system that allows each processor to have access to every channel in the system.

controller, disk, a printed circuit card that contains the integrated circuit (IC) chip necessary to activate and control a computer's disk drive.

controller, disk drive, A hardware interface between the disk drive and the computer, which controls the operation of the disk drive.

controller, dual channel, The controller that permits tape reading and/or writing at the same time.

controller, multiposition, A controller that has two or more discrete values of output.

controller, on-off, A controller that has two discrete values of output, fully on or fully off.

controller, proportional, A controller that only produces a proportional control action.

controller, ratio, A controller that maintains a ratio between two or more variables.

controller, three position, A multiple position controller having three discrete values of output.

controller, two position, A multiposition controller with two discrete values of output.

controls, built-in, Error checking devices built into data processing equipment.

controls, hold, The hand controls on a CRT (television-like device) that control the picture horizontally and vertically.

controls, linearity, Manual controls on a CRT (cathode ray tube, a television-like device) that help correct distortion of the picture (display).

controls, peripheral, Regulate the transfer of data between peripheral devices and the central processor.

conventions, Standards and accepted procedures in programming and systems work.

convergence, The three primary colors for television (red, blue, and green) overlapping perfectly to form an ideal picture, graph, chart, schematic, or other computer terminal output.

conversational algebraic language (CAL), A language designed for small numerical problems in an interactive environment.

conversational language, One of several programming languages that use a near-English character set which facilitates communication between the user and the computer.

conversational language, A nearly English language used to communicate with a computer from a terminal.

conversational mode, Generally concerns communication between a terminal and a computer in which each entry from one elicits a response from the other, maintaining real-time man-machine communications.

conversational mode, A mode of operation of man-machine communication, generally from a terminal.

conversational processing, Processing in a conversational mode (man-machine communication from a user terminal).

conversational time sharing, Use of a computer system by many users in a conversational mode.

conversion, (1) The changing of data from one form to another. (2) The changing of equipment. (3) The changing of programming languages.

conversion, binary-to-decimal, Conversion of a binary number to its equivalent decimal number.

conversion, code, A procedure for changing the bit grouping of a character in one code into the corresponding bit grouping in a different code, such as a change from EBCDIC code to ASCII code.

conversion, code, Changing from one coding structure to another.

conversion costs, The set of one-time costs associated with converting from one thing to another, e.g., one computer system to another.

conversion, data, Changing data from one form to another.

conversion, data code, Translating alphanumeric data into computer representation of data; usually done by the computer.

conversion, decimal-to-binary, The process of converting a number written in the base ten to its equivalent in the base two.

conversion device, A device used to convert data from one form to another without changing content.

conversion, file, Taking source document information and putting it onto magnetic tape or disk.

conversion, media, Putting data from one form into another form, such as punched card to magnetic tape.

conversion programs, Computer programs used to convert other computer programs from one system to another.

conversion routine, A computer program routine used to change data from one form to another.

convert, To change from one thing to another.

converter, A device that converts representation of information from one form to another.

converter, language, A device designed to change one form of data (on some medium) to another (on another medium).

converter, signal, A particular transducer used to convert one standardized signal to another.

conveyor, paper document, A device that carries or conveys paper documents.

cooperation index, Used in facsimile image transmission, it is the product of the drum diameter (in inches) and the line scan advance (in lines per inch).

cooperative installation, A computer installation serving many users (perhaps from different companies).

coordinate paper, Continuous form graph paper used for printout on an XY plotter.

coordinate storage, Two dimensional storage that needs two coordinates to access a location, e.g., cathode ray tube storage.

coordinates, rectangular, A set of axes (lines) that intersect (used for making graphs, etc.)

copies, facsimile, Copies of a document made by a copying machine.

copy, The process of transferring information from one location to another.

copy, To reproduce information into a new location.

copy and correct, A particular record is copies from one tape to another and corrected as specified.

copy, document, The original that is being photographed, also called hard copy.

copy, hard, A document, report, anything on paper, as opposed to a visual display that will appear off the screen, so you can't take the information with you.

copy, soft, A copy of a computer's output which appears on the screen of a visual display device. Soft copies, unlike hard copies, cannot be carried away from the computer by a user. Soft copy can also refer to output in audio format or in any other form that is not hard copy.

copying machine, diazo, A copy machine whose originals must be on translucent paper.

cordless plugs, A connector with no flexible portion (no "cord").

core, Magnetic material made of iron oxide or ferrite used extensively but formerly in internal computer hardware.

core, ferrite, The magnetic core used in core storage in computers (also used in other electronic functions).

core, fiberoptics, The light conducting portion of the fiber, defined by the high refractive index region, the core normally being in the center of the fiber, bounded by the cladding material.

core, magnetic, A magnetic material capable of assuming two or more conditions of magnetization.

core memory, A storage device using ferromagnetic cores.

core tape, The tape used in bobbin core. (See bobbin core.)

CORELAP, Computerized Relationship Layout Planning.

correct and copy, A particular record is copied from one tape to another and corrected as specified.

correcting signal, A signal sent recurrently for the correction of data (in synchronous systems).

correction, Something done to correct an error condition.

correction, automatic error, A technique used to correct transmission errors automatically.

correction from signals, A system used to control synchronous equipment.

correction routine, A computer program routine used in or after a computer failure or program or operator error.

correction routine, error, A computer program routine used to correct a detected error while processing.

corrective maintenance, The repair or correction of a known malfunction of equipment.

correlation, fact, An analysis process used to examine the relations of data in files.

cost effectiveness, A ratio of measurement of cost to performance of a system, product, etc.

cost, marginal, The rate of change of cost related to quantity.

cost/cubic foot, Cost per cubic foot is used for measuring costs to users of a records center.

costs, conversion, The set of one-time costs associated with converting from one thing to another, e.g., one computer system to another.

coulomb charge, Electric current is caused by the motion of electric charges in the wires of circuit. The coulomb is the basic electric charge unit.

count, To increase or decrease a total of the number of times something occurs; also the count is the number itself.

count, dropout, The number of dropout detected in a specific length of tape.

count pulse interrupt, An interrupt triggered by pulses from a clock source.

count zero interrupt, an interrupt triggered when a count pulse interrupt has produced a zero in a clock counter.

countdown, A counter or total "counted down" to zero from an initial value.

counter, Refers to a register or computer storage location used to represent the number of occurrences of an electronic switch or an event.

counter, A device used to store a number that is added to or subtracted from to keep track of events.

counter, binary, (1) A counter that counts using the binary number system. (2) A counter that can assume one of two stable states.

counter, control, The computer address counter that contains the address of the next instruction to be executed.

counter, microfilm, A counter on a microfilm camera to keep track of the number of exposures made.

counter, program, The program counter or instruction counter is a register in the central processing unit (CPU), which contains the address of the instruction currently being executed.

counter, program, A computer register that contains the identification of the next instruction to be executed.

counter, program address, Same as instruction counter.

counter, repeat, A counter used to control repeated operations.

coupled computers, Computers that are connected to each other for back up or other purposes.

coupler, acoustic, A device that converts electrical signals into audio signals, enabling data to be transmitted over the public telephone network via a conventional telephone handset.

coupling, The process of connecting two systems or components together so that they can communicate with each other.

coupling, capacitive, Alternating current coupling by a capacitor instead of a transformer.

coupling, zener diode, Circuit modules that use zener diodes for coupling circuits.

CP, An abbreviation for Central Processing.

CP/M, Control Program for Microcomputers formerly was the most popular operating system for small computers. CP/M commands are used to keep track of the data and programs stored on disks and to determine the programming language being used, among other tasks.

CP/M disk operating system, Formerly one of the most popular control program systems that is a disk operating system for dynamically allocating and releasing file storage.

CPE, See central processing element.

cps, 1 Characters per second. 2 Cycles per second. Now referred to as hertz (Hz).

CPS, An abbreviation for characters per second or cycles per second.

CPU, See central processing unit.

CPU (Central Processing Unit), The main part of a computer control system where arithmetic and logical operations are performed. It also contains the main memory and instructions to carry out system control functions.

CPU chip, These perform the functions of numerous individual chips; the chip often requires two sets of input signals to generate one set of output signals. Instruction signals tell the CPU chips which logic to emulate according to design and processing procedures. The chip is a computer in itself, having all the components in miniature that are found on most mini and standard units.

CPU chip architecture, Principal elements are control section for interpretation and execution of instructions as processed by the ALU, arithmetic-logic unit, timing and register control, scratch-pad memory, decoding, parallel data handling, input/output, and other bus control and memory management.

CPU handshaking, The interaction between the CPU (central processing unit) and the various peripheral devices but sometimes meaning users as well.

CPU time, The actual time needed for a particular operation.

crash, Concerns inoperable systems. Computer systems crash when there is a malfunction in the basic equipment. Programs crash when they contain serious errors.

crash, A "crashed" system is one that becomes inoperative or lost in a loop, or is blocked most often due to a hardware failure or a software malfunction.

CRCL, An abbreviation for Cyclic Redundancy Check Character.

crimp, To bend or deform, e.g., to squeeze a connector barrel to connect.

crippled leap frog test, A variation of the leap frog test.

criteria, sequencing (sorting), The field or fields of data used to determine the order of records in a file (e.g., employee number within department number).

criterion, A value used to compare against; to test or to judge.

criterion, cycle, The number of times a cycle is to be repeated.

critical path, The longest path of several paths of activity in project completion. (See PERT.)

critical path scheduling, A project planning and monitoring system used to check progress toward completion of the project.

CRO, An abbreviation for cathode ray tube oscilloscope.

cross assembler, A program run on one computer for the purpose of translating instructions for a different computer, usually a microcomputer.

cross bar, A type of automatic telephone-switching system using movable switches mounted on bars.

cross channel switching, A feature that permits program access to input/output devices through two channels.

cross fire, Interference in telegraph and telephone circuits.

cross isle, The place where operators tear off tape and transfer it to an outgoing circuit in a torn tape system.

cross program, A specific program in software development in which a program for computer X resides in (executes) on computer Y as used for tests, program development, simulations, etc.

cross reference, A notation showing that a record has been stored elsewhere.

cross sectional testing, Tests used to get a representative sampling of system performance.

cross talk, Interference on circuits.

cross tracking, An array of bright dots on a display device (in a cross-like form).

cross validation, A method of verifying results of an experiment.

cross-assembler, An assembler that translates a program into a form that can be run on a different computer than the one on which the cross-assembler runs.

crosscheck, To check calculations using two different ways.

crossfoot, To add across (horizontally) several fields of numeric information.

crossover network, The device between audio amplifier output and speakers dividing the high and low frequencies.

crosspoint, An electronic circuit that can electrically connect or disconnect two conductors in response to some external control signal. Synonymous with contact pair.

crowding, character, The reduction of space between characters on magnetic tape.

CRT, See cathode ray tube.

CRT (Cathode Ray Tube), A device whereby electrons form patterns onto a viewing screen under the direction of magnetic fields to form patterns. CRT is often used as a synonym for visual display screen.

CRT display, ultraprecision, A type of CRT with a high degree of accuracy, stability, and resolution. (See CRT.)

CRT highlighting, Process to distinguish between variable data and protected data such as field labels or error messages, completed by blinking, underlining, or varying the intensity of the characters in the display.

CRT inquiry, An inquiry made at cathode ray tube (CRT) terminal whose response is displayed on the screen (television-like screen).

CRT, nonscrollable, Refers to a line or portion of the CRT screen that does not scroll off the top as new information is written at the bottom. When a nonscrollable message reaches the top of the screen, it stays there, while subsequent messages continue to scroll underneath it.

CRT, raster-scan, Generation of pictures the same way an ordinary TV set does. They scan their screens line by line and refresh the information on those screens 60 times per second. Storage tube terminals, on the other hand, require no refreshing retaining the image until users clear the entire screen.

CRT refresh, On raster screen terminals, all video information must be refreshed, and a block of static RAM sufficient to store at least one full page of data is often used.

CRT, shadow mask, A type of CRT used in color monitors and color TV sets, in which a screen, the shadow mask, is used to align the phosphor dots on the screen with their respective electron guns.

CRT, thermionic emission, Thermionic emission occurs where a heated metal surface gives off electrons. It is by thermionic emission that the electron gun in a CRT gives off electrons which illuminate the screen-surface.

CRT, X, Y coordinates, A point plotting CRT used for graphic forms.

cruncher, number, Number cruncher is the name given to a large computer specifically designed to perform a large number of scientific calculations. A number cruncher's arithmetic-logic unit (ALU) is capable of performing up to 12 million arithmetic operations per second.

crunching, Often refers to number operations. Also, a way of condensing programs to pack the most instructions into the smallest space. By crunching a program, it uses less memory space and runs more efficiently.

cryogenic element, High speed circuits that use the superconductivity of materials at or near absolute zero temperatures.

cryogenic memory, Superconductive memory that operates at very low temperatures.

cryogenic storage characteristics, A modern storage that depends on superconductivity of certain materials when their temperatures are below absolute zero.

cryogenics, The study and use of devices using properties of materials at or near absolute zero temperatures.

cryostat, A device used to achieve extremely low temperatures; often used to liquify gases.

cryotron, A device using properties of metals at near absolute zero temperatures to obtain large current changes by relatively small magnetic field changes.

cryptographic (crypto), Pertains to equipment that changes data to conceal its meaning such as a secret code conversion.

crystal diode, A diode containing crystalline elements.

crystal, piezoelectric, A crystal that converts mechanical pressure into an electrical signal or vice versa.

crystal, quartz, A piezoelectric crystal that regulates an oscillator frequency.

CSP (control switching points), The class 1, 2, and 3 offices (regional, sectional, and primary centers) used for nationwide dialing.

CTC, An abbreviation for conditional transfer of control, a term used by programmers.

ctn, An abbreviation for cotangent.

CTR, An abbreviation for Central Tumor Registry or Computerized Tumor Registry or California Tumor Registry.

cumulative, indexing, Assigning two or more indices to a single address in a computer instruction.

cupping, Curvature of magnetic tape in a lateral direction.

circuit, side, One of two circuits in a phantom group.

current, A flow of electrons through a conductor.

current, The flow of electrons through a circuit.

current instruction register, A computer register that contains the instruction currently being executed.

current rating, The maximum continuous current that can be carried by a conductor without degradation of the conductor or its insulation properties.

current, sneak, A leakage current that gets into telephone circuits from other circuits; can cause damage if allowed to continue.

current time, See real time.

cursor, Generally, this is the small 'blip' of light that traverses the CRT screen indicating where the next character typed will appear. Usually a cursor is a square or rectangle the size of a character, or a dash the width of a character, and in many cases it flashes off and on to draw the operator's attention to it.

cursor, A display position indicator to emphasize a character to be corrected or a position in which data are to be entered or erased, often a solid underscore that may appear under any character location on the screen. In some systems, the cursor always appears under the location where the next character appears.

curvature, longitudinal, A deviation from straightness of a length of magnetic tape.

curve, A graphical representation of the relationship between two variables.

curve fitting, A representation on a CRT of a curve by a mathematical expression.

curve follower, A peripheral device used to read data represented on graphs.

custom IC, Integrated circuits that are manufactured to a specific customer's requirements.

customer engineer, manufacturers', See customer engineer.

customer station equipment, Communications equipment located on the customer's premises.

cutoff, The frequency of transmission in communications.

CUTS, A specific cassette user tape system.

CWP, See communicating word processor.

cyberculture, A word derived from cybernetics and culture.

cybernation, Basically, the use of computers coupled with automatic machinery to control and carry out complex operations.

cybernetics, The study of control theory and communication between and among people and machines.

cybernetics, A field of science relating the operation of automatic equipment to functions of the human nervous system.

cycle, A set of operations that may be repeated.

cycle criterion, The number of times a cycle is to be repeated.

cycle, execution, The part of a machine cycle during which execution of an instruction occurs.

cycle, grandfather, Saving magnetic tape for a period of time to provide a means of data file reconstruction in case of lost information.

cycle index, A register (counter) in a digital computer, set to a value and reduced by one (in each cycle) until it reaches zero.

cycle, instruction, The set of steps necessary to process an instruction (getting, interpreting, decoding, and checking it).

cycle, machine, The time that it takes for a sequence of events to be repeated.

cycle, memory, The process of reading and restoring information in memory.

cycle, operation, Same as execution cycle.

cycle reset, The returning to an initial value in a cycle index.

cycle, search, The time required or the sequence of events used to complete a search operation.

cycle stealing, Cycle stealing is the taking of an occasional machine cycle from a CPU's regular activities in order to control such things as an input or output operation.

cycle stealing, data channels, A technique used to "steal" a memory cycle; a data channel steals the cycle for an input unit to use.

cycle, storage, The cycle (sequence of events) occurring when information is transferred to and from storage in a computer.

cycle time, The time used to call for and deliver information from a storage unit or device.

cycle, work, A sequence of memory elements needed to perform a task, job, or execution to yield production.

cycled interrupt, The change of control to the next (or a specific) function (in an interrupt condition).

cyclic code, A special type of binary code.

cyclic feeding, The feeding of documents at a constant rate (in character recognition readers).

cyclic shift, Same as circular shift.

cyclic storage access, A storage unit designed so that access to any location is possible only at specific, equally spaced times.

cycling tape, An updating procedure in which a new tape file is created.

cylinder, A term related to magnetic disks recorded on vertical parallel tracks.

cylinder concept, The concept that data is recorded on parallel tracks that are available by merely switching read/write heads (an imaginary cylinder).

D

DA, An abbreviation for differential analyzer.

DAB, An abbreviation for display assignment bits or display attention bits.

DAC, A system that handles real-time applications in process control and data acquisition. (See data acquisition and control system.)

daisy chain, Often used with computer devices such as in applications in which devices not requesting a daisy-chained signal respond by passing a signal on. The first device requests the signal to respond by performing the action and breaks the daisy-chained signal continuity system by allowing the assignment of device priorities based on the electrical position of the device along a chain or bus.

DAM, An abbreviation for data association message or descriptor attribute matrix.

damper, A diode in a power supply that prevents ringing.

DAS, An abbreviation for digital analog simulator.

DASD, An abbreviation for direct access storage devices.

DASD, direct-access storage device, A direct-access storage device is a device with each physical record having both a discrete location and a unique address.

data, Basically, data is factual information. 'Data' is the plural of the word 'datum,' which means 'a single fact.' Data processing is the act of using data for making calculations or decisions. Strictly speaking, 'data' is a plural noun, but in practice it is almost invariably used in the singular. For example: 'After the data has been input...' A computer uses various types of data, such as words and numbers.

data, A general term used to describe numbers, facts, letters, symbols, names, etc.

data acquisition (DA), The methods and techniques used to acquire or gather data.

data acquisition and control system, A system designed to handle the acquisition of data, process control, and a variety of real-time applications.

data acquisition, high-speed (HS-DA), A monitoring and controlling facility used to acquire, evaluate, and record data in a testing situation.

data acquisition system, A system used to gather data from remote locations.

data, air movement, Date relating to flight plan information such as position and estimated time of arrival, etc.

data array, A data structure containing two or more logically related elements of the same type which are identified by a single name. In general, elements in an array are stored in consecutive locations in the main memory.

data array, An arrangement of data on magnetic tape, punched cards, or computer storage, etc.

data automation, source (SDA), The methods of recording data so that it can be used over and over again.

data bank, A collection of data that is accessible by a computer.

data base, The set of data accessible to a computer.

data, biased, A distribution of data records in a file that is being sorted which affects sorting time.

data buffer, A temporary storage device used between two devices of different rates of data flow.

data capture, direct, Automatic recording of transaction data such as at a cash register.

data capture, speech synthesis, A method of using speech as a direct form of input.

data reliability, A ratio used to measure a degree to which data is error free.

data representation, pictorial, Representation on graphs, charts, maps, etc.

data retrieval, The finding of data by searching in a file, data bank, or storage device.

data rules, The rules governing data elements, data sets, data files, etc.

data scrambler, Not as efficient as encryption devices, scramblers protect data being transmitted by large dispersed databases, as well as data in central processors accessed by remote terminals. Scores of systems are available with various coding and numerical weighing schemes.

data, secondary, Data published by other than the same source that collected it.

data set, A group of data elements that are related.

data set, concatenated, A set of data formed by combining the data from several independent data sets.

data set control block (DSCB), A standard control block needed to manipulate the data set in a direct access device.

data set, partitioned, A data set that is divided internally (into parts).

data sets, Groups and combinations of data elements.

data signaling rate, In data transmission, the bits per second data transmission capacity of a particular channel.

data sink, In a data transmission system, the equipment that accepts data.

data, source, (1) Data that will become computer input. (2) Data transmission equipment supplying the data.

data station console, In communications a console (generally remote) that performs reading, printing, and data sending and receiving.

data station console, remote, See data station console.

data switching center, A location where messages are automatically or manually directed to outgoing circuits.

data system, communications, Usually a real-time system of data communication between a computer and remote terminals.

data tablet, In using a data tablet, a pen shaped stylus is moved over a flat electromagnetically sensitive board; the pen's position over the board is monitored by a controller that relays information to a computer. In this way it is possible to "draw" images directly into a computer's memory.

data terminal, (1) A device that modulates and/or demodulates data. (2) A device for inputting or receiving output from computers.

data terminal equipment (DTE), The modem or unit at either end of a data communications channel.

data terminal, multiplex, A data transmission device that modulates and demodulates, encodes and decodes between two or more I/O devices and data transmission stations.

data terminal, remote, A data terminal not on site of the central processor, i.e., in a remote location.

data, test, A set of data used to test a program or system.

DATA TEXT, A language used by social scientists to perform computations and analyses.

data time, The time needed to fulfill a single instruction.

data, transaction, The data associated with a transaction, i.e., an event.

data transcription, A process for copying data from one media to another, such as tape to disk, etc.

data transfer rate, The rate at which data may be read or written. It is generally measured in characters per second.

data transmission, The sending of data from one place to another in a system.

data transmission equipment, The communication's equipment associated with the data processing equipment in a communications system.

data transmission, synchronous, A system in which timing is derived through synchronizing characters at the beginning of each message.

data transmission terminal installation, The installation consisting of data terminal equipment, signal conversion equipment, etc.

data transmission utilization ratio, The ratio of useful data to total data in data transmission.

data transmission, video display units, Any input or output equipment capable of displaying information on a screen, usually a CRT. (See CRT.)

data unit, A set of one or more characters treated as a whole.

data validity, (1) A measure of acceptability of data, e.g., if male was coded a 1 and female coded a 2, a code of 3 would not be valid; or (2) An unacceptable code pattern.

data word, A unit of information that is composed of a predetermined number of bits depending on the particular computer.

data-adapter unit, This device can be attached to either a selector channel or a multiplexor channel to greatly expand the input/output capabilities of the system in communications.

database, A collection of data arranged in files used for more than one purpose.

database management, A systematic approach to storage and retrieval of information in computers.

database-management system (DBMS), A system whose components include: database design, system interface, input and recovery models, special languages, access techniques, administration, performance measurement, security, integrity and privacy requirements.

datamation, A combination of the words data and automation.

dataphone, A trademark of the AT&T company to identify the data sets it manufactures and supplies for use in the transmission of data over the telephone network.

dataphone, A generic term describing a family of devices used in data communications.

dataphone adapters, Transceivers, transmitters, and receivers are dataphone adapters or components of digital-plotting communication systems.

dataplotter, A plotting device providing automatic plotting of digital information.

date, calendar, The date in the usual form, including month, day, and year.

date, delivery, The date that equipment is to be delivered, not necessarily unpacked or installed.

date, installation, The date a new computer system is installed. (See installation, computer (2).)

date, Julian, The day of the year, e.g., February 1st is day 32, as contrasted to calendar date.

date, scalar, Representation of a date by a number that is a displacement from a starting point; used in date calculations in a computer.

dating routine, A computer program routine that calculates and stores dates.

datum, The singular form of data, i.e., a unit of information.

day clock, An electronic clock used in real-time processing in a computer.

dB, An abbreviation that stands for decibel, a unit of power.

DBMS Data Base Management System, The primary control software for manipulating information files in which data dictionaries have become primary tools together with other structures of input, access, and retrieval.

DBMS, database management system, Generally refers to a software package used to keep track of a database. The system must be able to locate particular items in the database, to add new data or change old data when needed, and be flexible so that people with different needs can have access to the database.

DBOS Disk-Based Operating System, Software to provide disk-based processing for program generation, maintenance, and operation. Some have "menu" systems for user topic or search selection.

dBRN, A unit of measure of electrical circuit noise.

DC, An abbreviation for any of the following: data conversion, decimal classification, design change, detail condition, digital computer, direct coupled, direct current, direct cycle, direction cycle, or display console.

d-c coupled, flip-flop, A flip-flop in which the active elements are coupled with resistors. (See flip-flop.)

dc, dump, The intentional or accidental removal of all direct current power from a system or component.

dc erasing head, An electronic device capable of removing or erasing magnetic bits from magnetic tape.

dc, pulsating, Electric current that flows in one direction and varies in intensity.

dc signaling, A transmission method using direct current.

DC1, DC2, DC3, etc., Abbreviations for device control characters.

DCR, An abbreviation for any of the following: data conversion receiver, digital conversion receiver, design change recommendation, or detail condition register.

DD, An abbreviation for any of the following: delay driver, digital data, decimal display, digital display, or data demand.

DDA, See digital-differential analyzer.

DDA (digital-differential analyzer), A specific incremental differential analyzer, generally electronic.

DDC, An abbreviation for direct digital control.

DDCE, An abbreviation for digital data conversion equipment.

DDD, An abbreviation for direct distance dialing.

DDG, An abbreviation for digital display generator.

DDP, An abbreviation for digital data processor.

DDS, An abbreviation for digital display scope.

DDT, An abbreviation for digital data transmitter; also the name of a debugging package.

DDT (debugging package), A versatile, sophisticated, on-line debugging set of routines.

DE, An abbreviation for any of the following: display element, digital element, decision element, display equipment, or division entry.

dead band, A range of values in which the incoming signal can be altered without changing the outgoing response.

dead file, A file that doesn't have any current use but is not destroyed.

dead halt, A halt command to the computer from which there is no recovery, and the computer can't go on.

dead line, A telephone line disconnected from a central office.

dead space, The range of values that a signal can be altered without changing the outgoing response (synonymous with switching blank, dead zone and similar to neutral zone).

dead time, A delay between two related actions.

dead zone, The range of values that a signal can be altered without changing the outgoing response. It is synonymous with switching blank, dead space, and similar to neutral zone.

deadlock, A state of affairs in which two or more processes are waiting for events that will never occur.

debit card system, Terminals are equipped with keyboards and display panels that are activated by magnetically encoded plastic "debit" cards issued by various banks and credit companies. Operators insert cards with personal identification numbers (PIN) followed by amounts to be deposited or withdrawn. The device updates the values on the stripe.

debit magnetic stripe reader, These are generally self-contained, hand-fed readers of ABA, THRIFT, and IATA formats that are important for debit and credit card systems and electronic funds transfer systems (EFTS).

deblocking, The process of breaking up a data block into its individual records.

debug, To locate and correct errors and their sources in a computer program, either manually or through the use of special debugging routines.

debug, The process of locating and correcting errors in a computer program or a computer system.

debug macroinstruction, The type of instruction that generates a debugging capability in a computer program.

debug macros, Aids for debugging that are built into a program.

debug on-line, Debugging while the computer is performing on-line functions.

debugging, A procedure or process of isolating and removing bugs from computer programs. Also, a process of determining the correctness of a computer routine and correcting any errors.

debugging aids, reference, A set of routines that help the programmer debug computer programs.

debugging, console, Using the computer console to debug (find errors in) a computer program by stepping through instructions (very) slowly.

debugging package (DDT), A versatile, sophisticated, on-line debugging set of routines.

debugging, program, The process of finding and correcting errors in a computer program.

debugging, remote, The use of a remote terminal to debug computer programs.

debugging, snapshot, A technique of computer program debugging in which "snapshots" of contents of registers and accumulators are recorded.

debugging, source language, Detecting and correcting computer program errors by looking at the source language program instead of the machine language version.

debugging statements, Special computer program statements available to aid in debugging a computer program. (See debugging.)

decade, A group of ten units of something.

decade counter, A counter capable of counting to ten or counting to nine and resetting to zero.

decay time, The time that a voltage decreases to one-tenth or its maximum value.

decimal, The number system with a base of ten.

decimal, packed, Storing two digits in a storage area that usually stores a letter or special character.

decimal point, actual, A decimal point that is printed as an actual character or, if in computer storage, requires a position of storage.

decimal point, assumed, A place in a computer stored number where the decimal point is assumed to be.

decimal-to-binary conversion, The process of converting a numeral written to the base ten to the equivalent numeral written to the base two.

decimal-to-binary conversion, The process of converting a number written in the base ten to its equivalent in the base two.

decision, To make a choice among alternates.

decision box, Used in flowcharting to indicate a choice between one or more paths. (See flowchart.)

decision element, A circuit that performs a logical operation.

decision elements, gates, A circuit with two or more inputs and one output that is determined by the combinations of the inputs.

decision, instruction, A conditional branch instruction.

decision, logic, A decision of binary type (yes or no type) relating to equality, inequality, and relative magnitude (less than, equal to, or greater than).

decision, logical, In computers choosing between alternatives or selecting paths of flow in a program.

decision mechanism, The mechanism in an optical character reader that identifies a character.

decision plan, A procedure used for making management decisions.

decision rules, The programmed criteria to make operating decisions in an on-line real-time system.

decision table, A table of possible courses of action, selection, alternatives; serves a purpose such as the flowchart.

deck, tape, The mechanism used to control the movement of tape.

declarative statement, An instruction in symbolic coding used to define areas, constants, and symbols, etc.

declaratives, Same as declarative statement(s).

decode, A procedure to determine the meaning of individual characters or groups of characters in a message through the reversal of some previous coding.

decode, The opposite of encode, i.e., to interpret and determine meaning, also to translate a code into a more understandable form.

decoder, Basically, a circuit which translates data from one coded form to another, or interprets a specific code.

decoder, A device that ascertains the meaning of a set of signals.

decoder, command, The computer program that preprocesses commands from a user console.

decoding, The interpretation of the operation code of an instruction.

decollate, Separating the parts of a multipart form, generally in continuous forms.

decollator, The machine that decollates. (See decollate.)

decrement, The quantity used to decrease a variable; also, to decrement is to decrease a variable by a quantity.

decrement field, A part of a computer instruction used for modifying a register or storage location.

decryption, A procedure for the deciphering (interpretation) of coded data.

dedicated, Generally, a communications line or other device such as a printer used for a specific purpose only.

dedicated channel, A communications channel reserved or committed for a specific use.

dedicated storage, Storage that is reserved and committed to some specific purpose.

deduce, To draw a conclusion.

defect, An imperfection.

deferred processing, Processing that can be delayed, i.e., is considered low priority.

define, To establish a value for a variable or a constant.

definition, problem, Identifying the elements of a problem in an organized way.

definition, recursive, A definition which defines something partly in terms of itself.

degauss, To demagnetize or erase magnetic tape.

degradation, The condition in which a system continues to perform at a reduced level of service.

degradation, graceful, In case of equipment failure, the computer system falls into a degraded mode of operation instead of no response at all. It is also called fail softly.

degradation testing, Measuring performance of a system at extreme operating limits.

degree of multiprogramming, The number of transactions that can be handled in parallel in a multiprogramming system.

delay, The difference in time between a cause and its effect, such as the transmission and receipt of a pulse.

delay, The length of time after an event to another determined event.

delay counter, A counter used to delay a program long enough to complete an operation.

delay, data, (1) A delay attributable to something in the data itself. (2) The time spent waiting for information between two points in processing.

delay differential, The difference between maximum and minimum frequency delays across a band.

delay, digit, A logic element that delays its input signal.

delay distortion, Distortion resulting from the nonuniform speeds of transmission frequencies.

delay element, The electronic mechanism that temporarily delays data flow.

delay, envelope, Characteristics of a circuit that result in frequencies arriving at different times even if they were transmitted together.

delay, equalizer, A corrective network to make envelope delay constant over a desired frequency range.

delay, external, A delay caused by an external factor such as failure of the public power supply.

delay line, Devices designed to retard or hold back a pulse of energy.

delay loop stores, A method of storing information by transmitting bits or no-bits through a loop.

delay, operating, Computer time loss due to operator error.

delay, propagation, The time needed for a signal to travel from one point to another on a circuit.

delay, report, The time between the cutoff of activity to be reported and the delivery off the report.

delay time, The amount of time between two events.

delay unit, A unit in which the output signal is a delayed version of the input.

delays, external, See delay, external.

deleave, Same as decollate.

delete, To remove, e.g., to delete a record from a file.

delete character, A character used to get rid of erroneous or undesirable characters.

delete code, A code used to correct errors.

deletion record, A record used to delete a matching record from a master file.

delimit, To make a boundary or fix the limits of something.

delimiter, A delimiter is a character responsible for separating units of information, such as strings of characters.

delimiter, A character used to define the end of a data string or series.

delimiter, data, A character that marks the end of a series of bits or characters.

delivery date, The date that equipment is to be delivered, not necessarily unpacked or installed.

demand processing, The processing of data as fast as it becomes available.

demarcation strip, An interface between a machine and the common carrier in communications.

demodulation, Generally, a process of retrieving intelligence (data) from a modulated carrier wave, the reverse of modulation.

demodulation, The process of recovering an original signal from a modulated wave.

demonstration testing, A performance to show capabilities and limitations of a system.

demultiplexer, A logic circuit that can route a single line of digital information to other lines, the device acting to switch information to many different points.

denominator, In a fraction, the bottom number (the divisor).

density, The compactness of distribution of space on a storage medium.

density bit, A measure of bits recorded per unit of length (e.g., bits per inch, bpi).

density in bits, Bits per inch that may be written on data media.

density, packing, The number of units of information in a length, e.g., units per inch.

density, peak flux, A maximum magnetic condition of magnetic materials.

density, quad, A technique that records four times as much binary information per unit area of a storage medium as compared to the standard density for that particular medium. Quad density usually applies to floppy disks.

density, recording, The bits per unit length in a recording medium.

density, storage, The number of bits, bytes, characters, etc., per unit length such as characters per inch, etc.

density, track, The number of adjacent tracks per unit distance.

departure time, The time at which control is returned to the supervisory program.

dependent variable, A variable whose value depends on the function of another quantity.

derivative (rate) control action, A control action in which the output is proportional to the rate of change in the input.

derivative control, Control in which the output is proportional to the rate of change of the input.

descending sort, A sort in which the output records are in a descending order, the highest key being first, then each following less than the previous. (See key.)

description, problem, The statement of a problem and possibly a solution.

descriptor, A significant word that helps classify information.

design, The specification of working relations between parts of a system.

design and monitoring simulation, A procedure designed for developing a model of a system using special languages.

design, data, A layout or format of data to be used as input or output and in storage.

design, forms, Relates to designing (planning the layout) of a form to be used in data processing procedures.

design, functional, The design of a machine, computer program procedure, etc., in terms of broad components and describing their interrelationships.

design, interface, Design work done by engineers to interface units of on-line systems.

design, item, The set of records or fields that composes an item as delineated or the sequence in which they are recorded.

design, logic, Specification of the working relationships between parts of a system in terms of symbolic logic and without any major regard for the hardware implementation of it.

design, logical, (1) The basic logic for a system, machine, or network. (2) Pre-engineering design. (3) Data flow design (within the computer). (4) Design that will be implemented by hardware.

design objective, The planned performance goal or expectations, i.e., standards to be met.

design, solid-state, The design of solid-state devices having characteristics of lower power, cooling, and space requirements.

design, systems, The design of the nature and content of input, files, procedures, and output and their interrelationships.

design verification, The tests used to determine that a design meets the required specifications.

design, worst case, A circuit design (or other) designed to function with all the worst possible conditions occurring at the same time.

designation register, A computer register into which data is being placed.

desired value, A hoped for or chosen value.

desk check, Checking a program for errors without the aid of the computer.

desktop computer, Computer with a keyboard display memory, microprocessor all built into a single unit or system, although keyboards may be detachable. Some have printers built into the unit and can accept attachments of many peripherals such as disk drives, tape drives, plotters, and so on. Most have functions for immediate execution of sophisticated financial, statistical, or scientific programs.

destination file, The device (magnetic tape or disk) that will receive the file of information output from a computer run.

destination warning marker (DWM), A reflective spot on magnetic tape that is sensed photoelectrically to indicate the end of the tape is coming.

destruction notification, A notice sent out to departments indicating that records are to be destroyed.

destructive addition, The sum replaces the augend (the value of the augend is lost) in the execution of an add instruction in the computer.

destructive read, The destruction of data that is read from storage; generally the data is regenerated.

destructive reading, Reading of data that destroys the source data.

destructive readout, See destructive read.

destructive storage, Storage that needs to be regenerated to be retained, e.g., CRT, cathode ray tube storage.

destructive test, A test of equipment in which part of it is destroyed or damaged.

detail card, A punched card containing transaction information.

detail chart, A flowchart done in detail, step by step.

detail file, A file in which information changes more frequently than a master file.

detail printing, A listing of each record as contrasted to group printing.

detail record, A record containing single transaction data.

detecting code, error, A code in which errors produce a forbidden code combination.

detection, photoelectric, Mark reading by a photoelectric device in optical character recognition.

detection system, error, In communications a system that uses an error detecting code to delete error signals.

detection, transmission error, Errors are detected by parity and long channel checks in communications.

detector, A circuit that receives an input pattern and produces a designated output.

detent, A raised or depressed part of a surface.

deterministic simulation, A simulation in which there is a fixed relation between elements as contrasted with stochastic simulation.

development system, universal, Some types support many microprocessor chips and include assemblers and high-level languages, relocating macroassemblers, disassembling debuggers, in-circuit emulators, logic analyzers, and other tools for developing and debugging software for microcomputer systems.

development time, The time used to test and debug routines or hardware.

deviation, A departure from a desired or expected value or pattern.

deviation, offset, A deviation from a steady state of the controlled variable.

deviation, standard, A statistical term used to compare to a normal distribution.

device, A mechanical, electrical, or electronic contrivance or appliance.

device, analog, A device that represents numbers as physical quantities, e.g., by lengths as in a slide rule, or by voltage currents as in an analog computer.

device, asynchronous, A unit that has an operating speed not related to anything it's connected to.

device compatible, Two devices are compatible if they can work together without special hardware or software having to be used to make this possible.

device, conversion, a device used to convert data from one form to another without changing content.

device, direct access, Sometimes called random access device; magnetic disk, drum, etc., as contrasted to serial access.

device independence, The capability to express input and output independent of what device will actually be used.

device, input/output, In communications any user equipment that sends or receives data in a data communications system.

device status word (DSW), A computer word containing bits whose condition indicate the status of devices.

Dewey decimal system, A classification system used in libraries to indicate the arrangement of books.

DF, An abbreviation for any of the following: decimal fraction, direction finder, direction finding, or dual facility.

DFT, An abbreviation for Diagnostic Function Test.

diad, A group of two items that generally refers to digits.

diagnosis, The process of determining the cause of an error or problem.

diagnosis, continuous system, A system in which there is a collection of diagnostic tasks that are processed when other higher priority things are not running.

diagnostic function test (DFT), A program used to test overall system reliability.

diagnostic routine, A computer program routine used to locate a malfunction in a computer or a program.

diagnostics, Listings of detected errors.

diagnostics, system, A program used to detect overall system malfunctions.

diagram, A schematic representation of data flow, a circuit or logic, etc.

diagram, block, A graphic representation of operations, a planning and design chart, shows paths of information flow.

diagram, computer, A functional diagram of computing elements.

diagram, electrical schematic, A representation (drawing) of electric circuit elements and their relationships.

diagram, energy level, A drawing that shows increases and decreases in electrical power.

diagram, engineering logic, A diagram relating to circuitry, etc., in logic elements.

diagram, flow, Same as flowchart.

diagram, flow-process, A flowchart of the major steps of work in process, synonymous with process chart. (See flowchart.)

diagram, functional, A diagram showing functional relationship of parts of a system, process, etc.

diagram, logical, A diagram of logical elements and their interconnections.

diagram, run, A graphic representation of information to be handled under program control.

diagram, schematic electrical, A graphic representation of electrical circuits.

diagram, set up, A graphic representation showing necessary preparation for a computer run.

diagram, Veitch, A table or chart showing information contained in a truth table.

diagram, Venn, A diagram showing set relationships; shows overlapping relationships.

dial exchange, An exchange in which all subscribers can dial a call.

dial, print timing, A control knob on a printer.

dial pulse, Pulse contacts in telephone dialing.

dial up, The service using a dial telephone capability.

dialing, direct distance, An exchange service permitting users to dial outside of their local area.

dialing, pushbutton, Touching buttons instead of a rotary dial to place a call.

dialing, tone, See pushbutton dialing.

dialing unit, automatic, A modem or device that is capable of automatically generating dialed digits for a call.

dichotomizing search, Same as binary search.

dichotomy, A division into two classes or subgroups.

dictionary, A book or list of code names used in a system.

dictionary, automatic, The component of computer language translating that provides a word-for-word substitution from one language to another.

dictionary code, An alphabetical arrangement of words and terms and their meanings.

dictionary, database, Used to permit better documentation, control, and management of the data resource; goals may or may not be achieved through the use of a database management system (DBMS).

dictionary, external symbol, A list of symbols that are external (outside the current program) but defined by another.

dictionary, mechanical, A language translating machine component that provides word-for-word substitution.

dictionary, relocation (RLD), The part of a program that contains information necessary to change addresses when it is relocated.

dielectric, A non-conducting material.

difference, The result of the subtraction process.

difference engine, A machine built by Charles Babbage in 1812.

difference reports, Reports showing changes that result from a computer program change.

differentiate, To find the derivative of a function or to distinguish between objects (or ideas).

differentiating amplifier, A specific amplifier in analog computers.

digit, A symbol representing a positive integer in a given numbering system. For example, a bit is a binary digit representing 0 or 1 in the binary number system. Also, the numbers 0 to 9 are all digits in the decimal number system.

digit, One of the symbols of a numbering system, such as 0, 1, 2, 3, etc.

digit, binary, The digits used in the binary numbering system, 0 (zero), or 1 (one).

digit, check, The use of one or more redundant digits used for checking purposes.

digit, decimal, One of the numbers zero through nine, i.e., 0, 1, 2.......9.

digit delay, A logic element that delays its input signal.

digit emitter, A character emitter that generates and emits digits.

digit, forbidden, Same as forbidden code. It is not valid in a specific data processing system.

digit, hexadecimal, A digit of the hexadecimal numbering system; the digits 0 through 9, and A, B, C, D, E, F are used.

digit, least significant, The digit in a number contributing the smallest amount to the total quantity.

digit, octal, A digit in the octal numbering system; 0, 1, 2, 3, 4, 5, 6, or 7.

digit period, The magnitude of the time interval between signals that represent consecutive digits.

digit place, The position of a digit in a number.

digit, sign, Same as sign bit.

digit, significant, A digit of significant value to the accuracy of the number.

digital, (1) Data in discrete quantities. Contrasts with ANALOG. (2) Pertaining to data in the form of digits.

digital, Pertaining to use of discrete integral numbers.

digital cassette, Off-line operations for recording and storing alphanumeric information that can be accepted asynchronously such as from a keyboard. Many such devices are especially designed for home and very small computer system operation.

digital channel, A channel capable of carrying direct current, as opposed to analog channels, which do not.

digital circuit, An on-off switchlike circuit. It is called a binary circuit.

digital clock, A clock having output signals in digital representation.

digital communications, Such systems have quickly become economical due to low cost microprocessors and codes that aid in converting from and reconverting to analog signals. With all-digital systems, the conversion equipment and time used for conversion are not needed; error discovery and corrections are simpler, faster, cheaper.

digital computer, A computer in which information is represented in discrete values as contrasted with analog computer.

digital computer, serial, A computer in which digits are handled serially in the arithmetic.

digital control, direct, Control obtained by a digital device.

digital data, Data represented by digits such as 0, 1, etc.

digital   dataphone   service (DDS), AT&T's DDS allows users to transmit digitized voice at rates up to 9,600 bits per second from most major American cities.

digital differential analyzer, See DDA.

digital display, A visual display (CRT) of alphabetic and/or numeric data.

digital PBX applications, Applications of electronic PBX include: call forwarding, camp-on, trunk call-back, automatic route selection, queuing, automatic number identification, detailed station message accounting, etc.

digital readout, A lighted display in decimal digits.

digital recorder, A device that records data as discrete points.

digital representation, A representation of data by means of digits.

digital signal, A discrete or discontinuous signal whose various states are discrete intervals apart.

digital subtracter, The unit capable of calculating a difference between two numbers.

digital system, man-machine, The combination of people, digital computers, and equipment used to achieve system objectives.

digital-analog decoder, A device in an analog computer used to translate digital data in electrical flow.

digit-coded voice, A coded voice response that is output from an ARU (audio response unit).

digitize, To convert an analog measurement of a physical variable into a number expressed in digital form.

digitize, To convert to digital form.

digitizer, Any device that can convert analog measurements into digital quantities for digital computer processing.

digitizer, The device that converts analog data into digital form (synonymous with quantizer).

digits, check, Digits used in processing for checking purposes.

digits, equivalent binary, The number of binary digit places required to express a number written in another number system form.

diode, An electronic device used to permit current flow in one direction in a circuit and to inhibit current flow in the other.

diode, A device that permits the flow of electricity in one direction only.

diode, crystal, A diode containing crystalline elements.

diode, silicon, A type of crystal diode containing crystalline silicon.

DIP-Dual-In-Line Package, A packaging for ICs - integrated circuits and chips which are enclosed taking on a "bug-like" appearance with parallel rows of leads (legs) that connect to the circuit board.

diplexer, A coupling device that allows two radio transmitters to share an antenna.

dipole, A double antenna used in UHF and VHF systems.

direct access, The ability to read or write information at any location within a storage device in a constant amount of time. Every site available for data storage on a direct access device is identified by its own unique, numeric address.

direct access arrangement (DAA), The use of modems on the dial-up facilities of the telephone; the device is often rented from the phone company and limits the signaling power of the attached modem.

direct access device, Sometimes called random access device; refers to magnetic disk, drum, etc., as contrasted to serial access.

direct access inquiry, Making an inquiry to a file on magnetic disk or other direct access device.

direct access library, The librarian portion of the control program in an operating system where the program library is on a direct access device. (See librarian.)

direct access storage, Storage devices in which the access of position data is not dependent on the last position accessed.

direct access storage devices, Storage devices, such as magnetic disk and drum, that are capable of fast and direct access to storage locations.

direct access storage inquiry, Directly requesting and obtaining information from a storage device such as from a magnetic disk file.

direct address, An address in a computer instruction that indicates where the location of the operand is without any other references. It is synonymous with first-level address.

direct addressing, A method for specifically citing an operand in a computer instruction by the operand's location in storage.

direct code, Same as absolute code.

direct control, Control of one device by another without human intervention.

direct coupled flip-flop, A flip-flop made of electronic circuits in which the active elements are coupled with resistors.

direct current (DC), An essentially constant-value current that flows in only one direction.

direct data capture, Automatic recording of transaction data such as at a cash register.

direct distance dialing, An exchange service permitting a telephone user to dial directly out of the local area.

direct distance dialing, See DDD.

direct insert subroutine, Same as in-line subroutine and open subroutine as contrasted with closed subroutine.

direct memory access (DMA), The on-chip circuit that provides for those applications that require data to be transferred directly into memory at a very high rate rather than going through the CPU.

direct output, Output, printed, visual, etc., from on-line output equipment which is directly connected to the computer.

direct video storage tube (DVST), A CRT which holds a constant image. Some types of DVSTs have very high resolution and picture quality and are used in computer-aided design.

directing character code, Routing indicator(s) at the start of a message to indicate destination.

direction, flow, Direction of flow in a flowchart usually indicated by arrows.
(See flowchart.)

direction, grain, Direction of the fibers in paper relative to the way the paper travels through an optical character reader.

direction, lateral (magnetic tape), Across the width of the tape.

direction, longitudinal, Along the length (not width) as in magnetic tape.

direction, normal flow, In a flowchart the normal flow directions are left to right and top to bottom.

directive, A pseudo-instruction in a computer program used to control translation.

directly proportional, Two quantities increasing or decreasing together at a constant ratio as contrasted with inversely proportional.

director, Equipment used to control processes.

directory, A description of a file layout.

disable, A repression of an interrupt feature. (See interrupt.)

disabled interrupt, An armed interrupt waiting for enablement. (See interrupt.)

disarmed state, The state of an interrupt level in which it cannot accept an input signal.

disassembler, A program to translate from machine language to assembly language, e.g., it generally is used to decipher existing machine language programs by generating symbolic code listings of a program.

disaster dump, A dump (printout) that occurs when there is a non-recoverable computer program error.

disc (or disk), A magnetic storage device consisting of rotating discs that have magnetic surfaces.

disconnect signal, A signal sent to a terminal from a central computer that results in the ending of the line connection.

discrete, Separate and distinct parts of data.

discrete circuits, Electronic circuits built from separately manufactured components as contrasted with integrated circuits.

discrete data, A representation for a variable that may assume any of several distinct states, i.e., sex or race, and is usually coded.

discrete programming, A class of optimization problem using only integer data.

discrete sampling, A sampling process in which each sample is sufficiently long in duration and the accuracy is not decreased by the sampling process in communications.

discrete, series, A series of numbers that have no values between them (such as dress sizes 8, 10, 12, 14 or 7, 9, 11, 13, etc.).

discrete simulation, Simulation using discrete events such as in a queuing network. It is also called event oriented simulation as contrasted with continuous simulation.

discrimination instruction, Same as conditional branch or conditional jump instructions

disjunctive search, A type of search defined in terms of a logical sum which uses the inclusive or instruction as contrasted with conjunctive search.

disk alignment notches, Two small semicircular notches in the floppy disk jacket which ensure the disk is properly inserted in the disk drive.

disk controller board, Most boards allow computer memory to be extended by permitting the computer to be connected to more floppy disk drives; the boards also contain additional input/output capability.

disk controller board, intelligent, Some controller boards accept software commands from the program in execution, decode them, and manage the disk drive in such a way as to produce the required operation.

disk crash, A disk read-write head making destructive contact with the surface of a rotating disk which loosely refers to any disk unit failure that results in a system malfunction.

disk, data organization, Data on various disks are organized in sectors and tracks, the latter being concentric rings on the surface of the disk.

disk, double-sided, Using both sides of the disk, recording doubles the on-line storage capacity of many types, especially floppy disks, while adding only about 25 percent extra cost.

disk drive, Typical disk drives are highly reliable random access, moving head memory devices, compactly designed for use as peripheral units in large and small, and recently microcomputer systems.

disk drive, Winchester-based, A sealed-housing, two-sided, lubricant-coated, 8-1/4-inch aluminum disk qualifies for this connotation.

disk file, A magnetic disk pack or a logical file on magnetic disk.

disk file addressing, A method of locating information on magnetic disk storage.

disk files, A magnetic storage medium consisting of layers of disks which rotate. Each disk may contain stored information.

disk, fixed head, Consists of a rotating magnetically coated surface and an arm that can position a head over any section of the disk. As the disk rotates, every position on the tracks under the head become available for read or record.

disk fragmentation, This is the phenomenon that occurs on disks (and other storage devices) most often during processing that requires frequent updating of files. The continuous process of storing and erasing data on a disk tends to break up files into small pieces, called extents, which become scattered over the disk. This leads to an ever-decreasing efficiency in the search-retrieval and storage algorithms in the program. Because of this loss of efficiency due to fragmentation, special compaction algorithms are needed to periodically find and regroup a file's extents.

disk, magnetic, A storage device consisting of a magnetized recording surface on a metal disk.

disk, nondismountable pack, A pack (disk or other storage medium) that cannot be removed from its read/write device. Generally, nondismountable packs refer to hard, fixed disks.

disk operating system (DOS), A versatile operating system for computer systems having disk capability.

disk operating system capabilities, Typical file-oriented routines can: read a byte, write a byte, read a block, write a block, update a block, open file for input, open file for output, find a file, and so on.

disk pack, A number of magnetic disks connected by a central spindle and enclosed in a protective package.

disk pack, A removable, portable set of magnetic disks that contains information and may be put on a disk drive attached to a computer.

disk reader, A device that converts information stored on disks into signals that can be sent to a computer.

disk sector, A sector is generally preceded by a small block of information containing the track number and sector number both normally verified by the disk controller prior to disk access.

disk, sorting, Using a disk memory device for auxiliary storage during sorting (see sorting).

disk storage, Storage of data on surfaces of magnetic disks.

disk storage unit, A random-access data storage device which provides rapid access to data.

disk track, Information is stored on a magnetic disk in one of a number of concentric circles, each of which is called a track.

disk types, A computer memory device which looks something like an audio record. It is either hard or floppy. See FLOPPY DISK, HARD DISK, MAGNETIC DISK.

disk write protect, An option that inhibits writing to prevent the accidental overwriting of recorded information. Writing is inhibited when a hole in the flexible jacket is open. A sticker covering the hole will enable writing.

diskette operating systems, Substantially reduces the time required to assemble, edit, and execute programs which include the disk controller, disk drive, and management software.

diskette sectoring, Two main methods of sectoring: hard sectoring and soft sectoring. The former identifies each sector by holes punched in the diskette (one hole per sector), the latter identifies the sectors by magnetic codes written on the diskette. Both have a hole called the index hole in the diskette to identify the beginning of the tracks.

dismount, To remove a magnetic storage medium from its read/write device.

dismountable pack, A floppy disk or other storage medium that can be dismounted from its read/write device and replaced by another. Dismountable packs contrast with nondismountable packs, such as fixed disks.

dispatcher, (1) A computer program routine used to control communication between the computer and its input/output devices. (2) A person that coordinates the input and output of a system.

dispatcher, task, A computer program routine that selects the next task to be processed.

dispatching system, In a real-time system the dispatching system responds to demand by assigning resources, e.g., a system that assigns inventory to fill orders.

dispatching systems, In a real-time system, responding to demand by assigning resources to meet it.

disperse, The distribution of items.

dispersion, The distribution of oxide particles in magnetic media.

display, The visual representation of information on a CRT or other display device.

display, Visible representation of data on a screen or in lights.

display adapter unit, A unit that controls the transmission of data for CRT devices.

display category, The type or class of data to be visually displayed.

display center, A position on a display screen.

display console, A CRT (cathode ray tube, television-like device) that permits visual display of computer contents.

display console, message, A computer console containing a symbol generator and a CRT (cathode ray tube, a television-like device).

display control unit, The control unit for display devices.

display controllers, Provide an integrated solution to the problem of display-support circuitry. Combined on a single chip in some systems are data latching, seven-segment decode, segment drive, and digit multiplex control.

display, CRT, A cathode ray tube (television-like device) used to display messages and graphic information.

display cursor, A moveable mark that locates a character on a screen. Cursor control keys permit operators to move the cursor from line to line and from character to character.

display, digital, A visual display (CRT) of alphabetic and/or numeric data.

display, forced, A display made by the system that wasn't requested by the operator.

display, horizontal, The width in inches of the display screen.

display, incremental, A newer, more versatile and accurate incremental CRT (cathode ray tube) display.

display lights, storage address, The indicator lights on the operator's console that display the bit pattern in an address.

display, plasma panel, A flat display device composed of tiny neon bulbs. It is used as an alternative to the CRT for graphics displays.

display, points per frame, The measurement of minimum and maximum flicker free points on a CRT.

display, protected fields, On some systems, when fill-in forms are displayed on a video screen, some material like "Name," "Address," and other instructive items — should not normally be altered by the operator.

display refresher rate, The manufacturer's recommended number of frames per second for regeneration of a display.

display, reverse field, A function that shows dark characters on a background of light screen area, often used when material is being edited to show which characters are being inserted or deleted, and for special comments and warnings to the operator.

display screen, word processing, This type of screen usually shows text as users create and assemble or edit it before it is printed.

display scrolling, A feature permitting text to be moved up or down, so as to show material that does not fit on the display screen, usually with a scrolling key causing the first line in the direction of motion to disappear.

display station, A cathode ray tube (CRT) television-like terminal.

display, translate, To move an image on the screen up or down or side to side.

display tube, A cathode ray tube (CRT) a television-like device.

display types, Common types are cathode ray tube (CRT), plasma, liquid crystal displays (LCD), light emitting diodes (LED), incandescent and fluorescent plus the standard "Nixie" types.

display unit, A unit that is capable of visual representation of data.

display unit, graphic, A communications terminal (linked to a computer) that displays data on a (television-like) screen.

display, vector-mode, A mode in which straight lines between two points can be displayed.

display, vertical, The height in inches of the display screen (CRT).

dissector, image, A mechanical or electronic device that detects the level of light in optical character recognition.

distributed computer systems, The arrangement of computers in an organization that are not all at one location.

distributed data processing (DDP), Data processing in which two or more connected computers share the work load.

diversity reception, A method used in radio reception to minimize the effects of fading.

DMA bus, single chip systems, Feature Direct Memory Access that means fast, direct transfers are possible from memory to peripherals, peripherals to memory, and peripheral to peripheral.

DML, Data Manipulation Language.

DNC, Direct numerical control systems of factory automation or process control with a common memory and provisions for on-demand distribution of data to the machines.

document, (1) A form or paper containing information about a transaction. (2) To record information for evidence or instruction.

document copy, The original that is being photographed, also called hard copy.

document leading edge, The edge of a document that goes into the machine first (optical character recognition).

document reader, optical, An input device that can read characters on documents.

document sorter-reader, magnetic, A device that reads and sorts magnetic ink documents such as checks.

document, source, The document that is used to make data into machine readable form.

document transportation, Moving a document to the read station in an optical character reading device.

documentation, Descriptions that accompany a computer program to explain to people how the program works.

documentation, (1) The process of organizing documents containing information about a procedure or program; (2) the group of documents themselves.

documentation, graphic, A process for recording data on film and graphs.

documentation, program, Information about a computer program to aid programmers and computer operators and others.

documents, software, All the documents related to the computer operation such as manuals, diagrams, also compilers, library routines, etc.

docuterm, A word or phrase that is descriptive of an item of information that is used for retrieval.

domain, In terms of relational models of database management systems, the domain is the collection of field occurrences in a file.

dopant, Chemical elements that are introduced into lattice structures as impurities to form desired chip properties.

DOS (disk operating system), A versatile operating system for computer systems having disk capability.

dot matrix CRT, A type of display that operates by illuminating selected dots on a grid of points.

dot matrix printer, A type of impact device which uses a column usually of seven pins to strike the ink ribbon five times for a 5 x 7 dot matrix and for each character symbol. With a typical 5 x 7 matrix character display, the exact dot patterns for all characters are stored in Read Only Memory (ROM) allowing selection of a number of optional character fonts.

dot printer, Same as matrix printer.

dots, phosphor, Elements in a screen of a cathode ray tube (CRT) which glow.

double density, Twice the amount of binary information that can be stored per unit area as compared to the standard density for that particular medium. Double density usually applies to floppy disks.

double modulation, Modulation of one wave by another wave.

double precision, A quantity using twice as many positions as are normally used in a computer.

double precision arithmetic, Uses two computer words of memory to represent one number when a single word doesn't provide enough accuracy in arithmetic calculations.

double sideband transmission, In communications, the sidebands are not related to each other, but are related separately to two sets of modulating signals (see sideband).

double-length, Twice the length of a unit of storage or data, e.g., double-length word, double-length register, etc.

doubleword, program status, A double word indicating all programmable control conditions of the CPU (central processing unit) of a computer.

double-word register, Two computer registers used together to hold a double word (see double word).

down time, The time a computer is not working because of machine failure.

down time, scheduled, Time the computer or other machine is being serviced for regular maintenance; also known as preventative maintenance time (PM).

download, Refers to various procedures to transfer a copy of a program, file, or other information from a remote database or other computer to the user's own terminal over a communications line. Download is synonymous with down-line loading.

downtime, Generally, the period of time during which a computer system is down, or not operating. Downtime usually refers to the operating time lost due to an error or malfunction.

DPM, An abbreviation for documents per minute or data processing machine.

DPMA, Data Processing Management Association.

DPMA certificate, A certificate given by the association to indicate that a person has a certain level of competence in the field of data processing.

drift , The change in the output of a circuit that is caused by voltage fluctuation.

drills, network, The final level of testing in a real-time system in which the entire network is tested.

drive, A device that moves tape or disk past a read/write head.

drive, disk, An electromechanical device into which a disk is inserted to read or write information.

drive, disk, The disk drive itself is responsible for implementing the commands from the controller and supplying the required status information.

drive, tape, The device that moves magnetic tape past the recording heads; same as tape transport.

driven, key, Any device that requires an operator to depress keys to translate information into machine-sensible form.

driver, device, Usually an operating system (OS) module that controls a specific input/output peripheral.

drives, start/stop, Start/stop drives pause in inter-record gaps on the tape surface as they read or write data.

DRO, Stands for destructive read-out.

drop, A subscriber's telephone connection.

drop, subscriber's, The line from a telephone cable that "drops" to the subscriber's building.

drop-dead halt, Same as dead halt.

dropout count, The number of dropouts detected in a specific length of tape.

drum, A cylinder with a magnetic surface used to store data

DSW (device status word), A computer word containing bits whose condition indicate the status of devices.

DTR, An abbreviation for distribution tape reel.

dual channel controller, The controller that permits tape reading and/or writing at the same time.

dual systems, Two computers, one is used for total back up. This is a desirable situation for air traffic control and other critical activities.

dual-in-line package (DIP), The packaging of integrated circuits (see DIP).

dumb terminal, Usually has no augmentation. The various degrees of smartness are generally related to arbitrary characteristics such as memory size, ROM or RAM storage of firmware, and so on.

dummy, Generally, an artificial element in a program used only to fulfill specifications in the program and not to actually perform a function. Examples of dummy items are dummy variables, dummy instructions, dummy addresses, and dummy blocks.

dummy address, An artificial address used to show an example to someone.

dummy instruction, An artificial instruction that may be used to define constants or to hold a place that will later contain a usable instruction.

dump (noun), A list of the contents of a computer's main memory.

dump (verb), To copy the contents of all or part of memory, usually from an internal storage device into an external storage device.

dump, ac, The intentional, accidental, or conditional removal of all alternating current power from a system or component.

dump, core, A printed listing of the contents of storage or part of storage (synonymous with memory dump and memory printout).

dump, dc, The intentional or accidental removal of all direct current power from a system or component.

dump, disaster, A dump or printout that occurs when there is a non-recoverable computer program error.

dump, memory, A list of the contents of a storage device.

dump, monitor control, A memory dump that may be specified in the job control information.

dump, port mortem, A dump or printout of the contents of storage at the end of a computer run.

dump, power, The removal of all power.

dump, rescue, To dump or record the contents of computer memory onto magnetic tape.

dump, selective, A dump or printout of contents of a selected area of internal storage of a computer.

dump, snapshot, A dump of a computer program at various points in a machine run. A dump is a printout of storage contents.

dump, static, A printout of the contents of computer memory at a particular time during a machine run.

dump, storage, A printout of the contents of internal storage. It is the same as memory dump, memory printout, and dump.

dump, tape, The transfer of the contexts of tape to another storage medium (may be a printout).

dumping, storage, The process of transferring data from one storage device to another. (See also storage dump.)

duodecimal, Pertaining to the number system of the base 12.

dup (or dupe), The abbreviation for duplication.

duplex, Concerns a pair or any combination of two things.

duplex, full, Simultaneous (at the same time) communications between two points in both directions.

duplex, half, A communication system in which information can travel in only one direction at a time as contrasted to full duplex.

duplex system, Two computers, one being used and the other standing by in case of failure of the first.

duplicate, To reproduce data without changing the original data.

duration, pulse, The length (in time) of a pulse.

duration, run, The length of a run (in time).

dyadic, See BINARY.

dynamic, A transient or unstable condition.

dynamic analysis, The study of effects on controlled variables in a control system with disturbance inputs.

dynamic instruction, The sequence of machine steps performed by a computer in a real-time or simulated environment.

dynamic loop, A specific loop stop designed to stop the machine (see loop stop).

dynamic memory, The movement of data in memory such that it is circulated and not always instantly available.

dynamic printout, A printing that occurs during a computer run instead of after, as contrasted with static printout.

dynamic RAM, Data that is stored capacitively and must be recharged (refreshed) periodically (every 2 microseconds, or so) or it will be lost.

dynamic relocation memory, A process that frees the user from keeping track of the exact locations of information in memory.

dynamic response, A specific behavior of the output of a device as a function of the input, both with respect to time.

dynamic scheduling, Scheduling changes are made based on demands on the system rather than being fixed as in the conventional way.

dynamic stop, An instruction that branches to itself in a computer program.

dynamic storage, The mobility of stored data in time and space.

dynamic storage allocation, A method of making storage capacity available to programs and data based on actual, immediate needs.

dynamic storage allocation, A feature in which storage for a subroutine is assigned to the first available storage; results in storage saving.

dynamic storage, permanent, Storage in which the maintenance of data doesn't depend on a flow of energy such as magnetic disk, drum, etc.

dynamic storage, volatile, A storage medium that depends on external power to retain stored information.

dynamic subroutine, A computer program subroutine that uses parameters to adjust its processing.

dynamiciser, A logic element of a specific capability.

dynamic control, The operation of a computer so that it can alter instructions as computation proceeds.

dynamizer, Same as dynamiciser.

E

E value, The difference between the radius of the outer edge of tape in a roll and the radius of the outer edge of a tape reel flange.

EAM (electrical accounting machine), Punched card equipment such as sorters, collators, accounting machines, etc. (clarified by tabulating equipment).

EAROM, EAROM-stored data is electrically alterable and can easily be updated, reprogrammed electrically in the system and become non-volatile memory.

earth stations, satellite, Special communications ground terminals use antennas and associated electronic equipment to transmit, receive, and process communications via satellite. Many cable and computer systems are able to interconnect by domestic communications satellites creating regional and national networks, with international ones being implemented.

EBCDIC (Extended Binary Coded Decimal Interchange Code), A computer code in which a character is represented by a particular pattern of eight binary digits.

EBCDIC code, Stands for extended binary coded decimal interchange code, a standard code used in data processing.

echo attenuation, The ratio of transmitted electrical power at an output terminal to the amount reflected back to the same terminal.

ECL-Emitter-coupled logic, A chip logic approach that is very uniform, fast, and stable and offers advantages in packing density and low power.

ECMA, Stands for European Computer Manufacturing Association.

edge, stroke, An imaginary line equidistant from the stroke centerline in optical character recognition.

edge, trailing, The drop in voltage at the end of a pulse.

edge, twelve, The top edge of a punched card.

edit, Refers to the rearrangement of data or information. Editing may involve the deletion of unwanted data, the selection of pertinent data, the application of format techniques, the insertion of symbols, and the testing of data for reasonableness and proper range.

edit, To rearrange data, may include deleting unwanted data.

editing functions, terminal, Allow removal of characters, words or larger pieces of text, insertion of new text, and movement of text from one position to another, functions essential to word processing operations, particularly the facilitation of mistake correction.

editing keys, Allow the insertion or deletion of characters or lines in the screen display, among other functions.

editing, post, An editing procedure on the output of a previous operation.

editing subroutine, A computer program subroutine used with input/output operations to perform editing.

editor, A computer program routine that performs editing operations.

editor, symbolic, A computer program that permits the adding or deleting of lines in a source language program.

editor, tape, A computer program used to edit, correct, etc., symbolic program tapes.

editor, text, A program that facilitates changes to computer-stored information; assists in the preparation of text.

EDP (electronic data processing), Data processing performed by electronic equipment.

EDPE, An abbreviation for electronic data processing equipment.

EDPM, An abbreviation for electronic data processing machine.

EDPS, An abbreviation for electronic data processing system.

education, simulation, Using simulation computer programs so people may be exposed to effects of environmental change, e.g., management games.

edulcorate, (1) To eliminate worthless information; (2) To weed out.

EEROM, Electrically erasable read only memory similar to EAROM — electrically alterable ROM, EEROM can be erased in one second and reprogrammed up to a million times.

effect, rain barrel, An echo-like effect developed into an audio signal.

effective address, The address actually used in execution of a computer instruction. It may be different from the address in the instruction in that it is modified in some way prior to execution of the instruction.

effective byte location, The actual storage location indicated in an address in a byte addressing instruction.

effective doubleword location, The actual storage location indicated in an address in a doubleword addressing instruction.

effective halfword location, The actual storage location that is indicated in an address in a halfword addressing instruction.

effective instruction, An altered computer instruction containing effective addresses prior to execution.

effective time, The time that equipment is in actual use.

effective word, The word actually accessed in a computer operation on a single word.

effectiveness, cost, A ratio of measurement of cost to performance of a system, product, etc.

efficiency, computer, The ratio of the number of hours of proper machine operation to the total hours of scheduled operation.

efficiency, information, A computed ratio of actual negative entropy to maximum possible entropy (see entropy).

efficiency, multiprogramming, Reduced turnaround time, increased computations per dollar, and other efficiencies of multiprogramming.

EFTS-Electronic Funds Transfer Systems, Various electronic communications systems that transfer financial information from one point to another and related to automated tellers, point of sale (POS) terminals.

EHF, Extremely high frequency.

EIA interface, A set of signal characteristics (time duration, voltage, and current) for connection of terminals to modem units, and specific physical coupler dimensions specified by the Electronic Industries Association.

EIA-Electronic Industries Association, A national trade association representing manufacturers of electronic products with committees engaged in developing EIA Standards and Engineering Bulletins.

eight level, Any teletypewriter code that uses eight pulses (plus a start and stop pulse) to describe a character.

eighty column card, A standard punched card with 80 columns for data recording.

electric delay line, See delay line.

electric pulse, A momentary rise or fall in voltage level.

electrical accounting machine (EAM), Punched card equipment such as sorters, collators, accounting machines, etc., that is clarified by tabulating equipment.

electrical communications, Communications using material with relatively low electrical resistance such as copper wire.

electrical connector, Any of many devices used to connect conductors, join cables, etc.

electrical contact, The joint or touching of two halves of a connector or the point of electrical connection.

electrical schematic diagram, A representation or drawing of electric circuit elements and their relationships.

electricity, A fundamental quantity consisting of two oppositely charged particles, the electrons being negatively charged, and the protons positively charged. A substance with more electrons than protons is said to be negatively charged; conversely, one with more protons than electrons is positively charged.

electrode, A metal body capable of having an electric charge.

electromagnetic communications, Communications in which the electromagnetic conductor is space, e.g., radio, television, radar.

electromagnetic deflection, The swerving of the beam in writing tubes by means of a magnetic field.

electron, A subatomic particle with a negative electric charge.

electron, A part of an atom having a negative charge.

electronic data processing, Using electronic equipment to process data.

electronic data processing system, The aggregation of machines, people, and methods used to perform data processing functions.

electronic message service (EMS), Acceptance of mail electronically from facsimile devices, word processing units using magnetic tape and disk media plus other types of communication by computer such as computer conferencing.

electronic office, Generally refers to an office which uses electronic equipment, such as computers, word processors, etc., to process, store, and deliver information.

electronic statistical machine, A punched card sorter that can print and add data while sorting.

electronic stylus, A light pen used with a CRT (cathode ray tube) for inputting and changing information.

electronic switch, A high speed circuit element causing a switching action.

Electronic Switching System, A switching system designed by Bell Laboratories.

electronic switching system (ESS) operation, A type of telephone switching system that uses a special purpose stored program digital computer to direct and to control the switching operation. ESS permits the provision of custom calling services such as speed dialing, call transfer, three-way calling, and so on.

electronic tutor, A teaching machine using programmed instruction.

electronics, A branch of science dealing with the behavior of currents of free elections.

electrostatic storage, Storage on a dielectric surface such as the screen of a CRT (cathode ray tube, television-like device) or storage using electric charges to represent data.

elegant, Generally a program is considered elegant if it uses the smallest amount of main memory possible. Thus, an elegant program contains no statements which are not essential.

element, A component part.

element, active, A circuit or device that receives energy from a source other than the main input signal.

element, cryogenic, High speed circuits that use the superconductivity of materials at or near absolute zero temperatures.

element, data, A combination of one or more data items that forms a unit or piece of information.

element, data, (1) A group of characters specifying an item; (2) an item of information; (3) or the smallest unit of data to which reference is made such as a customer code, unit price, etc.

element, decision, A circuit that performs a logical operation.

element, delay, The electronic mechanism that temporarily delays data flow.

element, function, A device that performs a function of logic.

element, logic, A device that performs a logic function.

element, negation, A device capable of reversing a signal, condition, or state to its opposite.

element, sequential, Devices having at least one output channel and one or more input channels; the state of the output channel is determined by the states of the input channels.

element, start, The first element in data transmission used for synchronization.

element, threshold, A specific type of logic element.

element, unit, An alphabetic signal element having a duration equal to a unit interval of time.

elements, solid-state, Electronic components using solid material to convey electrons as opposed to space or a vacuum.

elimination, zero, A process used to eliminate leftmost zeros before printing a number.

else rule, A catch-all rule to handle conditions not covered by explicit rules.

embossment, (1) A "raised up" or engraved surface on a document; (2) in optical character recognition, a specific measure of distance related to characters.

emitter, A device that is capable of emitting pulses at certain times.

emitter coupled logic (ECL), A circuit technology for computer construction (see ECL).

emitter, digit, A character emitter that generates and emits digits.

emitter, pulse, A device in some punched card machines.

EMMS, An abbreviation for Electronic Mail and Message Systems.

empirical, In scientific methods, documentation of evidence without the use of theory or deduction.

emulate, The capacity of one computer system to imitate another.

emulation, The situation in which one computer behaves like another.

emulator, The specific hardware in a computer that permits it to emulate or behave like another computer.

enable, A procedure used to restore a suppressed interrupt feature (see interrupt).

enable pulse, A pulse when combined with a write pulse is strong enough to switch a magnetic cell.

encipher, The same as encode.

encode, To translate data into a particular code.

encode, To apply a code to represent characters.

encoding strip, On blank checks the area where magnetic ink is used to represent characters.

encryption, A coding of sensitive data that is to be stored or transmitted often according to officially acceptable procedures and standards.

encryption algorithm, Any algorithm that implements a cipher.

END, The computer program statement used at the end of a program.

end instrument, In communications a device connected to one terminal of a loop that is capable of converting usable intelligence signals into electrical signals or vice versa.

end, leading, The end of a wire, tape, ribbon, etc., that is processed first.

end mark, An indicator that signals the end of a unit of data.

end of data, The signal that is generated or read when the last record of a file is written or read.

end of file, A mark at the end of a data file.

end of line, A machine code character that indicates the end of a group of records.

end of message (EOM), A set of characters to indicate the end of a transmitted message.

end, physical, The last statement in a computer program or the last data record in a file.

end printing, The printing of large characters on the end of a punched card that is done by a reproducing punch.

end, trailing, The last end of a tape or ribbon, etc., to be processed.

end value, A value to be compared with an index, count, etc., to see if the end of that processing has been reached.

end-of-file indicator, An indicator that turns on when an end-of-file condition is reached. It is used to inform the computer program or programmer.

end-of-file mark, A code indicating the last record of a file has been read.

end-of-text character, A character used to indicate the end of the text in data communications transmission.

endorser, A feature on a magnetic ink character reader (MICR) that is an endorsement record of each bank.

energy control system, Energy management, allocation, and control are achieved by monitoring power demand and regulating electrical devices to meet preprogrammed energy loads. Various packaged systems are programmed through a CRT console using a special purpose language in some wide-ranging systems.

energy level diagram, A drawing that shows increases and decreases in electrical power.

engaging force contact, The force necessary to insert pins into electrical sockets.

engineer, field, A field engineer is a person who repairs computer equipment. Field engineers usually work for computer vendors or computer repair services and are often called FEs or CEs (customer engineers).

engineering logic diagram, A diagram relating to circuitry, etc., in logic elements.

engineering, service, Covers the board range of support to a customer of a computer vendor.

engineering time, Total machine downtime due to failure, preventative maintenance, etc.; same as servicing time.

engineering time, scheduled, Same as scheduled downtime and preventative maintenance time.

engineers, software, A specialized group of programmers who work for computer manufacturers and usually create the systems software that operates the equipment for the user.

ENQ, An abbreviation for enquiry character.

enter key, This is a key on a computer terminal which is pressed at the end of each line in order to enter the contents of that line into the computer. Also called return key.

entropy, (1) A measurement of unavailable energy in a system; (2) also, unavailable information in a set of documents; (3) an inactive state.

entry, (1) An input through a terminal; (2) a location (cell) in a table; (3) a member of a list.

entry, data, The entering of data into a system from a terminal or other media.

entry, index, A one item entry in an index.

entry instruction, Usually the first instruction to be executed in a subroutine. There may be several entry points within the routine.

entry, keyboard, An element of information entered manually into a computer.

entry, manual, Keyboard entry of data into a computer by a person.

entry, page, The point in a flowchart where the flowline continues from a previous page.

entry password, A secret group of characters that a user must input to log-on to a computer system. This prevents unauthorized persons from obtaining access to the computer or to specific information.

entry point, The address of the first instruction executed in a computer program or in a section of one, such as a routine or subroutine.

entry point, Usually the first instruction in a program, routine, or subroutine.

entry, remote job (RJE), A situation in which a central computer accepts and processes jobs from a remote location.

entry time, That time when control is transferred from the supervisory program to an application program.

envelope delay, Characteristics of a circuit that result in frequencies arriving at different times even if they were transmitted together.

environmental monitoring systems, Electro-optical equipment has been developed to provide analyses of atmospheric conditions to determine trace concentrations of specific gaseous pollutants. Techniques employed represent state-of-the-art capabilities in sensitivity and specificity for certain common pollutants.

EOF, Stands for end of file.

EOJ, Stands for end of job.

EOM (end of message), A set of characters to indicate the end of a transmitted message.

EOT, Stands for end of transmission.

epitome, A concise summary of a document.

EPROM, ultraviolet, Erasable Programmable Read Only Memory erasable by being exposed to ultraviolet light for a minimum of 20 minutes. Usually, the memory block is completely erased and must be fully reprogrammed for further use.

equal zero indicator, An indicator that turns on when the result of an arithmetic computation is zero (see indicator).

equation, computer, A mathematical equation derived from a model that is more conveniently used on a computer.

equation, differential, An equation that contains differentials of an unknown function.

equation, linear, A mathematical equation that has linear expressions on both sides of the equal sign.

equations, independent, A set of mathematical equations that can't be expressed as a linear combination of each other.

equations, simultaneous, Mathematical equations that are solved together that contain the same unknown quantities.

equipment, A general term for machines and parts of machines and systems.

equipment, ancillary, Same as peripheral equipment.

equipment, auxiliary, Various devices or units used with a computer such as data processing sorters, printers, etc.

equipment, COAM, Stands for customer owned and maintained communication equipment, disks, cassettes, etc.

equipment compatibility, The ability of equipment to accept and process data and/or programs prepared by another piece of equipment.

equipment complex, Any large mixture or group of computing equipment used for a large scale specific purpose missile tracking, etc.

equipment, customer station, Communications equipment located on the customer's premises.

equipment, data terminal, The modem or unit at either end of a data communications channel.

equipment, data transmission, The communications equipment associated with the data processing equipment in communications systems.

equipment failure, Something goes wrong in the equipment and it doesn't work properly.

equipment, input, (1) Same as input device, (2) data preparation equipment such as keyboard.

equipment, input-output, All the devices of a computer system that read (input) and write (output) data.

equipment, output, Any equipment used to transfer information out of a computer.

equipment, peripheral, Input/output or auxiliary equipment in a computer installation.

equipment, remote control, Control apparatus that works from a distance by electronic means.

equipment, standby, Data processing equipment that is available in case other equipment breaks down or is overloaded.

equivocation, The measure of difference between received and sent messages in communications.

erasability, A measure of the ease with which a printed image can be removed without impairing the surface of the document.

erasable PROM-Programmable Read Only Memory, A type of memory circuit with capability for pattern experimentation, ultraviolet light erasability of bit patterns, and low power operation.

erase, To replace data with zeros (or blanks), to clear.

eraser, bulk, A device used to erase or destroy the information on a reel of tape.

erasing head, dc, An electronic device capable of removing (erasing) magnetic bits from magnetic tape.

error, A general term indicating a deviation from correctness.

error, absolute, The magnitude (size) of an error disregarding whether it is a plus or minus error, or if it is an error in a vector, disregarding the direction of the error.

error, balanced, A range of error that can be the same amount in either a plus or minus direction.

error burst, A data transmission method using designed error bits.

error correction, automatic, A technique used to correct transmission errors automatically.

error correction routine, A computer program routine used to correct a detected error while processing.

error data, Wrong or incorrect data.

error detecting code, A code in which errors produce a forbidden code combination.

error detection, automatic, A characteristic in a computer program that permits detection of its own errors.

error detection system, In communications a system that uses an error detecting code to delete error signals.

error detection, transmission, In communications, errors are detected by parity and long channel checks.

error diagnostic message, A message the computer prints in case of an error to help the programmer or engineer identify the cause of the error.

error diagnostics, A listing of computer program statements containing errors.

error, fatal, Any error during the execution of a program that causes the program's execution to halt.

error, inherited, The error in an initial value. It is synonymous with inherent error.

error, intermittent, An error which occurs at random. This type of error is usually caused by an external condition, such as dust on a recording medium's surface, and may disappear when the recording medium (disk or tape) is moved.

error interrupts, Special interrupts that are provided in response to certain error conditions in the central computer.

error, logic, An error in a program caused by faulty reasoning of the programmer.

error, machine, An error that occurs because of equipment failure.

error messages, The messages in a computer program that designate errors.

error, overflow, 1 An error condition that arises when the result of a calculation is a number too big to be represented on the computer. 2 The portion of the result of an operation that exceeds the capacity of the intended unit of storage.

error, overrun, An error occurring when a transmitted character arrives at its destination before the previously transmitted character has been read. When an overrun error occurs, an error signal is generated so that the previous character will be retransmitted.

error, parity, A machine-detected error in which a bit or bits are lost.

error, permanent, An error that cannot be corrected. Such errors usually cause the program to stop prematurely. An example of a permanent error is a data check.

error, probable, A statistical term related to standard error.

error, program, A mistake made by a programmer in a computer program.

error, quiet, Errors that are quickly discovered and corrected before they spread throughout a process or system.

error, rate of keying, The ratio of the number of signals incorrectly sent to the total number of signals of the message.

error, recoverable, A recoverable error is either an error which can be corrected or one that does not result in a program's execution terminating abnormally. For example, a rounding error is a recoverable error.

error, select, A tape-transport unit error.

error, sequence, When a record is out of sequence; may be data or instructions.

error, side effect, This occurs when operations performed in one section of a program have an unintended effect on another section of the program.

error, single, An error bit that has at least one correct bit in front and in back of it.

error, size, An error that occurs when the number of positions in a data field is greater than allowed by the machine or program.

error, squared, A mathematical technique of error correction.

error, syntax, A programming error in the structure, or syntax, of an instruction or set of instructions. All syntax errors in a compiled program must be corrected before the program can be executed. In an interpreted program, only those syntax errors pertaining to individual instructions must be corrected before the program can be executed. During execution, syntax errors in groups of instructions, such as loops and subroutines, can then be detected.

error tape, A special tape used to record errors for analysis at a later time.

error, timing, An error caused by devices being "out of time" with what is expected.

error, unbalanced, A condition in which the average of all error values is not zero.

errors, catastrophic, When so many errors have occurred that the job is terminated.

errors, coding, Errors caused by the programmer writing the instruction incorrectly.

errors, consistency, remote computing system, One of the types of syntax errors in which statements conflict with previous definitions.

errors, instrumentation, Errors in a system due to instruments used, such as pressure gauges, etc.

errors, intermittent, Sporadic or intermittent equipment errors that are difficult to detect as they may not occur when trying to diagnose their cause.

errors, operator, Any errors caused by the person operating a device.

errors, precautionary, Warning messages printed during computer programing compilation.

errors, semantic, Errors in meaning or intent of meaning made by a programmer in programming.

errors, static, Errors that are independent of time; contrasted with dynamic error which depends on frequency.

errors, transient, Errors that seem to "come and go."

ESC, Represents an escape character which, when received by a terminal from the host, introduces an escape sequence.

escape, The departure from a code or pattern.

ESD, An abbreviation for electrostatic storage deflection.

ESI (externally specified index), A feature in communications that provide control for many systems.

ESS, An abbreviation for electronic switching system.

ETB, An abbreviation for end of transmission block character.

etched circuit, An integrated circuit construction technique as a geometric design or pathing arrangement to form active elements by an etching process on a single piece of semiconducting material.

ETX, Abbreviation for End-of-TeXt. It is a control character used to designate the end of text in a message or text file.

ETX, An abbreviation for end of text character.

evaluation, data, The examination and analysis of data.

evaluation, performance, An analysis of accomplishments compared to initial objectives.

even parity, A type of parity checking in which the parity bit's value is set to make the total number of on bits in the byte even.

even, parity, The count of binary ones is an even number (see parity bit).

event, An occasion or action that is processed to alter data files.

event, file, A single activity of reading or writing from or on a file of magnetic disk or tape.

EVOP (evolutionary operations), A statistical technique used to improve plant operations.

exception principle system, An information system in which results are reported only when they differ from some predetermined criteria.

exception reporting, A record of only the exceptions that is, changes, values, over or under certain limits, or anything that needs to be noted.

exchange, automatic, A communications exchange with no intervention by operators (people).

exchange buffering, A technique for input/output buffering (see buffered computer).

exchange, central office, Same as central office.

exchange, dial, An exchange in which all subscribers can dial a call.

exchange, input/output, An electronic switch used in routing input/output messages in communications.

exchange, manual, A telephone exchange where calls are completed by an operator.

exchange, memory, The switching of the contents of two storage areas or devices.

exchange, message, A device between a communications line and a computer to perform some communications functions.

Exchange, Private Automatic (PAX), A private telephone service within an organization, not connected to the public telephone network.

exchange, private automatic branch, A dial exchange that provides private telephone service within a company and also connection to the public telephone network.

Exchange, Private Branch (PBX), A telephone exchange on a customer's premises that is also connected to the public telephone network.

exchange, service, A service providing the interconnection of any customer's telephones using switching equipment.

exchange, single office, In communications an exchange that is served by only one central office.

exchange station, In communications a type of system in which any two customers can be interconnected by an exchange.

exchange storage, Interchanging of contents of two storage areas. Also the exchange of data between storage and other elements of a system.

exchange system, A communications system that can interconnect any two customers through an exchange.

exchange, trunk, An exchange devoted mainly to interconnecting trunks.

EXEC, An abbreviation for execute or executive system.

executable form, A program written or translated into machine language, which is ready for the computer to execute.

execute, To execute an instruction is to do what the instruction states.

execute, To perform or carry out operations on a computer.

execute phase, The part of a computer operation cycle when an instruction is being performed.

execute statement, A job control statement that indicates execution of a job.

execution, Performance of computer operations in a computer program sequence.

execution control, program, The control function involved in interrupt processing.

execution cycle, The part of a machine cycle during which execution of an instruction occurs.

execution, instruction, The set of steps necessary to perform the operation of the instruction.

execution, interpretive, A procedure in which source (program) statements are retained to be used for debugging. It is used in a conversational mode of operation.

execution, looping, Repeating a set of instructions, but using different data values each time or modified instructions.

execution time, (1) The time during which actual execution of an instruction takes place in the computer. (2) The time a program is being actually performed or executed.

executive, A master controlling computer program routine.

executive control language, A set of control commands used in an executive system.

executive diagnostic system, A diagnostic system within an executive system to help in the checkout of programs.

executive, real-time, A system that controls, sequences, and provides for allocation of facilities in a real-time system.

executive resident, A specific computer program in an operating system that is a permanent resident of internal computer memory.

executive routine, Most such routines control loading and relocation of routines and in some cases make use of instructions which are unknown to the general programmer.

executive supervisor, In large systems, the computer program routine that controls sequencing, setup, and execution of all runs on the computer.

executive system, (1) An integrated system that provides for multiple programs running at the same time. (2) It is the same as monitor system.

executive system control, An executive system in which control information is fed to the system on-line or from remote locations.

executive termination, The termination of an operating program by the executive program in an operating system.

executive, time sharing, The executive program that processes all the user's requests in the time sharing system.

exit, The time or place of leaving a sequence of instructions in a computer program.

expression, A series of symbols which forms a unit to which meaning is assigned.

external interrupts, Interrupts caused by external devices needing attention or by the timer going to zero.

external labels, Labels in a computer program that are defined in another program.

external memory, A device not connected to a computer but which contains data usable by a computer.

external reference, A reference made to a name outside of the computer program.

external registers, Registers that can be referenced by a program.

external signals, Equipment failure warning signals to the operator.

external sort, The second phase of a multipass sort in which strings of data are merged.

external storage, Storage on devices such as magnetic tape, disk, drum, and so on as opposed to internal storage (memory) in the CPU, central processing unit of a computer.

external symbol dictionary, A list of symbols that are external or outside the current program but defined by another.

externally specified index (ESI), A feature in communications that provides control for many systems.

external-signal interrupt, Allowing external equipment to interrupt the computer program to process the interrupt.

extract, To select a set of items from a larger group.

extraction, The reading of selected portions of a record.

extraneous ink, Ink on a computer printout other than where it belongs; that is, other than the printed characters.

extrapolation, A mathematical technique.

F

F, When used as a subscript means "final."

fabricated language, A language designed for ease of use in a particular application area as contrasted with natural language.

face, A character style in optical character recognition as contrasted with type font.

facilities, library, A basic set of general purpose computer programs used to perform common jobs.

facility, A general term for communication paths.

facility assignment (executive), A computer programming routine capable of assigning computer memory and other facilities to meet the requirements of the job.

facility, compare, The ability of a computer to execute instructions based on the outcome of various combinations.

facility, hard, A place that is built to protect the contents such as a vault or a protected room, etc.

facility, hold, The ability of a computer to keep or hold values of data when calculations are interrupted.

facility leased, A communications facility reserved for one customer to use.

facsimile, (1) A reproduction of a document, (2) a method of sending images by electrical means.

facsimile copies, Copies of a document made by a copying machine.

facsimile networks, Fax networks and electronic mail service includes Western Union's TWX and TELEX but recently other services as well including Graphnet for both terminal-to-fax and SPC's SPEEDFAX and ITT's FAXPAK and others scheduled for the early 1990's.

facsimile posting, A data processing function of transferring by duplicating a printed line to a ledger or other sheet.

fact correlation, An analysis process used to examine the relations of data in files.

fact retrieval, Recognizing, selecting, and interpreting data words, phrases, etc., and relating the data for useful results.

factor, blocking, The number of records per block (see blocking).

factor, elimination, A fraction calculated by dividing the number of documents in a file that haven't been retrieved by the total number in the file.

factor, mission, A fraction calculated by dividing the number of documents in a file that haven't been retrieved by the total number in file.

factor, packing, The number of units (words, bits, characters, etc.) that can fit in something of defined size (per inch, per record, etc.).

factor, scaling, A number used to scale other quantities in a calculation.

factor, time, The comparison of the time between two events in a simulated computer run and the actual real-life time it would take for the same.

factorial, A calculation of multiplying together all the numbers up to a limit, i.e., 5 factorial equals 1 x 2 x 3 x 4 x 5.

factorial sign, An exclamation point (!), e.g., 5! (see factorial).

factoring, A mathematical process of separating a quantity into factors. That is, 2 and 3 are factors of 6 as 2 times 3 equals 6.

fading, A change in radio field intensity caused by change in the transmission equipment.

fading, selective, Fading in which the different frequencies are affected differently (see fading).

fail softly, In case of equipment failure the computer system falls into a degraded mode of operation instead of no response at all. It is also called graceful degradation.

fail-safe system, The ability in some computer systems to "lock in" vital information in case of power failure so that the information isn't lost.

fail-soft system, A computer system which will continue to run with deteriorated performance despite failure in parts of the system.

fail-soft, time sharing, A graceful degradation or fail-soft in a remote computer system (see fail-soft).

failure, equipment, Something goes wrong in the equipment and it doesn't work properly.

failure, incipient, A failure in equipment that is about to happen.

failure, induced, A failure in equipment caused by an external condition such as temperature, etc.

failure logging, A procedure in which the computer keeps track of its errors to help the person who fixes the problem.

failure, mean-time-between, A means of evaluating equipment failures related to operating time.

failure, mean-time-to, The average time a computer system or part of the system works without failing.

failure, skew, A document in machine readable form is not aligned properly to be read.

fall time, A measure of time required to change the output voltage of a circuit form a high to a low level.

fallback, Using a backup in another computer or section of a computer or a manual backup during degraded operation of a computer system.

fallback, double, (1) Having two procedures for backup, (2) being able to handle two types of failures.

fallback, recovery, The recovery of a computer system from a fallback mode of operation (see fallback).

false code, A character which is not accepted as a valid combination of bits by a machine (computer).

fan-in, The number of devices that can be connected to an input terminal of a circuit without impairing its function.

fan-out, The number of circuits that can get input signals from an output of a circuit or unit.

farad, The unit of measure of capacitance.

farad, A unit of electricity capacity.

fast-access storage, Computer storage with the fastest access relative to other types of storage.

fast-time scale, The comparison of time used in a computer program simulation of a system to the real-life time required to accomplish the same thing.

fault, A physical break or other problem that causes a device to fail or not work at all.

fault, pattern sensitive, A fault that responds to a particular pattern of data (see fault).

fault, permanent, A fault that repeatedly occurs as contrasted with intermittent or sporadic faults (see fault).

fault, program sensitive, A fault that responds to a particular sequence of computer program steps (see fault).

fault, sporadic, Same as intermittent fault.

fault time, The period of time the computer isn't working correctly due to some mechanical or electronic failure.

fault-location problem, A problem used to obtain information about faulty equipment (see fault).

fault-tolerant, Those programs or systems where parts may fail and which will still execute properly.

fax, An abbreviation for facsimile transmission of pictures (see facsimile).

FCC (Federal Communications Commission), A federal government commission having the authority to regulate communications systems.

FD or FDX, Stands for full duplex (see full duplex).

FDOS, Floppy Disk Operating System — Provides complete program development capability including editing, assembling, linking, and debugging, in the usual case.

feasibility study, A study made to determine how a proposed system or computer might work in a company or department.

feasible solution, (1) A solution to constraint equations in which all variables satisfy their sign restrictions in linear programming, (2) in a loose general sense, a possible solution that is practical.

FEB (Functional Electronic Block), Another name for monolithic integrated circuit, which is used in computers.

feed holes, Holes along the sides of computer printer paper that allow the paper to be driven by a sprocket wheel.

feedback, One type occurs when a control device uses information about the current state of the system to determine the next control action.

feedback, Using output of a machine or process as input into the same machine or process in another phase. It is used for its self-correcting capability.

feedback and reports (factory), A system in which feedback of data is collected and analyzed to control and predict stock requirements.

feedback control, A type of control in which a part of an output is fed back as input in the system.

feedback control signal, The part of an output signal that is returned as an input to accomplish some effect, such as a fast response.

feedback, degenerative, A type of feedback in which a larger quantity is deducted from the input and it increases output results (see feedback).

feedback loop, The loop that connects the input and output (see feedback).

feedback, positive, The returned output is input in a way that increases the output results (see feedback).

feeding, cyclic, The feeding of documents at a constant rate in character recognition readers.

feeding form, The positioning of paper forms on a computer or business machine printer in a fast, accurate way.

ferromagnetic, A property of substances which can cause an electric force of current with a change in polarity.

ferromagnetism, A property of a substance, the capability to retain one or more magnetic states.

ferrous oxide spots, Used to represent information on magnetic tape.

FET, Abbreviation for field effect transistor (unipolar) and as part of the acronym MOSFET, Metal Oxide Semiconductor FET.

fetch, Obtaining data from computer storage.

FF, An abbreviation for flip-flop (see flip-flop).

fiber optic material dispersion, The spreading of a light pulse inside an optic fiber due to the different wavelengths of light emitted by a source. Because different light wavelengths travel at varying speeds through a material, material dispersion occurs when the light source, such as a light-emitting diode (LED), emits a wide interval of bandwidth.

fiber optic modal dispersion, A form of pulse spreading caused by the different path lengths of light rays entering a core (fiber optic cable) of uniform optical density at different angles.

fiber-optic cable, Generally, a bundle of thin, coated-glass rods. Light introduced into one end of a rod travels the rod's length, emerging at the other end. Variations in light intensity travelling through a fiber-optic rod relay information in the same way as variations in electrical current travelling through a wire.

fiberoptic cable, Offers significant advantages over coaxial cable including electrically isolated communications immune to noise, secure communications that do not radiate their signals, cables that do not spark or short circuit, and others.

fiberoptic cable applications, These communication cables are suitable for use inside buildings, between buildings, for aerial, underground or field cable installations, as laid under carpet, in cable trays, or pulled through ducts.

fiberoptics handling, Various fiberoptic cables are anywhere from 10 to 80 times smaller in diameter than copper wire or coaxial cables with the same information carrying capacity. Due to their smaller size, weight, and high crush resistance, they are easy to handle, install, and store.

fiche, Microfiche storage and computer retrieval of large amounts of alphanumeric and/or graphic data, a piece of film mounted on an aperture card of standardize sizes.

field, A group of adjacent characters is called a field. See DATA ELEMENT.

field, A set of data positions treated as a unit. Examples are a name field, a social security number field, etc., defined to hold that data.

field, common, A field of data that is accessible to two or more computer program routines.

field, control (sorting), A data processing card which contains the parameters for a sort.

field, decrement, A part of a computer instruction used for modifying a register or storage location.

field effect transistor (FET), A transistor whose internal operation is unipolar in nature and widely used in integrated circuits due to a small geometrics, low power dissipation, ease of manufacture, and low cost. Usually related to MOSFET, Metal Oxide Semiconductor Field Effect Transistor.

field, fixed, A specific field set aside for a given type of information as contrasted to a free field.

field name, A symbolic name used in computer programming, assigned to data field by a programmer.

field, operation, The part of a computer instruction that indicates the computer operation to be performed.

field protect, terminal, Screen formatting of protected and unprotected fields displayed often in dual intensity, a mode that is specified by delimiters at start and end of the field to be protected.

field, register address, The part of a computer instruction that contains a register address.

field, sort, A specified field in a record used to sort the records of a file.

FIFO, See FIRST-IN FIRST-OUT.

figures, significant, Digits in a number which may be not be rounded off without losing accuracy.

file, Generally, file is a collection of information stored as records. Files are stored on peripheral memory devices, such as a disk memory or a tape memory.

file, A group of related records such as payroll file, student file, inventory file, etc.

file, active, A file to which entries or references are made on a current basis.

file, active master, A master file containing relatively active items.

file address checking program, A computer program that checks to see that it is not writing information on the wrong area of disk storage.

file addressing, A method of addressing, using the key or code of a data record to locate the record (see key).

file addressing, disk, A method of locating information on magnetic disk storage.

file addressing, randomizing, One method of calculating addresses for records to be stored in a random-access file as on magnetic disk.

file analysis, A study of data file characteristics.

file, chained, A procedure used to retrieve data in which each data record contains the address of another record with the same key.

file, change, A file of transactions to be processed against the related master file.

file checks, magnetic tape, Automatic checking for faulty magnetic tape without losing computer time or using any manual intervention.

file, closed, A file is closed when data cannot be read into it or written from it.

file compatibility, Generally refers to data-file disks for a particular program that can be moved between two computers. This is one of the main criteria in assessing the compatibility between two microcomputers.

file composition, Filing records within a computer storage unit.

file control system, A system designed to aid in the storage and retrieval of data without restriction as to types of input/output devices.

file conversion, Taking source document information and putting it onto magnetic tape or disk.

file, dead, A file that doesn't have any current use but is not destroyed.

file, destination, The device (magnetic tape or disk) that will receive the file of information output from a computer run.

file, detail, A file in which information changes more frequently than a master file.

file, direct, A method of file organization in which records are stored sequentially but, unlike a sequential file, each record is of a fixed length. Fixing the length of the records allows the retrieval time to be reduced.

file, directory, A file containing the names, sizes, locations, and other relevant information about all the files contained on a disk.

file event, A single activity of reading or writing from or on a file (magnetic disk or tape).

file, forms, A file of samples of all the forms needed in some activity procedure.

file gap, A space containing nothing to indicate the end of a file.

file identification, The coding or marking on the outside of a tape reel or disk pack to identify it. It is readable by humans, not machines.

file, index, A file on magnetic disk that indicates locations of data records in another disk file.

file index, disk, A disk file table of keyfields that identifies the records in another disk file.

file, indexed sequential, A method of file organization in which each record has a variable length and is stored sequentially, similar to a sequential file. Unlike a sequential file, however, the indexed sequential file reserves a portion of memory to serve as an index to the locations of all records in the file. Thus, only a small amount of memory is used for nonuseable data, and the index serves to lessen the average retrieval time of a particular file.

file label, A label written on magnetic tape describing the file name, tape reel number, and various dates.

file label beginning, A label in the beginning of a file that describes the contents of the file on magnetic tape and disk, etc.

file, logical, A set of records that are logically related or of the same type.

file, magnetic disk, A data file on magnetic disk or may be the magnetic disk pack itself.

file, magnetic strip, Devices containing strips of material with magnetic surfaces for recording data.

file maintenance, graphic, The process used to update such things as microfilm, film prints, and other graphic material.

file management, A set of procedures for creating and maintaining files.

file, mass storage, A type of slower storage than main computer storage (internal memory). It may be magnetic tape, disk, cassette, etc.

file, master, A file which contains relatively permanent information as contrasted to file, detail.

file, master program, A file containing all the computer programs used for a system that may be on magnetic tape.

file, member, A file which acts as a record to a partitioned file. Each member has an individual name and can be altered in any way without affecting the other members of the partitioned file.

file name, A set of characters (name) assigned to identify a file (e.g., PAYRL for payroll, etc.).

file, on-line (central), A large data file available to computer terminal users in a central computer.

file, open, A file is open when it is ready to have data transferred into it or out of it.

file organization, Structures of files differ for a given application. Generally, there are four different types of file organization, each of which has its own advantages and disadvantages. These are, in order of increasing complexity: sequential, direct, indexed sequential, and partitioned. Usually, file organization is considered on the level of program development, so that each program uses the one file organization (or more than one) that best suits its intended application.

file organization, The way a file is set up (e.g., sequential, random, etc.). The best way to organize a file of data based on its method of use.

file packing density, The ratio of available file storage space to the amount already stored in the file.

file, partitioned, A method of file organization in which the file is divided (partitioned) into portions called 'members,' each of which is itself a file. The partitioned file has a directory that displays the names, locations, and other relevant information about the files. Partitioned files are less often used for data storage than for storage of related programs.

file preparation, Getting data ready in a form to be put on magnetic storage such as tape, disk, etc.

file, problem, The documentation needed for a computer program.

file, program, A system designed to maintain and keep up to date the entire software library of all the computer programs.

file protection, A hardware or software device to keep sections of memory (computer) protected by preventing writing onto it.

file reconstruction procedures, Processes to safeguard against the loss of data that is accidentally destroyed by programmer or operator error.

file security, Processes of keeping files unavailable to people who shouldn't have access to them. It may contain private or confidential information.

file separator, Identifies logical boundaries between files. It is abbreviated as FS.

file, sequential, A data file whose records are stored sequentially. Each record is written immediately after the previous record. This is perhaps the most straightforward method of file organization. Because sequential files are stored sequentially, they use less memory space per byte of usable data than any other method of file organization. However, the average retrieval time of a particular record is slow, since the computer must search each record, starting from the beginning, until it finds the desired record. Similarly, the average time to store a record is slow, since the computer must search each record to the end of the file in order to determine where the next record will be written.

file, sequential, A data file in which each successive record has a higher key. It is normally processed by accessing each record after the previous one (see key).

file, source, Same as input file.

file, specification, Same as forms file.

file storage, A type of storage designed to contain a relatively large file.

file string, A string used to order or arrange records for convenient reference (see string).

file, suspense, A file of information needing attention at certain times, i.e., things to be processed at particular times.

file, tape, (1) A file on magnetic tape; (2) a group of magnetic tapes in a tape library.

file, test, A file of data that is used to check a computer program for errors during its development. Sometimes called a 'program test file' or 'program test data.'

file, transaction, A batch or file of transactions ready to be processed against a master file. It is used to update the master file.

file, volatile, A rapidly changing file or very active file.

file, work, A temporary hold file used for interim storage, e.g., in a sort as contrasted to destination file.

filemark, An identification mark for the last record of a file to indicate the end of a file.

filemark, end of, A code indicating the last record of a file has been read.

file-oriented programming, When the input/output computer instructions are file oriented as opposed to device oriented.

file-oriented system, When file storage reference is the principal basis of a system.

files, permanent, Relatively permanent data file as contrasted with working data files that are destroyed after being used.

files, protected, Files having file security (see file security).

files, shared, Two systems that have access to the same file on a direct access device.

filing system, A method or set of plans to identify records so that they may be retrieved, e.g., in alphabetical order, numeric order, etc.

fill, Filling up some unused space in storage with the same character or symbol.

fill, character, See fill.

filler, One or more non-data characters placed in a field so that all the positions in the field are occupied. Fillers are used to bring fields to a standard size.

filler, Using a fill character or other method to achieve uniform size of data records.

fill-in-blanks data entry, Applications that experience a high rate of error rejection because of inability to perform basic validation of data at time of entry often allow for formats that will ensure the input of reasonable, accurate data. Filling in blanks on terminal screens eases the entry procedure and reduces errors significantly.

film, A thin base less than one micron that contains a layer of magnetic material that is used for logic or storage elements.

film frame, A single photograph on a strip of film such as microfilm.

film, magnetic (thin), A thin layer of magnetic material commonly less than a micron in thickness (see film).

film reader, A device that is designed to scan patterns on film and enter information about the patterns into a computer.

film recorder, A device that receives information from a computer and records it on film as contrasted to film reader.

film storage, magnetic, A thin film magnetic storage used for high speed internal memory.

film, thin, An ultrahigh speed storage device.

filmorex system, A system for electronic selection of microfilm cards.

filter, A device used to eliminate or separate things such as parts of a pattern of characters, data, signals, or material of some sort. It is also called an extractor or mask.

fine index, A supplemental index used to locate a file record as contrasted with gross index.

fine sort, An off-line sorting especially used in banks to arrange checks and deposits into customer account number order.

finished stock, A production item that requires no further processing.

finite, A quantity that has a limit that can be reached, as contrasted to infinite, which has no limit.

firmware, Most often this refers to the computer programs encoded permanently into ROM. These programs are referred to as microprograms and cannot be altered or erased. Common examples of firmware are microcomputer operating systems and video game cartridges.

firmware, Logic circuits in computer read only memory that may be altered by software under certain conditions as contrasted with hardware or software.

first generation computer, Computers built in the technological era of development when the vacuum tube was the main electronic element.

first level address, An address in a computer instruction that indicates where the location of the operand is without any other references. (Synonymous with direct address.)

first order subroutine, A computer program subroutine that is entered directly from the main computer program and later returned to it.

First-In-First Out (FIFO), Generally refers to a technique of storing and retrieving data in certain data structures. The most common data structure that uses the FIFO method is the queue. In FIFO, the first data item stored in the queue is the first one to be retrieved. Thus, a data item stored in the queue must wait until all data items 'in line' ahead of it are retrieved before it can be retrieved. FIFO is contrasted with LIFO. (See LAST-IN-FIRST-OUT.)

fitting curve, A representation on a CRT of a curve by a mathematical expression.

fixed, Something is said to be fixed if it is not allowed to change. For example, a fixed disk is a disk that is permanently mounted on a disk drive.

fixed area (FX), A specific area on magnetic disk where data files or computer programs may be stored and protected.

fixed cycle operation, A type of computer operation performed in a fixed amount of time.

fixed data name, A reserved name for a piece of data.

fixed field, A specific field set aside for a given type of information as contrasted to free field.

fixed format, A specification of information content or a format that can't be changed.

fixed head, A reading and writing mechanism that is rigidly mounted and stationary that is used on some direct-access storage.

fixed length, A computer concept that relates to a fixed number of characters that can be in a data element or storage location as contrasted with variable length.

fixed point, A numeration system in which the bit position of one decimal is fixed with respect to one end of the numerals.

fixed-form coding, Every part of computer instruction coding has to be in a certain field as contrasted to free-form coding.

flag, Generally, this is a symbol that marks some computer output messages, such as error messages, to indicate that they deserve special attention. Also, any of various types of indicators used for identification, such as word mark, or a character that signals the occurrence of some condition, such as the end of a word.

flag, An indicator that is set to indicate that a particular condition occurred and that is checked for at a later time in a computer program.

flag bit, overflow, A flag set when an arithmetic result is too large to be held in memory.

flag, skip, A bit set in a position in storage that causes bytes to be skipped.

flange, connector, A metal or plastic projection around a connector.

flip-flop, A type of electronic circuit which can assume one of two states. Flip-flops are used as memory elements, and state changes are produced by electrical signals.

flip-flop, A circuit capable of assuming either one of two stable states. It is synonymous with binary pair, with bistable circuit, with toggle, with bistable multivibrator, and with bistable trigger circuit.

flip-flop, dc coupled, A flip-flop in which the active elements are coupled with resistors (see flip-flop).

flip-flop string, A sequence of flip-flops in a row (see flip-flop).

float, To shift a character(s) to the right or left that is to float asterisks or dollar signs.

floating point arithmetic, This uses a variable location for the decimal point in each number.

floppy disk, Refers to a disk made of some nonrigid magnetic material upon which data can be stored.

floppy disk controller, Device to provide control of data transfer to and from a floppy (flexible) disk memory system. It provides user-defined and/or IBM compatible formats and serve often up to four drives, usually, single or double density.

floppy disk drive, Consists of a mechanism within which the disk rotates and a controller containing electronic circuitry that feeds signals into and from the disk and that allows the disk unit to work together with the computer CPU.

floppy disk operating system (FDOS), See FDOS.

flow, A generalized term for a sequence of events.

flow, bi-directional, Flow that can occur in either or both directions. It is represented by a single flowline in flowcharting.

flow control, The sequence in time of computer instruction executions that relate to control of a computer system.

flow diagram, Same as flowchart.

flow diagram, data, Usually refers to a data flowchart that shows the flow of data (see flowchart).

flow direction, Direction of flow in a flowchart usually indicated by arrows (see flowchart).

flow, normal-direction, A flow direction on a flowchart either left to right or top to bottom as contrasted with flow, reverse direction.

flow, parallel, A system of operations in which several are taking place at the same time.

flow, reverse-direction A flow other than left to right or top to bottom as contrasted with flow in a normal direction.

flow, serial, Flow of a system of operations that are performed one step at a time, each after the one before.

flow tracing, A type of debugging of computer programs (see debugging).

flowchart, A graphical representation of a process, problem, flow of data, computer program instructions, etc., using symbols.

flowchart (noun), A pictorial representation of an algorithm used in a computer program. Flowcharts are composed of symbols that represent the different types of operations - for example, a diamond represents a decision, and a parallelogram represents an in-put statement. The completed flowchart depicts graphically the overall logic and flow of control that is used in the program.

flowchart (verb), To describe and document the individual steps in a process.

flowchart connector, A symbol used in a flow chart to show flow and connection of other symbols.

flowchart, data, A flowchart showing data flow in a system.

flowchart flowline, A line linking two flowchart symbols. The flowline has an arrowhead to represent the direction data transfer or program control proceeds.

flowchart, logical, A flowchart showing the logical sequence of operations in a computer program (see flowchart).

flowchart, program, A flowchart describing a single project written by a programmer. Program flowcharts are written before the actual program is written and serve as a means of communication between programmers working on the project.

flowchart, program, A flowchart showing the sequence of instructions in a computer program (see flowchart).

flowchart symbols, Symbols such as squares, diamonds, circles, rectangles, etc., that are labeled to show different functions in a flowchart (see flowchart).

flowchart, systems, A flowchart which describes a computer system and which is written and used by systems analysts.

flowchart, systems, A flowchart of a system showing data flow (see flowchart).

flowcharts, structure, Generalized flowcharts showing input, processing, and output without indicating specific methods of processing (see flowchart).

flowline, A line connecting symbols on a flowchart (see flowchart).

flow-process diagram, A flowchart of the major steps of work in process. It is synonymous with process chart (see flowchart).

fluorescent screen, The coating on the inner wall of a CRT (cathode ray tube) that converts electrical energy into light. CRT is a television-like computer terminal.

flutter and wow, Terms used to describe changes in output frequency caused by tape speed variations at low and high rates, respectively.

flux, The lines of force in a magnetic field.

flying head, The read/write heads used on magnetic disks and drums that "fly" above the magnetic surface supported by a film of air (they don't touch the surface).

flying spot, A small spot of light that rapidly moves in a CRT (cathode ray tube) which is a television-like computer terminal.

flying-spot scanner, In optical character recognition, a device using a flying spot to scan a space (see flying spot).

FM, See FREQUENCY MODULATION.

focusing coil, The coil in a writing tube that guides electrons in the beam.

folder, problem, All the materials used to document a computer program.

follower, curve, A peripheral device used to read data represented on graphs.

font, A family or assortment of type characters of a particular size and style.

font, type, A type face of a specific size, e.g., 12-point GOTHIC.

forbidden, Usually this refers to al illegal character or operation.

forbidden code, A representation of data that has no accepted equivalent.

forbidden combination, A code character set or symbol that seems to be the proper element but isn't. It is judged to be a mistake.

forbidden digit, Same as forbidden code. It is not valid in a specific data processing system.

force, To manually interrupt the operation of a computer routine.

force, contact separating, The electrical force necessary to remove pins from sockets.

forced display, A display made by the system that wasn't requested by the operator.

foreground, (1) A high priority computer program that uses parts of the computer when and where needed (gets first priority of resources), (2) the partition (section) of computer storage that contains the foreground program.

foreground processing, Allows for high priority computer programs to be run while other activities or programs run in the background.

foreground program, The computer program that gets priority treatment delaying progress of a background program.

foreground routine, Same as foreground program.

foreign-exchange service, The central office or service connecting a customer's telephone to a location. It is not normally serving the customer's location.

form, A document that has space for the printing (or writing) of information.

form, blank, A form that records no data.

form control, Some units have a designed manual control for the print gap that allows the user to click-adjust the gap for one-to-six part forms, a control that assures uniform density of the character impression whatever the number of forms to be handled.

form, graphic, A pictorial representation of data such as plotted graphs, engineering drawings, etc.

form, standard, A prescribed arrangement of data elements.

form stop, On a data processing printer, a device that causes the printer to stop when it runs out of paper.

format, Format is a term often used to refer to the specific arrangement and location of information within a larger unit of storage.

format, A predetermined method of arranging characters, lines, punctuation, etc.

format, address, The arrangement of the address parts of a computer instruction.

format, horizontal, The arrangement of data across a document (page, paper) as opposed to vertical which is up and down.

format, instruction, The makeup of an instruction, i.e., how many addresses it has and in what order, etc., according to a set of rules.

format statement, WP, Shows horizontal spacing, line length, left margin, paragraph indentation, vertical spacing between lines and paragraphs, top margin, lines per page, assumed page length, and justification and other characteristics on many systems.

format, vertical, Arrangement of data up and down on a page or paper as contrasted with format, horizontal.

forms creation, terminals, Forms are created with display features to make data entry easier and reduce the chance of errors, such forms are similar to paper forms except that they are displayed on the terminal screen. Forms are made by defining "fields" of one or more characters, each character given one or more of the display features and the created forms are stored and called when needed.

forms design, Designing or planning the layout of a form to be used in data processing procedures.

forms file, A file of samples of all the forms needed in some activity or procedure.

FORTRAN, One of the most widely used scientific computer programming languages, FORTRAN stands for FORmula TRANslation language. It was developed for IBM computers in the late 1950s.

Fortran compiler system, The two elements of a source language computer program and a compiler that translates the program into machine language.

Fortran language, A computer programming language written in algebraic expression and arithmetic statements. It also has input/output, control, and other statements.

forward-and-store, A type of message switching system.

fourier analysis, The decomposition of a signal into its simples harmonic curves (sines and cosines).

fourth generation computer, A modern digital computer that uses large-scale integration circuitry.

four-wire circuit, A system in which the transmitting and receiving paths are separate channels.

fox, The word form of the digit in the hexadecimal numbering system that corresponds to the decimal value of 15. It is written as 'F.'

fox message, A standard message used to test all characters in a transmission of data. That is, the quick brown fox jumped over a lazy dog's back, etc.

FPLA device (Field Programmable Logic Array), A programmed logic array in which the internal connections of the AND and OR gates can be programmed by passing current through fusible links by other than factory personnel.

fractionals, The places to the right of the decimal (or other) point.

fragment, part of a document, program or routine.

fragmentation, Breaking a whole, such as a computer program, into smaller parts.

frame, A vertical strip on magnetic or paper tape on which a single character, or byte, can be stored.

frame, A group of bits or punches on magnetic or paper tape.

frame, distribution, A structure used for terminating wires and connecting them in any order desired.

frame, film, A single photograph on a strip of film such as microfilm.

frame, main, The CPU (Central Processing Unit) of a computer that doesn't include any of the other devices such as input/output, etc.

frame, microfilm, A length of microfilm with one exposure.

frame, time, A reference to a block of time. The beginning and end is defined and required to accomplish something.

frames, data, Data on magnetic tape, i.e., a frame of data.

framing, The process of selecting bits from a continuous stream of bits and determining the characters from the groupings.

free access floor, A raised floor that provides concealment of computer cables. Floor panels are removable to get to the cables.

freeze mode, Sam as hold mode.

frequency, The measurement of the number of cycles of an audible tone or alternating current per second. One cycle per second is known as a Hertz, abbreviated Hz.

frequency band, The range of frequencies.

frequency clock, The frequency of periodic pulses that schedules the operation of a computer (see synchronous).

frequency distribution, A table showing the number of occurrences of each value or the frequency of occurrences. It is used in statistics.

frequency divider, A circuit that reduces the frequency of an oscillator.

frequency division multiplexing (FDM), The use of an electrical path to carry two or more signals at different frequencies. One computer-related example is the full-duplex modem, which carries signals to and from terminals.

frequency division multiplexing (FDM), A multiplex system in which the available transmission frequency range is divided into narrower bands, each used for a separate channel, channels being derived by allocating or "splitting up" a wider bandwidth into several narrower bandwidths

frequency, master clock, The time between pulses of the master clock (see frequency, clock).

frequency, maximum operating, The highest clock rate at which modules will perform reliably.

frequency modulation, The process for varying frequencies in a carrier (communications).

frequency modulation (FM), A means of conveying information by modifying the frequency of a carrier signal. The most common use of FM is in radio broadcasting, although it is also used in data communications.

frequency pulse repetition, The number of electric pulses per unit of time.

frequency, relative, The ratio of the number of observations in a class (subset) to the total number in the population. It is a statistical term.

frequency shift keying, The most popular form of frequency modulation. FSK techniques are generally quite suitable for low-speed devices such as teleprinters and allow for operation at speeds as high as 1,800 bits per second (BPS).

frequency shift., In a teletypewriter operation, the use of one frequency for marking and the use of a different frequency for spacing.

frequency side, A frequency in a sideband.

frequency spectrum, The range of frequencies of electromagnetic radiation waves.

frequency, voice, A frequency within the range used for transmission of speech as in telephone lines.

front end processing, Minor processing as related to host computing, microprocessors are used to interface communication terminals to a host computer and to perform other protocol matching, compaction, and input/output functions.

FS (file separator), Identifies logical boundaries between files.

FSK-Frequency Shift Keying, An effective method of modulation with the advantages that it can be coded simply and inexpensively, is affected less by noise than amplitude sensitive coding. It has become almost universally acceptable for low and medium-speed data transmission over phones using acoustic couplers.

full duplex, Simultaneous communications between two points in both directions.

full duplex operation, Communication between two points in both directions as the same time.

full duplex service, A service using full duplex capabilities (see full duplex).

full speed, The top speed of data transmission equipment in communications.

full-duplex, See DUPLEX TRANSMISSION.

function, A relationship of two items, one to the other. Also, a type of arithmetic relationship in computer instructions.

function codes, Codes used to operate machine functions such as (printer) carriage return, skip, tabulate, etc.

function, control, An operation to control a device, e.g., the starting and stopping of a printer carriage, a rewind of tape, etc.

function element, A device that performs a function of logic.

function generator, A computing element whose output is a (non-linear) function of its input(s).

function, information, A mathematical function that describes an information source.

function keys, Fixed and variable function keys have been added to various CRT terminals and other computer keyboards which provide special program calls with examples being airline agent's sets, badge readers, stock broker's inquiries, and so on.

function keys, user programmable, Keys that enable the operator to issue a string of display and device commands with a single keystroke often as designed for the system by the user with programs using ROM chips and/or boards.

function, logic, An expression representing an operation that includes one or many logic operators.

function switch, A circuit whose output is a function of the input.

functional design, The design of a machine, computer program, procedure, etc., in terms of board components and describing their interrelationships.

functional diagram, A diagram showing functional relationship of parts of a system, process, etc.

functional electronic block (FEB), A monolithic integrated circuit used in computers.

functional interleaving, The process of having input/output and processing go on independently of each other but interlaced or interleaved in their sharing of computer memory.

functional symbols, A block diagram representation used in functional design (see functional design).

functional unit, A unit in a computer system capable of performing arithmetic, storage, control, input, or output functions.

fuse, A protective device, usually a short piece of wire or chemical compound, constructed to melt and break a circuit when the current exceeds its rated capacity.

G

G, The force of gravity.

gain, The ratio between the output and input signals of a device.

gain, static, The ratio of output to input after a steady state has been reached (see gain).

game theory, Mathematical game playing as done on a computer.

gap, An interval in space or time.

gap, block, The space or distance between blocks of data on magnetic storage media. The same as interblock gap.

gap, file, A space containing nothing to indicate the end of a file, e.g., on magnetic tape.

gap, head, The space between the read/write head and the magnetic disk, drum, etc.

gap, interblock, A gap on tape or disk which separates blocks or physical records.

gap, interrecord, The space between records on a magnetic tape.

gap, interrecord (IRG), The blank space between records on magnetic tape.

gap, interword, The space between words or magnetic tape, disk, or drum.

gap length, The size of space between records on magnetic tape.

gap, record, An area in a storage medium devoid of information that indicates the beginning and end of a physical record. On tape, the record gap delimits records and allows the tape to stop and start between records without losing data.

gap, record, On magnetic tape, the space between records.

garbage, This general term refers to faulty data, acquired noise from a communications line, incorrect computer commands, any other useless or undesirable input, or data already in the computer which is no longer needed.

garbage collection, A procedure that makes more memory available by locating those storage units in main or virtual memory that contain data no longer needed by the current program.

garbage in, garbage out (GIGO), GIGO is a term meaning that if a program is given bad data (garbage) for input, it will produce bad results (garbage) for output.

gate, A circuit that contains one or more input signals and produces a single output depending on its function.

gate, logic, An electronic switching component which accepts one or more values as input, evaluates them, and produces one output value according to a specific logical operation.

gate, synchronous, Usually a time gate designed so the output intervals are synchronized with an input signal.

gate, time, A specific date that gives output only at certain chosen times.

gates (decision elements), A circuit with two or more inputs and one output that is determined by the combinations of the inputs.

gather-write, Refers to the placement of information from non-adjacent locations in memory into a physical record such as a tape block. Opposite of scatter-read.

gather-write, An operation that "gathers" non-consecutive locations in computer memory to form an output record.

gather-write/scatter-read, Scatter-read is placing the record back into the computer memory in non-consecutive locations (see gather-write).

gaussian noise, Noise that implies that voltage distribution is specified in terms of probabilities.

gear, integrating, A device used in analog computers.

general program, A computer program designed to solve a class of problems as specified.

general purpose languages, Generally machine independent languages that are widely used for many purposes, such as Fortran, Cobol, Basic, and Pascal.

General Purpose Simulation Program (GPSS), A simulation language developed by IBM.

general registers, Very fast registers used for general purposes in a computer.

general utility functions, Same as functions, utility.

generalized routine, A computer program routine used to process a large range of jobs in an application area.

generalized sort, A sort (computer) program that may be used in varying ways as specified.

generalized subroutine, A computer program subroutine that is general in nature and may be used by many computer programs.

generate, To develop a computer program using a generator for a special language processor.

generator, A computer program or routine that constructs another computer program from sets of specifications supplied by a programmer.

generator, character, A chip which stores the pixel patterns the computer uses to display the character set onto the screen.

generator, compiler, A generating computer program that constructs another computer program that can be used to translate computer programs for another computer.

generator function, A computing element whose output is a (nonlinear) function of its input(s).

generator, line (display), A device used in a cathode ray tube; dotted, dashed, or blank lines can be generated.

generator, program, A program that permits a computer to write other programs automatically.

generator, random number, A computer program or routine used to produce random numbers. A technique used in statistical work.

generator, report program, A computer program that provides the capability of creating reports from a set of specifications.

Generator, Report Program (RPG), A programming method (language) used for relatively easy generation of reports from data file information (see generator, report program).

generator, time base, A digital clock used for calculation and control.

gibberish, Same as garbage (see garbage).

GIGO, Garbage in, garbage out; refers to computer input and output.

GIGO (garbage in-garbage out), If you put bad data full of errors in a computer, you will get bad results out (see garbage).

glass, electronic, Offers versatile products with applications ranging from touch control panels to visual display devices, most activated by the touch of a finger, using no moving parts. One type is a glass touch control panel that has been replacing other electromechanical devices.

glitch, Generally refers to a small bug that causes an error in data transmission. Glitches are usually caused by electrical noise or by a voltage surge.

glitch, A pulse or burst of noise in that such a small pulse of noise or other nuisance item becomes an annoyance to cause error drop-outs, various types of crashes, or failures.

global knowledge, In artificial intelligence, global knowledge is the knowledge of a problem's complete solution. It is responsible for instructing the control system which rules or pieces of knowledge are applicable to the problem.

global variable, A variable with a name that has the same meaning throughout all the subroutines of a program.

global variable, A variable whose name may be referred to by a main computer program and all its subroutines.

glossary, A listing of words related to a particular subject.

go ahead, A signal sent from a computer to a terminal saying, in effect, go ahead and send in information. Also means to start transmission.

GOTO statement, An instruction in a high-level language.

GP, Abbreviation for generalized programming or general processor or general purpose.

gpa, interblock, The space separating two blocks of data on magnetic tape.

GPC-general purpose computer, (See general purpose computer.)

graceful degradation, In case of equipment failure the computer system falls into a degraded mode of operation instead of no response at all. It is also called fail softly.

grade channel, Refers to the relative bandwidth of a channel: narrowband, voiceband, wideband.

grade, circuit, The information carrying capability in speed or type of signal in communications.

grade, teletype, The lowest grade circuit in terms of speed, cost, and accuracy.

grain direction, Direction of the fibers in paper relative to the way the paper travels through an optical character reader.

grammar, The order of words in communication or a portion of communication.

grandfather cycle, Saving magnetic tape for a period of time to provide a means of data file reconstruction in case of lost information.

grandfather tape, A backup tape that was made two cycles ago, i.e., two updates were made since then.

graph, A display or document of things such as curves, points, and explanatory information.

graph, acyclic, A graph with no cycles. Acyclic graphs are also loop-free and simple.

graph, complete, A graph in which any two distinct nodes are adjacent. Thus, every node is adjacent to every other node.

graph follower, An optical sensing device that reads data in the form of a graph.

graph, standard, A plotted graph with an X scale and a Y scale.

graphic console, A CRT, cathode ray tube, television-like device used as the primary control console for the system.

graphic data reduction, The process of converting graphs, plotter output, engineering drawings, etc., into digital data.

graphic display, A computer terminal that displays information, such as drawings and pictures, on a screen, usually a cathode ray tube, TV terminal, or video terminal.

graphic display unit, A communications terminal that is linked to a computer which displays data on a television-like screen.

graphic documentation, A process for recording data on film and graphs.

graphic file maintenance, The process used to update such things as microfilm, film prints, and other graphic material.

graphic form, A pictorial representation of data such as plotted graphs, engineering drawings, etc.

graphic panel, A master control panel that graphically displays with lights, etc.

graphic solution, A solution to a problem obtained with graphs or other pictorial devices, contrasted with solutions obtained by number manipulation (arithmetic calculations).

graphics, The field in which computers are used to manipulate data in the form of pictures, charts, diagrams, etc.

graphics, The use of written symbols and visual displays to obtain information. Often the displays are on CRTs, a television-like display.

graphics, bitmapped, In bitmapped graphics, each pixel on the screen is represented by its own bit in memory. Bitmapped graphics are used to create detailed, high resolution graphics.

graphics, business, Computer graphics images produced to aid businesses in either analysis or presentation of information to clients, especially slides or large transparencies for projection.

graphics, computer, The processing and generation of visual information using a computer linked to a keyboard and CRT.

graphics display, vector, A display system in which the electron beam 'paints' the desired image on the display screen. Unlike raster-scan displays, vector-graphics displays do not scan horizontal lines to create images.

graphics, interactive, Graphics in which the user interacts with the graphics display to control the content of the display. Examples include computer simulations and computer-aided design.

graphics primitive, Refers to a specific pre-programmed basic shape available to the user of a computer graphics program which, when combined with other primitives from the program, can be used to construct a more complicated composite image. Typical primitives in a two-dimensional computer graphics system are rectangles, circles, ellipses, and lines. Typical primitives in a three-dimensional computer graphics system are boxes, spheres, ellipsoids, and cones.

graphics, random scan, A video display system in which the cathode ray tube traces out the individual screen images in a series of random lines.

graphics, raster scan, A video display system in which the screen is composed of a set of horizontal lines. The screen is then drawn one row at a time, from the top of the screen down. Raster scan is the display system used in TV and many kinds of computer graphics.

graphics tablet, An input device used with interactive graphics to locate a place on the screen. The tablet is used with a stylus or hand cursor which locates screen position.

grid, A device used for measuring characters in optical character recognition.

grid spaced contacts, Rows and columns of contacts on connectors and printed circuit boards.

grommet, An insulating or protective material.

gross index, The most major index, the first one checked when trying to locate a record as contrasted with fine index.

group indicate, The printing of identifying information from the first record of a group of related records.

group indication, Printing only from the first record of a group (data pertinent to all the records in the group) rather than repeating the common information for each record.

group, link, Those data links that use the same multiplex equipments (see data link).

group mark, A special character used at the end of a record in storage in some computers.

group printing, Printing one line of information for each group, as opposed to listing or detail printing in which there is at least one line of print for each record.

group separator, Identifies logical boundaries between groups of data. It is abbreviated GS.

group theory, The theory of combining groups (a mathematical technique).

group, trunk, A set of trunk lines (communications) between two switching centers or points that use the same terminal equipment.

group, user's, An organization of people who use the same kind of equipment.

grouping, A mass of data arranged into related groups, each group having common characteristics.

grouping of records, Same as blocking of records.

guard band, Any unused frequency band. It is used to guard against interference.

guard bands, Bands which protect the head carriage from the sudden jarring of the disk drive assembly against the chassis at the limits of carriage movement.

guard bit, A bit contained in a computer word (or group of words) to indicate that the contents of memory cannot be altered. It is used in file protection.

guard, memory, Electronic or program guards preventing access to sections of storage.

guest operating system, In a piggyback operating system mode, the guest operating system is the operating system that is being simulated by the 'host' operating system.

guide edge, The edge along which a document is guided while being fed into a machine.

guide margin, The distance between the guide edge and the center of the closest track of paper tape (see guide edge).

gulp, A slang expression referring to a small group of bytes (see byte).

gun, holding, An electron gun used to produce the holding beam in a CRT, television-like terminal (see holding beam).

H

half adder, A computer circuit capable of adding two binary digits.

half, drop-dead, Same as dead halt.

half-duplex transmission, Mode of transmission used for communication which is capable of sending and receiving data in both directions, but not simultaneously. During transmission, one modem is the transmitter and the other modem is the receiver.

halt, To terminate the execution of a program via an instruction, error, or interrupt.

halt, dead, A halt command to the computer from which there is no recovery.

halt instruction, A computer instruction that stops execution of a computer program.

halt, non-programmed, When the computer stops from other than encountering a halt instruction, e.g., power failure as contrasted with programmed halt.

hamming code, An error correction code.

handling, data, The production of records, also the common activities such as data sorting, input/output operation, etc.

handling, interrupt, The process following an interrupt. How the interrupt condition is handled.

handshaking, A slang term that means exchanging of data between sending and receiving communications equipment.

hanging prevention, Refers to computer logic which prevents any set of legal or illegal instructions from hanging the system.

hang-up, See LOOP, HANGING.

hang-up, A slang term used for the situation when a non-programmed halt occurs (see non-programmed halt).

hard copy, A printout on paper of computer output.

hard copy, A document, report, or anything on paper as opposed to a visual display that will disappear from the screen.

hard copy device, color, A type of peripheral output device that provides the user with hard copies (charts, graphs, drawings, or text) in multiple colors. These devices include pen plotters; electrostatic, impact, and ink jet printers; and almost any normal hard copy device with the incorporation of additional colors.

hard disk, A storage device made of ceramic or aluminum using a single disk or a stack of several disks in contract to floppy disks.

hard facility, A place that is built to protect the contents such as a vault or a protected room, etc.

hard failure, Failure of a device or component that cannot be resolved without first repairing the device. For example, a sudden power surge may be enough to burn out a chip, causing a hard failure and requiring repair of the equipment.

hardware, Consists of all the physical elements in the computer, such as integrated circuits, wires, and keyboard.

hardware, Computer and data processing equipment, the electronic and mechanical devices, the equipment itself as contrasted with software and firmware.

hardware check, Use of checking features built into computers to check for any changes in data as it's moved around in the computer system.

hardware, common, Hardware such as plugs, sockets, etc., that are commonly used.

hardware, compatible, Equipment that can be used on several different systems and are compatible from one system to another.

hardware configuration, The arrangements, relationships, and general architecture of the various devices (disk drives, printers, modems, and so on) that make up a computer system. Hardware configurations also include all physical and electrical paths which connect these devices, including their interface devices.

hardwired logic, Logic designs for control or problem solutions that require interconnection, usually completed by soldering or by printed circuits and are thus hardwired in contract to software solutions achieved by programmed microcomputer components.

hartley, A unit of measure of information content.

hash, Useless information present within a storage medium. Hash can be data that is no longer being used, or serves as a 'filler' for fixed-length blocks of data. Hash is often synonymous with garbage after use.

hash, Same as garbage.

hash total, The addition of all of a specific field in a group of records which, when compared to a previous hash total, can help ensure that all the records are present.

hash total, A sum formed for error-checking purposes by adding fields that are not normally related by unit of measure, e.g., a total of invoice serial numbers.

hash total, A total that is meaningless except for verification control, e.g., a total of all customer numbers that is meaningless except to compare to that same total calculated at another time.

HD, High density.

HDLC multiplexer, Intelligent time-division multiplexer enhanced so that it has high level data link control (HLDC) and statistical multiplexing, as well as the capability of combining synchronous and asynchronous traffic.

head, A device that reads or writes information on a magnetic medium such as magnetic disk, drum, tape, etc.

head access window, An oblong slot in the floppy disk jacket which allows the disk-drive head access to the information stored magnetically on the disk.

head crash, A physical collision which occurs when a read/write head touches the surface of a disk.

head, disk drive, An electromagnetic device which sends and receives data pulses allowing it to create magnetic fields on a storage system.

head, fixed, A reading and writing mechanism that is rigidly mounted and stationary. It is used on some direct access storage devices as contrasted to moveable head.

head, flying, The read/write heads used on magnetic disks and drums that "fly" above the magnetic surface supported by a film of air. They don't touch the surface.

head gap, The space between the read/write head and the magnetic disk, drum, etc.

head, magnetic, A small electromagnet used to read and write on magnetic surfaces.

head, playback, A reading head (see head).

head, pre-read, An additional read head encountered before the read head of a device (see head).

head, read, A magnetic device which reads data from the storage medium (usually disk or tape).

head, read, A head used for reading from various media (see head).

head, read/write, A magnetic device which can read from or write onto a storage medium.

head, report, Description of a printed report, often at the beginning.

header, A file record containing identifying information about the file (see file).

header (message heading), In communications the first characters of a message indicating who the message goes to, the time, etc.

header record, A file record that contains a description of the file.

heading, (1) Same as header as for message heading, (2) titles at the top of a report as for page heading.

heading, page, The titles and descriptions that appear at the top of each page of a printed report.

head-per-track, Magnetic disk equipment with a read/write head over each track of information.

height control, The hand control on a CRT (television-like device) that controls the height of the picture.

HELP program, time-sharing, A special program designed to help the user use the system.

hermaphroditic connector, A connector having no male or female parts but whose mating parts are identical.

hertz, A unit of frequency equal to one cycle per second. Cycles are referred to as Hertz in honor of the experimenter Heinrich Hertz. It is abbreviated Hz.

Hertz (Hz), A measurement of the frequency of an audible tone or alternating current. One Hertz is equal to one complete cycle per second and is abbreviated as Hz.

hesitation, A temporary suspension of operations in a computer to wait until something else has been completed.

heuristic, Concerns a method used when there are several approaches to a solution, but no one approach is known to solve a problem consistently. This method examines the problem and then tries an approach that seems most appropriate in solving the problem at hand. A solution is found by trial and error.

heuristic, Pertaining to exploratory methods of problem solution, evaluating progress as you go along as contrasted with algorithmic.

heuristic approach, A trial and error method of problem solving as opposed to the algorithmic method.

heuristic program, A computer program that simulates the behavior of humans in approaching similar problems.

hexadecimal, Number system based on 16 digits, 0-9, A, B, C, D, E, F, designating 16 different possible values.

hexadecimal notation, Notation of numbers in the base 16 (see hexadecimal digit).

hexidecimal digit, A digit of the hexadecimal numbering system; the digits 0 through 9 and A, B, C, D, E, F are used.

HF, An abbreviation for high frequency as in UHF and VHF.

hierarchy, A ranking order, classifying items by rank or order.

hierarchy, data, The structure of data, i.e., subsets of data within a data set.

hierarchy, memory, A set of computer memories of varying sizes and speed and cost.

higher order language, Computer programming languages that are less dependent on the computer they run on, such as Fortran, Cobol, and Basic.

high-level language, Refers to various computer programming languages designed to allow people to write programs without having to understand the inner workings of the computer. High-level languages do not translate from one high-level instruction to one machine instruction. It is not unusual for one high-level instruction to translate to a dozen machine-code instructions.

high-order bit, The left-most bit in a word.

high-speed loop, A capability on some magnetic disk and drum storage devices.

high-speed memory, Computer memory with input and access speeds in microseconds.

high-speed printer, A printer that runs at a speed more compatible with the speed of processing (e.g., 1500 lines per minute).

high-speed reader, A reader that reads more than 1000 cards per minute.

high-speed storage, Storage devices that are relatively high speed compared to the other storage devices.

hit, Finding the record that is being looked for as in information retrieval.

hit-on-the-fly system, A printer in which either the paper or the print head or both are constantly moving.

hit-on-the-line, A momentary open circuit (teletypewriter).

hits, Momentary line disturbance that can cause mutilation of the transmitted characters as in communications.

hold, To retain information in a storage (device) location after transferring it to another storage (device) location, in contrast to clear.

hold controls, The hand controls on a CRT (television-like device) that control the picture horizontally and vertically.

hold facility, The ability of a computer to keep or hold the values of data when calculations are interrupted.

hold instruction, A type of computer instruction used to retain information in its original location, as well as copy it in a new location.

hold mode, A mode in an analog computer in which variables are held at a current value. It is also called freeze or interrupt mode.

holding beam, A beam of electrons in a cathode ray tube (CRT) used to keep holding the picture on the screen.

holding gun, An electron gun used to produce the holding beam in a CRT, television-like terminal (see holding beam).

holistic masks, A unique set of characters in a character reader that represent all possible characters that could be accepted.

Hollerith, The standard punched card coding system, named for Herman Hollerith.

holographic-based systems, One type is Holofile data storage and retrieval, a system that utilizes laser and holographic technology in a microform setting to cut both the cost and the space requirements of massive databases.

home loop, It is an operation at a local terminal only.

home record, The first record of a chain of records in a data file.

homeostasis, A condition of a system (same as steady state).

hook switch, The switch on a telephone that is under the ear and mouth piece and opens when one lifts the receiver.

horizontal display, The width in inches of the display screen.

horizontal format, The arrangement of data across a document such as a page or paper as opposed to vertical that is up and down.

horizontal parity check, A checking procedure counting bits along a horizontal direction to compare them with a previous count (see parity).

horizontal raster count, The number of positions across the width of a CRT (cathode ray tube), a television-like terminal.

horizontal system, A computer programming system in which instructions are written horizontally across the page.

horizontal tab, A machine function that causes the print mechanism or cursor to move to a specific column while staying on the same line.

host computer, A computer that is connected to a stored-program multiplexor, that is dependent upon it for certain vital functions.

host operating system, Concerns various piggyback operating system modes. The host operating system is that which the computer hardware traditionally uses and which runs as one of its tasks a 'guest' operating system.

housekeeping, Pertaining to overhead operations such as setting up constants and variables to be used in a computer program.

housekeeping operation, A general term for the operation which must be performed for a machine run, usually before actual processing begins.

housekeeping operation, Operation(s) in a computer program that must be done before the actual processing begins, such as initializing, file identification, etc.

housekeeping routine, The first instructions in a computer program that are only executed one time.

housekeeping runs, Operations that are required for file processing such as sorting, merging, and other maintenance procedures.

Houston Automatic Spooling Processor (HASP), A type of operating system mostly used on IBM equipment, it is totally batch oriented and it an alternative to other operating systems (OS).

hunting, Repeated attempts in an automatically controlled system to find desired equilibrium conditions.

hunting, trunk, An arrangement in which a call is switched to the next number in sequence if the first number is busy.

hybrid computer, input/output, A group of programs used to control operation of analog/digital conversion equipment.

hysteresis, (1) The lagging in the response of a unit of a system following a change in the strength of a signal; (2) a phenomenon of materials whose behavior is a function of the history of the environment they've been in.

hysteresis loop, A specific graphic representation showing magnetic forces.

Hz (Hertz), Cycles per second.

I

I/O, The abbreviation for input/output.

I/O buffer, The temporary storage area for input and output of a computer.

I/O cable, A wire or wires or bus, etc., used to connect input or output devices to the computer.

I/O equipment, All the devices of a computer system that read (input) and write (output) data.

I/O handler, A routine that either handles input/output operations or controls the operation of an input/output device.

I/O port, A connection to a CPU that is designed and configured for provision of data paths between the CPU and the external devices, such as keyboards, displays, readers, and so on. An I/O port of a microprocessor may be an input port or an output port, or it may be bidirectional.

I/O spooling, Programs requiring a significant amount of communication with ''slow'' peripheral devices may have their data routed at high speed transfer rates to the disk for later rerouting to the intended devices. This is called spooling and results in faster task completion, freeing main memory for other tasks.

IAD, An abbreviation for initiation area discriminator, a type of CRT, or cathode ray tube.

I-address, The location or address of the next computer instruction to be executed.

IC, integrated circuit, An electronic device consisting of many miniature transistors and other circuit elements on a single silicon chip. An important type of integrated circuit is the microprocessor.

IC-Integrated Circuit, typical, A miniaturized circuit developed by using microphotography and mounted inside a special package, most often a DIP, Dual In-Line Package, that has pins (legs) along its sides that allow the package to be plugged into a socket or soldered to a printed circuit card or board.

icon, A geometric symbol often displayed on a user's terminal during the execution of a program which is used to give information to the user as a supplement to or in place of verbal information. Icons are often found in engineering or computer graphics creation software. Generally menu options are selected by positioning the cursor over the icon which represents the desired option.

identification, file, The coding or marking on the outside of a tape reel or disk pack to identify it. It is readable by humans, not machines.

identifier, (1) A symbol (name) used to identify data; (2) a key (see key).

identifier, location, A label assigned to a location in computer storage or in the broad sense of a location such as a city, street, address.

identify, To attach a name to a unit of information.

idle characters, In communications, control characters used in data transmission for synchronization.

idle time, Time a computer is available but is not being used.

IDP (Integrated Data Processing), (1) A system that treats all data processing needs as a whole; (2) processing in which all operations are connected or associated with a computer.

IEEE bus controller (488), Standardized by the Institute of Electrical and Electronic Engineers, a bus that may be connected to talkers, listeners, talkers/listeners or controllers, that performs functions depending upon its role: handshake, single address talk or listen, service request, parallel poll, device clear, and device trigger.

ier register, The register that contains the multiplier during a multiplication operation.

ignore gate, Same as gate A ignore B and gate B ignore A (see gates).

illegal character, A combination of bits (a character) not accepted as valid by a data processing machine.

illegal code, A character or symbol which seems to be proper but is not a true element of a defined alphabet.

illegal operation, Inability to perform what is indicated by a computer instruction. It will either do nothing or do it wrong and it occurs because of built in computer constraints.

image, An exact logical duplicate of something stored in a different medium.

image dissector, A mechanical or electronic device that detects the level of light in optical character recognition.

image processing, Most often concerns computer enhancement of photographs to increase clarity and detail.

image processing, Areas of image science that include image transforms, image coding, image enhancement, image restoration, feature extraction, image understanding, and hybrid optical/digital image processing, all with the aid of computer capability.

immediate access, Pertaining to the ability to obtain data from or place data in a storage device or register directly, without serial delay due to other units of data, in a relatively short period of time.

immediate address, A computer instruction address that is used as data by the instruction of which it is a part. It is synonymous with zero-level address.

immediate address instruction, A type of computer instruction that contains the value of the operand in its address part instead of the address of the operand.

immediate addressing, An instruction addressing mode in which the memory reference specifies not a memory address but the actual data to be operated on.

impact printer, A printer which operates by striking individual raised characters or wire ends against an inked ribbon and paper. Impact printers print either fully-formed characters or dot-matrix characters at a rate of one character at a time or one line at a time. Some types or impact printers are: bar printers, chain printers, drum printers, wire-matrix printers, train printers, thimble printers, and daisy-wheel printers.

impact strength, The ability of magnetic tape to withstand sudden stress.

impedance, Total opposition offered by a component or circuit to the flow of an alternating or varying current, a combination of resistance and reactance.

imperative statement, Action statements of a symbolic program that are converted into actual machine language.

implementation, The installation and starting of operation of computer systems.

implicit address instruction format, This format contains no address part of the instruction as it is not needed or implied by the operation itself.

implied addressing, The addressing method used in certain computers in which instructions having a zero address instruction format refer automatically to the location following that effected by the last instruction executed.

imprinter, The device that causes the name and account number on a credit card to be transferred to a sales slip as used in department stores, gasoline stations, etc.

impulse, A change in intensity in a short time of an electrical pulse.

impulse noise, A pulse from an outside source in an output of a circuit that wasn't in the input.

inaccuracies, systematic, Inaccuracies caused by limitations in equipment design.

inactive mode time sharing, A user in this mode is not logged onto the system.

inadmissable character, automatic checking, An internal checking done by the computer to guard against errors made by the computer operator.

incidentals times, Time used by staff for training, demonstrating, etc., things other than program development.

incipient, failure, A failure in equipment that is about to happen.

in-circuit emulation, Concerns hardware/software facilities for real-time I/O debugging of chips and other circuits, where the microprocessor is replaced by a connection whose signals are generated by an emulation program and where programs reside in (simulated) RAM memory or they can actually be ROMs or PROMs.

in-circuit testing, Process in which the innards of a circuit board are probed and tested to reveal component defects and manufacturing errors, in-circuit testing is attractive as a screening operation, for weeding out gross defects early and thus reducing the burden on the more expensive functional test systems.

incomplete program, A computer program or routine that is not complete by itself (a subroutine, subprogram, etc.).

inconnector, A symbol used on a flowchart that shows an entry into the flow path from somewhere else.

increment, An amount to be added to something else. It may be positive or negative.

index, (1) A table in a computer, (2) a reference list, (3) a reference in an array, or (4) pertaining to index register.

index addressing, A mode of addressing in which the effective address is found by adding the contents of an index register to the given memory reference.

index, channel utilization, The ratio of the information rate (per second) to the channel capacity (per second).

index, citation, A reference list of documents that are mentioned or quoted in a text.

index, cycle, A register or counter in a digital computer, set to a value and reduced by one in each cycle until it reaches zero.

index file, A file on magnetic disk that indicates location of data records in another disk file.

index, fine, A supplemental index used to locate a file record as contrasted with gross index.

index, gross, The most major index, the first one checked when trying to locate a record as contrasted with fine index.

index, permutation, An index that lists all the words in a title so that each word appears as the first word, followed by the others (many entries per title).

index register, A register within a computer's CPU, decremented each time through a loop that uses the index registered. Generally, an index register may be used within a loop to access consecutive locations in memory, such as arrays, or to serve as a counter to monitor the number of times the loop should be performed.

index register, A register in a computer that contains an amount to be used to modify an address in an instruction.

indexed address, An address in a computer instruction that is modified by the contents of an index register.

indexed sequential access method (ISAM), Provides advanced keyed accessing for fast, on-line retrieval of large databases. Programmers use ISAM's variable length record keys to save index space; ISAM permits keyed and keyed-relative processing.

indexing, The method of address modification used to access data in an array or table.

indexing, application, (1) Using an index file for data retrieval (see index file), or (2) modifying a computer instruction address by the contents of an index register.

indexing, aspect, A method of indexing by use of two or more terms so that all information relating to an item may be found.

indexing, association, A study of words usage following two approaches.

indexing, cumulative, Assigning two or large indices to a single address in a computer instruction.

indexing, data code, A unique library system of indexing documents.

indication, group, Printing only from the first record of a group the data pertinent to all the records in the group rather than repeating the common information for each record.

indicator, A device in a computer that can be on or off depending on certain conditions and may be displayed to the operator.

indicator, branch-on, Branching takes place dependent on indicator settings, a conditional branch.

indicator, check, A device in a computer that displays or otherwise indicates that an error has occurred in a checking operation.

indicator, machine check, See indicator, check.

indicator, overflow, An indicator that turns on when an overflow occurs, such as a number generated that is too big for a register (see indicator).

indicator, read/write check, An indicator that shows that an error took place in reading or writing into or from the computer (see indicator).

indicator, routing, In communications an identifier on label that indicates the route and destination of a message.

indicator, sign check, A device indicating no sign or an improper sign (plus or minus) in a field after an arithmetic operation.

indicators, comparison, Indicators that are set after a compare instruction such as high, low, equal (see indicator).

indicators, operator, The displayed lights showing indicator conditions on the console of the computer (see indicator).

indirect address, An address in a computer instruction that refers to another address to be actually used.

indirect addressing, (1) A method of addressing that points to the address of the address to be used, (2) any level of addressing other than first level or direct addressing.

indirect control, As contrasted with direct control in which one computer is controlled by another without human intervention. If a human is involved, it is not indirect control.

indirect output, Output that is obtained from an off-line device instead of directly from the computer.

individual line, A subscriber line that serves only one main station in communications.

induced failure, A failure in equipment caused by an external condition such as temperature, etc.

inductance, Represents the energy stored in the magnetic field set up by an electric current. In order to concentrate the magnetic field, inductors are made by winding a conductor into a coil, sometimes with a core of a ferromagnetic material.

industrial data processing, Data processing designed as industrial applications, often numerical control (n/c).

industrial process control, Computer controlled processes in many industrial applications.

infinity, In data processing, any number larger than the maximum number that a given computer is capable of storing in its registers.

information, (1) Knowledge not previously known, (2) an aggregation of data, or (3) the meaning assigned to data.

information bit, Bits that are genuine data bits, not check bits or others in data communications (see bit).

information channel, In communications the transmission equipment between two terminals.

information, computer, Information is data previously processed by a computer and produced as meaningful output.

information efficiency, A computed ratio of actual negative entropy to maximum possible negative entropy (see entropy).

information function, A mathematical function that describes an information source.

information, machine-sensible, Same as machine readable information.

information processing, (1) The manipulation of data so that new data appears in a useful form. (2) The processing of data and analysis of its meaning.

information processing system, A system that receives, processes, and delivers information.

information rate, The average information content per symbol times the average number of symbols per second.

information requirements, The questions that may be posed to an information system.

information retrieval, (1) A method used to catalog data in such a way that it is easily retrieved, (2) a branch of computer science.

information science, The study of the creation, manipulation, and communication of information in all its forms.

information source, An information generator.

information system, The combination of all communication methods in an organization (computers, telephones, personal contact, etc.).

information system, management, A communication process providing information for decision making that is fed back to top management of an organization.

information theory, An area of mathematical theory dealing with information rate, channels, etc., and other factors affecting information transmission.

information transmission system, In communications a system that receives and sends information without changing it.

information word, A computer word that isn't an instruction (data as opposed to instructions).

information-feedback system, In communications an error-control system.

information-retrieval system, A system in which data is located, selected, and printed or displayed.

infrared, The electromagnetic wavelength region between approximately 0.75 micrometers and 1000 micrometers. For fiberoptic transmission, the near infrared region between these areas is most relevant because glass, light sources, and detector techniques are most nearly matched in this wavelength region.

inherent storage, Automatic storage, e.g., internal storage in the CPU, central processing unit of a computer.

inherited error, The error in an initial value. It is synonymous with inherent error.

inhibit, (1) To prevent something from happening, or (2) to prevent a device from producing a certain output.

inhibit counter, A bit in the program status double word that indicates whether or not all count zero interrupts are inhibited.

inhibit, external interrupt, A bit in the program status double word that indicates whether or not all external interrupts are inhibited.

inhibit pulse, A pulse that prevents an action from occurring.

inhibiting input, An input that may inhibit an output.

inhibiting signal, A signal that may prevent a circuit from exercising its normal function.

in-house line, A privately owned or leased line that is separate form public right of ways.

initial condition, The value of a variable prior to computation.

initial program loading (IPL), The initial entry of an operating system or program into computer memory.

initialization, Generally, the act of setting variable information - such as storage locations, counters, and variables - to starting values. Initialization of variables is usually the first step in a computer program.

initialize, (1) To preset a variable or counter to its proper starting values before commencing a calculation. (2) In computer programming to set values (addresses, counters, registers, etc.) to a beginning value prior to the rest of processing.

initiator/terminator, A computer program routine that performs housekeeping tasks (see housekeeping).

ink, extraneous, Ink on a computer printout other than where it belongs, i.e., other than the printed characters.

ink, magnetic, A special kind of ink containing a magnetic substance that can be sensed by a magnetic sensing device (MICR).

ink, reflectance, The reflecting characteristic of ink used in optional character recognition.

ink smudge, The overflow of ink beyond the outline of a character in optical character recognition.

ink-jet printers, Do not require special paper, print on about anything, approach is the drop-on method in which each individual drop is cued, released, and accelerated by a piezoelectric shockwave nozzle.

in-line coding, A portion of computer program coding in the main path of a routine program.

in-line data processing, Data processing in which changes to records and accounts are made at the time the transaction occurs.

in-line subroutine, A computer program subroutine that is inserted wherever it is needed and recopied each place it is used in a program.

in-plant system, A data handling system in one location as in a building or group of buildings.

input, (1) Information or data to be entered into internal computer storage from card, tape, or disk devices. (2) The devices used to input data, such as card readers, tape readers, etc.

input (communications), (1) Current voltage or power applied to a circuit or device.   (2) The terminals where (1) is done.

input (noun), The input to a computer is the data or programs fed into the computer for it to process. The data or programs may be entered into the computer via a keyboard, magnetic tape, disk, and so on.

input (verb), To enter data into a computer or data-processing system.

input area, A specified section of computer storage reserved for receiving data that comes into the computer.

input block, Synonymous with input area.

input buffer register, A device that receives data from input devices (tape, disk) and then transfers it to internal computer storage.

input data, Data upon which processing is to be done, such as computing, summarizing, reporting, recording, etc.

input limited, The situation in which the input speed is the limiting factor or the slowest part.

input loading, The amount of load upon the sources supplying signals to the input.

input, manual, Entering data by hand into a data processing device.

input port, Physical arrangement of wires and electronic circuitry that is provided in a computer system so that data may be passed into the computer input devices.

input queue, new, A queue or waiting line of new messages waiting to be processed.

input, real-time, Instantaneous input to a real-time system, i.e., input that goes into the computer as the activity occurs.

input reference, A reference point used to compare to. Also referred to as set point or desired value.

input routine, A routine to control input into the computer; may be hardware or software in the machine or in a program.

input section, Same as input area or input block.

input state, The state of a channel condition, i.e., positive, negative, etc.

input storage, A storage area to receive input.

input tape, problem, A magnetic tape or punched paper tape containing problem data to check out a computer system.

input terminal, The unit used to get data to be processed available to the computer, such as a card reader, a tape reader, etc.

input work queue, The line of jobs to be submitted for processing.

input/output area, A specified section of computer storage reserved for data that comes into the computer or goes out of the computer (to and from input/output devices).

input/output channel selection, Pertains to the capability of a computer to select a particular channel for use.

input/output channels, multiple (time-sharing), In a time-sharing computer serving many communications lines multiple channels are required.

input/output control program, The control of input and output operations by the supervisory computer program.

input/output exchange, In communications an electronic switch used in routing input/output messages.

input/output interrupt, The use of the interrupt capability allows input/output equipment to be kept running at full capacity.

input/output interrupt indicators, The indicators that can be tested to see which device and what reason caused an interrupt.

input/output processor (IOP), A unit that handles control and sequencing of input/output.

input/output programmed, Program control information used to speed processing of input/output.

input/output random access, Input/output control processing that permits random processing of records on a device like magnetic disk.

input/output referencing, symbolic, The method by which magnetic tape and disk are referred to by a computer program, i.e., symbolically instead of actual addresses.

input/output registers, Registers that temporarily hold input and output data.

input/output remote message, In sending and receiving messages to and from remote terminals, pertains to the input/output control.

input/output request words, Control words in the computer used in input/output request processing.

input/output routines, Computer program routines used to simplify the programming task.

input/output storage, A storage area in the computer used in processing input and output.

input/output table, A plotting device used to record one variable as a function of another one.

input/output traffic control, A method in which time-sharing of main memory is directed by the peripheral devices and the central processor.

input-bound, Generally, a device is said to be input-bound if it can output data at a faster rate than data is being input to it. For example, a computer using paper-tape input is input-bound.

Input-Output (I/O), Input is data and instructions entered into a computer, perhaps via a keyboard or magnetic tape. Output is all information received from the system, perhaps as hard copy printout or as a display on the screen.

inputs, synchronous, Terminal inputs entered upon command of a clock.

inquiries, banking, Inquiry into the status of a bank account. (See inquiry.)

inquiry, A technique by which the interrogation of the contents of a computer's storage may be initiated at a keyboard.

inquiry application, A computer application that involves the interrogation of stored information.

inquiry, CRT, An inquiry made at cathode ray tube (CRT) terminal whose response is displayed on the television-like screen.

inquiry, direct-access, Making an inquiry to a file on magnetic disk or other direct access device.

inquiry, keyboard, Making an inquiry using a keyboard on the typewriter console or a terminal.

inquiry, remote, An inquiry made from a remote terminal or the capability to do so.

inquiry station, The location of a device from which an inquiry is made.

inscribe, The act of reading a document then writing the same information back onto the document in a machine-readable form.

inscribing, Preparation of a source document for optical character recognition.

inserted subroutine, A computer program subroutine that is inserted into the main computer program each place it will be used.

insertion method sorting, A method of internal sorting in which records are moved so other records can be inserted.

insignificant, A characteristic of that data that has little effect on the output values.

instability, magnetic, A property of magnetic material in that it is changed somewhat by temperatures, time, and mechanical flexing in magnetic tape.

installation, computer, (1) The whole computer facility itself including machines, people, etc. (2) The process of delivering and installing, connecting and setting up, a computer system.

installation date, The date that a new computer system is installed. (See installation, computer (2)).

installation, terminal, The location of a terminal or terminals and related equipment at one place.

installation time, The time required for installing and testing and correction of errors in an initial installation situation of a new computer system.

instantaneous access, Getting and putting data from and to a storage device in a relatively short period of time.

instantaneous storage, Computer storage media with an access time that is slight compared to operation time.

instruction, (1) A coded computer program step that tells the computer how and what to perform for a single operation. (2) A set of characters that defines an operation and causes the computer to operate accordingly. The instructions may be in machine language as in (2) or programming language as in (1).

instruction, absolute, A computer instruction that is used in absolute coding. (See absolute coding.)

instruction address, The location or address where an instruction is in computer storage.

instruction address registers, A register that contains the address of an instruction and other registers that contain the addresses of the operands of an instruction.

instruction, alphanumeric, A computer instruction that can be used as well with numeric or alphabetic data.

instruction, blank, A computer instruction that tells the computer to do nothing but go on to the next instruction. The purpose is to hold a place for another instruction to replace it later.

instruction, branch, A computer instruction that may instruct the computer to jump or skip to another part of the program.

instruction, branch test, A test indicated by the computer instruction testing for greater than, negative, less than, etc., conditions.

instruction, branch-on-zero, A conditional branch instruction that tests the arithmetic accumulator for zero.

instruction, breakpoint, An instruction that may cause branching to a supervisory routine or a type of conditional branch.

instruction, check indicator, A computer instruction that directs a signal device to be turned on for the purpose of calling the computer operator's attention to the instruction in use.

instruction code, The set of symbols that are intelligible to a given computer.

instruction, conditional jump, Same as conditional branch.

instruction control circuits, The circuit used to control the carrying out of instructions in the proper sequence.

instruction counter, The computer register that keeps track of the next instruction to be executed.

instruction cycle, The set of steps necessary to process an instruction: getting, interpreting, decoding, and checking it.

instruction, decision, A conditional branch instruction.

instruction, discrimination, Same as conditional branch or conditional jump instructions.

instruction, dummy, An artificial instruction. It may be used to define constants or to hold a place that will later contain a usable instruction.

instruction, dynamic, The sequence of machine steps performed by a computer in a real-time or simulated environment.

instruction, effective, An altered computer instruction containing effective addresses prior to execution.

instruction, entry, Usually the first instruction to be executed in a subroutine. There may be several entry points within the routine.

instruction execution, The set of steps necessary to perform the operation of the instruction.

instruction format, functional address, This format contains no operation part of the instruction as it is implied by the address parts.

instruction format, implicit address, This format contains no address part of the instruction as it is not needed or implied by the operation itself.

instruction, hold, A type of computer instruction used to retain information in its original location as well as copy it in a new location.

instruction, immediate address, A type of computer instruction that contains the value of the operand in its address part instead of the address of the operand.

instruction, internal manipulation, A computer instruction that causes a change in format or location of data.

instruction, jump, Same as branch instruction.

instruction length, How much computer storage is required to contain a particular instruction. The length varies based on the number of addresses contained and the form in which they are represented.

instruction, logic, A computer instruction performing a logic operation, such as in Boolean logic the AND and the OR operations as contrasted with arithmetic instruction.

instruction, look up, A computer instruction designed to permit reference to arranged data, such as a table.

instruction loop, closed, A group of instructions that will be repeated and repeated and there is no exit point.

instruction, machine, An instruction in the machine's own language instead of a programming language. The form that the machine can recognize and execute.

instruction, macro, (1) One symbolic instruction that is translated into several machine instructions. (2) Several operations in one instruction.

instruction, micro, A small, single, short command.

instruction, microprogrammable, Instructions which do not reference main memory can be microprogrammed.

instruction mix, The selection of different types of instructions to determine speed and accuracy.

instruction modification, Changing the instruction prior to its execution so that it will perform differently than before.

instruction, multiple address, A computer instruction containing two or more addresses.

instruction, no-address, A computer instruction that requires no address to perform the operation.

instruction, no-op, A computer instruction that performs no operation.

instruction, presumptive, A computer instruction that will be modified.

instruction, reference, Same as instruction, look-up.

instruction register, control, A specific register that contains the address of the next instruction to be used.

instruction register, current, A computer register that contains the instruction currently being executed.

instruction, repetition, A computer instruction that is repeated a specified number of times before going on to the next instruction.

instruction, short, A shorter than usual form of an instruction.

instruction, single-address, A computer instruction having one operand address.

instruction, skip, (1) Synonymous with no-op instruction. (2) May cause a skip (jump) to another location.

instruction, source destination, Same as functional address instruction format.

instruction, stop, A computer program instruction that stops the computer.

instruction, storage, The area in computer storage used to store a computer program.

instruction, supervisory, A computer instruction unique to the supervisor used to control operation.

instruction, symbolic, An instruction written in a programming language that must be translated into machine language before it can be executed.

instruction, table look-up, Same as look-up instruction.

instruction tape, master, A specific magnetic tape containing computer programs and routines for a run or run series that is used in a tape operating system.

instruction time, The part of an instruction cycle in which the instruction is accessed plus the time used to execute an instruction.

instruction, transfer, A computer instruction such as a branch.

instruction, unconditional transfer, Synonymous with unconditional branch.

instruction word, A word of computer storage containing an instruction or one that will be treated as an instruction.

instruction, zero-address, A computer instruction with no addresses.

instructional constant, A constant to be used in a computer program that is written in the form of an instruction but is really a piece of data. It is one form of a dummy instruction.

instructional cycle, The steps necessary to process an instruction to get it ready for use.

instructions, control, Computer instructions used for control functions.

instructions, IOT, A class of instructions dealing with IOT, input/output, and transfer.

instructions, privileged, Computer instructions that can only be executed in the supervisor state when the supervisor routine has control.

instructions, return, Use of a return instruction permits return to a main computer program from a subroutine.

instructions, shift, Computer instructions used to shift data to the left or right in a register in the computer.

instructions, interpretive, Parts of interpreters that automatically translate an old program code to a new one. (See interpreter (2).)

instrument, end, In communications a device connected to one terminal of a loop that is capable of converting usable intelligence signals into electrical signals or vice versa.

instrumentation errors, Errors in a system due to instruments used, such as pressure gauges, etc.

insulation, In electricity a nonconducting material.

integer, A number in the set of all positive and negative whole numbers. 18, -43, and 0 are all examples of integers. However, 18.76,/, -43.93, and 0.32 are not integers.

integral, The number of places to the left of the decimal point. The decimal number 426.12479 has three integral places.

integrated circuit, microprocessor, The basic underlying element of microcomputers. Solid state microcircuits that consist of integrated (interconnected) active and passive semiconductor devices diffused into a single silicon chip, e.g., a slice or wafer.

integrated circuit, monolithic, One of several logic circuits that are etched on chips of material. (See integrated circuit.)

integrated data processing (IDP), (1) A system that treats all data processing needs as a whole. (2) Processing in which all operations are connected or associated with a computer.

integrated injection logic (I²L), A technology with advantages of increased density, good speed-power product, versatility, and low cost that can handle digital and analog functions on a single chip and is made with a mask process without the need for current-source and load resistors.

integrated system, A system in which the data is not repeated when additional related data enters the system.

integrating gear, A device used in analog computers.

integration, analog, A process performed in an analog computer by means of an operational amplifier with a capacitor instead of a resistor in the feedback loop.

intellectronics, The use of electronic devices to extend man's intellect, e.g., use of a computer to recall facts.

intelligence, A developed capability of a device to do things normally associated with human intelligence, such as reasoning, learning, etc.

intelligence, artificial, (1) The concept that machines can be improved to assume some capabilities normally thought to be like human intelligence, such as learning, adapting, self-correction, etc. (2) A comparison of man extending his intelligence using computers as he extended his physical powers with tools. (3) In a more restricted sense, the study of techniques to use computers more effectively by improved programming techniques.

intelligent copier, Types of copiers offer the combined features of a copier with a laser printer and provide the ability to receive and transmit documents over phone and other communication lines, bridging both word processing and data processing.

intelligent terminal, Any functionality or combination of functions in the terminal that relieves any processor to which it might be connected from some of the operations that the processor would otherwise be required to handle if connected to the basic or "dumb" terminal. Degrees of "intelligence" vary from manufacturer to manufacturer.

INTELSAT V satellite series, A satellite series launched in 1979. The systems are designed for global service comprising seven satellites, each able to carry 12,000 telephone conversations plus television.

intensity, The density of a black or colored image on paper in optical character recognition.

intensity, dual, A method whereby some characters are displayed on a monitor more brightly than others, under the control of the program displaying the characters. In simple terms, this method allows certain data to be emphasized.

interactive, An interactive computer system is a system in which the user communicates with the computer through a terminal, and the computer presents the results immediately after an instruction has been entered.

interactive system, A system capable of real-time man-machine communications.

interblock, To prevent operation of a machine, device, or element.

interblock gap, The space separating two blocks of data on magnetic tape.

interblock space, The space on magnetic tape between blocks of data on which nothing is written.

intercept, willful, In communications intercepting messages when there is station equipment or line trouble.

intercepting trunk, In communications a trunk where a call is connected for action by an operator (telephone) in cases of a vacant number, changed number, or line out of order.

interchangeable connector, Connects from different manufacturers that can be used interchangeably.

interchangeable type bar, A type bar on a data processing printer that can be removed by the operator to change the alphabet available to a print position.

intercomputer communication, Data is transmitted from one computer to another computer.

interconnecting device, A device used with multiple systems to switch peripheral units from one system to another.

interconnector, A flow chart symbol showing continuation of a broken flowline.

intercouple, To connect two or more units of hardware.

intercoupler, The connection of two pieces of hardware, electronically or electrically.

interface, A common boundary between data processing systems or parts of systems. In communications and data systems it may involve formal, speed, code, or other changes as needed.

interface converter, transmission, A device that controls transfer of information between a channel and adapter.

interface design, Design work done by engineers to interface units of on-line systems.

interface design, system, The engineering design of specialized input/output equipment for a computer system.

interface, Kansas City standard, Named for the meeting place of the symposium at which it found acceptance. The standard describes a modem technique for reading and writing digital data on audio cassette recorders.

interface, RS-232-C, A bit serial interface for teleprinters, terminals, and modems. Data transfer rates, data formats, and parity are all selectable, and current loop operation is also provided. All communication is in an asynchronous mode.

interface, standard, A device used to connect two or more units, systems, etc. that matches a standard.

interface, standard types, Use of standardized interface signals and low-speed peripherals, such as CRT terminals, that generally conform to the EIA RS-232 standard; some medium-speed devices, including digital instruments and floppy disk drives, conform to the IEEE-488 bus, and so on.

interference, The presence of undesirable energy in a circuit.

interference, adjacent channel, Such interference occurs when two modulated carrier channels are placed too close together in frequency.

interfix, In communications a technique used to avoid false retrievals.

interior label, A label that accompanies the data it identifies.

interleave, A method used to merge parts of one computer program into another so that they can in effect be executed at the same time, e.g., a technique used in multiprogramming.

interleaving, Refers to the mixing of actual data with control information when transmitting data on a communications path. Control information includes identically spaced check characters to assist the computer in detecting data transmission errors. The receiving terminal must be able to interpret the interleaved information according to set rules and formats, so that if it finds an error it can signal the sending terminal to retransmit the block of data.

interleaving, functional, The process of having input/output and processing go on independently of each other, but interlaced or interleaved in their sharing of computer memory.

interleaving memory, Two or more computer memory banks operating at a fraction of a cycle apart to reduce cycle time and improve memory speed.

interleaving, multiprocessing, The special process of addressing storage modules that are adjacent in an even/odd method.

interlock, An interdependent arrangement of control of machines and devices to assure proper coordination.

interlock (communications), Any protective feature that helps in preventing interference to normal transmissions.

interlock switch, An automatic circuit breaker that cuts off power.

interlock time, print, The time necessary for the printer to accept data from storage and complete the printing of it.

interlude, A small computer subprogram used for preliminary operations that may be written over after used.

intermediate, language, (1) A language that is a compromise between machine language and a higher-level language. (2) A language that acts as a go-between in translating from source language to one of many languages.

intermediate memory storage, Used as an electronic scratch pad for temporarily holding data.

intermediate pass (sorting), The parts of a sort that isn't the first or last pass.

intermediate total, A total somewhere between a major total and a minor total.

intermittent errors, Sporadic or intermittent equipment errors that are difficult to detect as they may not occur when trying to diagnose their cause.

intermittent fault, A fault that occurs seemingly in no predictable or regular pattern.

intermix tape, A feature of some computers that permits combinations of different models of tape units on one computer.

internal arithmetic, The arithmetic calculations performed by the arithmetic unit in the CPU of a computer.

internal checking, The features of equipment that help improve accuracy by checking for things such as hole counts, parity checks, validity checks, etc.

internal code, The data representation structure of a computer, e.g., in the IBM 360 a byte is 8 bits, a half-word is 2 bytes, etc.; the internal code is an 8-bit character.

internal control system, Programmed controls built into the system that govern the flow of computer operations.

internal interrupt, A feature of peripheral equipment that causes equipment to stop and perform a designated computer program subroutine.

internal memory, The storage in a computer that is in the machine itself and that is capable of retaining data.

Internal Telecommunications Union (ITU), A 156 member specialized agency of the United Nations responsible for the international coordination of matters related to telecommunications, including telephone, telegraph, radio, and TV.

internally stored program, The compute program or set of instructions that is stored in computer internal memory as contrasted with those stored on disks, magnetic tape, etc.

interpret, (1) To translate non-machine language to machine language. (2) To decode. (3) To translate coded characters into letters, numbers, and symbols.

interpretative language, A computer program language used to translate and execute each source language statement as it encounters it.

interpreter code, An interim code that must be translated to computer coding before use.

interpreter routine, A computer program routine that translates a stored program from a pseudocode into machine language.

interpreter/reader, A specialized computer program routine that reads an input stream (series of jobs) and stores the programs and data on a random access device for later processing.

interpretive instructions, Parts of interpreters that automatically translate an old program code to a new one. (See interpreter (1).)

interpretive mode, A mode of processing used for error tracing.

interpretive programming, Writing computer programs in a pseudo-machine language that needs translation to machine language before execution.

interpretive routine, A computer program routine that translates instructions in pseudo-code to machine language and executes the instructions immediately.

interpretive trace program, A computer program that is used to trace or check another program in an interpretive mode.

interrecord gap (IRG), The blank space between records on magnetic tape.

interrecord gap length, The length of the space between records on magnetic tape.

interrogation, An inquiry into a system for which a quick reply is expected.

interrogators, video-data, In communications a device comprised of a keyboard and separable associated display.

interrupt, operator, Signals the operation to type in some data on the console typewriter.

interrupt, (1) A break in normal flow of a routine that can be continued from that point at a later time. (2) A control signal that diverts the attention of the computer from the main program; to stop the current sequence.

interrupt, automatic, An automatic computer program controlled interruption of operations that causes a branch to a specified computer storage location.

interrupt, batch-processing, A feature of a real-time system where the computer's batch-processing program may be interrupted to permit handling of a real-time transaction.

interrupt, contingency, An interrupt caused by operator request at the keyboard, typing in a character, operator requests a program stop, etc.

interrupt control routine, A computer routine entered when an interrupt occurs for analysis of the interrupt cause.

interrupt, count pulse, An interrupt triggered by pulses from a clock source.

interrupt, count zero, An interrupt triggered when a count pulse interrupt has produced a zero in a clock counter.

interrupt, cycled, The change of control to the next or a specific function in an interrupt condition.

interrupt, disabled, An armed interrupt waiting for enablement. (See interrupt.)

interrupt, external inhibit, The bit in the program status double word that tells whether or not all external interrupts are inhibited.

interrupt, external-signal, Allowing external equipment to interrupt the computer program to process the interrupt.

interrupt handling, The process following an interrupt or how the interrupt condition is handled.

interrupt indicators, input/output, The indicators that can be tested to see which device, and for what reason, an interrupt was caused.

interrupt, input/output, The use of the interrupt capability allows input/output equipment to be kept running at full capacity.

interrupt, internal, A feature of peripheral equipment that causes equipment to stop and perform a designated computer program subroutine.

interrupt log word, Contains bits set to indicate the number and types of interrupts that occur in a segment of a program.

interrupt logging, The listing or logging of interrupts during the testing of programs.

interrupt mask, The process of ignoring certain types of interrupts until a later time.

interrupt, master control, A type of interrupt in which control is given to a master control program.

interrupt, not busy, A response sent from a device to the computer if the device is not busy.

interrupt, override, A group of power on/off interrupts that have highest priority.

interrupt, parity, An interrupt that occurs because of a parity check (parity error).

interrupt, peripheral, A stop resulting from a peripheral device completing a task or signalling of readiness for a task.

interrupt, power-fail, A design in which only a priority interrupt can interrupt a non-priority interrupt routine and the power-fail is the highest priority interrupt.

interrupt, priority, The levels of priority assigned to various interrupts. (See interrupt.)

interrupt priority table, A table that lists the priority sequence of handling and testing interrupts used when a computer doesn't have fully automatic interrupt handling capability.

interrupt processing, A feature in a real-time system that permits interruption of batch-processing programs to allow for processing of real-time transactions.

interrupt routine, A computer program routine that performs interrupt action.

interrupt, scanner, A method in which external devices are continuously scanned for interrupt requests.

interrupt signal, The control signal that demands the attention of the central computer.

interrupt system, A system in some computers in which an interrupt source meets automatic and immediate response.

interrupt, trapped program, A system in which there is an interrupt trap associated with each type of interrupt that may be set to either respond or ignore an event when it occurs.

interrupt traps, A program-controlled trap is provided for each type of interrupt to prevent or allow the corresponding interrupt.

interrupt trigger signal, A signal that is generated to interrupt the normal sequence of events in the central processor of the computer.

interrupt vectoring action, That action of providing a device an ID number or an actual branching address in response to the interrupt acknowledge signal from the processor.

interrupter code, A code requiring translation to be in machine language.

interruption, A brief suspension of operations in order to process something else.

interruption, machine, An interruption caused by an error being detected in the machine checking circuits.

interrupts, automatic check, These interrupts permit automatic checking for error conditions and initiation of recovery routines where practical.

interrupts, error, Special interrupts that are provided in response to certain error conditions in the central computer.

interrupts, external, Interrupts caused by external devices needing attention or by the timer going to zero.

interrupts, external device (ED), Interrupts that occur due to external device conditions such as a real-time event occurred, an error condition exists, or responding on completion of an operation, etc.

interrupts, machine, Interrupts that occur because of a malfunction in the processor of the computer.

interrupts, machine-check, Interrupts caused by detection of an error by the checking circuits.

interrupts, priority ordered, The levels of priority; may be over 200 priority ordered interrupts in some time-sharing computers.

interrupts, standard, Those program interrupts standard in a system (See interrupt.)

interrupts, supervisor, Same as supervisor-call interrupts.

interrupts, supervisor-call, Caused by the program giving an instruction to turn over control to the supervisor (operating system).

interrupts, system, Programmed requests from a processing program to a control program for some action.

interrupts, system-call, Caused by programmed requests from a processing program to the control program for some action.

interval, significant, In communications the period of time during which a given significant condition and the signal to be transmitted is (or should be) transmitted.

interval timer, A timer in a computer with the ability to keep track of the time of day and to interrupt as specified. (See interrupt.)

interval, time-write, The amount of time required to get ready to transmit output such as printing or writing on tape.

interval, unit, In communications a unit of measure of time.

interword gap, The space between words on magnetic tape, disk, or drum.

interword space, Same as interword gap.

intrinsic function, A standard function built into a computer language.

introspective program, A self-monitoring computer program.

inventory master file, A file of permanently stored inventory information.

inventory, real-time processing, A system that can be depended upon to provide up-to-the-minute inventory information.

inventory stock report, A printed report showing the current amount of each item carried in inventory that is on hand.

inversion, (1) The process of reversing the state of binary digits by changing the magnetization of each bit. (2) In Boolean (algebra) operations, refers to the NOT operator.

invert, To change any two-state value to the opposite state.

IOC, An abbreviation for input/output controller.

IOCS, An abbreviation for input/output control system.

IOP (input/output processor), A unit that handles control and sequencing of input/output.

IOP-Input-Output processors, A set of flexible and specialized I/O instructions that often include bit manipulation and testing, to permit simple and efficient I/O data transfers between two components residing anywhere in the system.

IPC, An abbreviation for industrial process control.

IPL, (1) An abbreviation that is used for initial program loading. (2) An abbreviation that is used for information processing language.

IPL (Initial Program Loading), The initial entry of an operating system or program into computer memory.

IPL-V, An abbreviation that is used for information processing language-five, a list processing language used to manipulate tree structures.

IPS, An abbreviation that is used for inches per second.

IRE, An abbreviation that is used for Institute of Radio Engineers.

IRL, An abbreviation that is used for information retrieval language.

irregularity, stroke edge, Deviation of the edge of a character from its stroke edge in optical character recognition.

ISAM, indexed sequential access method, An access method in which indices, which can be used to provide direct access to a file that would otherwise only provide sequential access, are stored with sequential files. The index, for each file, contains keys for every record in the file as well as their corresponding location, such as the track number on a disk.

ISAM-Indexed Sequential Access Method, See Indexed Sequential Access Method.

ISO (International Standards Organization) code, The codes authorized by ISO to represent characters.

isochronous, Having a regular periodicity.

item, A field or set of fields of related data.

item, addition, An item to be added to a file in a designated place.

item, advance, A technique to group records for operating successively on different records in memory.

item, data, A data item is the smallest unit of named data and may consist of any number of bits or bytes. Data items are often called fields or data elements.

item design, The set of records or fields that composes an item as delineated or the sequence in which they are recorded.

item, line, An item of data that could logically be printed on the same line as a related given set of items, e.g., identification number, description, quantity, etc.

item separation symbol, A control symbol that indicates the beginning of an item.

item size, (1) The magnitude expressed in number of words, characters, or blocks. (2) The number of characters in an item.

iterate, To repeat execution of a series of computer program steps until some condition is met.

iteration, An iteration is one pass through a sequence of computer program instructions. Several passes through the same sequence of instructions, such as in a loop, are called reiterations.

iterative, Used to describe the process of repeatedly executing a series of computer program instructions until a condition is met.

iterative operation, Using automatic repetition, e.g., repeating the same computing process, but with different values.

iterative process, (1) Any process that requires more than one repetition (iteration) of the same procedure or set of instructions. A loop is one such example of an iterative process in computer programming. (2) A process for reaching a desired result by repeating a series of operations that comes closer and closer to the desired result.

ITS, In communications an invitation to send.

ITU, Abbreviation for International Telecommunications Union.

ITU-International Telecommunication Union, The telecommunications agency of the United Nations.

Iverson notation, A special symbolic notation developed by Dr.Kenneth Iverson that is used in APL.

J

jack, A connecting device to which wires of a circuit may be attached.

jackplug, A type of electronic connector.

jargon, A vocabulary used by an associated group of people; the words are generally not known to others. The jargon of the computer industry is known as computerese.

JCL, An abbreviation that is used for job control language.

jitter, (1) The electrical short-time instability of a signal. (2) The loss of synchronization caused by electrical or mechanical changes.

jitter, phase, Brief, unwanted distortions in a communications signal. When the duration of such distortions is long enough, of if they are numerous enough, phase jitter can cause loss of information.

job, A specified group of tasks prescribed as a unit of work for a computer. By extension, a job usually includes all necessary computer programs, linkages, files, and instructions to the operating system.

job control, stacked, The jobs that computer programs are performed in the sequence that they enter into the system.

job control statement, Individual statements in the job control language (JCL) that provide information to the operating system as to how the job is to be run.

job description, A listing of the duties, responsibilities, and qualifications for a particular job position.

job flow control, Control processes including input/output transition between jobs and job segments, unit assignments, initialization when the computer is turned on, control between jobs and much more.

job input stream, The input consisting of programs that usually is the first part of an operating system. The stream contains the beginning of job indication, directions, programs, etc.

job management, Special functions of job management are performed by specific computer programs such as job schedulers or master schedulers, etc.

job processing, master file, Computer programs necessary for job processing. There are four categories: (1) input/output drivers, (2) system programs, (3) utility routines, (4) library subroutines.

job processing, stacked, A technique that permits multiple jobs to be stacked for presentation to the system which automatically processes the jobs onc aftcr the other.

job schedule, A control (computer) program used to examine the input work queue and determine the next job to be processed.

job stacking, The ability of a monitor system to batch process compilations, assemblies, etc., that is, jobs can be stacked and left to run without human intervention.

job step, A measured unit of work from the viewpoint of the computer user.

job-oriented language, A computer programming language designed to relate to a particular type of job.

job-oriented terminal, (1) A specific terminal designed for a particular application. (2) A specially designed terminal to fit into the environment associated with the job.

job-processing control, A portion of the control computer program that starts job operations and performs functions necessary to go from one job to another.

job-processing monitor, Computer programs that are processed by computer routines contained in the monitor system. The processes may include compilation, assembly, loading, executing, etc.

job-processing system, A monitor system composed of a set of computer programs that together form an operating system.

job-program mode, A mode of operation in which job programs are limited to those sections of storage assigned by the executive (routine).

job-request selection, Selection of the next job to be started based on its priority, available facilities needed for the job, etc.

JOSS, A time-sharing language developed by Sperry-Rand.

JOVIAL, A type of language designed by System Development Corp. for real-time command and control.

joystick, (1) Basically, an input device which consists of an upright lever mounted in a ball and socket joint together with an activating button. When a joystick is used in conjunction with an output display screen, the lever can be tilted in any direction in order to move a cursor in a corresponding direction on the screen. The activating button is used to perform a desired action at a specific cursor position, such as selecting an item from a menu or drawing a point at the cursor position. (2) A stick or lever that can be tilted in various directions to control or indicate direction of movement of cursors, game activities, and other movement or measurement of data or graphics.

JUG, Stands for Joint Users Group. A group of computer users with common interests.

jump, Basically this refers to the process by which a computer interrupts its normal sequence of processing instructions in a program and abruptly starts processing from a different location in the program. Jumps are also referred to as branches.

jump, conditional, Same as conditional branch.

jump instruction, Same as branch instruction.

jump operation, An operation in which the computer departs from the sequence of instructions and "jumps" to another program, routine, or instruction in the same program.

jump, unconditional, Same as unconditional branch.

junk, Garbled or unintelligible data, especially as received from a communications channel, i.e., hash or garbage.

justification, The act of shifting digits to the left or right as prescribed.

justified margin, Arrangement of data on a printed page so that the left and/or right end of each line are "lined up."

justified, right-hand, When an amount in storage or in a register has no zeroes in the right hand positions.

justify, (1) The process used to space a set of characters so they are aligned. (2) The process used to align margins.

justify, left, (1) The process of setting a left margin on a printed page just as one does in typing. (2) In input and output data, starting to record at the left most position of a field.

juxtaposition, Placing of items side by side or adjacent to each other.

K

K, The letter 'K' represents the number 210 or 1024. Also, the letter K is usually used in the expression representing a computer's capacity. For example, a personal computer's capacity, the number of bytes in its main memory, might be expressed as 64K (65,536 bytes). K is also used loosely to mean 1000.

Kansas City audio cassette standard, Names for the symposium meeting place, provides for computer data encoding on standard audio cassettes using standard cassette recorders. (See interface, Kansas City standard.)

Karnaugh map, An arrangement in tabular form that permits combination and elimination of duplicate logical functions by listing similar logical expressions.

KB, Kilobytes per second (1,000 bytes per second).

KCS, Stands for 1,000 characters per second, a measurement of data transmission rate.

kernel, memory use, Allocator and manager of memory in an operating system. It shares CPU time among programs, coordinates inter-program signals, and accepts and hands out jobs to appropriate I/O chips.

kernel, secure, A well-defined segment of the system software which is carefully protected by specific, often elaborate, access controls.

key, (1) A group of characters used in identification or location of an item. (2) That part of a word, record, file, etc., by which it is identified and controlled. (3) The field by which a file is sorted such as employee number, department number, etc.

key, carriage restore, A button on a printer that returns the printer carriage to a start position.

key, check reset, A push button on a computer used to reset some error conditions.

key, load, A control key or push button used to activate the input of data or instructions.

key, major, The most significant key level in a record as used in sorting.

key, protection, The use of indicators to allow access to sections of memory and deny access to all other parts of memory. It is related to storage protection and memory protection.

key, sequencing, The field in a record that is used to determine the sequence of records in a file.

key, single cycle, A push button on a computer printer that causes an additional line to print in spite of an end-of-form condition.

key, stop, A push button that will cause a stop of processing after completion of the instruction being processed at that moment.

key, storage, A set of bits associated with every word or character in a block of storage.

key, symbolic, A type of key used in the Cobol programming language as contrasted with actual key.

key, tape-load, A push button control used to initiate loading of information from tape into storage to start processing.

key typeout, respond, A push button on a console inquiry keyboard used to lock the keyboard to permit automatic processing to continue.

key, write, A code in the program status double word that may be tested to determine whether or not a program may write into specific storage locations.

key, write-field, The part of the program status double word that contains the write key.

keyboard, A device used to enter data by depressing a key similar to the typewriter keyboard.

keyboard, companion, An auxiliary keyboard that is usually located remotely away from the main unit.

keyboard computer, A computer that has keyboard input fundamentally.

keyboard, display console, The keyboard (similar to a typewriter keyboard) on a display console. (See display console.)

keyboard entry, An element of information entered manually into a computer.

keyboard inquiry, Making an inquiry using a keyboard on the typewriter console or a terminal.

keyboard labels, On some systems labels can be placed on special keys to identify user-defined escape and other sequences and programs called up by individual keys.

keyboard lockout, In communications an interlock feature that prevents sending from the keyboard of a terminal while the circuit is busy. (See interlock.)

keyboard, optical display, A display control device whose keys may be covered with specific order overlays for particular jobs.

keyboard printer, In communications a device with keyboard input and printed output operating at speeds related to the common carrier service available.

keyboard, programmable function, A button keyboard commonly used with graphics systems to provide input selection for graphics commands.

keyboard, PROM-encoded, Some terminals are developed with PROM-Programmable Read Only Memory, to permit custom keyboard layouts, including special function keys as defined by users to meet specific applications

keyboard send/receive set (KSR), In communications a combination transmitter and receiver with transmission from the keyboard only.

keyboard, supervisory, The supervisory console consisting of an operator's control panel, a keyboard and type-printer, and a control unit.

keyboard time out, In communications a feature that causes the keyboard to lock if there is more than 15 seconds between the sending of characters.

key-driven, Any device that requires an operator to depress keys to translate information into machine-sensible form.

keyed sequential access method (KSAM), A file structure and a group of library routines that together allow users to directly read records from a file based on content of key fields or in sequential order, based on the ordering of key field contents.

keying error, rate of, The ratio of the number of signals incorrectly sent to the total number of signals of the message.

keylock, A lock on a terminal which prevents it from being used unless a key is in the lock and turned to the 'on' position. Keylocks are useful in preventing the use of a terminal by unauthorized persons.

keypunch, (1) A machine used to record data in cards or paper tape by punching holes. (2) To operate the machine in (1).

key-verify, The process of using a verifier machine to check what was supposed to have been punched. It looks like a keypunch machine and is used to check what has actually been punched.

keyword-in-context index (KWIC), An index that lists available computer programs in alphabetical order with entries for each keyword in the title.

keywords, The most informative words in a title; the significant words.

killer, noise, An electrical device used to reduce interference with other communications circuits.

kilo, A prefix meaning one thousand. It is often abbreviated as K.

kilobauds, Higher capacity data channels. (Kilobaud is 1,000 bauds.)

kilobit, One thousand binary digits.

kilobyte, See K.

kilomega, A prefix meaning one billion.

kludge, A slang term that refers to a make-shift hardware and/or software system. A kludge is made from various mismatched parts and is consequently both temporary and rather unreliable.

KSAM-Keyed Sequential Access Method, See Keyed Sequential Access Method.

KSR-keyboard send/receive set, In communications a combination transmitter and receiver with transmission from the keyboard only.

KWIC, keyword-in-context index, An index which lists titles alphabetically according to their keywords. There is an entry for each keyword in the title. An index of this type is prepared by highlighting each keyword of the title and aligning the keywords in a vertical column alphabetically.

KWIC-keyword-in-context index, An index that lists available computer programs in alphabetical order with entries for each keyword in the title.

L

label, (1) A name, in a program, that identifies an instruction, a data value, a file, a record, a device, or a storage location. (2) A marker used to designate the location in a PASCAL program to which a GOTO statement will cause a jump to occur.

label, examples, (1) An identification device that records address, etc. (2) A name that is symbolic of an instruction or data group. (3) A set of symbols used to identify or describe an item, record, message, or file. (4) To assign or to label as a means of identification a body of data, tape, card, record, file, etc.

label, file, A label written on magnetic tape describing the file name, tape reel number, and various dates.

label, interior, A label that accompanies the data it identifies.

label, operational, Procedure in which tape files are identified by a label for the computer operator's information.

label record, A record in a file that identifies the contents of the file.

label, scale, The number labels placed on the scale at various points.

label, tape, An identifying label on the first record of a magnetic tape.

labels, external, Labels in a computer program that are defined in another program.

labels, future, Labels that are referenced by a programmer but have not previously been defined.

labels, tab, Labels on or in a continuous form that can be processed on a computer printer, then are detached and put on an envelope, etc.

laboratory instrument computer (LINC), A computer used by the laboratory research worker for data recording, monitoring, controlling, and analysis.

lag, (1) The relative time delay between two mechanisms, programs, etc. (2) The delay between two successive events.

landline facilities, Communications facilities within the continental United States.

language, (1) A set of characters, symbols, etc., and the rules for using them. (2) A combination of vocabulary and syntax. Examples of computer languages are Cobol, Fortran, Algol, Basic, and Pascal.

language, assembly, Low-level symbolic language used for writing source programs. The symbolic instructions are translated into machine-language commands before being used by the computer.

language, common business oriented, The Cobol programming language, the most widely used business applications programming language.

language, common machine, A machine-sensible representation that is common to a group of machines.

language, computer, A programming procedure in which instructions are in machine language.

language, computer-oriented, A term used for relatively low-level languages, i.e., requiring a low degree of translation.

language, conversational, A near English language used to communicate with a computer from a terminal.

language declaration, procedure, The act of naming and writing a procedure. Some programming languages require that a procedure be declared, that is, given a formal name along with its code so that it can be called later by using its name in lieu of an instruction.

language, interpretive, A computer program language used to translate and execute each source language statement as it encounters it.

language, job-oriented, A computer programming language designed to relate to a particular type of job.

language, machine, (1) Formations of the binary code which a computer can immediately understand. All high-level languages must be translated into machine language before the commands can be executed by the computer. (2) The language in symbols and format that is directly understandable to a machine, i.e., does not need translation.

language, object, The language form that is the output of an automatic coding routine, usually the same as machine language.

language, PL/1 programming, A computer programming language that has some features of Fortran and some features of Cobol, plus others.

language precedence rules, Refers to that part of a programming language that determines in what order the computer will perform the operations if a single expression contains more than one operation.

language program, macro-assembly, A language processor that has characteristics of both an assembler and a compiler.

language, programming, A way of communicating with a computer that is much easier than writing programs in machine language binary code. FORTRAN, COBOL, BASIC, and PASCAL are examples.

language, pseudo, An artificial language.

language, source, The language written by a programmer that is translated into machine language by an assembler, compiler, etc.

language subset, A part of a language that can be used independently of the remainder of the language.

language, symbolic, Use of symbols to express formal logic.

language, symbol-manipulating (LISP), A powerful list processing language.

language, synthetic, A fabricated language, a pseudocode or symbolic language.

language, target, The language that some other language is to be translated to.

language theory semantics, Meaning of words as opposed to syntax which refers to structure of a sentence.

language translator, (1) A computer program used to translate a program from one language to another. (2) A program that helps to translate languages such as French to English. (3) An assembler or compiler that translates "human" coding into machine language.

languages, low-level, Refers to symbolic programming languages that are coded at the same level of detail as machine code and can be translated in a ratio of one symbolic instruction to one machine-code instruction.

large scale integration, The accumulation of a large number of circuits (say 1,000 or more) on a single chip of silicon. It is characteristic of microprocessor and memory circuits of the late 1970's and in preparation of VLSI-Very Large Scale Integration, with hundreds of thousands on a single chip in the 1980's.

LARP, An abbreviation representing Local and Remote Printing, used in Word Processing.

laser emulsion storage, A data storage medium using a controlled laser beam to expose very small areas of a photo-sensitive surface.

laser scanners, Found in many applications in recording systems, optical character readers (OCRs), film readers, and data digitizers; monochromaticity and coherence of the laser beam make it possible to focus the wavefront to a diffraction limited point image to then become the recording or analyzing spot.

laser-computing applications, Low cost lasers find wide ranges of utility in data processing: facsimile equipment, video discs, high-speed printers, copiers, and so on, as well as the base for many types of fiber optics communications.

Last-In-FIrst-Out (LIFO), A very specific technique for storing and retrieving data in certain data structures. The most common data structure that uses the LIFO technique is the stack. In LIFO, the last data item stored in the data structure is the first to be retrieved. A close analogy is a stack of plates, in which the last one placed on the stack must first be removed before any of the subsequent plates can be removed.

latch, A device or circuit that maintains an assumed position or condition until it is reset to its former state by external means.

latch tules, small systems (PROM), On some systems the even address channel outputs to a "control latch" in the programmer, odd outputs to either an "address latch" or a "data latch" depending upon the state of the fourth bit in the "control latch" and so on.

latches, single chip system, Are useful in expanding addressing and peripheral interface capabilities. They provide tri-state bus interfacing and buffer expansion.

latching, Arrangement whereby a circuit is held in position, e.g., in read-out equipment, until previous operating circuits are ready to change this circuit. It is also called locking.

latency, A delay time.

latency time, A time lag or the rotational delay time in magnetic disk or drum processing.

lateral direction (magnetic tape), Across the width of the tape.

latest start date (PERT), In PERT (Program Evaluation and Review Technique), the latest date a task can start so that the whole job is completed on time.

layer, barrier, An electrical layer at the contact surface between a metal and a semiconductor or between two metals.

layout, data, Definition of arrangements of characters, fields, lines, printouts, etc.

layout, file, The file format, i.e., the size, structure, and sequence characteristics of the file.

layout, record, Shows the design of the contents of a record, such as size, arrangement of data, etc.

LCD, liquid crystal display, Generally, a type of video display that consists of a sandwich of two glass sheets, spaced approximately .0005 inches apart and sealed at the perimeters. Between the two plates flows a liquid crystal solution.

LCD-Liquid Crystal Display type, Consists of a thin sandwich, or cell, of two glass plates, with sealed edges, containing nematic liquid-crystal material.

LD, An abbreviation for long distance.

LD trunk, A long distance (LD) trunk permits connection with local, secondary, primary, and zone centers.

LDRI, An abbreviation for low data-rate input.

LDT, An abbreviation for logic design translator.

leader, An unused length of tape at the beginning of a reel of tape in front of the recorded data.

leader (Fortran), A computer program used to load Fortran programs into storage.

leader record, Same as header record.

leading control, A title of a control group of records that appears in the front of the group.

leading edge, document, The edge of a document that goes into the machine first in optical character recognition.

leading end, The end of a wire, tape, ribbon, etc., that is processed first.

leakage, A "leakage" of electricity when there is insufficient insulation.

leap frog test, A computer program used to discover computer malfunctions.

learning, machine, The ability of a machine to improve its performance based on its past performance.

learning, programmed, Instructional methodology based on alternating expository material with questions coupled to branching logic for remedial purposes becoming "programmed text" or "tutorial computer-assisted instruction," and so on.

leased channel, In communications a channel reserved for sole use of a leasing customer.

leased facility, A communications facility reserved for one customer to use.

leased-line network, A communications network reserved for the sole use of one customer.

least frequently used memory (LFU), Often when information must be read into main memory, other already resident information must be overwritten. Algorithms may be used to decide which page or segment of memory is expendable, and the LFU algorithm replaces the area that is being or has been accessed the least. Another type is least recently used (LRU), and so on.

least significant character, The character in the right-most position of a field or word.

least significant digit, The digit in a number contributing the smallest amount to the total quantity.

LED, Abbreviation for Light Emitting Diode. An LED device will light up when the proper current is passed through it.

ledgers, magnetic-striped, A magnetic stripe with data recorded on it.

LED-Light Emitting Diode, A semiconductor chip that emits energy when stimulated by a low-voltage dc current and is more efficient than an incandescent bulb. Its light output is not created by a superheated filament but by electrons jumping from higher to lower energy states at the semiconductor's junction; most often they're found in calculators, but are currently widening their utility.

left justify, (1) The process of setting a left margin on a printed page just like one does in typing. (2) In input and output data, starting to record at the left most position of a field.

leg, A path of instructions followed in a computer program after a branch point.

legal retrieval, Retrieving information related to law such as court decisions, citations, references, etc.

length, The number of bits or characters, etc., in a word.

length, block, Expressed in total number of records, words, etc., contained in a block. (See block.)

length, double, Twice the length of a unit of storage or data, e.g., double-length word, double-length register, etc.

length, field-selected, The design of a fixed length data field. (See fixed length.)

length, fixed, A computer concept that relates to a fixed number of characters that can be in a data element or storage location as contrasted with variable length.

length, gap, The size of the space between records on magnetic tape.

length, instruction, How much computer storage is required to contain a particular instruction. The length varies based on the number of addresses contained and the form in which they are represented.

length, interrecord gap, The length of the space between records on magnetic tape.

length, pulse, The time interval as a pulse is measured.

length, record, The number of characters or words in a data record that may be expressed in characters or words, etc.

length, register, The number of positions in a register.

length, string, The number of records in a string.

length, variable, A varying number of words per block or records per block.

length, wave, The distance between peaks of two consecutive waves.

length, word, The number of bits or characters in a word or the size of a field.

letter, One of a set of symbols that are used to represent words.

letter shift, Shifting on a teleprinter from upper case to lower case.

level, reorder, The amount of stock left when stock should be reordered (inventory).

level, transmission, A ratio expressing transmission units.

lexicon, A vocabulary with definitions of terms.

LF, See LINE FEED.

LF, An abbreviation for low frequency.

LFC-Local Forms Control advantages, Facilitates off-line data entry, reduced operator waiting time, increases data throughput, reduces dependence on host computer, permits more efficient scheduling, and so on. Forms are displayed on the screen, often with dual brightness levels, etc.

librarian, A person who has responsibility for safekeeping of all computer files, such as programs and data files on magnetic tapes, disk packs, microfilm, punched cards, and so on.

librarian, In an operating system a computer program makes a collection of programs, routines, and data available.

librarian, magnetic tape, Used to arrange programs on the library tape. (See librarian.)

librarian program, The computer program that provides maintenance of library programs used in an operating system.

librarian system, A person who maintains records of files and programs in the installation.

library, (1) The area of a magnetic disk that is used to hold programs. (2) A collection of documents or a group of computer programs. A group of computer program routines and subroutines.

library, direct access, The librarian portion of the control program in an operating system where the program library is on a direct access device.
(See librarian.)

library facilities, A basic set of general purpose computer programs used to perform common jobs.

library, macro, A group of computer program routines available in mass storage that may be incorporated into user written computer programs.

library, program, The set of computer programs and routines that are available for use. The media on which they are stored.

library, source program, A collection of computer programs in source language form.

library, subroutine, A collection of subroutines that can be used in conjunction with various routines with little or no modification.

library, subroutine, A set of computer program subroutines kept on file for use to be incorporated into computer programs.

library tape, A "library" of programs and routines on magnetic tape.

library track, A track or tracks on magnetic disk, drum, etc., used to store reference data such as titles, key words, etc.

LIFO-Last In, First Out, A push-down stack procedure, a buffer procedure and a queue discipline wherein the newest entry in a queue or file is the first to be removed.

light, check, A computer or other machine indicator light that is lit when there is an error condition of some kind.

light emitting diode, See LED.

light emitting diode-LED, See LED.

light, NIXIE, A patented glowing bulb that is used to visually display decimal numbers.

light pen, A small pen-like input device used with a CRT to make a selection from a list of choices, create a drawing on the CRT, and so on.

light pen, A pen-like device used with a cathode ray tube (television-like device) to modify or change a display.

light, thermal, A display signal that is visible to a computer operator when the temperature in a piece of equipment is higher than it is supposed to be.

limit check, Checking data in a computer program to see that it is within predetermined limits.

limit, priority, The upper bound to a priority list.

limit, velocity, A limit that the rate of change of a variable cannot exceed.

limited, Generally used with another word to indicate the activity that takes the most time such as tape-limited, processing-limited, I/O limited, etc.

limited, computer (sorting), Sort programs that are limited in time by the internal processing of instructions.

limited, input, The situation in which the input speed is the limiting factor (slowest part).

limited, input/output, The condition in which the time for input and output operations is longer than that for other operations.

limited, output, The situation in which the output speed is the limiting factor. Other parts of the system have idle time while waiting for the output.

limited, printer, The relatively low speed of the printer is holding up the processing.

limited, tape, The relatively low speed of the tape unit is the limiting factor in processing.

limited, tape (sorting), Sort programs that are limited by the relatively low speed of tape as contrasted with limited by computer.

limiter, A device used to reduce the power of an electrical signal when it exceeds a certain value.

limits, scanning, Comparing inputs against high or low limits.

LINC (laboratory instrument computer), A computer used by the laboratory research worker for data recording, monitoring, controlling, and analysis.

line, (1) A printed line or row of characters. (2) In communications, a channel or conductor capable of transmission of signals.

line, code, One computer instruction written by a programmer on one line.

line conditioning, A process by which the telephone company maintains the quality of a specific privately-leased line to a certain standard of permissible delay distortion and signal attenuation. Types include C and D.

line control, In communications a control that tells each terminal when to start transmitting.

line coordination, The process of making sure that the equipment at both ends of a circuit is ready for a specific transmission.

line, dedicated, A specially conditioned line, so as to be used exclusively for a precise use or by a single customer.

line, delay, Devices designed to retard (hold back) a pulse of energy.

line driver, analog (ALD), A device in an analog computer (a power amplifier).

line, electric delay, See delay line.

line, end of, A machine code character that indicates the end of a group of records.

line feed (LF), The control character used to advance the paper in a printer or the cursor on a screen to the next line. In ASCII, the LF character is represented by the ASCII code '010.'

line finder (data processing), A device attached to the platen of a printer that automatically line-feeds it to a specific line on a printed form.

line generator (display), A device used in a cathode ray tube; dotted dashed, or blank lines can be generated.

line, hit-on-the, A momentary open circuit (teletypewriter).

line, individual, In communications a subscriber line that serves only one main station.

line, in-house, A privately owned (or leased) line (separate from public right of ways).

line item, An item of data that can logically be printed on the same line as a related given set of items, e.g., identification number, description, quantity, etc.

line level, In communications the signal level (in decibels) on a transmission line.

line misregistration, In optical character recognition, the unacceptable appearance of a line compared to an imaginary horizontal baseline.

line, multidrop, A circuit that interconnects several stations.

line, narrow band, A communication line similar to a voice grade line but operating on a lower frequency.

line noise, Noise in a transmission line.

line, print, A row of printed characters and spaces.

line printer, A printer that produces a line at a time as opposed to a character printer, which prints a single character at a time.

line, private, A line leased for exclusive use by one customer.

line, program, An instruction on one line of a coding sheet (same as code line).

line protocol, Set of rules for controlling the sequence of transmissions on a synchronous line, explaining bidding for a line, methods for positive and negative acknowledgments, requests for retransmissions, receiver and transmitter timeout constraints, etc., to provide an orderly flow of message blocks.

line, skew, A type of line misregistration (in optical character recognition) in which the line appears slanted or skewed.

line status, The status of a communications line, e.g., receive, transmit, or control.

line, subscriber, A telephone line between a central office and some end equipment.

line, switching, A technique of switching in which the connection is made between the calling party and the called party prior to the start of a communication.

line, telephone, A general term used in communication practices relating to communication channels (conductors and circuit apparatus).

line terminals, communication (CLT's), Input and output devices used when data is to be transmitted to or from the central processor using a communications line.

line, tie, In communications a leased line between two or more PBX's.

line, transmission, A communication path for (electrical) signals.

linear, An order of algebraic equation in which the variables are in the first degree.

linear equation, A mathematical equation that has linear expression on both sides of the equal sign.

linear list, A linear list is a list with no sublists, where a sublist is a list within a larger list.

linear predictive coding (LPC), A method of analyzing speech and digitally encoding the signal to reduce the bandwidth required to carry information from source to destination. The encoding method results in blocks (packets) of encoded speech data.

linear programming, A technique used to find a best solution for a particular problem, e.g., in mixing to find an optimum mixture.

linear programming (product mix), Using linear programming to determine the best mix of materials, e.g., blending of gasoline.

linear programming control language, The language consisting of verbs (agendum names) and embodying the desired algorithm to be used prescribes the course of linear programming on a computer.

linearity controls, Manual controls on a CRT (cathode ray tube, a television-like device) that helps correct distortion of the picture (display).

line-feed code, A code that causes page teleprinters (and others) to move the platen up one line.

line, shelf, The length of time a device or supply will remain usable "sitting on a shelf."

link bit, A special one bit register in a computer. (See bit.)

link, communication, The physical connection between one location and another used for data transmission.

link, data, The equipment used to transmit information in data format.

link group, Those data links which use the same multiplex equipments. (See data link.)

link, information, The physical means of connection of two locations for the purpose of transmitting information.

link, library, A special set of data used by execute statements such as attach, link, load, etc.

LINK macro-instruction, A macro-instruction used in OS/360 (an operating system) to load a program module.

link, radio, The channel provided by a radio emitter and receiver.

linkage, (1) The instructions related to entry and re-entry of subroutines. (2) The interconnections between a main computer routine and a closed routine.

linkage, basic, A linkage (interconnection of computer routines, programs, etc.) that follows the same set of rules each time it is used.

linkage, communications, Common carrier equipment providing high-speed communications facilities for data transmission.

linkage editor, A linkage editor is a device to combine into a single module a set of program instructions that have been independently compiled.

linkage macro-instruction, A macro-instruction used to provide logical linkage between computer programs. It saves data needed by the next program.

linked list, A data structure in which each item in the list is composed of two elements: the information itself, and a pointer to the next element in the list. The advantages of linked lists are that new elements are created as they are needed and that items can be easily added to or deleted from the list.

linked subroutine, A computer program subroutine that is linked by special instructions to a main computer program.

linking loader program, A special computer program used to combine links as they are loaded into computer storage for execution.

LIPL (Linear Information Processing Language), A version of IPL, a high order programming language.

liquid crystal display, See LCD.

liquid crystal display, color-pigmented, A display that uses liquid crystal solutions that appear as colors other than black when electrically excited. (See LCD.)

LISP, A computer programming language used in artificial intelligence whose basic data structure is a binary tree.

LISP (List Processing), Types of interpretive languages used to develop higher level languages.

list (to), To print a line for each item.

list, assembly, A computer-printed listing of a computer program that was processed by an assembler.

list, command, A sequence of steps generated by the CPU (Central Processing Unit) for the performance of an input/output operation.

list, dense, A dense list is a list that fills up all the available storage space. A record cannot be added to a dense list until either more storage space is allocated to the list or until a record is deleted from the list.

list, indexed, In the Fortran programming language an instruction used to read and write indexed arrays.

list, memory map, A listing of variable names, array names, etc., and their addresses in computer memory.

list processing, A special technique used in computer programming that uses list structures to organize storage.

list processing languages, Languages developed by symbol manipulation used in construction of compilers and in simulations, etc.

list, push-down, In a list of items, an item entered in the first position "pushes down" in position all the items in the rest of the list as contrasted with push-up list.

list, push-up, In a list of items, an item is entered at the end of the list and all other items remain in the same relative position as contrasted with push-down list.

list structure, Many lists contain one or more sublists. A sublist is a list within a larger list. For example, the list (a, b, c, (aa, bb)) is a list structure because the last item in the list (aa, bb) is a sublist.

list, waiting, A list of programs waiting to be processed (synonymous with queue).

listing, assembly-language, A computer printed listing of the computer program that was processed by an assembler.

listing, proof, A listing of a computer program or data that is used for check out purposes.

listing, selective, A listing of data of various sets of predetermined criteria.

literal, A symbol, number, etc., that defines itself and not something it might represent (not a label). It is used in computer programming.

literals, Refers to data or messages to be output exactly as they are indicated in the instruction.

literature search, An organized and exhaustive search for published material related to a specific subject.

lithography, A method of printing in which character images are ink receptive and blank areas are ink repellant. It may be used in optical character recognition.

live keyboard, On some units this lets users interact with the system while a program is running to examine or change program variables or even perform keyboard calculations.

LOAD, A command that causes information to be transferred from a peripheral storage device to the computer's main memory.

load, To put information from auxiliary storage into internal storage (of a computer). It may be programs or data.

load and go, Computer operation and compiling technique in which pseudo language is converted directly to machine language, and the program is then run without the creation of an output machine language; also relates to bootstrap loaders which provide for immediate entry of data or parameters.

load key, A control key (push button) used to activate the input of data or instructions.

load key, tape, A push button control used to initiate loading of information from tape into storage (to start processing).

load line, A percentage of maximum circuit capability that the actual use reflects (during a period of time).

load mode, A mode in which data has delimiters carried along with it.

load module, A computer program developed for loading into storage and being executed whose output is a linkage editor run.

load on call, Loading program segments into storage as they are needed.

load point, The point on magnetic tape where it is positioned under the read/write head.

load sharing, Computers placed in tandem to share the peak period processing load of a system.

load, work, An amount of work to be accomplished in a given period of time.

load-and-go, A procedure that achieves rapid response and simple operation because no delays or stops occur between the loading and execution phases of a program.

loader, bootstrap, A computer subroutine built (usually into the hardware) to initiate reading of another computer subroutine.

loader program, linking, A special computer program used to combine links as they are loaded into computer storage for execution.

loader, system, A computer program designed to load output from compilations and assemblies into sections of computer memory.

loading, block, A technique in which sections of programs are loaded into adjacent sections in main memory.

loading, input, The amount of load upon the sources supplying signals to the input.

loading procedure, Selection of one of various methods used to load programs and routines into memory.

loading program and allocation, A program that links together relocatable binary elements for execution or future use.

loading, program, In general refers to reading a computer program into memory prior to program execution.

loading scatter, A procedure used to load parts of program into memory not necessarily in order.

LOCAL, An abbreviation for load on call. (See load on call.)

local format storage, Allows frequently used formats to be stored at a terminal controller instead of being repeatedly sent down the communications line to speed up transaction response times and reduce delays caused by heavy line loading.

local forms control (LFC), Software for use in some emulation systems that make possible off-line data entry operations by diskette storage of fixed formats and data at the local site. LFC reduces operator dependence on the host computer and lets the work continue even when the host computer or communication line is down.

local loop, The channel that connects a subscriber to a central office exchange; also refers to the type of service provided. It is sometimes called a subscriber station.

local service area, In communications the area one can call without toll charges.

local side, Data terminal connection to input/output devices.

local variable, A data variable whose name is only defined in a subroutine or subprogram and not known to the main computer program.

locate, To find a record of specified information (in a search).

location, Is a position in computer storage or a place in storage from which data may be retrieved.

location, bit, A storage position on a record capable of storing one bit. (See bit.)

location, effective double word, The actual storage location (indicated in an address in a double word addressing instruction).

location, effective half word, The actual storage location (indicated in an address in a half word addressing instruction).

location, effective word, The actual storage location (indicated in an address in a word addressing instruction).

location identifier, A label assigned to a location in computer storage or in the broad sense to a location such as a city, street, or address.

location run, A routine used to locate the correct run on a program tape.

location, specific addressed, In random access devices, an address that may be directly accessed without a sequential search.

location, storage, A storage position designated by an address (or a register).

locations, buffer storage, A set of storage locations used to temporarily hold data to compensate for differences in data rate going from one device to another.

locations, protected, Storage locations available only to specific users (others cannot get access to it).

locator run, Same as location run.

locking shift character, A control character that indicates all characters that follow should be of the shifted set of characters (compares somewhat in concept to the locking of the shift key on a typewriter).

lockout, A portion of a buffer cycle in which operation of the logic or arithmetic unit stops or neither is able to communicate with memory.

lockout, keyboard, In communications an interlock feature that prevents sending from the keyboard of a terminal while the circuit is busy. (See interlock.)

lockout, write, A situation in time-sharing that prevents programs from writing at that time.

log, To record events that take place.

logarithm, The exponent indicating the power necessary to raise a number (the base) to produce the number.

logger, A machine that records physical processes automatically with respect to time.

loggers, system utilization, A computer program or a device that records statistical data about how the system is running.

logging, failure, A procedure in which the computer keeps track of its errors (to help the person who fixes the problem).

logging, interrupt, The listing or logging of interrupts during the testing of programs.

logic, The science of the formal principles of reasoning or the basic principles, relationships, of propositions, the interconnection of on-off circuits for manipulation in a computer.

logic analysis, The analysis used to determine what specific steps are required to produce the desired computer output.

logic, binary, Digital logic elements which operate in two states (such as on and off, 1 and 0, high and low, etc.).

logic, Boolean, Logic used in applications of information retrieval and circuit-switching designs.

logic card, A functional card containing electrical components and wiring circuitry (not a punched card), several of which are in a computer.

logic chart, Same as program flowchart, showing the logical steps used to solve a problem.

logic circuit, One of many types of switching circuits such as AND, OR, etc., that perform logic functions.

logic circuits, silicon transistors, Logic circuits using silicon transistors instead of germanium components.

logic, computer, The logic capabilities of a computer.

logic, control, Generally relates to the sequence of steps needed to perform a function.

logic decision, A decision of the binary type (yes or no type) relating to equality, inequality, and relative magnitude (less than, equal to, or greater than).

logic design, Specification of the working relationships between parts of a system in terms of symbolic logic and without any major regard for the hardware implementation of it.

logic device, A semiconductor device which performs a logical operation in a computer. Gates, combinational circuits, and sequential circuits are all examples of logic devices.

logic diagram, A diagram representing logic design or the later hardware implementation. (See logic design.)

logic, double-rail, Circuits in which each logic variable is represented by a pair of electric lines.

logic element, A device that performs a logic function.

logic expression, An expression containing variables, constants, function references, etc., separated by logical operators and parentheses.

logic, formal, An objective study of structure, form, and design of valid arguments.

logic function, An expression representing an operation that includes one or many logic operators.

logic instruction, A computer instruction performing a logic operation (such as in Boolean logic the AND and the OR operations) as contrasted with arithmetic instruction.

logic, machine, The capabilities of the computer (that are built in) to make decisions.

logic, mathematical, Exact reasoning concerning non-numerical relationships.

logic multiply, A Boolean operation performed by an AND operator.

logic operation, Non-arithmetic operations performed by a computer, such as compare, branch, etc.

logic operator, Any of the many switching operators or gates such as AND, OR, etc.

logic product, The result of an AND operation.

logic product gate, Same as gate, AND. (See gates.)

logic shift, A non-arithmetic shift. (See shift instruction.)

logic, solid-state, Microelectronic circuits are the product of solid logic technology (SLT). These microminiaturized circuits are called logic circuits.

logic sum gate, Same as gate, OR. (See gates.)

logic symbol, See logical symbol.

logic, symbolic, The study of formal logic, mathematical logic, and Boolean algebra.

logic types, Some of the most regular types are transistor-transistor-logic (TTL), emitter-coupled logic (ECL), and complementary metal-oxide semiconductor (CMOS), each with families and each encountered in many modern microprocessor applications, TTL being the oldest.

logic, variable, Alterable internal logic design (electronic).

logical add, Combining two numbers in a logical sense to produce a result as opposed to adding them in an arithmetic add. Used in Boolean algebra.

logical choice, Making the right decision from a group of alternate possibilities.

logical circuit, A type of switching circuit such as AND, OR, and other Boolean logic operations gates.

logical comparison, Comparing two elements to see if they are the same or different.

logical connectives, The fundamental operators, gates, switches, or words like AND, OR, IF THEN, etc. (used in Boolean operations).

logical decision, In computers choosing between alternatives or selecting paths of flow in a program.

logical design, The basic logic for a system, machine, or network, pre-engineering design, data flow design (within the computer), and design that will be implemented by hardware.

logical diagram, A diagram of logical elements and their interconnections.

logical file, A set of records that are logically related (of the same type).

logical flowchart, A flowchart showing the logical sequence of operations in a computer program. (See flowchart.)

logical instruction, An instruction that carries out a logical operation such as AND and OR. (See instruction, logic.)

logical one or zero, The "computer people" term used to represent the two possible states of binary systems.

logical operation, An operation in which a decision is made to determine the sequence of instructions to be taken next; also, an operation of Boolean logic such as an OR.

logical operator, Such operators as AND, OR, and NOT, etc.

logical product, Same as intersection, conjunction, and AND operation results.

logical record, A group of related fields making up a record. One logical record may also be one physical record, but a physical record may be a block of logical records.

logical sum, The result of the inclusive OR operation, (a Boolean logic operation).

logical switch, An electronic device (used in switching).

logical symbol, A symbol used as a logical operator or a symbol used to represent a logical element.

logical tracing, Tracing the paths followed after branch, jump, or transfer instructions (a debugging technique).

logical variable, A variable which may only have a "true" or "false" value.

log-off, Procedure to enter into a computer the information needed to end a session on a terminal.

long term storage, A relative term referring to data stored in internal memory for a long time.

long word, The longest element a computer can process in computer words, such as double word, full word, etc.

longitudinal check, A checking process done by counting bits.

longitudinal circuit, A circuit of one or more telephone lines with the return through the earth.

longitudinal curvature, A deviation from straightness of a length of magnetic tape.

longitudinal direction, Along the length (not width) as in magnetic tape.

longitudinal parity check, A parity check made in a longitudinal direction (as opposed to vertical). (See parity check.)

longitudinal redundancy check, An error control check based on the arrangement of data according to a rule.

longitudinal transmission check, A parity check at fixed intervals of data transmission. (See parity check.)

look up, A process in which a table of stored data is searched for a particular item.

look up instruction, A computer instruction designed to permit reference to arranged data such as a table.

look-up table, (1) A collection of data in a form easily referenced by computer programs. (2) Can also be taken to mean the process of searching for data that is stored in an organized fashion.

loop, The repeated execution of a series of instructions or a line or series of lines that are connected back to where they started.

loop, central scanning, A loop of instructions that determine what is to be performed next.

loop checking, A method of checking data transmission by sending data back to the sender.

loop, closed, A technique, system, or device involving feedback of data for control or checking purposes.

loop, control, A path used by control signals.

loop, dynamic, A specific loop stop designed to stop the machine. (See loop stop.)

loop, feedback, The loop that connects the input and output. (See feedback.)

loop, hanging, A condition in which the computer will not respond to input, because it is unable to escape from a loop, attempting to execute an illegal or non-existent instruction, or trying to access a non-existent peripheral device. Hanging of the system usually results in the computer continuously repeating the instructions which caused it to hang. Sometimes referred to as hang-up.

loop, home, In communications an operation at a local terminal only.

loop, hysteresis, A specific graphic representation showing magnetic forces.

loop, line, A communication line from an input at one terminal to output units at a remote terminal.

loop, open, An information system that makes no provision for automatic error correction or data modification. Such a system requires the operator to make any necessary modification or adjustments.

loop operation, A set of instructions that are modified prior to each entry to the loop.

loop, rectangular, A type of hysteresis loop that is more rectangular than "S"-shaped.

loop, square, A type of hysteresis loop that is more square than "S"-shaped.

loop stop, A small closed loop in computer programming used to indicate an error to the operator, etc.

loop storage, A particular storage device using loops of magnetic tape as a storage medium.

loop stores delay, A method of storing information by transmitting bits or no-bits through a loop.

loop, subscriber's, Same as local loop.

loop system, closed, A system in which a computer controls a process without human intervention.

loop termination, Ending the execution of a loop of instructions because of some condition.

loop testing, Checking to see if further looping is required in computer program execution.

looping, A computer operation in which a sequence of steps is repeatedly executed.

looping execution, Repeating a set of instructions, but using different data values each time (or modified instructions).

loops, outside, Loops that are larger and on the ''outside'' of the loops in computer programming.

loss, transmission, A general term to note a decrease in signal power in transmission.

low order, The right-most position of a number or field of data.

low punch, The zero zone punch in a punched card.

low-activity data processing, A small number of transactions processed against a very large master file.

lowpass, The passage of low frequency signals.

low-performance equipment, Equipment having insufficient characteristics to permit their use in trunk or link circuits.

low-speed storage, A storage device with access time longer than the speed of the arithmetic operations in the central processing unit; also, slower than other peripheral units.

LRC-longitudinal redundancy check, An error-checking technique based on an accumulated exclusive OR of transmitted characters, accumulated at both the sending and receiving stations during transmission of a block, an equal comparison indicating a good transmission of the previous block.

LRU, See Least Frequently Used.

LSI communication equipment, The use of Large Scale Integrated chips and thus microprocessors and programmable LSI receiver/transmitter and conversion chips in data communications service and devices such as multiplexers, data concentrators, front-end pre-processors, network diagnostic equipment, intelligent terminals, and message switching systems.

LSI, large scale integration, LSI refers to the process of putting large numbers of transistors and components on a very small chip, thereby reducing the size of main memory storage.

LSI memories, Many are available that are developed with Large Scale Integration techniques including RAM, ROM, PROM, EAROM, each having its own characteristics and advantages.

LSI microprocessor, Essentially a complete system on a chip, or at most a few chips, and with RAM, I/O, and control ROM; some timing circuits become a full-fledged microcomputer, the microprocessor being the

CPU, the central processing unit. ROMs are predesigned and can customize the processor or expand or change its power, control and versatility.

LSI, programmable, Large Scale Integration has simplified the phases of the design cycle to automate engineering work while the implementation of the microcomputer from LSI chips has automated tens of thousands of consumer and industrial products, as each year adds more power and capability to LSI chip technology, packing more control, memory, and manipulated intelligence in each chip.

LSI-Large Scale Integration, An ambiguous acronym but usually refers to more than 100-gate complexity in circuit development. More generally regarded as judicious packing of thousands of transistors and associated components on a single integrated circuit that has produced "dedicated" microprocessor devices with low-price-performance to thousands of consumer, industrial, and scientific products.

luminance signal, The signal that controls light values in the color CRT receiver (a television-like screen).

M

M, Mega (1,000,000).

MAC, An abbreviation for any of the following: multiple access computer, machine-aided cognition, memory-assisted cognition.

Mach, A term designating the speed of sound, i.e., Mach 3 is three times the speed of sound.

machine check, An automatic check or a programmed check of machine functions.

machine check indicator, See indicator, check.

machine code, As the fundamental language of the computer, it is written as strings of binary Is and Os. Machine code instructions tell the central unit of the Central Processing Unit (CPU) what to do first and next.

machine coding, Writing code in the computer's own language (machine language).

machine cognition, A type of artificial learning by a machine, i.e., perception and interpretation based on previous experience.

machine cycle, The amount of time necessary for the computer to perform one operation. Machine cycle is also called cycle time.

machine cycle, The time that it takes for a sequence of events to be repeated.

machine error, A deviation from correctness due to equipment failure in design or operation.

machine instruction, Refers to instructions written in machine language. Machine instructions can be read and directly executed by the computer. However, because they are composed only of Is and Os, they are extremely difficult for a person to read and understand.

machine instruction, An instruction in the machine's own language instead of a programming language. The form that the machine can recognize and execute.

machine language, The language in symbols and format that is directly understandable to a machine, i.e., does not need translation.

machine learning, The ability of a machine to improve its performance based on its past performance.

machine logic, The capabilities of the computer (that are built in) to make decisions.

machine operation, Any of the particular operations a specific computer is designed to perform.

machine operator, The person who manipulates and controls computer and input/output device activities.

machine run, The execution of one or more programs that form a job.

machine, scanning, Either an optical scanner or a magnetic ink scanner.

machine, self-organizing, See self-organization.

machine sensible, Has the capability of being sensed or read by a machine such as ROM, magnetic tapes, disks, etc.

machine word, An information unit of a particular computer.

machine-check interrupts, Interrupts caused by detection of an error by the checking circuits.

machine-dependent, A machine-dependent program works on only one particular type of computer.

machine-independent, A machine-independent program can be used on many different types of computers and is not dependent upon one type.

machine-independent language, A language not written for use of a specific computer or computers, generally high-level languages.

machine-readable, Machine-readable data generally has been recorded in such a way that it can be read or sensed directly by the computer. For example, data recorded on tape is machine-readable.

machine-sensible information, Same as machine-readable information.

macro code, A coding method that permits single words to generate many computer instructions during translation.

macro library, A group of computer program routines available in mass storage that may be incorporated into user-written computer programs.

macro system, A computer programming system having the capability of many-for-one (or macro) instruction development.

macro trace, A program debugging aid.

macro-assembly program, A language processor that translates macroinstructions.

macroelement, A set of data elements handled as a unit.

macroinstruction, An instruction consisting of a sequence of short micro instructions which are inserted into the object routine for performing a specific operation. A macroinstruction usually combines several operations in one instruction.

macroinstruction, One symbolic instruction that is translated into several machine instructions or several operations in one instruction.

macroinstruction, debug, Generates a debugging capability in a computer program.

macroinstruction, LINK, A macroinstruction used (an operating system) to load a program module.

macroinstruction, linkage, A macroinstruction used to provide logical linkage between computer programs and that saves data needed by the next program.

macroprogramming, Writing computer program statements in terms of macroinstructions.

macrostatement number, A number label on a macrostatement that permits reference to it.

MAD, An abbreviation for Michigan Algorithmic Decoder, a programming language.

MADCAP, A language used for mathematical problems.

mag tape, The slang expression for magnetic tape.

magnetic (thin) film, A think layer of magnetic material commonly less than a micron in thickness. (See film.)

magnetic bubble memory, Used as extensions or replacements for disks and some semiconductor types, storage is a very thin layer of magnetic garnet material with a process of converting bubbles into information bits.

magnetic card storage, A type of storage using the magnetized surface of flexible plastic cards.

magnetic cell, A basic storage element.

magnetic cell, static, A binary storage cell in which two values of one bit are represented by patterns of magnetization.

magnetic character, A character that is imprinted with magnetic ink.

magnetic character sorter, A machine that reads magnetic ink and sorts the documents with this ink on them.

magnetic core, A magnetic material capable of assuming two or more conditions of magnetization.

magnetic disk, A flat, often circular, plate with a magnetic surface on which data can be stored by selective magnetization of portions of the flat surface. May be made of rigid material (hard disk) or flexible plastic (floppy disk)

magnetic disk file, A data file on magnetic disk or may be the magnetic disk pack itself.

magnetic disk storage, A storage device consisting of several circular surfaces of magnetic material upon which data is recorded and that can be used for direct access.

magnetic document sort-reader, A device that reads and sorts magnetic ink documents such as checks.

magnetic drum storage, A drum-like (cylindrical) storage device with a magnetic surface upon which data is recorded. It can be accessed by a computer.

magnetic film storage, A thin film magnetic storage used for high-speed internal memory.

magnetic head, A device incorporating a small electromagnet that reads, records, or erases data on a storage medium, such as a magnetic disk or tape.

magnetic ink, A special kind of ink containing a magnetic substance that can be sensed by a magnetic sensing device (MICR).

magnetic ink character recognition (MICR), The sensing of characters written in magnetic ink used in banking for checks.

magnetic ink scanner, An optical scanner (machine) that can read characters printed in magnetic ink.

magnetic instability, A property of magnetic material in that it is changed somewhat by temperature, time, and mechanical flexing (in magnetic tape).

magnetic memory, Any of several memories used to store information in computers.

magnetic path, The route followed by magnetic flux lines.

magnetic recording, The recording of data by magnetization (in a pattern) on magnetic material.

magnetic stripe systems, Used on bank credit and debit cards, their development pushes automated banking and shopping from the future to the present. Terminals update the coded figures on the magnetic stripe to record amounts, dates, and other symbols of the type of transaction; used extensively in POS (Point of Sale) systems.

magnetic tape, A ribbon of flexible material used as a storage medium, described by a qualifying adjective such as paper, magnetic, oiled, and so on. The word 'tape' is most commonly used to refer to magnetic tape.

magnetic tape, A plastic tape with a magnetic surface on which data can be stored by selective polarization of portions of the surface. Often referred to as 'mag tape' or merely 'tape.'

magnetic tape drive, A device that converts information stored on magnetic tape into signals that can be sent to a computer and that receives information from the computer and stores it on magnetic tape.

magnetic tape file check, Automatic checking for faulty magnetic tape without losing computer time or using any manual intervention.

magnetic tape unit, Generally a type of secondary storage unit used for backup. Magnetic tape units are low in cost but are accessed sequentially which gives slow data-access time.

magnetic track, The part of a moving magnetic medium (disk, drum, tape) that is read (or written on) by a head.

magnetic-ink character recognition, A form of input for an electronic data-processing system using special characters printed with ink which can be magnetized. Magnetic-ink characters read and transmit the data electronically to a conventional storage device, such as magnetic tape.

magnetic-strip file, Devices containing strips of material with magnetic surfaces for recording data.

magnetic-striped recording, Recording of data on magnetic stripes on a document as in magnetic-striped ledgers.

magnetostriction, A phenomenon by which certain materials increase in length in the direction of the magnetic field and restore to original length when demagnetized.

magnetostrictive delay line, A delay line using the principle of magnetostriction. (See delay line.)

magnetron, A uhf diode oscillator in which electrons are whirled in a circular path.

magnitude, A measurement of size or mass.

magnitude, relative, The comparative size of one quantity to another.

main memory, The internal storage in a computer.

main path, The principal line of direction in a computer program; the main logical direction.

main program, The primary processing computer program as contrasted with a routine or subroutine.

main station, A telephone station with a distinct number that connects directly to a central office.

main storage, Generally the internal (fastest) storage in a computer as contrasted with auxiliary storage.

mainframe, A mainframe computer is a large, often complex, computer system. Its capacity is much greater than that of a minicomputer or microcomputer. It is the basis for supercomputers.

maintainability, The ease with which a system can be kept in operating condition.

maintenance, The process of keeping equipment (or programs) in working order.

maintenance contracts, preventive, The arrangement between the customer and manufacturer for periodic maintenance of equipment.

maintenance, corrective, The repair or correction of a known malfunction of equipment.

maintenance, preventive (PM), Periodic maintenance of equipment to prevent potential machine problems

maintenance, program, The process of changing computer programs when necessary.

maintenance programmer, The person who makes changes and corrections to production programs.

maintenance, remedial, A maintenance function performed following equipment failure.

maintenance time, routine, Time devoted to maintenance on a regular schedule; includes preventative maintenance.

maintenance time, scheduled, Time used for machine repair on a regular pattern or schedule, also includes preventative maintenance time.

maintenance time, unscheduled, The time between discovery of a machine failure and the return of equipment to normal operation.

major control change, In a report, a change of the major level as contrasted with intermediate and minor.

major key, The most significant key (level) in a record (as used in sorting).

major state, The control state of a computer.

major total, The most significant level of totals.

majority decision gate, A gate that has the capability of implementing the majority logic operation. (See gates.)

makeup time, Time needed for reruns of job previously run with error or malfunction.

malfunction (noun), A failure in a portion of the computer's hardware, causing it to operate incorrectly. When there is a malfunction in a computer system, the computer stops operating and the system is said to be 'down.' Various continuous power systems prevent this.

malfunction (verb), To operate incorrectly.

malfunction, program sensitive, A malfunction that occurs only during execution of a particular program sequence.

malfunction routine, A particular routine used to locate a malfunction in a computer.

management, data, A general collective term referring to the functions of a system which provide access to data, enforce storage conventions, and regulate the use of input/output devices.

management, database, A systematic approach to storage and retrieval of information in computers.

management, file, A set of procedures for creating and maintaining files.

management information system, A communication process providing information for decision making that is fed back to top management of an organization.

management, record, Programming the most efficient methods of record processing.

management science, The study and use of management techniques and procedures of decision making.

management services, Consulting and other assistance provided by a consulting firm.

management, task, The set of functions in a control program that controls the use of system resources.

manager, computer center, The person with responsibility for the entire computer center related activities.

manager, operations, The person who is responsible for operation of equipment; generally not responsible for the programming staff.

manager, programming, The person who manages and supervises programming activity.

manifolding, Multiple part paper (carbon in between).

manipulated variable, A variable that is changed to regulate a condition.

manipulation data, Same as data handling.

manipulation, simulation, Using inputs and generating outputs analogous to those of the system being simulated.

manipulation, string, The procedure used to manipulate (process) strings of characters, records, bits, etc.

manipulation, symbolic, A technique used in list processing languages.

man-machine dialogue, Man-machine interaction in processing.

man-machine digital system, The combination of people, digital computers, and equipment used to achieve system objectives.

man-machine simulation, A simulation environment with man and the machine interacting.

mantissa, The fractional part of a logarithm, i.e., in 2.5, the 5 is the mantissa.

manual address switches, External control switches used by an operator to select a storage address.

manual backup, A manual method of processing that may be used if the computer isn't available.

manual control, Control of a computer function using manual switches.

manual entry, Keyboard entry of data into a computer (by a person).

manual exchange, A telephone exchange where calls are completed by an operator.

manual input, Entering data by hand into a data processing device.

manual input unit, A set of manual controls (devices) which can be used by a computer operator to set a computer word for input.

manual mode, A mode of operation in which automatic features are off and the computer accepts operator instructions.

manual operation, Processing of data manually in all or part of a system.

manual read, An operation in which the computer reads (senses) switches that were manually set.

manual switch, A hand operated switch as contrasted with electronic switch.

many-to-one, Many instructions translate to one instruction in language translation.

map, A list of the contents of a storage device.

map, Karnaugh, An arrangement in tabular form that permits combination and elimination of duplicate logical functions by listing similar logical expressions.

map, memory, A printout provided to aid in processing scattered program fragments in memory.

map, storage, An aid to the programmer used to estimate the amounts of storage needed for data, etc.

mapped memory, In some multiprogramming systems, mapped memory allows several blocks to be assigned to various users, each with access to his or her own block, the blocks being correlated with multiple-mapping registers that translate addresses for various blocks.

mapping, Procedures for transforming one set to another set (of information) or a correspondence.

margin, A difference or a range.

margin, guide, The distance between the guide edge and the center of the closest track of (paper) tape. (See guide edge.)

margin, justified, Arrangement of data on a printed page so that the left and/or right end of each line are "lined up."

margin-adjust mode, WP, In some word processing systems, a mode making it possible to properly adjust the right-hard margin while preserving the desired left-hand indentions, the system automatically looking ahead 7 or more characters to activate line feed or pause for hyphens.

marginal check, A technique used in preventative maintenance.

marginal cost, The rate of change of cost related to quantity.

marginal revenue, The rate of change of income as a function of quantity.

marginal testing, A type of testing used in computer preventative maintenance to check the equipment (also called bias testing).

mark, In communications a particular impulse (opposite of a space impulse). A sign or symbol to indicate a place in space or time.

mark detection, Mark reading and mark sensing in character recognition.

mark, end, An indicator that signals the end of a unit of data.

mark, group, A special character used at the end of a record in storage in some computers.

mark matching, A method used in optical character recognition.

mark page reader, optical, A device that can read 8-1/2″ x 11″ paper with marks on it.

mark reading, A form of mark detection using a photoelectric device.

mark, record, A special character used in some computers at the end of a record.

mark, record storage, A symbol used to indicate the length of a record being read.

mark, registration , A character recognition term for a preprinted indicator on the page.

mark scan, To mark scan is to read a specific mark in a particular location on a document.

mark, segment, A special character used on magnetic tape to separate each section of a file.

mark sensing, To mark cards or pages with a soft pencil to be read directly into the computer via a special reader.

mark, tape, A character that is written on tape to signify the physical end of recording.

mark to space transition, In communications the switching from a marking impulse to a space impulse.

mark, word, An indicator used to denote the beginning (or end) of a word.

marker, A symbol on a magnetic tape, placed for sensing to indicate beginning or end of a file or piece of information.

marker, beginning-of-information (BIM), A mark on magnetic tape that indicates the beginning of the magnetic recording area (may be a reflective strip, a perforation, or a transparent section).

marker, destination warning (DWM), A reflective spot on magnetic tape that is sensed photoelectrically to indicate the end of the tape is coming.

marking bias, A bias distortion that lengthens the marking impulse. (See bias, internal.)

marking-end distortion, End distortion that lengthens the marking impulse.

Markov chain, A model used to determine the sequence of events in which a given event is dependent on the preceding event.

mask, A machine word that specifies what parts of another word are to be operated on; to inhibit a function that might otherwise take place.

mask, IC, Sometimes a pattern "printed" on glass that is used to define areas of the chip on the silicon wafer, used for diffusion, oxidation, and metallization steps in chip manufacture.

mask, interrupt, The process of ignoring certain types of interrupts until a later time.

mask matching, In character recognition, a method used in character property detection.

masks, holistic, A unique set of characters in a character reader that represent all possible characters that could be accepted.

masks, peephole, A set of characters in character recognition used to show all input characters as unique.

masks, words, Words of particular bit patterns used in logical operations.

mass data, A quantity of data too large to be contained in internal computer memory; usually stored in a mass storage device.

mass-data multiprocessing, A large system in which all types of data are handled in a multiprocessing environment.

master, Files of semi-permanent data; also may refer to a record (of data).

master clock, The electronic source of timing signals in a computer.

master clock frequency, The time between pulses of the master clock. (See frequency, clock.)

master control interrupt, A type of interrupt in which control is given to a master control program.

master control program, The computer program that controls all phases of job set up, directs all equipment function and flow of data, directs the operator, etc.

master data, A set of data that is changed less frequently than transaction data.

master file, A file that contains records that are to be preserved.

master file, inventory, A file of permanently stored inventory information.

master file job processing, Computer programs necessary for job processing. There are four categories: (1) input/output drivers, (2) system programs, (3) utility routines, and (4) library subroutines.

master payroll data file, The file in which payroll required information for each employee is contained, such as number of dependents, deduction amounts, etc.

master program, The controller program in an operating system.

master program file, A file containing all the computer programs used for a system (may be on magnetic tape).

master record, A record in a master file; contains semi-permanent data.

master station, A station that sends data to a slave station under its control.

master synchronizer, The main source of timing signals; a clock-like device.

master tape, A master file on magnetic tape.

master time, The electronic or electric source of timing signals (clock pulses).

master/slave modes, time sharing, In time sharing, the executive program can operate in master mode and the user programs operate in slave mode (under control).

master/slave system, A two computer system in which one is the master, i.e., has control over the other, the slave.

match, The process of comparing two sets of records to see if there are matching records from each set.

match gate, Same as gate, exclusive NOR.

matched filter, A character recognition term that refers to a method of determining a character's identity.

match merge, A process of comparing two files and separating records that don't match.

mate, To combine or unite units of a computing system.

mathematical logic, Exact reasoning concerning non-numerical relationships.

mathematical model, The characterization of a process, concept, or object in terms of mathematics.

mathematical operator, A symbol that expresses a mathematical process.

mathematical power, The number of times a number is multiplied by itself.

mathematical programming, The series of techniques used in operations research to find an optimum solution to linear or nonlinear functions. The optimum solution is found by calculating either the maximum or the minimum value of the function, subject to certain restrictions.

mathematical simulation, Using a model of mathematical equations; computing elements are used to represent the subsystems.

mathematics, floating-point, An automatic method of determining the location of the decimal (or other) point.

matrix, A lattice-work of input and output leads with logic elements connected at some of their intersections.

matrix, constraint, A matrix of constraint equations in linear programming.

matrix, dot, See dot matrix.

matrix printer, A wire printer that prints a matrix of dots for characters.

matrix, semantic, A graphical procedure in semantic analysis.

matrix storage, Same as coordinate storage.

matrix table, A set of quantities in a rectangular array, mathematically arranged.

maximal, The highest or greatest.

maximum operating frequency, The highest clock rate that modules will perform reliably.

maximum transfer rate, The maximum number of digits per second that can be accommodated on a channel.

MB, Megabytes (per second).

mean-time-between-failures, A means of evaluating equipment failures related to operating time of the machine.

mean-time-to-failure, The average time a computer system or part of the system works without failing.

mean-time-to-repair, The average time to repair a faulty component of system.

mechanical dictionary, A language translating machine component which provides word-for-word substitution.

media, The material used to record information on such as ROM cartridges, paper tape, magnetic tape, etc.; the plural of medium.

medium, The physical substance upon which data is recorded.

medium, data, The material or mode in or on which data is represented.

medium, virgin, A storage medium with no data recorded on it.

medium-scale integration, A medium scale or density integration of circuits, containing logic functions more complex than small-scale integration (SSI) but less than large-scale integration (LSI), or very large-scale integration (VLSI), examples being 40-bit counters, latches, data multiplexers, etc.

megabit, One million binary bits.

megabuck, A slang term for $1,000,000 (a million "bucks").

megacycle, A million cycles per second.

member, print, A print bar, type bar or wheel, or other element that forms the printed character.

memorize, In data processing, to transfer data to internal storage.

memory, The part of the computer where data and instructions are stored as electronic boards (semiconductor) or various magnetic or laser-readable surfaces.

memory access, direct, A procedure used to transfer data between a computer and a high- speed storage device without using the CPU.

memory, acoustic, Computer memory that uses a sonic delay line.

memory, add-on, add-in, Add-on memory is generally supplied with an enclosure, power supply, and a cable to connect the memory to the mini or microcomputer. Add-in memories are normally circuit boards that slip into the chassis or expansion cabinets of the computer, whatever its size.

memory, annex, Same as buffer.

memory, associative, Same as memory, content addressed, or CAM. Data stored by content and not its location, the design permits access of all information that matches a certain "tag" organized in bits.

memory board, A typical semiconductor memory board provides addressing for from 4-k to 64-k bits or more and includes refresh and standby logic if needed, plus the bus interface, and is often driven by a microprocessor.

memory, bubble, A memory system that consists of tiny cylinders of magnetization whose axes are perpendicular to the crystal sheet on which they are located. Bubble memory allows a very high density of data storage.

memory bus, The CPU usually communicates with memory and I/O devices over a memory bus. In various computers this bus has different names, including an I/O bus, data bus, or one of many types of proprietary names.

memory, cache, Has limited capability and capacity but is usually a very fast semiconductor type. Its virtue is that it can be used with slower, less expensive memory, using look-ahead procedures to affect locating and depositing the correct information into the last memory when it is required.

memory capacity, The number of units of storage that can be used for data.

memory chip, Either RAM, ROM, PROM, or other types of semiconductor memory developed as chips and usually mounted on boards or cards to affect efficient operation with the CPU.

memory contamination, The storage of data in the wrong place in the memory can cause destruction of important data, or even the program itself. In most cases, if the program does not abend, further processing will result in unpredictable output. Contamination is loosely synonymous with corrupt.

memory, content addressed, A memory in which storage locations are identified by their content.

memory, core, A storage device using ferromagnetic cores.

memory cycle, The process of reading and restoring information in memory.

memory, dedicated, A section of memory committed to a particular purpose.

memory dump, A printout or screen display of the contents of the memory.

memory, dynamic, The movement of data (in memory) such that it is circulated and not always instantly available.

memory, dynamic relocation, A process that frees the user from keeping track of the exact locations of information in memory.

memory exchange, The switching of the contents of two storage areas or devices.

memory, external, A device not connected to a computer, but which contains data usable by a computer.

memory guard, Electronic or program guards preventing access to sections of storage.

memory hierarchy, A set of computer memories of varying sizes, speed, and cost.

memory, high-speed, A computer memory with input and access speeds in microseconds.

memory, interleaving, Two or more computer memory banks operating at a fraction of a cycle apart to reduce cycle time and improve memory speed.

memory, internal, The storage in a computer that is in the machine itself and that is capable of retaining data.

memory, laser, A mass storage device on which information is stored and read by a laser.

memory locations, standard, Reserved areas of storage for special purposes.

memory, magnetic, Any of several memories used to store information in computers.

memory, main, The internal storage in a computer.

memory map, A printout provided to aid in processing scattered program fragments in memory.

memory map list, A listing of variable names, array names, etc., and their addresses in computer memory.

memory map, virtual address, The drawing or table that shows the allocation of memory areas to devices but is also a procedure for memory segmentation as well as an automatic device for transforming virtual addresses into physical addresses in some time-sharing systems.

memory, mass, Usually refers to disk or bubble memory; also the same as bulk memory.

memory module, A magnetic core module (in increments of a constant amount).

memory, non-volatile, Storage that retains information when power is removed.

memory, normal, A standard set of main memory positions that are contiguous.

memory overlap, Putting information "on top of" other information in memory effectively replacing it.

memory, permanent, Memory that retains information when the power is removed; same as non-volatile memory.

memory, photo-optic, A memory unit that uses an optical medium such as film.

memory pointer, virtual, Pointers or lists used to keep track of program segments in virtual memory.

memory printout, Same as a memory dump.

memory protect, A feature that protects certain parts of memory from user access.

memory protection, time-sharing, A feature which prevents users from getting into executive protected areas and each other's areas.

memory, quick-access, A part of memory that has a relatively short access time.

memory, read-only (ROM), A special memory that can be read from but not written into.

memory, real, A computer's actual memory that is directly addressable by the central processing unit (CPU).

memory, refresh, A high speed storage unit used in CRT display systems to regenerate the picture being displayed.

memory, regenerative, Memory devices that need to be refreshed or the contents will gradually disappear.

memory register, A register in computer storage rather than other units of the computer; same as storage register.

memory, scratch pad, An area of computer memory used for temporary storage of the intermediate states of computation.

memory, secondary, A special storage which is usually larger and slower (in access time) than main memory.

memory, semiconductor, A computer memory that uses semiconductor circuits for storage.

memory, serial-access, A memory device in which, in order to find the desired item, all the items which occur before it must be read first.

memory, shared, A memory chip (usually RAM) that can be accessed by two different CPUs. This allows the CPUs to use the same data and communicate with each other. Shared memory chips are also called dual-port memory chips.

memory, single level, A method of memory organization that combines fast internal memory with slower external memory, and they appear to be a single memory.

memory, slow, Computer memory that has a slow access rate, relatively speaking.

memory storage, Any device into which information can be copied, stored, and retrieved.

memory, virtual, (1) Using disk storage as an extension of main computer memory. (2) A type of memory in which paging or segmenting is used to simulate larger memory.

memory, volatile, A storage medium that depends on power to retain stored information.

memory, working, The memory that stores information for processing and releases it after it is used.

memory-addressing mode, In some systems, refers to the way in which an instruction can address memory - that is, call up or place data into a memory location. The different addressing modes include direct, indirect, immediate, relative, and indexed.

memory-mapped video, Generally refers to the mapping of a screen to an area in memory. Screen display is determined by what is in the corresponding screen memory location.

menu, This often is used as a list of options which is displayed on a monitor screen during a computer program and from which the user of that program must make a choice. The result of an initial choice is often, but not always, another menu of options.

menu, device advantages, An aid to the operator in managing input, a list of programs, questions, ordered procedures, or other information can be displayed for selection of the computer user; several operators can use the same or varied menus at the same time on some systems. Light pens are often used with or without keyboards.

menu-driven program, A computer program is menu-driven if its various parts are accessed through choices made from menus which are arranged in a definite hierarchy.

merge, A merge describes the combination of two or more sets of records with similarly ordered sets into one set that is arranged in the same order.

merge, order of, The number of input files to a merge program.

merge sort, A procedure for sorting two or more sets of records in order.

merge sorting, A method of sorting by merging two or more sequences of data.

mesh, To combine in an arrangement according to a rule, two or more sequences of items.

message, In data communications, a message is an item of data with a specific meaning transmitted over communications lines. A message is composed of a header, the information to be conveyed, and an end-of-message indicator.

message, A sequence of letters, symbols, etc., of some meaning.

message, automatic, Incoming communications messages are automatically directed to a selected outgoing circuit based on the content of the message.

message diagnostic, Refers to a message generated by a compiler or interpreter to assist in program error correction.

message display console, A computer console containing s symbol generator and a CRT (cathode ray tube, a television-like device).

message, end of (EOM), A set of characters to indicate the end of a transmitted message.

message, error, A brief message displayed to the user when the program in execution encounters an abnormal situation or an error in the data. The error message contains a brief explanation about the nature of the error.

message exchange, A device between a communications line and a computer to perform some communications functions.

message, fox, A standard message used to test all characters in a transmission of data (the quick brown fox jumped over a lazy dog's back, etc.).

message heading header, In communications the first characters of a message indicating who the message goes to, the time, etc.

message, multiple-address, A message that is to be sent to more than one location

message processing, remote, A system in which messages are received from remote locations by way of communications lines.

message queuing, The control of the waiting line (queue) of messages to be processed.

message routing, The process of selecting a route or alternate route for a message.

message, single-address, A message that is only deliverable to one address as contrasted with multiple-address message.

message, switch, One of the routing points in a store and forward switching system.

messages, error, The messages in a computer program that designate errors.

metal oxide semiconductor (MOS), Part of the acronym MOSFET, the FET meaning Field Effect Transistor. MOS LSI devices are Large Scale Integrated transistors and allied components designed for computer memory, peripheral, or other devices, including the microprocessor itself.

method, See approach.

method, access, The method used to transfer data in or out of the memory of a computer by a program.

method, bottom-up, A (computer) compiling technique. It is the reverse of top-down method. (See compiling.)

method, insertion (sorting), A technique of internal sorting in which records are inserted during the process.

method, monte carlo, A trial-and-error method of repeated calculation to reach the best solution.

Mickey Mouse, A slang term referring to something that is not sophisticated or well done.

MICR code, The code used in magnetic ink character recognition, developed by the American Bankers Association.

micro instruction, A small, single short command.

microcircuits, Miniaturized circuitry common to third generation computer equipment.

microcode, A coding system of sub-operations (parts of operations) in a computer.

microcomputer, A computer whose processing unit is based on a microprocessor chip. Microcomputers originally had an increasing variety of applications in the home, office, and many other areas. Although they are smaller than minicomputers and mainframe computers, multiprocessor and parallel micro systems now compete in power and price.

microcomputer architecture, The basic interrelationships between the principal parts of the micro system and the methods (or paths) by which data can be made to flow within a system. Architecture includes: number of registers available, how registers are used, instruction sets, input/output operations, number of stacks available, how stacks are used, hardware interrupt structure, data paths into memory (number and types), data paths into CPU (number and types), and others. Most architectures are classified into either CPU oriented, memory oriented, or bit-slice.

microcomputer, components, A general term referring to a complete tiny computer system, consisting of hardware and software whose main processing blocks are made of semiconductor integrated circuits and that is similar in function and structure to a minicomputer but is at least several orders cheaper due to mass production. Components are: ALU - arithmetic-logic unit, memory, peripheral circuits, such as input/output, clock, and control devices.

microcomputer development system, Often purchased by large users of microprocessors for program development and debugging. They are specially designed tools to employ software such as exercisers, emulators, etc., to eliminate manual I/O and the need for the user to be fluent in hexadecimal. They often include terminals, tape systems, floppy disks, and other peripherals.

microcontroller, A type of all-purpose word for a microprogrammed machine containing a microprocessor or a microcomputer used for control purposes often designed to make changes in processes or control of other devices.

microcontroller chip, Usually a complete computer-on-a-chip, with program storage, data memory, input/output circuitry, and CPU, all etched on a single chip of silicon, the integration of these features designed to control rather than "number-crunch."

microelectronics, Electronics using extremely small electronic parts.

microfarad, One millionth of a farad, the unit of electrical capacity.

microfiche, A unit of film that is divided into rectangles, each typically representing a page of information. The average microfiche contains about 250 pages of information.

microfilm, A fine grain, high-resolution film containing an image that is greatly reduced in size as compared to its original paper form. Recording of microfilm (images) utilizes numerous techniques and film types.

microfilm computer output (COM), Outputting information onto microfilm.

microfilm counter, A counter on a microfilm camera to keep track of the number of exposures made.

microfilm frame, A length of microfilm with one exposure.

microfilm reader, A device used to view a microfilm image.

microfilm reader-printer, A machine that permits viewing of microfilm and printing a copy of it by pushing a button.

microfloppy disk, A 3 in., 3-1/4 in., or 3-1/2 in. disk similar to the 5-1/4 in. floppy disk.

microfloppy disk drive, A data storage device similar to a floppy disk drive except that it uses 'microfloppy' disks.

micrographics, Combinations of microforms and multiple CRT computer terminals, graphic buffers and programs, central automatic-microfilm selector and video generator modules, and various programs to search, index, and update information.

microinstruction, A small, short command such as 'add' or 'delete.'

microminiaturization, The process of reducing the size of photographs, circuits, etc.

micron, One thousandth of a millimeter, i.e., one millionth of a meter.

microphotography, A photographic reproduction so small that magnification is needed to read it (see it).

microprocessor, A complex electronic chip which is at the heart of a microcomputer, in effect providing the CPU of the system. The term is not synonymous with microcomputer which refers to the total system built around the microprocessor chip. Microprocessors are also used for control purposes on many machines and appliances and domestic and industrial equipment.

microprocessor advantages, MPUs are particularly adaptable and versatile for control of processes, procedures, and machines. They eliminate the need for designing special-purpose logic to solve specific problems because they can be programmed, thus shortening design times, making changes easier, faster. Other advantages include the lower cost of standardized hardware and added flexibility in planning, operation, and control execution.

microprocessor cards, Typical microprocessor cards are often flexible, low-cost, self-contained 8-bit parallel processors and controllers. They are designed for computer-oriented equipment such as data terminals, test systems, communications equipment, machine tool controllers, process control systems, and peripheral device controllers. With them the system designer can have a proven, totally debugged processor that he may customize to his immediate application by programming rather than by hard-wiring. This technique can save considerable cost, both in terms of money and developmental time - in contrast to costly in-house-developed processors or controllers that use hard wired or permanent logic.

microprocessor unit (MPU), The primary part of a microcomputer, it consists of an ALU, arithmetic-logic unit, some main memory, usually for control, input/output interface devices, a clock circuit, plus buffer and driver circuits and passive-circuit elements. It does not contain power supplies or cabinet and is normally understood to be in a dual in-line package (DIP) and mounted on some type of circuit board.

microprogram, Refers to various programs that are often stored in ROM. A microprogram is often permanently burned into ROM and is unalterable in most cases. Examples of microprograms are video game programs and BASIC interpreters. EEPROMs are electrically erasable.

microprogrammable instruction, Instructions that do not reference main memory can be microprogrammed.

microprogrammed, As a general rule, a computer is microprogrammed if its control unit within the central processing unit (CPU) activates its circuits through microinstructions stored in the control memory, instead of through permanently wired circuitry.

microprogramming, A type of programming that became very popular with the introduction of micro and minicomputers and generally refers to computer instructions that do not reference the main memory. It is rather a technique to design subroutines by programming the very minute computer operations.

microsecond, One millionth of a second.

MIDAS, A digital simulated analog computing program.

middle punch, Same as 11 punch; also known as the "X" punch.

migration, A movement of atoms within a metal.

millisecond, Abbreviation msec. A millisecond is .001 (one thousandth) of a second.

minicomputer, A small digital computer not usually based on a single processor chip, which is larger than a microcomputer and smaller than a mainframe computer.

mirror writing/shadow reading, On some systems, the host computer treats two physical disks as a single logical unit and writes data on both. Reading on one or the other is done according to their respective angular positions, to shorten access time. This technique improves data reliability.

MIS (management information system), A communication process providing information for decision making which is fed back to top management of an organization.

misregistration, line, In optical character recognition, the unacceptable appearance of a line compared to an imaginary horizontal baseline.

missile, ballistic, A guided missile that is self-powered on the way up and becomes free-falling on the way down.

mission factor, A fraction calculated by dividing the number of documents in a file that haven't been retrieved by the total number in the file.

mistake, Generally taken as the use of faulty logic or faulty syntax in program.

mixed mode expression, An arithmetic expression within a program that contains operands of different types. For example, a statement might contain both real and integer type variables.

mnemonic, Symbolic name used for various operations and instructions and used to reference a particular register, certain memory locations, fields, files, and subroutines in a program.

mnemonic automatic programming, A computer programming system which allows for mnemonic expression.

mnemonic code, Code that assists people in remembering what things stand for, such as ACC for accumulation, NET for net pay, etc.

mode, alter, A mode of operation of a computer which permits altering to take place.

mode, analysis, A mode of computer operation in which program testing data or statistical data may be automatically recorded.

mode, binary, A mode in which operations use the binary number system, allowing use of 1 and 0 only.

mode, burst, A mode of communications between the computer and the input/output devices as contrasted with byte mode.

mode, byte, An alternate mode of communications between the computer and the input/output devices as contrasted with burst mode.

mode, command, The time when no program is active for a given terminal (in time-sharing).

mode, compute, Also called operate mode as contrasted with hold mode.

mode, conversational, A mode of operation of man-machine communication, generally from a terminal.

mode, freeze, Same as hold mode.

mode, hold, A mode in an analog computer in which variables are held at a current value; also called freeze or interrupt mode.

mode, interpretive, A mode of processing used for error tracing.

mode, job-program, A mode of operation in which job programs are limited to those sections of storage assigned by the executive (routine).

mode, load, A mode in which data has delimiters carried along with it.

mode, manual, A mode of operation in which automatic features are off and the computer accepts operator instruction.

mode, off-line, A mode in which devices are not hooked together.

mode, on-line, A mode in which all devices are hooked up to a computer.

mode, operate, Same as compute mode; contrasted to hold, freeze, or interrupt modes.

mode, simplex, A mode of communications operation of one direction only that can't be reversed.

mode, substitute, A method of exchange buffering (see buffer).

mode, supervisor, A mode of operation in which the supervisor program is in control.

mode, training, A mode used for the training of terminal operators.

model, A representation in mathematical terms or a pictorial representation of a system.

model, mathematical, The characterization of a process, concept, or object in terms of mathematics.

model, pilot, A model of a system that is not as complex as a complete model.

model, process, A model of a process.

modelling, The process of representing an object system or idea in some briefer form other than that of the entity itself.

models, utility, A model that is studied and restudied to improve the system.

modem, A communication device which alters data in digital form into wave form suitable for transmission over telephone lines and which carries out the reverse process when receiving data. Stands for modulator/demodulator.

modem, An abbreviation for modulator/demodulator.

modem, A MODulator/DEModulator connects communications systems and devices from the remote outlet to the near device or system converting the signals or pulses to the right codes to ready them for transmission in alternating current. At the receiving end a modem reconverts the signals to direct current for communications to the computer. In effect, from the computer it converts from digital to analog - and to the computer it converts from analog to digital.

modes, display, Modes such as vector, increment, character, point, etc., that indicate the manner in which points are displayed on a screen.

modes, time-sharing master/slave, In time sharing, the executive program can operate in master mode and the user programs operate in slave mode (under control).

modes, user, time-sharing, One of the following modes a user may be in: inactive, command, ready, running, waiting.

modification, A change in words or parts of words (in a computer).

modification, address, The process of changing an address in a computer instruction during the running of the computer program containing the instruction.

modification instruction, Changing the instruction prior to its execution so that it will perform differently than before.

modifier, A quantity used to change an address of an operand in a computer instruction.

modify, To alter a part of a computer instruction.

modular, A degree of standardization of computer components to permit combination and expansion.

modularity, The ability of a system to be expanded or changed with minimal difficulty.

modulate, In communications, conversion of signals to a standard.

modulation, dipole, A method of magnetization used in representation of binary digits on magnetic surfaces.

modulation, double, Modulation of one wave by another wave.

modulation factor, A percentage calculated by using heights (amplitude) of waves (such as signals).

modulation, frequency, In communications, the process for varying frequencies in a carrier.

modulation, phase, A variation of frequency modulation.

modulation, pulse, The use of a series of pulses to convey information.

modulation rate, The reciprocal of the units interval measured in seconds (expressed in bauds).

modulation, two phase, A method of phase modulation in which two significant conditions are different.

modulator/demodulator, A basic device that converts data from a digital form which is compatible with data processing equipment (parallel) to an analog form that is compatible with transmission facilities (serial-by-bit) and vice versa.

module, A module is any independent unit which is part of a larger system. Microcomputer and other similar systems may be made from several modules.

module, A piece or segment of a whole; an incremental block.

module, control output, A device that can store computer commands and translate them for control purposes.

module, load, A computer program developed for loading into storage and being executed whose output is a linkage editor run.

module, program, A set of program instructions treated as a unit by a translator, loader, etc.

module, source, A set of source language statements in a machine-readable form.

modulo-two sum gate, Same as gate, exclusive OR (see gates).

MOL (machine-oriented language), Synonymous with assembler language and contrasted with problem-oriented language.

molecule, A group of atoms.

monitor, Most often this is the screen of a cathode ray tube (CRT). Monitors are usually used with microcomputers. Consequently, people who buy a home computer or personal computer may buy a monitor to go with it. With most home computers, the domestic television set can be used as the monitor.

monitor control dump, A memory dump that may be specified in the job control information.

monitor, job-processing, Computer programs that are processed by computer routines contained in the monitor system. The processes may include compilation, assembly, loading, executing, etc.

monitor, operating system, A software system (an operating system) that controls the operation of a computer system.

monitor program, A supervisory computer program (not related to high-density TV).

monitor, real-time, The monitor program in a real-time system.

monitor routine, Same as the supervisory routine or supervisory program.

monitor system, time-sharing, A collection of programs remaining in memory to provide coordination and control of the total system.

monolithic, A single silicon substrate in which an integrated circuit is constructed.

monostable, A device that has only one stable state.

Monte Carlo, A type of simulation method that uses random numbers to determine the evolution of a system.

monte carlo method, A trial and error method of repeated calculation to reach the best solution.

morpheme, A basic element of language relationships, e.g., the relation between a noun and verb.

morphology, A specific branch of linguistic study.

mother board, Often considered the main printed circuit board (PCB) in a computer. Other printed circuit boards plug into the mother board so that power and electronic signals can be conducted among the boards.

mouse, A hand-held object with rollers on its base used to control the cursor position on the screen. The typical mouse is rolled across a flat surface, and this produces a corresponding movement in the cursor on the screen.

move, To copy data from one storage location in main memory to another.

MPS or MPU, Acronyms for Microprocessor System and Microprocessor Unit.

MPU applications, The microprocessing unit (MPU) performs the central control function of a microcomputer, and its architecture determines the eventual applications for which the system is best suited. Some MPUs are especially oriented toward the process control and data communications fields; others are designed for alarm functions, games, calculators, and thousands of other purposes. Some guiding characteristics for superior systems are maximum power, versatility, system throughput (operating speed) and design ease.

multiaccess computing, More than one identical input/output terminal attached to a system.

multidrop line, A circuit that interconnects several stations.

multifile sorting, The sequencing of more than one file automatically without operator intervention.

multipass sort, In various sort programs many passes of the data are required to complete the process.

multiple access, A capability of a system to send or receive (input and output) from many locations.

multiple precision, Using two or more computer words to represent a single quantity.

multiple programming, Programming that allows two or more operations to be executed at the same time.

multiple station, high-speed communications, The number of high speed stations that can be connected to a CTS (communications terminal station) over DDD (direct distance dialing) network circuits.

multiplex, Refers to the act of combining input signals from many sources onto a single communications path, or the use of a single path to transmit signals from several sources.

multiplex data terminal, A data transmission device that modulates and demodulates, encodes and decodes between two or more I/O devices and data transmission stations.

multiplex, time division, The connection of more than one terminal to a common channel (see time division).

multiplexer, A device that receives input signals from various sources and combines them into a single transmission, sending the signals out over one line. In some cases, the multiplexer receiving the signals then reverses the process by separating the signal components from the stream and redistributing them to their respective destinations.

multiplexer, data channel, Allows multiple data break capability (see data break).

multiplexing, byte, A process of delegating time to input/output devices to use the channel to get information into main memory.

multiplexor terminal unit, A unit used to connect multiple terminal stations to and from the central processor of a computer.

multipoint circuit, A circuit that interconnects several that must communicate on a time-shared basis.

multiposition controller, A controller that has two or more discrete values of output.

multiprecision arithmetic, A form of computer arithmetic in which two or more computer words may be used to represent each number.

multipriority, A queue of items (of different priorities) waiting to be processed.

multiprocessing, The use of two or more computer processing units in the same system at the same time.

multiprocessing interleaving, The special process of addressing storage modules that are adjacent to an even/odd method.

multiprocessing, mass-data, A large system in which all types of data are handled in a multiprocessing environment.

multiprocessing sharing, Communication between two computer processors; the sharing of storage, a control unit, or other devices.

multiprocessing system, A system of two or more interconnected computers that perform specialized functions.

multiprocessor, overlapping, A processor capable of determining whether its current operand and next instruction are in different storage modules.

multiprogramming, A system with the ability to effectively process programs concurrently.

multiprogramming, degree of, The number of transactions that can be handled in parallel in a multiprogramming system.

multiprogramming efficiency, Reduced turnaround time, increased computations per dollar, and other efficiencies of multiprogramming.

N

N, May stand for a number of terms such as nano, number or number of bits.

N/C (numerical control), A method of machine control by paper or plastic tape containing digital instructions.

NAK, See NEGATIVE ACKNOWLEDGEMENT.

NAK, negative acknowledgement, The control character that the receiving terminal of a data transmission sends to the transmitting terminal to indicate that a transmission error occurred in the last data block sent. The transmitting end then resends the data block to correct the error. In ASCII, the NAK character is represented by the ASCII Code '021.'

name, data, A word or group of characters identifying an item of data, a tag or a label.

name, file, A set of characters (name) assigned to identify a file, e.g., PAYRL for payroll, etc.

name, procedure, A label used to refer to a catalogued procedure.

name, record, A name assigned to a record in a file of data.

name, variable, The alphanumeric name assigned by a programmer to represent a variable in a computer program.

nanosecond, One thousand millionth of a second.

nanosecond, One billionth of a second, same as billisecond.

nanosecond circuit, A circuit with a pulse rise or fall time measured in billionths of seconds.

narrow band line, A communication line similar to a voice grade line but operating on a lower frequency.

NASA, An abbreviation for National Aeronautics and Space Administration.

natural language, A language whose rules reflect current usage rather than prescribed usage.

natural language processing, The capability of a computer to understand everyday language, such as English.

NDRO, Stands for Non-destructive Read Out.

negation element, A device capable of reversing a signal, condition, or state to its opposite.

nest, A subroutine or block of data embedded in a larger unit.

nest of subroutines, The situation in which one subroutine calls another and that perhaps calls another, etc., each time returning to the calling subroutine.

net, data, A standard name of a device that can be used for production control, data collection, and sending information or data over a phone line.

network, Basically, a system in which terminals and computers are linked together according to such factors as the distance between them, the amount of message traffic expected between them, and the existence of appropriate communications facilities needed to connect them. In some networks there are alternate paths (communication links) from every computer or terminal to every other.

network, analog, An arrangement of circuits representing physical values to express mathematical relationships through electric or electronic means.

network analyzer, An analog device that is used to simulate electrical networks.

network, awareness, The condition in which the central processor of a computer is aware of the status of the network.

network, computer, Two or more interconnected computers.

network drills, The final level of testing in a real-time system by which an entire network is tested.

network load analysis, A listing of characteristics such as volumes of documents, frequency of processing, and special time requirement in a station to station message sending environment.

network, packet, Systems in which groups of bits including data and control elements called packets, are switched and transmitted as a composite whole, in a specified format, each packet with its own address being dropped off or switched as it travels along its specified route.

network, private telephone, A network (leased) operated by the customer.

network, ring, A network in which terminals and computers are linked together in a circular pattern with each being connected to the two closest to it, one on each side, in the circle.

network, sorting, A device used for sorting data. In these networks, data is inputted into the network in an 'unordered' spatial relationship and output from the network sorted into a specific spatial order.

network types, Most basic are: dedicated, dial, multipoint, multiplexer, data concentrator, distributed, and centralized. The groups within these might be: star, loop or ring, and hierarchical.

network, value-added, Those that accept raw data and perform some special service such as preprocessing and with timesharing networks, special routing such as packet systems, or types with special branching, or some types of intelligence reporting.

new input queue, A queue (waiting line) of new messages waiting to be processed.

nibble, Half a byte. More specifically, a nibble is a string of 4 bits seen as a unit.

node, Any terminal, station, or communications computer in a computer network.

noise, Generally, any disturbance which would tend to interfere with the normal operation of a device or system. Also, spurious signals which can introduce errors in the transmission of data.

noise, carrier, Residual modulation, i.e., undesired variations in frequency in a signal.

noise, interference, Noise or some other disturbance in data transmission which may result in errors or in the loss of data.

noise, types, (1) Extra bits that must be ignored, (2) errors introduced into data in communications channels, (3) random variations of current, and (4) loosely, any disturbance.

nominal bandwidth, The maximum range of frequencies, including guard bands, assigned to a channel. Only the range between the guard bands is usable for data transmission under most circumstances.

nondeletable, Refers to a message or portion of the screen that scrolls off the top of the screen, but can be called to be redisplayed by a specific command.

nondestructive read, A reading process that does not erase the data in memory.

number, base, Same as radix. The number of characters available for use in a numbering system.

number, binary-coded decimal, A number consisting of successive groups of four binary digits (e.g., 0110 1001 1010).

number, complex, The combination of a real number and an imaginary number.

number, control, A number used to compare results to prove accuracy of a process or problem.

number, hexadecimal, A number whose place values are based on powers of 16 (see hexadecimal digit).

number, mixed-base, Same as mixed-base notation.

number, mixed-radix, Same as mixed-base number.

number, positional, A number of which each successive position (right to left) has a higher value.

number, radix, Same as the base number of a numbering system.

number, random, A number selected at random from an orderless set of numbers.

number, self-checking, A number with an extra digit on the end that is used for checking purposes as in credit card numbers.

number, sequence, A number assigned to an item to show its relative position in a set of items.

number sequence, pseudorandom, A sequence of numbers that is random enough for statistical purposes.

number, serial, The number that is unique to a machine and identifies it as a serial number on a car engine.

number, sexadecimal, Synonymous with hexadecimal number.

number, statement, A number assigned to a computer program statement to allow reference to it from other parts of the program.

numbering, serial, Numbering items with successive numbers such as paychecks, purchase orders, etc.

numeral, A digit or digits used to represent a number.

numeral, binary, A set of digits that represents a quantity written in binary form (all 1s and 0s).

numeralization, Use of digits to represent alphabetic data.

numeric, Composed of numerals.

numerical analysis, The study of methods that may be used to obtain solutions to mathematical problems and of the potential errors in such solutions.

numerical control, The control of machine tools or drafting machines through servomechanisms, tapes, and/or control circuitry.

numerical tape, A punched paper or plastic tape used in numerical control (N/C).

numerical word, A word containing only numeric digits.

numerically controlled machine tools, Computer controlled machinery in manufacturing.

O

object code, The code produced by a compiler or assembler (after translation from source code) in computer programming.

object computer, The computer that executes the object program, as contrasted with source computer.

object language, As the output after a translation process, usually object language and machine language are the same, i.e., direct use languages.

object machine, The computer that the object program will be executed on (may be different than the source machine or computer).

object module, Refers to the output of a compiler or assembler which contains a program module in instruction form and also control information to guide the linkage editor.

object phase, When the target program is run (see target program).

object program, A program that has been translated into machine language and is ready to be run.

object program, A computer program that has been translated from a source language into machine language or an intermediate language.

objective, design, The planned performance goal or expectations, i.e., standards to be met.

OCR (optical character recognition), Using photosensitive (optical) devices to sense (read) characters.

octal, A numbering system that uses the base, or radix, of eight. The symbols used in the octal system are the digits 0, 1, 2, 3, 4, 5, 6, and 7. The octal numbering system was widely used in earlier computers but is seldom used in computers today.

octal, binary coded, A system of representation of octal numbers where binary numbers represent each octal digit.

octal digit, A digit in the octal numbering system, 0, 1, 2, 3, 4, 5, 6, or 7.

octet, Eight binary digits considered as a unit, such as an 8-bit byte.

octonary, Pertaining to the number system of the base 8 (see octal).

odd parity, A type of parity checking in which the parity bit's value is set to make the total number of on bits in the byte odd.

OEM-Original Equipment Manufacturer, Firms that purchase components or semifinished equipment to add to its product before distribution to various markets, such as firms that purchase microprocessors to add to their weighing scales, refrigerators, etc.

off premise, Equipment or data in a location other than the computer installation.

off-demand system, A system in which information is available at the time it is requested.

office, central, A common facility that performs switching in a communications network.

offline, Generally output not directly connected to the computer and, therefore, not under the control of the central processing unit (CPU)

off-line mode, A mode in which devices are not hooked together.

off-line processing, Processing done by equipment not under computer control.

off-line storage, Storage that isn't under control of the central processing unit of a computer.

on, sign, The instruction(s) the user begins with at a terminal to begin communication with the system.

one address, A method of machine instruction in which each instruction describes one operation and involves one storage location. It is synonymous with single address.

online, Refers to a procedure which is under the direct control of the central processing unit (CPU). This condition usually allows data to be processed immediately, as opposed to batch processing.

on-line adapter, A device that permits a high speed computer memory to computer memory linkage.

on-line data reduction, Processing data as rapidly as it is generated by the source.

on-line, debug, Debugging while the computer is performing on-line functions.

on-line diagnostics, The running of diagnostic routines while a system is on-line.

on-line mass storage, Mass storage devices that are available to the computer system (connected) for processing.

on-line mode, A mode in which all devices are hooked up to a computer.

on-line operation simulated real-time, The processing of data in a system along with a physical process so that the results of the data processing are useful to the physical process.

on-line processing, Processing done by equipment under computer control.

online storage, Usually refers to secondary storage devices that are under direct control of the central processing unit (CPU) such that data is available immediately when required.

on-line typewriter, A typewriter device connected to a computer.

onomasticon, A special vocabulary of proper or special names (a list of titles).

op code, The part of an instruction that indicates to the computing equipment what function to perform.

op register, A computer register used to hold the operation code of computer instructions.

open ended system, A system in which the input data are taken from sources other than a computer (in optical character recognition).

open shop, A computer installation in which any qualified individual may operate the computer as contrasted with closed shop.

open-ended system, Generally, a system which permits new programs, instructions, subroutines, modifications, terms, or classifications to be added without disturbing the original system.

open-loop control system, A control system without feedback as contrasted to closed loop.

operand, The item on which an operation is performed.

operand types, Any quantity resulting from or entering into an operation (in a computer) or the address portion of a computer instruction.

operate mode, Same as compute mode as contrasted to hold, freeze, or interrupt modes.

operating delay, Computer time loss due to operator error.

operating ratio, The ratio of the number of hours of correct machine operation to the total hours of scheduled operation.

operating system, Basically a collection of routines, usually software or firmware, used in overseeing the input, and output processing, of a computer's program. The tasks of an operating system include: compilation, interpretation, debugging, input/output, garbage collection, memory allotment, and file management.

operating system, disk (DOS), A versatile operating system for computer systems having disk capability.

operating system, monitor, A software system (an operating system) that controls the operation of a computer system.

operating system, Pick, A machine-independent operating system named after its developer, Dick Pick.

operating system, piggyback, An operating system that runs as a task of another, different operating system. This enables a program to be run on a computer system whose operating system is other than that which the program was written for.

operating system routines, A collection of integrated service routines used to control the sequencing of programs by a computer. It is synonymous with monitor system and executive system.

operating system supervisor, The part of the operating system that is the supervisor program.

operation, An action specified by a computer instruction or the process of executing an action.

operation, auxiliary, An operation performed by equipment which is not controlled by the central processing unit (CPU).

operation, full-duplex, Communication between two points in both directions at the same time.

operation, half-duplex, A communications circuit that operates in only one direction at a time.

operation, independent, An operation that does not directly affect another operation.

operation, iterative, Using automatic repetition, e.g., repeating the same computing process but with different values.

operation, jump, An operation in which the computer departs from the sequence of instructions and "jumps" to another program, routine, or instruction in the same program.

operation, logic, Non-arithmetic operations performed by a computer, such as compare, branch, etc.

operation, loop, A set of instructions that are modified prior to each entry to the loop.

operation overhead, Same as housekeeping.

operation, parallel, The use of two or more operations or data lines at the same time.

operation part, The part of a computer instruction that specifies the kind of operation to be performed.

operation, peripheral, Operation, not under computer control, of input/output devices.

operation, polar, Circuit operation where the flow of current is reversed as electrical pulses are transmitted.

operation ratio, The proportion of the total time that equipment is operating to the total number of hours scheduled.

operation register, Same as op register.

operation, scatter write, Getting data from one place but transferring parts of it to several output areas.

operation, scheduled, Time used by the computer that has been planned (for productive work).

operation, sequential, The performance of operations one after another.

operation, serial, An operation in a computer in which the digits are handled sequentially.

operation use time, The time that equipment is in actual use (not all the time it is turned on).

operation, variable cycle, Action in which any cycle may be of different length (in a computer).

operational label, Procedure in which tape files are identified by a label for the computer operator's information.

operative limits, The range of conditions within which a device can operate without damage.

operator, (1) Designates the operation to be performed, (2) a person who operates a computer or other machine.

operator command, An instruction issued by a computer operator to the control program in a computer.

OPM, An abbreviation for operations per minute.

optic fiber, Optic fiber consists of a core surrounded by a cladding of lower optical density. Light entering the core at a sufficiently shallow angle with respect to the core axis will be reflected back into the core, travelling through the core until it emerges at the other end.

optical character reader, A device that can read information directly from a source such as a sheet of paper by sensing the locations of the marks in the paper.

optical character reader, videoscan, A unit that combines an optical character reader with mark sensing and card reading.

optical character recognition (OCR), The reading of information directly from paper using optical character readers.

optical character recognition (OCR), Using photosensitive (optical) devices to sense (read) characters.

optical communications, Also called light wave communications (see fiberoptics).

optical display keyboard, A display control device whose keys may be covered with owner-specified overlays for particular jobs.

optical display terminal, A terminal composed of an alphameric keyboard and a video screen.

optical document reader, An input device that can read characters on documents.

optical fiber characteristics, Optical fibers in general consist of a core of dielectric glass surrounded by a cladding of another material of (generally) lower refractive index. The material composition, core size, cladding thickness, etc., are design-parameters that influence the attenuation and dispersion characteristics of the system. Silica fibers currently show lower losses, but various forms of glass fibers and plastic-cladded fibers have some advantages in manufacturing.

optical journal reader, A specific optical reader that can provide input to a computer from journal tapes that can be output from adding machines, cash registers, etc.

optical mark page reader, A device that can read 8-1/2" by 11" paper with marks on it.

optical mark reader, An input device able to read and interpret marks on special input documents.

optical reader, A device that can sense (read) data optically from cards or documents.

optical scanner, bar-code, An optical scanning device that can read documents coded in a special bar-code.

optical scanning, Machine recognition of a character by its image.

optical type font, A font that can be read by both people and machines.

optima, alternate, Different solutions to the same optimization problem.

optimization, A method of continual adjustment to obtain the best set of conditions.

optimize, A procedure for removing inefficiencies and unnecessary instructions to make the program as short and as fast as possible.

optimizing control action, Control actions that seek the most advantageous value and maintain it.

optimum code, Computer code that is especially efficient.

optimum coding, Generally, the coding of a routine or program for maximum efficiency with regard to a particular aspect, such as reducing either retrieval time or execution, depending on the priority.

optimum merging patterns, A method of processing that minimizes the total number of merge passes needed to create a single file.

optional word, A Cobol programming language word that improves readability.

options, prewired, Optional equipment on the processor of a computer.

optoelectronics, Many consider this a technology that defies definition. Its many categories encompass the sciences of semiconductor wafer processing, glass tube fabrication, chemistry, and a score of others in such divergent areas as light-emitting diodes, incandescent bulbs, cathode ray tubes, liquid crystals, gas-discharge tubes, photo-conductive materials, etc.

OR (operations research), Using analytical methods to solve operational problems.

order, (1) an arrangement of elements or events, (2) to sequence or arrange in a series, and (3) the position of a digit in a number.

order of merge, The number of input files to a merge program

ordering bias, The degree to which data items are already in order (such as alphabetical or numerical order).

organization, data, The arrangement of data in a data set or file.

organization, file, The way a file is set up (e.g., sequential, random, etc.) or the best way to organize a file of data based on its method of use.

organizing, The ability of a system to arrange its structure.

origin, An address in a computer used for relative addressing.

original language, The original form (source form) of a computer language before it is processed (translated).

origination, data, The creation of machine readable data from some other form.

OS, The abbreviation for Operating System.

oscilloscope, An instrument used to show changes in voltage. It is used in equipment error detection, etc.

outconnector, A flowchart symbol showing a place on the flowline that will be continued somewhere else.

outer face, The side of magnetic or paper tape that does not contact the mechanism to read or write or punch (in contrast to inner face).

output, Refers to data which has been processed and is then made available to the user, perhaps through a printer or display screen, or put onto tape or disk for storage.

output area, A specified section of computer storage reserved for data that goes out of a computer (to a printer, tape drives, or other device).

output block, Synonymous with output area.

output data, That data that is "put out" (output) from a device or system.

output device, The machine unit that is capable of presenting computer output.

output, direct, Output, printed, visual, etc., from on-line output equipment. It is directly connected to the computer.

output equipment, Any equipment used to transfer information out of a computer.

output, indirect, Output that is obtained from an off-line device instead of directly from the computer.

output limited, The situation in which the output speed is the limiting factor. Other parts of the system have idle time while waiting for the output.

output, types, (1) Results from the computer, (2) information transferred from internal memory to another device, or (3) any signal, data, etc., coming out of a device.

output work queue, Output from computer jobs that are in line to be printed or communicated into final form.

output writer, A service program that moves data from the output queue to an output device.

output, zero, The output from a magnetic cell in the zero condition.

output-bound, A device is said to be output-bound if it outputs data at a slower rate than data is being input to it. For example, a computer that is attached to a slow printer is output-bound if data can be entered at a faster rate.

outside loops, Loops that are larger and on the "outside" of other loops in computer programming.

overflow, Occurs when an operation produces results that are too large for a register or storage area in a computer.

overflow indicator, An indicator that turns on when an overflow occurs, such as a number generated that is too big for a register (see indicator).

overflow position, An extra position in a computer register that can develop an overflow digit.

overhead, Generally, overhead is the amount of processing required to finish a certain task.

overlapping, Two operations or parts of operations taking place at the same time.

overlapping multiprocessor, A processor capable of determining whether its current operand and next instruction are in different storage modules.

overlay, (1) Using the same area of storage during different times in processing, (2) bringing a computer program routine into memory in place of (on top of) another.

overlay segments, Overlaying (replacing) one program segment with another.

overlay supervisor, A computer program routine that is used to control the overlaying of parts of computer programs.

overlays, memory, Putting information "on top of" other information in memory effectively replacing it.

overload, A condition caused by saturation of one or more parts of the computing element in an analog computer.

overload level, The limit of a system or component reached when it stops operating properly due to overheating, damage, or some kind of failure causing condition.

overload simulator, Used to test a device by creation of an artificial condition of overload or overflow.

overloads, Rate of input so concentrated into the computer that messages cannot be processed on a real-time basis (see real-time).

overprinting, Printing on top of other printing or printing in an area outside of the specified area.

override interrupt, A group of power on/off interrupts that have highest priority.

own coding sorting, Coding provided by a computer programmer that is used in combination with the sort coding.

oxide shed, The loss of particles of oxide on magnetic tape during its use.

P

PA, An abbreviation for paper advance.

PABX, Stands for private automatic branch exchange.

pack (noun), Generally refers to a magnetic disk or assembly of such disks.

pack (verb), To compress data so that it required less space in memory or other storage media.

pack, disk, A removable, portable set of magnetic disks (in layers) that contains information and may be put on a disk drive attached to a computer.

pack, tape, The way tape is wound on a reel; a good "pack" has a uniform wind and is free of cinching and layer to layer adhesion.

package, debugging (DDT), A versatile, sophisticated, on-line debugging set of routines.

package, program, A group of logically related programs.

packed decimal, A packed decimal is a decimal stored in a packed format in order to save storage space and reduce handling overhead.

packed decimal, Storing two digits in a storage area that usually stores a letter or special character.

packet, In communications, a short (1000-2000 bits) block of data prefixed with addressing and other information for control that is used to carry information through a packet-switching network.

packet switching, In data communications, packet switching is a method of sending data from one computer or terminal to another. In this method, data is sent in packets of fixed length with each packet being sent separately.

packing density, The number of units of information in a length, e.g., units per inch.

packing density, file, The ratio of available file storage space to the amount already stored in the file.

packing, sequence, A procedure used in packing data in an accumulator (squeezing 3 words of data into the accumulator).

pad, To fill in a unit of data such as a block with zeros or other fillers.

padding, Filling out a block of information with dummy records.

page, A block or unit of fixed length of memory. In low-cost microcomputers, a page is commonly 256 bytes.

page boundary, The point where one logical page of memory ends and the next logical page begins.

page boundary, The (computer) address of the first unit (bytes or word) in a page of memory.

page density, It is the percentage of a page that is covered by text. An average page has about 40 percent of its page devoted to text. The rest is empty space.

page printer, A unique printer that composes a full page before printing, such as xerographic and CRT printers.

page reader, An optical character reader that possesses "pages" of documents.

pagination, The process of breaking up a printed report into units corresponding to pages.

paging, Breaking a program and data into fixed blocks.

pair, binary, A circuit capable of assuming either one of two stable states (synonymous with flip-flop, with bistable multivibrator, and with bistable trigger circuit).

pair, trigger, A bistable circuit.

panel, control, (1) A removable board that can be wired to control operation of equipment; same as plugboard, (2) also a console (see console).

panel, graphic, A master control panel that graphically displays with lights, etc.

panel, maintenance control, A panel of lights and switches used by repair men.

panel, operator's control, The panel containing all the switches, lights, and indicators for computer operation.

panel, touch, A touch-sensitive screen that is mounted onto the face of a CRT. Allows users to input a choice of options to the computer by simply touching a location on the screen.

panel, wing, A panel that is added on sides of existing panels.

panic button, A slang term that suggests a "magic" button needs to be pressed to save a panic situation.

paper, coordinate, Continuous form graph paper used for printout on an XY plotter.

paper, safety, A special kind of paper used in checks (money) to prevent counterfeiting.

paper slew, A high speed printer skip (see printer skip).

paper slewing rate, The rate at which blank paper can be physically moved through the printer or the rate that output can be driven over the allowable range.

paper tape, A paper strip in which data is stored in the form of punched holes and other machine sensible forms.

paper tape, chadless, Perforated tape with the chad partially attached to permit interpretive printing to the tape.

paper tape channels, Information channels, e.g., 8-channel tape has 8 channels of code position.

paper tape, punched, Paper (or plastic) tape into which data is recorded by punching holes into prescribed.

paper tape reader, A device that senses (reads) holes that are punched in paper tape.

paper throw, The distance paper moves in a printer when it is further than normal line spacing.

paper-advance mechanism, Two sets of sprocketed tractors in a printer.

parabolic interpolation, A method associated with numerical control of a machine tool.

paragraph, A group of logically related sentences.

parallel, Having the same direction or occurring at the same time.

parallel access, Simultaneous access to all bits in a storage location comprising a character or word. It is the same as simultaneous access.

parallel arithmetic, Arithmetic operations in a computer where all digits of a number are operated on simultaneously as contrasted with serial arithmetic.

parallel computer, A computer in which data are processed at the same time (in parallel); as contrasted with serial computer.

parallel flow, A system of operations in which several are taking place at the same time.

parallel operation, The use of two or more operations or data lines at the same time.

parallel processing, Operation of a computer in which two or more programs are executed concurrently.

parallel running, The running of an old system and a new system (to test the new system) at the same time.

parallel search storage, Same as associative storage.

parallel storage, Storage in which characters or digits are processed simultaneously in parallel.

parallel transfer, All bits in a string are transferred at the same time in parallel.

parallel transmission, A method of transmission in which a block of bits are sent at the same time.

parallelism, Concurrent operations in several parts of a computer system.

parameter, A variable that is held constant during a particular application.

parameter, A quantity that may be assigned different values.

parameter, program, A parameter that is incorporated into a subroutine during computation.

parameter statement, A statement used to assign values to variables at compile time or translation time.

parameter testing, Using a parameter to test to insure that input produces the expected output.

parameter word, A word in a computer program subroutine used to specify certain data or conditions.

parametric, Of, using, or containing parameters.

parametric subroutine, Same as dynamic subroutine.

parametron, A special device composed of two stable states of oscillation.

parity, A checking feature of a computer based on counting bits (see parity bit).

parity bit, Parity can be even or odd. If a bit pattern has an odd number of bits in an even parity machine, the parity bit will be "turned on" (set to one) and vice versa. This method is used to permit internal checking in data transfer (see bit).

parity check, horizontal, A checking procedure counting bits along a horizontal direction to compare them with a previous count (see parity).

parity check, longitudinal, A parity check made in a longitudinal direction as opposed to vertical (see parity check).

parity error, A machine detected error in which a bit or bits are lost.

parity, even, The count of binary ones is an even number (see parity bit).

parity, odd, The count of binary ones is an odd number (see parity bit).

parity, storage, Parity checking during data transfer from one storage to another storage device.

parity, tape, The parity checking feature used in magnetic and paper tape data transfer.

parse, To break down the components of a sentence into parts of speech.

parsing, language theory, To break down the components of a sentence into structural forms.

part, operation, The part of a computer instruction that specifies the kind of operation to be performed.

partition, A segment of a computer's main memory set aside for a particular use.

partitioning, A fixed method of allocating available memory in which each computer device is given its own permanently allocated portion of the computer's memory.

partitioning, The process of subdividing a block (of storage) into smaller units.

parts programmer, A computer programmer that programs the physical machining of a part.

PASCAL, A computer language that is a generalization of ALGOL. PASCAL allows for many different types of data.

Pascal attributes, A language designed to enable teaching of programming as a systematic discipline and to do systems programming. Based on the language, Algol, it emphasizes aspects of structured programming. Pascal has risen in popularity in the early 1980s to become a favorite of tens of thousands of programmers, product designers, microcomputer users.

Pascal, Blaise (1623-1662), A French mathematician who built a digital calculating machine in 1642.

pass, (1) To move magnetic tape past a read head, (2) a machine run or completion of a cycle.

pass band, A range of frequencies attenuated less than one-half the midfrequency power value.

pass, sorting, One access of each of a series of records.

passive components, The components that play a static role in circuits and systems.

password, A set of characters used for identification in communications with a computer.

patch, A series of instructions used to correct an error or make a change.

patch bay, A concentrated assembly of electrical tie points.

patch routine, A computer program correction or change made at execution time.

patchboard, A removable panel that can be wired to control machine functions.

path, A logical course or line.

path, critical, The longest path of several paths of activity in project completion.

path, magnetic, The route followed by magnetic flux lines.

path, main, The principal line of direction in a computer program; the main logical direction.

path, sneak, An undesired electrical path in a circuit.

pattern, bit, The possible combination of bits used to represent data (number of possible patterns) (see bit).

pattern recognition, The recognition of shapes and patterns by a machine.

pattern sensitive fault, A fault that responds to a particular pattern of data (see fault).

patterns, optimum merging, A method of processing that minimizes the total number of merge passes needed to create a single file.

paycheck run, The processing that prints payroll checks.

payroll data file, master, The file in which payroll required information for each employee is contained, such as number of dependents, deduction amounts, etc.

payroll register, The document that contains employee payroll information including net pay.

PBX (Private Branch Exchange), A telephone exchange on a customer's premises that is also connected to the public telephone network.

pc board types, Printed circuit boards can be classified in many ways. Simple, complex, combinational logic, sequential logic — these are types of boards typically tested. All of these can be tested because all the logic components are readily understood and accessible. Recent LSI boards and devices caused some changes in testing procedures.

PCB, See PRINTED CIRCUIT BOARD.

PCM-pulse code modulation, Modulation of a pulse train in accordance with a specific code, now widely used in transmission as well as for digital sounds in entertainment systems.

peak flex density, A maximum magnetic condition of magnetic materials.

PEEK, A BASIC or other language command on many computers that allows users to find out the contents of a specified location in the computer's memory.

pen, light, A pen-like device used with a cathode ray tube (television-like device) to modify or change a display.

pen travel, The length of the path that a pen moves from one end of a scale to another.

penumbral, The headings that are partially relevant to the data being sought.

perforated paper tape, The recording of data by punched holes in a paper tape.

perforated tape, A tape (generally pape) on which data is recorded in the form of punched holes.

perforator, tape, A tape (generally paper) on which data is recorded in the form of punched holes.

performance evaluation, An analysis of accomplishments compared to initial objectives.

performance period, The time a device is to operate.

period, digit, The magnitude of the time interval between signals that represent consecutive digits.

period, performance, The time a device is to operate.

period, regeneration, Same as scan period.

period, reporting, The time period covered in a report.

period, retention, The time that records are kept before they can be destroyed.

period, sampling, The time interval used from the sampling is based on points in time.

period, scan, The length of time a screen is swept by an electron beam to regenerate or restore the image.

period, warm-up, The time needed after energizing a device, before its rated output is reached.

period, word, The amount of time (interval) between signals representing digits.

periodic dumping, time-sharing, A feature in which dumps (copies) of user files are placed on a backup medium to be saved.

peripheral, Generally input/output devices in a computer system.

peripheral control switching unit, A unit which permits any two processors to share the same peripheral devices.

peripheral control unit, A control unit that links a peripheral device to the central processor or to another peripheral unit.

peripheral controls, Regulates the transfer of data between peripheral devices and the central processor.

peripheral equipment, Refers generally to any unit of equipment, distinct from the central processing unit (CPU), which may provide the system with outside communication or storage.

peripheral interrupt, A stop resulting from a peripheral device completing a task or signaling of readiness for a task.

peripheral operation, Operation, not under computer control, of input/output devices.

peripheral processor, A second processor in a computer system.

peripheral transfer, A process used to transfer data between two peripheral devices.

peripheral types, The mechanical and electrical devices, other than the computer itself, found in a computer system. Peripherals include terminals, tape units, disk units, and printers.

permanent dynamic storage, Storage in which the maintenance of data doesn't depend on a flow of energy such as magnetic disk, drum, etc.

permanent fault, A fault that repeatedly occurs as contrasted with intermittent or sporadic faults (see fault).

permanent memory, Memory that retains information when the power is removed, same as non-volatile memory.

permanent storage, A media or device capable of retaining information such as ROM cartridges, punched paper tape, etc. It also refers to nonvolatile storage.

permutation, Any of a number of possible changes in form or position in a group.

permutation index, An index that lists all the words in a title so that each word appears as the first word, followed by the others (many entries per title).

permuted index, Same as permutation index.

persistence, The length of time a fluorescent screen holds an image.

personal computer, A microcomputer used, for example, in homes, schools, or offices to perform a wide variety of tasks or capabilities, including game playing, word processing, control functions, and business calculations.

personal computers, video- and cassette-based, Some users have a TV set as an output display, a full alphanumeric keyboard for input, and an audio cassette for program storage and exchange. Video-based systems provide full user to system interaction at minimal cost. The speed of system response is practically instantaneous. Operations may be performed in almost complete silence. Reliability is enhanced as electromechanical mechanisms are often limited to the keyboard and cassette recorder. Data media storage density is increased with audio cassettes and small disks.

personal computing, The use of a computer (usually a microcomputer) by individuals for applications such as education, game playing, business calculations, word processing, and entertainment.

personality cards, Inside some PROM programers, a microcomputer tailors the program to the PROM the development team has decided to use. A programmer often directs the data to be stored through "personality" cards that provide the appropriate timing patterns, voltage levels, and other requirements. The programmer is partitioned so that new personality cards can be inserted as new PROMs are developed.

PERT, An abbreviation for Program Evaluation and Review Technique.

PERT/COST system, A computer program designed to facilitate planning, scheduling, control, etc., of research and development projects.

PERT/TIME, A Pert program that allows planning, scheduling, and evaluation of projects.

PF, An abbreviation for page footing.

PH, An abbreviation for page heading.

phantom channel, A communications channel that has no independent conductive path.

phase, execute, The part of a computer operation cycle when an instruction is being performed.

Phase Modulation (PM), A variation of frequency modulation.

phase, object, When the target program is run (see target program).

phase, run, When the target program is run (see target program).

phase shift, A change in time relationship of one part of a signal waveform with another, with no change in the basic form of the signal. The degree of change varies with frequency as a signal passes through a channel.

phase shift, The time between the input and output signals in a control unit, circuit, etc.

phase sorting, Sorting done in three phases, initialization, internal, and merge phases.

phase, target, The running of a target program; called the run phase or the object phase.

phone, data, A generic term describing a family of devices used in data communications.

phoneme, The smallest unit of speech that distinguishes one utterance from another.

phones, standard data, Standard telephone company data sets used in data processing.

phonetic system, A system using equipment that can act on data from a voice source and having a voice-grade output.

phosphor dots, Elements in a screen of a cathode ray tube (CRT) which glow.

phosphorescence, A property of emitting light after the source of excitation is removed, e.g., in CRT's.

photocathode, The electrode in an image orthicon which emits the electron image when struck by light.

photocomposition, A procedure in typesetting that uses a computer and a film recording system and develops a photo on a CRT.

photoconductor, Material which varies its electrical conductivity under the influence of light.

photoelectric reader, A device that reads data photoelectrically (light through the holes).

photographic storage, Any storage using photographic processes.

photogravure, A method of printing in character recognition.

photomicrography, The process of making a large photograph of a much smaller original.

photo-optic memory, A memory unit that uses an optical medium such as film.

phototypesetting, Setting type from computer outputs to photographic film.

physical end, The last statement in a computer program or the last data record in a file.

physical record, The data between and beginning and ending boundaries of a record.

physical stimulation, Design and use of models of physical systems.

physical system time, The ratio of computer time to the problem time in simulation.

physical systems simulation, In analog or digital computers, a development representation of physical systems, such as a chemical process.

PI codes, Program indicator codes used for program selection.

pica, A unit of measure (approximately one sixth of an inch) used in printing for horizontal measuring.

picofarad, One millionth of one millionth of a farad. (See farad.)

picosecond, One-trillionth of a second.

pictorial, A "picture" of specifications, layouts, headings for formats.

pictorial data representation, Representation on graphs, charts, maps, etc.

Picturephone, A trademark of the AT&T Co. to identify a telecommunications service that permits the user or group of users to see as well as talk with persons or gatherings at the other end of phone lines, e.g., two-way TV over phone lines.

piece work programming, Charging for a program by accomplishment rather than an hourly rate.

piezoelectric crystal, A crystal that converts mechanical pressure into an electrical signal or vice versa.

pilot, An original or test program or a test signal in communications.

pilot model, A model of a system that is not as complex as a complete model.

pilot synchronizing, A signal used to maintain synchronization of the oscillators of a carrier system.

PIN-Personal Identification Number, Often assigned by banks to customers who wish to debit/credit their accounts or to make purchases, as designed to be entered (keyed) by the customer shielded from other's vision.

pipeline, instruction, The instruction pipeline is the direct information channel through which machine instructions pass from macro to micro level.

pitch, A measure of the horizontal density of letters, i.e., 10 pitch indicates there are 10 characters per inch.

pixel, A single element of resolution on a screen. A pixel or 'picture element' is the smallest portion of the screen which the computer can address as an individual unit.

pixel types, The basic element of a TV picture derived through various types of scanning processes. Joystick or other type cursors allow analysts to point to any pixel (minute point), and treat it as a single bit for further, usually computer, manipulation.

PL/1, A programming language that has the capacity both to solve complicated numerical problems and to manipulate complicated data files.

place, A position in positional notation of numbers.

place, digit, The position of a digit in a number.

place value, The position of digits in a number in any positional value numbering system.

plan; decision, A procedure used for making management decisions.

plasma display, Flat panel plasma displays becoming an alternative to CRTs due to the advantage in many cases of the flat screen they provide, their compact size, readability, low power consumption, inherent memory, and long life.

platen, The platen is the part of the printer, either a plate or a cylinder, responsible for supporting the paper on which information is printed.

platen, pinfeed, A platen that moves paper in a printer with "pins" engaging in the holes on the edges of the form.

playback head, A reading head. (See head.)

plot, To map or diagram; to connect points.

plotter, A device that can be controlled by a computer to draw graphs, etc.

plotter, ink, A device which outputs pictures and text from a computer onto paper by means of one or more ink pens in holders whose movements are controlled by the computer.

plotter mechanical resolution, Refers to the shortest line a pen plotter is mechanically capable of drawing. This is contrasted with addressable resolution, which is the shortest line a user can command the plotter to draw. Mechanical resolution should be as high as, and preferably higher than, addressable resolution. Otherwise the plotter would be accepting commands that it is incapable of performing.

plotter, pen, A hard-copy output device that uses ink pens to provide high-resolution hard copies. Although pen plotters can be slow and require a high degree of user interaction, they provide draftsman-quality graphics, low initial cost, wide selection of paper size, and extremely low cost per copy.

plotter, pen speed, The maximum speed the pen in a pen plotter can achieve. Pen speed is measured in inches per second (ips) and, for small plotters, varies between 12 and 20 ips; large format plotters achieve approximately 35 ips.

plotting, The process of drawing a graph and/or placing information on it.

plotting, automatic, The drawing of a graph under computer direction (control).

plotting board, That surface of a plotting machine on which the curves, graphs, charts, etc., are displayed.

plug board, A control panel or wiring panel inserted into a data processing machine to control its functions. (See board.)

plugboard, Generally, a panel containing a rectangular array of holes into which plugs are inserted to control the operation of equipment. Wires with a plug at each end are connected from hole to hole to form circuits.

plug-in unit, A set of electronic components that can be plugged in or out easily.

plugs, cordless, A connector with no flexible portion (no "cord").

point, binary, The arithmetic point that separates the whole from the fractional part in a binary number (similar to decimal point in a decimal number).

point of no return, The point in a program run in which a rerun is no longer possible.

point, radix, Same as base point.

point, re-entry, The address of the first instruction in the main program to be executed after a subroutine has been completed.

point, re-entry, The computer instruction by which a routine is re-entered.

point, rerun, A point in a computer program at which a rerun may start.

point, restart, One of several points in a computer program at which a restart or rerun may begin.

point, set, A specific and desirable value for a quantity being controlled.

point, summing, A point at which signals are added.

point, switching, That point where signals change from one position to another.

point, variable, The point (such as decimal point) in a number.

pointer, Usually an address of a record that is to be found.

pointer, virtual memory, Pointers or lists used to keep track of program segments in virtual memory.

points per frame display, The measurement of minimum and maximum flicker free points on a CRT.

point-to-point transmission, Data transmission between two points.

POKE, A BASIC or other program command on many computers that allows you to store a particular quantity in a specified location of the computer's memory.

POKE statement, One of the most popular statements in the Basic language, causes the computer to change part of its own program in the manner commanded by the programmer or user, a "self-modifying" feature but a risky one that can lead to crashes.

polarization, In optics, making light vibrate in a definite plane; in electronics, the direction of an electric vector.

polarization diversity, Transmission methods used to minimize fading of components of a radio signal.

poll, A method in which communications lines are "asked" in a sequence if they want to transmit.

polling, Refers to a technique by which each of the terminals sharing a communications line is periodically interrogated to determine whether it has some data to transmit or to locate a free channel.

polling, See poll.

polyester, As related to magnetic tape, an abbreviation for the base film material polyethylene glycol terephthalate.

polymorphic system, A system capable of assuming various forms.

polyphase, A sorting technique that permits use of either an odd or even number of magnetic tapes.

polyphase merging, A technique used in a sort program.

polyvalence, The property of being interrelated in many ways.

polyvalent notation, A method of describing salient characteristics.

pop, A procedure to remove an item from the top of a stack. When an item is removed from the top of the stack, it can be thought of as moving every other item up one position.

port, An output in a processor where a peripheral or communications link plugs in or which interfaces a program.

portable, Generally, describes software which can be executed on many different types of computers without major conversion problems. Also, refers to small, lightweight computers which can be easily moved and used in different locations.

portable computer, A microcomputer that can be taken almost anywhere because it is small, lightweight, and powered by a rechargeable battery pack and/or an AC adapter cord. Some are called 'lap top;' others, (larger) 'transportable.'

positional notation, Place values varying in a number based on a digit's relative position in the number.

positional number, A number in which each successive position (right to left) has a higher value.

positional representation, See positional number.

POS-Point of Sale, The thousands of retail terminals being installed in the U.S. and many foreign countries that often scan the UPC (Universal Product Code) bar codes on packages to ascertain the price and provide printed descriptive receipts to customers, while also automatically updating store records; also used in other cash or transaction points of operations.

post, To enter information on a record.

post billing system, A system in which the customer bills (invoices) are sent after the order has been shipped.

post editing, An editing procedure on the output of a previous operation.

post installation review, An examination of procedures and operation of a system after the original installation.

post mortem, A slang term relating to analysis of an operation after it is completed.

post-mortem dump, A dump (printout of the contents of storage) at the end of a computer run.

post-mortem routine, A computer program routine run after an operation is completed for analysis purposes.

postmultiply, To multiply one matrix (of numbers) by another matrix.

postprocessor, Generally, a program responsible for performing various final operations on data already processed. For example, a postprocessor prepares data for printing.

postulate, To assume something without proof.

potential, The degree of electrification of a body.

power amplifier, A circuit that amplifies both voltage and current.

power consumption, Maximum wattage used by a device in its operating range.

power dump, The removal of all power.

power level, The level of power in a transmission system compared to a reference level of power (expressed in dbm or dbw).

power, mathematical, The number of times a number is multiplied by itself.

power of a number, An exponent.

power supply, Most power supplies refer to the circuitry within a hardware unit responsible for converting electrical power into the voltages required for the unit's electronics.

power surge, A sudden, usually undesirable, voltage or current change in an operating circuit. Surges are generally caused by a shorted circuit component or the collapse of a magnetic field.

power-fail interrupt, A design in which only a priority interrupt can interrupt a nonpriority interrupt routine and the power-fail is the highest priority interrupt.

pragmatics, A study of practical use as contrasted to theoretical or idea.

preanalysis, An initial review of a task prior to change.

prebilling, Preparation of an invoice prior to shipping of the goods.

precautionary errors, Warning messages printed during computer program compilation.

precision, The accuracy to which a quantity is correctly represented or expressed.

precision, double, Precision obtained by coupling two computer words to represent one number in fixed-word-length computers.

pre-compiler program, A computer program run before a compile to detect some errors.

predefined process, A process that has been specified by name prior to its use.

predefined process symbol, A flowcharting symbol used to represent a subroutine.

pre-edit, To edit data before computation.

prenormalize, Normalizing operands of an arithmetic operation before performing it.

preparation, data, The process of preparing data into a machine readable medium.

preprocessor, A program responsible for preparing data for further processing. For example, preprocessors may arrange data into different formats, organize it into groups, and perform similar operations on it.

preread head, An additional read head encountered before the read head of a device. (See head.)

prerecorded tracks, Tracks on magnetic media containing timing or permitting word and block addressability.

preserve, To retain as contrasted to clear (in computer storage).

preset, To set a variable to an initial value in a computer program.

presort, The first part of a sort.

pressure transducer, A type of pressure-sensitive device that emits a greater current of electricity as the amount of applied pressure is increased. Pressure transducers are used in robotics as obstacle and weight sensors.

presumptive instruction, A computer instruction that is or can be modified.

preventive maintenance (PM), Periodic maintenance of equipment to prevent potential machine problems.

preventive maintenance contracts, The arrangement between the customer and manufacturer for periodic maintenance of equipment.

preventive maintenance time

prewired options, Optional equipment on the processor of a computer.

primary storage, Generally the fastest storage in a computer system, i.e., internal memory (contrasted with auxiliary storage).

primary storage unit, The main memory unit of a digital computer, usually consisting of a high-speed direct-access unit with moderate storage capacity.

primitive, The most basic or fundamental unit of data such as a single digit or letter.

print bar, Same as type bar.

print control character, A control character used to control printer feeding, spacing, etc.

print member, A print bar, type bar, or wheel, or other element that forms the printed character.

print positions, The number of characters that can be printed on a line by a printer.

print restore (PR) code, A code when encountered that causes a printer to resume printing.

print timing dial, A control knob on a printer.

print wheel, A single element in a wheel printer.

printed circuit, A circuit in which interconnecting wires have been replaced by conductive strips printed, etched, etc., onto an insulating board. It also includes resistors, capacitors, diodes, transistors, and other circuit elements that are mounted on cards and interconnected by conductor deposits.

printed circuit board, Generally, an insulating board onto which a circuit has been printed or etched.

printer, Basically, an output device which converts electronic signals from a computer into a permanent form readable by humans, called hard copy, by printing the information onto paper.

printer, band, A type of line printer that uses an embossed steel band to form the letters printed on the paper.

printer, bar, An impact printer which prints fully formed characters, one line at a time, by striking type bars against an inked ribbon and paper.

printer, braille, A printer that "prints" braille characters.

printer, chain, A printer that uses a chain mechanism for printing.

printer, character, Character printers print one character at a time, unlike line printers which produce an entire line print in one operation. Character printers are slower than line printers but can offer better quality printing.

printer, daisy-wheel, One of the main types of impact printer. Daisy-wheel printers print fully formed characters, one at a time, by rotating a circular print element composed of a series of individual spokes, each containing two characters, that radiate out from a center hub. Daisy-wheel printers are often used with word processors.

printer, dot, Same as matrix printer

printer, dot-matrix, A printing device that forms each character from rows and columns of dots. A matrix is an array of items organized into rows and columns. For example, a 5 x 7 printer forms characters 5 dots wide and 7 dots high.

printer, drum, An impact printer which prints a line of fully formed characters by striking an inked ribbon and paper against a rapidly rotating drum. The drum contains a complete set of embossed characters that circle it at each print position, forming a row of As, Bs, Cs, Ds, etc., across its surface.

printer, electrostatic, A high-speed printer that uses charged pins to form character matrices on chemically treated paper.

printer, electrostatic, A device used for printing an optical image on paper.

printer, electrothermal, A high-speed printer that uses heated elements to create characters as matrices of small dots on heat-sensitive paper.

printer, ink-jet, A printer which forms characters by spraying a fine jet of precisely directed ink onto the paper. It is almost silent in operation.

printer, keyboard, A device in communications with keyboard input and printed output operating at speeds related to the common carrier service available.

printer, laser, A non-impact printer which uses laser beams to form dot-matrix characters on a photoconductor. The characters are then transferred to paper, one page at a time.

printer, letter quality, A letter-quality printer uses type elements of sufficiently high quality that the output looks as though it came from a typewriter.

printer limited, The relatively low speed of the printer is holding up the processing.

printer, line, A computer printer in which an entire line is composed and printed.

printer, matrix, A wire printer that prints a matrix of dots for characters.

printer, page, A printer that produces a page at a time as opposed to a character or a line at a time.

printer, serial, A printing device that prints one character at a time as a typewriter does.

printer skip, Lines are skipped on a printer as designed or as programmed.

printer, thermal, A dot-matrix printer that forms characters by pressing hot wires onto special paper. A thermal printer does not use ink or ribbons.

printer, thimble, One of seven main types of impact printer. Thimble printers produce fully formed characters by pressing a print element, shaped like a thimble, against an inked ribbon and paper. The thimble contains two rows of characters and rotates and tips up and down to print the characters required.

printer vertical tab, A machine function that causes the print mechanism or cursor to move to a specific line while staying in the same column.

printer, wheel, A printer that has type face mounted on wheels or discs.

printer, wire, A type of printer that forms characters by forcing a set of wires against the ribbon or paper.

printer, wire-matrix, An impact printer which prints dot-matrix characters, one at a time, by pressing the ends of certain wires against an inked ribbon and paper.

printer, xerographic, A device used to print an optical image on paper.

printing, detail, A listing of each record as contrasted to group printing.

printout, Computer output printed on paper or other media.

printout dynamic, A printing that occurs during a computer run instead of after as contrasted with static printout.

printout, memory, Same as a memory dump.

printout static, This sort of printout doesn't occur at the same time as other operations, but afterwards.

priority, The order in which a sequence of events will take place. A high priority item coming before a low priority item.

priority interrupt, The levels of priority assigned to various interrupts. (See interrupt.)

priority limit, The upper bound to a priority list.

priority, multi-programming, The levels of priority assigned to functions in a multi-programming system.

priority ordered interrupts, The levels of priority; may be over 200 priority ordered interrupts in some time-sharing computers.

priority rules, The rules followed in determining priorities for interrupts. (See interrupt.)

priority selection, Selection of the next job to be run based on available facilities and the priority of the job.

priority switch table, A specific table in computer storage that contains the status of devices operating in interrupt mode.

private, In communications, a line leased for a customer's exclusive use.

private automatic branch exchange (PABX), A dial exchange that provides private telephone service within a company and also connection to the public telephone network.

Private Automatic Exchange (PAX), A private telephone service within an organization, not connected to the public telephone network.

Private Branch Exchange (PBX), A telephone exchange on a customer's premises that is also connected to the public telephone network.

private circuit, Same as private line.

private line, A line leased for exclusive use by one customer.

privileged instructions, Computer instructions that can only be executed in the supervisory state (when the supervisor routine has control).

probability, A long range or historical record of experience used for prediction.

probability theory, A theory pertaining to the likelihood of chance occurrences of events or elements.

probable error, A statistical term related to standard error.

problem, A set of circumstances or situations in which a solution to a condition is sought.

problem, benchmark, A problem used to evaluate the performance of computers (compared to each other).

problem, check, A problem used to see if a computer or program is working properly.

problem definition, Identifying the elements of a problem in an organized way.

problem input tape, A magnetic tape or punched paper tape containing problem data to check out a computer system.

problem language, A source language used for a particular class of problems.

problem program, A computer program designed to solve a specific problem.

problem, structured design, An approach to problem solving using a set of guidelines, techniques, and special symbols to determine a set of interconnected modules or procedures, organized in a hierarchical fashion that will resolve a certain problem.

problem, test, A problem used to check out a computer program.

problem time, In simulation, the time interval between events in the physical system.

procedural and exception tests, Tests are designed to check machine control and operations.

procedural testing, The testing of alternative human actions in a system; distinguished from hardware or software testing.

procedure, A step-by-step method of problem solution.

procedure analysis, An analysis of a business activity to determine precisely what must be accomplished and how.

procedure, by-pass, A procedure used to get the most vital information into a main computer when a line control computer fails.

procedure, control, Consists of administrative control of job schedules, workflow, computer usage records, data and program libraries, etc.

procedure name, A label used to refer to a catalogued procedure.

procedure, recursive, A procedure that calls itself or calls another procedure that calls the first one again (in the computer).

proceed-to-select signal, The signal returned in response to a calling signal that indicates that selecting information can be transmitted.

process, A generic term that may mean to compute, assemble, compile, generate, etc.

process, batch, a sequential processing procedure where items are held to be processed in a batch.

process bound, Generally refers to a program or system that spends most of its execution time in calculations and operations rather than input or output procedures.

process chart, A flowchart of the major steps of work in process. It is synonymous with flow-process diagram. (See flowchart.)

process control, industrial, Computer controlled processes in many industrial applications.

process control loop, Control devices linked to control a phase of a process.

process control system, A system in which a computer (generally analog) continuously controls a process automatically.

process, iterative, A process for reaching a desired result by repeating a series of operations that comes closer and closer to the desired result.

process, predefined, A process that has been specified by name prior to its use.

process time, Time available for processing of data in the computer as contrasted with time needed for input and output.

processing, Handling, preparing, manipulating, computing, and otherwise operating on data.

processing, background, Work that the computer handles when work of a higher priority doesn't require parts of the computer's resources.

processing, batch, A technique used where items are collected into groups prior to processing on a computer.

processing, centralized data, Processing (at one location) all data involved with a given activity.

processing, concurrent, Processing more than one program at a time on a computer.

processing, continuous, On-line or real-time processing as contrasted to batch processing.

processing, conversational, Processing in a conversational mode (man-machine communication from a user terminal).

processing, data, A general term referring to all activities related to data preparation, the processing of data, the production of reports; also refers to the functions of classifying, sorting, calculating, recording, etc.

processing, deferred, Processing that can be delayed, i.e., is considered low priority.

processing, demand, The processing of data as fast as it becomes available.

processing, information, The processing of data and analysis of its meaning.

processing, in-line, Processing of data in a random order (as transactions come).

processing, integrated data (IDP), A system that treats all data processing requirements as a whole.

processing, interactive, A mode of processing in which the computer is updated almost instantaneously. There is generally some form of dialogue between the system and its operators.

processing, interrupt, A feature in a real-time system that permits interruption of batch processing programs to allow for processing of real-time transactions.

processing, list, A special technique used in computer programming that uses list structures to organize storage.

processing, off-line, Processing done by equipment not under computer control.

processing, on-line, Processing done by equipment under computer control.

processing, overlap, Two operations being performed at the same time.

processing, parallel, Operation of a computer in which two or more programs are executed concurrently.

processing, random, The processing of records in an order other than that in which they are stored.

processing ratio, Calculation time related to total available time.

processing, real-time, A mode of processing data in which the computer is updated almost instantaneously rather than after the next batch of work is processed.

processing, real-time results, The processing of data fast enough so that the results affect the process being controlled or monitored.

processing, remote, The processing of data received from remote locations.

processing, sequential, Processing of information or data in the same order that they occur.

processing, serial, Processing of one item after another, one at a time.

processing, stacked job, The automatic transition from job to job on the computer with little operator intervention (or none).

processing unit, The part of a computer that performs arithmetic and logic functions.

processor, A microprocessor or central processor, usually a single microelectronic chip or chip set.

processor, attached support (ASP), Using multiple computers (usually two) that are connected to increase the efficiency of processing many short duration jobs.

processor, central, The part of a computer that contains arithmetic, logic, and control capabilities.

processor, graphics, Those computer hardware and software systems that follow and interpret operator commands that provide stored symbol information and integrate all instructions and commands to develop displays of charts, graphics, line drawings, etc.

processor, input/output (IOP), A unit that handles control and sequencing of input/output.

processor, language, A program which translates symbolic instructions to machine code. There are three types of language processors: assemblers, compilers, and interpreters.

processor, operating, (1) The unit in a computer system containing logic and control. (2) A program that translates other computer programs.

processor, peripheral, A second processor in a computer system.

processor, satellite, An additional computer used to support a larger processor (computer) to further increase productivity.

processor, storage relocation, A computer program routine used to relocate (put in a different place) computer programs during processing.

processor unit, central (CPU), Same as Central Processing Unit.

processor verbs, Verbs used by a language processor that do not cause action at object time.

processor-error interrupt, This interrupt occurs when there is a check bit error or an addressing error in the memory of the computer.

production control, A system that provides information for management of a production line process to improve production.

production run, The actual processing run to accomplish an objective as contrasted with a test run.

program, Basically, a set of instructions the system follows in order to carry out certain tasks.

program address counter, Same as instruction counter.

program, assembly, Same as assembler.

program, background, A program with a relatively low-priority level. Background programs will not be executed until higher-priority programs have finished being executed.

program, background, A computer program that is a lower priority than another program (foreground program) and has to wait its turn to use the computer.

program, blow up, A program is said to have blown up if it ends unexpectedly because of a bug or because it encounters data conditions it cannot handle.

program checkout, The process of determining that a computer program is performing as expected for all conditions.

program compilation, The process of compiling (translating) a high level computer programming language into machine language.

program, computer, A series of instructions usable by a computer to solve a problem or accomplish an objective.

program, control, A computer program that prescribes the action to be taken by a system, device, computer, etc.

program control transfer, The transfer of operational control from one computer program to another.

program counter, A computer register that contains the identification of the next instruction to be executed.

program debugging, The process of finding and correcting errors in a computer program.

program default, The assumption that will be made by a program if a contradicting statement is not made by the programmer. In other words, a variable will take in a default value unless a different value is specifically assigned to it.

program, device driver, A software package that controls the timing and operation of external devices.

program, diagnostic trace, A special diagnostic program used to trace the intermediate step-by-step operations in a program.

program, diagnostics, A computer program used to check malfunctions and locate the problem.

program documentation, Information about a computer program to aid programmers and computer operators and others.

program execution control, The control function involved in interrupt processing.

program file, A system designed to maintain (keep up to date) the entire software library (all the computer programs).

program flowchart, A flowchart showing the sequence of instructions in a computer program. (See flowchart.)

program, foreground, The computer program that gets priority treatment delaying progress of a background program.

program, heuristic, A computer program that simulates the behavior of humans in approaching similar problems.

program, incomplete, A computer program (routine) that is not complete by itself (a subroutine, subprogram, etc.).

program, internally stored, The computer program (set of instructions) that is stored in computer internal memory as contrasted with those stored on ROMs, magnetic tape, etc.

program interpreter, A program which translates a high level source code into machine language. Unlike a compiler, which produces an object program to be run later, the machine language produced by an interpreter is executed immediately.

program, interpretive trace, A computer program that is used to trace or check another program in an interpretive mode.

program interrupt, To stop the running program in such a way that it can be resumed at a later time, meanwhile permitting some other action to be performed.

program language, (1) A language used by programmers to write computer programs, routines, etc. (2) A language other than machine language used to write computer programs.

program, librarian, The computer program which provides maintenance of library programs used in an operating system.

program library, The set of computer programs and routines that are available for use or the media on which they are stored.

program line, An instruction on one line of a coding sheet; same as code line.

program, loader, A program which loads another program into memory. Loaders are often used on programs which are ready to be run.

program loading, In general, reading a computer program into memory prior to program execution.

program loading, initial (IPL), The initial entry of an operating system or program into computer memory.

program loop, A series of computer program instructions that are repeated a number of times.

program, macro-assembly, A language processor that translates macro instructions.

program, main, The primary processing computer program as contrasted with a routine or subroutine.

program maintenance, The process of changing computer programs when necessary.

program, master control, The computer program that controls all phases of job set up, directs all equipment functions and flow of data, directs the operator, etc.

program, micro, A program of computer instruction subcommands.

program module, A set of program instructions treated as a unit by a translator, loader, etc.

program, object, A computer program that has been translated from a source language into machine language or an intermediate language.

program package, A group of logically related programs.

program parameter, A parameter that is incorporated into a subroutine during computation.

program, partial, A program that is incomplete by itself.

program, portable, A program that is machine-independent, i.e., which can be used on more than one type of machine.

program, pre-compiler, A computer program run before a compile to detect some errors.

program, problem, A computer program designed to solve a specific problem.

program, recognizer, A program that determines whether a particular program is valid according to the rules of the specified language.

program, record control, The computer program used for input/output processing that is file oriented rather than device oriented.

program reference table, A section of storage used as an index for operations, subroutines, etc.

program register, Same as instruction register.

program, relocatable, A program that is written so it can be located and executed from many areas in memory.

program, resident, A program that resides permanently in the storage unit of the central processing unit (CPU).

program selection, Switching from one job to another in the computer.

program, self-modification, The ability within a computer program to change its own instructions prior to execution. It may be done repeatedly.

program sensitive fault, A fault that responds to a particular sequence of computer program steps. (See fault.)

program sensitive malfunction, A malfunction that occurs only during execution of a particular program sequence.

program simulator, A computer program used as an interpreter to permit programs written for one computer to be run on a different kind of computer.

program, snapshot, A specific computer program used to trace output on certain selected instructions of another program.

program sort/merge, A computer program used to accomplish the sorting and merging on magnetic tape or disk, a generalized program.

program, source, A program written in a high-level programming language (such as BASIC) which must be translated into machine language before it can be executed by the computer.

program, specific, A computer program used to solve one problem, generally used only once.

program specification, A program used to design precise definitions of logic of routines and routine segments.

program, standard, A computer program written in a standard language which provides a standardized solution to a problem.

program, star, A program designed by a programmer and checked so there are no mistakes, i.e., it should run the first time on the computer.

program statements, A computer program is made up of program statements (instructions).

program step, A single operation, one computer program instruction.

program stop, Using a computer program stop instruction to stop the computer under certain conditions.

program storage, The internal computer storage used to store programs, routines, and subroutines.

program, storage print, A computer program used to print the contents of storage. (See dump.)

program, stored, Instructions are kept in a computer's internal memory for execution in the same form that data is kept. A program can be designed to alter itself as required when stored in this way.

program, stored, Refers to a computer program that is in storage and ready to use.

program, stroke analysis, A method used to identify characters by dissecting them into prescribed elements. The sequence, relative positions, and number of detected elements are then used to determine the specific character.

program, subject, Same as source program.

program, supervisor, The part of the control program of the operating system that coordinates the use of resources and maintains the flow of operations for the central processing unit (CPU) of the computer.

program, supervisory, Computer programs used to control specific functions. (See supervisor, program test supervisor, etc.)

program switching interrupt, Refers to the switching to and from programs and the interrupt processing some programs and does other related activities.

programmer analyst, A person who is skilled in computer programming and problem definition and solution.

programmer, parts, A computer programmer that programs the physical machining of a part.

programmer, systems, A person who plans, generates, maintains, extends, and controls the use of an operating system to improve overall productivity of the installation.

programmer, systems, The person who writes operating systems and other systems programs (instead of applications programs).

programming, The process of creating a computer program for problem solution.

programming, automatic, The process by which a computer automatically translates a 'source' program, in programming language, into an 'object' program, in machine code. This is accomplished by an assembler or compiler loaded into the processor's memory.

programming, automatic, Techniques such as compiling and assembling computer programs.

programming, dummy variable, A dummy variable or dummy argument is a variable that is used as a spaceholder and type specifier in the definitions of subprograms. Dummy variables inform the computer how many arguments the subprogram will take, and specify the data type of these arguments. When a subprogram is called, the dummy arguments are replaced by the actual arguments used in the calling statement.

programming, dynamic, A mathematical procedure for optimization of a multistage problem solution used in operations research and systems analysis.

programming, file-oriented, When the input/output computer instructions are file oriented as opposed to device oriented.

programming language, automatic (APL), A programming language using mathematical notation (IBM).

programming language, PL/1, A computer programming language that has some features of Fortran and some features of Cobol, plus others.

programming, minimum access, Programming so that minimum waiting time is needed to obtain information from storage.

programming, multiple, Programming that allows two or more operations to be executed at the same time.

programming, piece work, Charging for a program by accomplishment rather than an hourly rate.

programming specifications, Generally refers to a document detailing the precise programming steps that must be taken to create a given application.

programs, control, Specialized computer programs that contain routines that would otherwise need to be included in each program.

programs, conversion, Computer programs used to convert other computer programs from one system to another.

programs, standard procedures, Computer programming methods set by the computer manufacturer.

programs, support, Computer programs that support or aid the supervisory programs and applications programs, such as diagnostics, data generators, etc.

programs, systems, The computer programs generally provided by the manufacturer to perform systems functions.

PROM, An acronym for Programmable Read-Only Memory, which is a computer memory that can be programmed once, but not reprogrammed or adapted. Exception, EPROM erasable types.

PROM attributes, (1) Programmable Read-Only Memory is generally any type that is not recorded during its fabrication but which requires a physical operation to program it. Some PROMs can be erased and reprogrammed through special physical processes. (2) A semiconductor diode array that is programmed by fusing or burning out diode junctions.

PROM programmer (microprocessor), The typical use of erasable PROMs that plug into "prototyping" boards for programming, generally through the use of a special keyboard that is part of the programmer device.

proof listing, A listing of a computer program or data that is used for check out purposes.

proof total, One of many totals used to check calculations.

proof, zero, The procedure of adding plus and minus values (to get a zero result) in verifying accuracies of totals.

propagation delay, The time needed for a signal to travel from one point to another on a circuit.

property, A characteristic quality.

proportional band, A range of values of a condition that is usually expressed by engineers in terms of percentage of instrument full-scale range.

proportional control, A control technique in which the action varies linearly as the condition being regulated varies.

proportional controller, A controller that only produces a proportional control action.

proportional, directly, Two quantities increasing or decreasing together at a constant ratio as contrasted to inversely proportional.

proposal, A statement of how a company or group provides equipment and/or programs to solve problems for a customer.

prosign, precedence, A group of characters that indicates (to communications personnel) how a message is to be handled.

PROSPORO, A fill-in blanks process control system.

protect, memory, A feature that protects certain parts of memory from user access.

protect, storage, A computer hardware function in which sections of storage are protected against destruction, i.e., nothing can replace the information in those areas.

protected files, Files having file security. (See file security.)

protected location, Storage locations available only to specific users (others cannot get access to it).

protection, asterisk, Printing asterisks (*) in front of dollar amount as in paychecks.

protection, file, A hardware or software device to keep sections of memory (computer) protected by preventing writing into it.

protection key, The use of indicators to allow access to sections of memory and deny access to all other parts of memory. It is related to storage protection and memory protection.

protection, storage, Protection against unauthorized writing in and/or reading from all or part of a storage device by means of codes, special programming, or instructions.

protection, storage, Preventing sections of storage contents from being replaced.

protocol, A relationship between modules or procedures in different communications systems or workstations which define the rules and formats for the exchange of messages.

protocol, networks, A set of conventions between communicating processes on the format and content of messages as well as the speed to be exchanged. In sophisticated networks higher level protocols may use lower protocols in a layered fashion.

protocol types, When it is desired to establish communication between processes in hosts processing different speeds, word lengths, architecture, operating systems, access controls, etc., users must deal with factors requiring the development of a higher level of protocol for a very large number of pairs of processes. The development of such protocols is still in a stage of relative infancy, although quite a few have been implemented.

proving time, Time used to insure that no faults exist in a machine (after repair).

psec, An abbreviation for picosecond, one trillionth of a second.

pseudo language, An artificial language.

pseudocode, An imitation of actual computer instructions. Instead of using symbols to describe the programming logic steps, as in flowcharting, pseudocode uses a structure that resembles computer instructions.

pseudorandom number sequence, A sequence of numbers that is random enough for statistical purposes.

PTS (Program Test System), A system that automatically tests programs and produces diagnostics.

PTT/8, An 8-level paper tape code.

public, Provided for general use (relates to telephone use).

public switched network, Any system that provides service to many customers such as TELEX, TWX, telephone, etc.

pulsating, dc, Electric current that flows in one direction and varies in intensity.

pulse, A change in intensity or level (related to electricity).

pulse amplitude, The maximum instantaneous value of a pulse.

pulse, clock, On pulse used for timing purposes.

pulse code, A code made up of patterns of pulses.

pulse code modulation (PCM), Signal is sampled periodically, and each sample is quanticized and transmitted as a digital binary code.

pulse, commutator, A special pulse used to mark, clock, or control a binary digit position in a computer word.

pulse, data, An electronic signal sent by the disk-drive head to create a tiny magnetic field on a disk.

pulse, digit, A particular pulse corresponding to a one digit position in a computer word.

pulse duration, The length (in time) of a pulse.

pulse, electric, A momentary rise or fall in voltage level.

pulse modulation, The use of a series of pulses to convey information.

punch, automatic, A punching device that automatically punches data processing cards or tape under the control of electrical or electronic signals.

punched paper tape, Paper (or plastic) tape into which data is recorded by punching holes into prescribed places.

punched paper tape channels, The parallel information tracks along the length of paper tape.

punch-EL, A special punch to indicate the end of a paper tape record.

purge, To remove unwanted data or records from a file.

purification, data, Processes used to reduce errors in data prior to introducing it to a data processing system.

push, A process to put an item onto the top of a stack. When an item is inserted at the top of the stack, it can be thought of as pushing the other items down one position.

push button switching, A switching system in which the operator can select the outgoing channel.

push down list, In a list of items, an item entered in the first position "pushes down" in position all the items in the rest of the list as contrasted with push up list.

push down queue, A last (record) in, first (record) out method of queuing.

push down stack, Access on a last in, first out basis.

push down storage, A technique used in which data enters at the top register and information is pushed down from register to register.

push up list, In a list of items, an item is entered at the end of the list and all other items remain in the same relative position as contrasted with push down list.

push up storage, A technique in which the next item of data to be retrieved is the oldest, i.e., been in the queue the longest.

pushdown dialing, Same as push button dialing.

putaway, A computer memory location used to store specific information.

Q

Q test, A comparison test between two or more units of quantitative data.

QCB, An abbreviation for Queue Control Block.

QED (text editor), A text editor computer program.

QTAM-queued telecommunication access method, Provides the capabilities of BTAM plus the capability of queued messages on direct access storage devices, may be employed for data collection, message switching, and many other teleprocessing uses.

quad, A group of four, e.g., four conductors (electrical).

quaded cable, A cable having conductors in groups of four.

qualifier, A name used to "qualify" another name; similar to an adjective in English grammar.

quantification, To give numerical values to the measurement of an item.

quantity, A constant, variable function or expression; a number or value.

quantity, re-order, In inventory, the amount of stock that is ordered when the re-order level is reached.

quantity, scalar, A quantity having magnitude but not direction as contrasted with a vector quantity that has both magnitude and direction.

quantity, variable, A quantity that may assume different values.

quantity, vector, A quantity that has both magnitude and direction.

quantization, The subdivision of a range of values into a finite number of subranges.

quantization uncertainty, A measure of uncertainty related to information loss.

quantize, Same as quantization.

quantizer, The device that converts analog data into digital form (synonymous with digitizer).

quantum, A unit of processing time.

quantum clock, A device that allocates a quantum or processing time (in time-sharing).

quartz crystal, A piezoelectric crystal that regulates an oscillator frequency.

quasi-instruction, Same as pseudo-instruction.

query, A request for data (in a time-sharing system).

query language, A class of English-like languages that allow non-programmers to inquire about the contents of a database and receive fast responses.

query station, The unit of equipment where inquiries are made for requests for data.

queue, Generally refers to a list of items in which additions are made at one end of the list and deletions are made at the other. A queue is like a waiting line - first come, first served. Queues are also called First-In-First-Out, or FIFO, lists.

queue, (any) sequence, A line of items (jobs) on a computer system waiting to be processed. Any sequence means they can be removed from the waiting line without regard to how they entered it.

queue discipline, The methods selected to determine order of service in a queue, e.g., LIFO (last in, first out), or FIFO (first in, first out), etc.

queue, FIFO, First in, first out, which means the first item is processed first; same as push-up list.

queue, input work, The line of jobs to be submitted for processing.

queue, LIFO, Last in, first out; that means the latest arrival is processed first; same as push-down list.

queue, new input, A queue (waiting line) of new messages waiting to be processed.

queue, operation, A waiting line; generally refers to a group of messages, jobs, etc., waiting to be processed.

queue, output work, Output from computer jobs that are in line to be printed or processed into final form.

queue, push down, A last (record) in, first (record) out method of queuing.

queue, push up, Same as FIFO queue.

queue, sequential, The first-in, first-out method of queuing items that are waiting in line for the processor.

queue, task, The queue (waiting list) that contains the task control for the system.

queue, work in process, Items that have been partially processed and are "queued" (waiting in line) to be completed.

queuing, A study of the patterns in waiting lines.

queuing, message, The control of the waiting line (queue) of messages to be processed (in communication).

queuing theory, A probability theory used in studying delays and the waiting in line of people or things.

quick disconnect, A type of connector shell that permits very quick locking and unlocking of connector parts.

quick-access memory, A part of memory that has a relatively short access time.

quick-access storage, Same as high speed storage.

quiescent, Generally concerns an inactive circuit or system. A quiescent circuit is one which at the time is not experiencing an input signal. A quiescent computer system is a system that is either inactive and waiting for input or a mainframe system whose activity has ceased by not allowing the input of new jobs.

quiescent-carrier telephony, A form of telephony in which the carrier is suppressed when there is no signals to be transmitted.

quiescing, The stopping of a multi-programming system by the rejection of new jobs.

quiet error, Errors that are quickly discovered and corrected before they spread throughout a process or system.

quinary, A mixed radix number system of radices 2 and 5.

Quip, To improve on the utility of the Dual-in-line package (DIP) used to package integrated circuits and other electronics, Intel Corp. and the 3M Company jointly developed a competing package. Quip can be inserted in PC boards, can be dismantled with a small screwdriver, and is shorter and has other advantages.

R

raceway floor, A raised floor that permits the concealment of cables of data processing equipment.

radial transfer, The process of transferring data between internal memory and a peripheral device (of a computer).

radiation, Energy propagated through space or other medium.

radio communication, Any communication using radio waves.

radio frequency interference (RFI), Interference, i.e., unwanted noise of electromagnetic radiation of radio frequency signals into operating circuits.

radio link, The channel provided by a radio emitter and receiver.

radix, The base of a number system. Binary numbers have a radix of 2, and decimal numbers have a radix of 10.

radix, floating-point, Same as floating point base.

radix, mixed, A numeration system using more than one radix, e.g., the biquinary system.

radix notation, An annotation of a decimal number and its base following as a subscript in parentheses; same as base notation.

radix number, Same as the base number of a numbering system.

radix point, A character, usually a full point, that separates the integer portion of a number from the fractional portion. For example, the decimal numbers 8.93, 63.45, and 1008.56 all have a radix point.

rain barrel effect, An echo-like effect developed into an audio signal.

RAM, dynamic, A class of random access memory that requires periodic servicing (a refresh cycle) in order for the contents to remain valid.

RAM, Random Access Memory, Refers to types of memory devices whereby any location in memory can be found, on average, as quickly as any other location. Computer internal memories and disk memories are random access memories. Data is usually stored in bytes, and the RAM storage capacity is measured in kilobytes.

RAM refresh cycle (dynamic), These memories require a small amount of inactive time between operations (or clocks), time sufficient to allow address translation and its associated delay to take place without system performance loss when the memory is equipped with a Dynamic Mapping System. Refreshing of the address space is often accomplished by the refresh timer, control circuitry, and memory modules.

RAM-Random Access Memory types, Random because it provides access to any storage location point in this memory immediately by means of vertical and horizontal coordinates. Information may be "written" in or "read" out in the same very fast procedure. Primary types are static and dynamic RAM.

random access, A method of accessing data from a storage device that is not dependent on the last access of data.

random access input/output, Input/output control processing that permits random processing; records (on a device like magnetic disk).

random access sorts, Sorts to be performed on random access devices such as magnetic disk.

random access storage, Storage in which the time required to access information is independent of the last location accessed, such as magnetic disk.

random number, A number selected at random from an orderless set of numbers.

random number generator, A computer program or routine used to produce random numbers. It is a technique used in statistical work.

random number table, A table of random numbers, used in statistical calculations.

randomize, The process of making data random.

range, All the values a data item can have or the difference between the highest and lowest values.

range check, Checking to see that a value falls between maximum and minimum values as defined.

range, dynamic, The difference in decibels between the noise level of a transmission system and its overhead level.

range finder, An adjustable mechanism on a teletypewriter receiver.

rank, A procedure used to arrange a series of items in ascending or descending order.

rapid memory, Sections of memory from which information may be obtained in the shortest time.

raster, This relates to a term used in computer graphics to refer to a display image consisting of a matrix or pixels arranged in rows and columns.

raster, basic, The bright white glow that covers the CRT when no signal is received.

raster count, horizontal, The number of positions across the width of a CRT (cathode ray tube), a television-like terminal.

raster count, vertical, The number of addressable positions across the height of a cathode ray tube.

raster scan CRT, The standard TV display technique in which an image is created by lines of dots of varying intensities.

rate action, A type of action in which the rate of correction is made proportional to how fast the condition is going awry.

rate, bit, (1) The speed at which bits are transmitted. (2) The rate at which bits pass a given point on a communications line. (See bit.)

rate, of clock, The frequency per unit time that pulses are emitted from the clock in a computer.

rate, information, The average information content per symbol times the average number of symbols per second.

rate joystick, A joystick which moves a cursor at a fixed rate over a display screen in a direction corresponding to the direction of the joystick handle. This kind of joystick is good for making slow, precise movements of the cursor.

rate, modulation, The reciprocal of the units interval measured in seconds (expressed in bauds).

rate of keying error, The ratio of the number of signals incorrectly sent to the total number of signals of the message.

rated capacity, General term for the output of an item of equipment that can continue indefinitely, in conformity with a criterion, e.g., heating, distortion of signals, or of waveform.

rated output, The output power, voltage, current, etc., at which a machine, device or apparatus is designed to operate under normal conditions.

ratio, The relation of one quantity to another.

ratio, activity, The ratio of the number of records that have activity to the total number of records in that file. (See active file.)

ratio, operating, The ratio of the number of hours of correct machine operation to the total hours of scheduled operation.

ratio, processing, Calculation time related to total available time.

ratio, sensitivity, (1) A measurement of the degree of response to change, or (2) a measured ratio of change in output to the change in input.

ratio, signal-to-noise, The ratio of information signals to no information (bad) signals.

raw data, Data that has not been edited, may not be in a machine readable form, has not been processed.

RDOS-Real-Time Disk Operating System, Used in both the development and implementation of programs, it includes all the file capabilities nominally available on disk operating systems, allowing the user to edit, assemble, execute, debug, compile, load-and-go, save, and delete files.

RDY, The control signal for slow memory to indicate that data are valid.

read, To sense recorded data; to transmit data into computer memory; to copy data from one place to another.

read, backward, A feature that some magnetic tape units have that permits the transfer of data to computer storage while moving the tape in the reverse direction.

read, destructive, The destruction of data that is read from storage; generally the data is regenerated.

read head, A head used for reading from various media. (See head.)

read, manual, An operation in which the computer reads (senses) switches that were manually set.

read, non-destructive, A reading process that doesn't destroy the source data (can be read over and over again).

read release, A feature of a reader that permits more processing time by releasing the read mechanisms.

read, reverse, Reading magnetic tape in an opposite direction.

read screen, A transparent part of most readers through which the document is read (in optical character recognition).

reader, A device capable of transcribing data from an input medium.

reader, Any device capable of sensing (reading) data, such as a wand reader, tape reader, optical reader, etc.

reader, badge, A device that reads information (such as employee number) from a badge-like card and enters the data into a computer.

reader, character, A device capable of locating, identifying, and translating into machine code, handwritten or printed data appearing on a source document.

reader, document, A device that can read holes in or marks on documents either optically or magnetically.

reader, film, A device that is designed to scan patterns on film and enter information about the patterns into a computer.

reader, page, An optical character reader that processes "pages" of documents.

reader/interpreter, A specialized computer program routine that reads an input stream (series of jobs) and stores the programs and data on a random access device for later processing.

readiness review, An examination of a site for a new computer to see that everything is ready (wiring, air conditioning, etc.).

reading, destructive, Reading of data that destroys the source data.

reading, mark, A form of mark detection using a photoelectric device.

reading, non-destructive, Reading in which the source data is not destroyed.

reading rate, The number of characters, words, blocks, etc., sensed (read) per unit time.

read-only memory (ROM), A special memory that can be read from but not written into.

readout, Processed information presented to the user, such as on a visual display, line printers, or plotter.

read-write, scatter, Reading a block of data, breaking it up for processing, then recombining it to write it.

ready, The status of being ready to run.

real time, Basically, this refers to an application in which the computer response is received immediately, so a user can make a decision at the time the results are received.

real-time application, Access of computer information in a real-time environment.

real-time, batch processing, A real-time system that is designed to automatically allow batch processing to take place as facilities in the computer are freed.

real-time clock, A clock that reflects actual time in contrast to fictitious time.

real-time control system, A system that processes data and makes decisions in real-time (automatic immediate control of a process).

real-time executive, A system that controls, sequences, and provides for allocation of facilities in a real-time system.

real-time monitor, The monitor program in a real-time system.

real-time output, Output from a system in time to be used to alter the program or process.

real-time processing, The processing of data fast enough so that the results affect the process being controlled or monitored.

real-time processing, inventory, A system that can be depended upon to provide up-to-the-minute inventory information.

real-time satellite computer, An additional computer in a real-time system that performs some of the tasks so that the main computer doesn't have to.

real-time simulation, A simulation environment in which simulated events occur at the same time they would occur in the actual system.

real-time, time-sharing, A system designed for providing data on a real-time basis with immediate response needed to continue the process.

rear projection, plasma terminal, The transparency of the plasma panel terminal enables rear projection; remote selection of 256 different full colors on some models can be remotely selected and projected on the display screen and alpha/graphic items can be superimposed.

rearrange, To change the sequence or location of items in a set of data.

receive only, A device that can only receive information from a computer but can't send it.

receive-only service, In communications service in which a channel is capable of receiving but not sending.

receiver signal, A device controlled by signals and used generally to send out new signals.

reception, diversity, A method used in radio reception to minimize the effects of fading.

recognition, The process of identification of input. Related to optical character recognition and magnetic ink character recognition.

recognition, character, Identifying or reading character optically, magnetically, etc.

recognition, optical character (OCR), Using photosensitive (optical) devices to sense (read) characters.

recognition, pattern, The recognition of shapes and patterns by a machine.

recognizer, syntax, A specialized computer program subroutine that recognizes the phase class in an artificial language.

record, A collection of related data items. A group of records is called a file.

record, addition, A new record in a master file being updated or a new record added to a file without moving or erasing any record in the file.

record, block, Same as physical record as contrasted with logical record.

record, change, A record used to change information in a master file record.

record control program, The computer program used for input/output processing that is file oriented rather than device oriented.

record, data, A record of data, a collection of data fields that form a unit for processing.

record, deletion, A record used to delete a matching record from a master file.

record, detail, A record containing single transaction data.

record equipment, unit, Punched card machines, such as sorters, collators, tabulators, etc.

record, fixed-length, A fixed-length record always contains the same number of characters.

record gap, On magnetic tape, the space between records.

record, header, A file record that contains a description of the file at the beginning of a file.

record, home, The first record of a chain of records in a data file.

record, label, A record on a file of magnetic tape that contains identifying information about that file.

record label, A record in a file that identifies the contents of the file.

record layout, Shows the design of the contents of a record, such as size, arrangement of data, etc.

record, leader, Same as header record.

record length, A measure of the size of a record, usually specified in units such as words, bytes, or characters.

record, logical, A group of related fields making up a record. One logical record may also be one physical record, but a physical record may be a block of logical records.

record management, Programming the most efficient methods of record processing.

record separator, A character used to mark logical boundaries between records.

recorder, A device that makes a permanent record of signals such as voltages.

recorder, digital, A device that records data as discrete points.

recorder, film, A device that receives information from a computer and records it on film as contrasted to film reader.

recorder, X Y, A recorder that makes a record of one voltage with respect to another.

recording density, Generally refers to the number of bits in a single linear track measured per unit of length of the recording medium. For example, the recording density of magnetic tape is measured in bits per inch (bpi).

recording density, The bits per unit length in a recording medium.

recording density, tape, The bits per inch recorded on magnetic tape.

recording head, A head used to transfer data to a storage device such as magnetic drum disks, tape, etc. (See head.)

recording, magnetic, The recording of data by magnetization (in a pattern) on magnetic material.

recording, magnetic stripe, Recording of data on magnetic stripes on a document.

recording surface, Storage of information on a surface such as the coating on magnetic tape, etc.

recording trunk, One used for communication between operators on long distance calls.

records, extent, A collection of physical records, continuous in secondary storage. The number of records in an extent depends on both the physical size of the volume and the user's request for space allocation.

records, vital, Records that are essential for legal and/or financial purposes in a company.

recovery, Generally, this concerns the process by which a system resumes processing, without irreparable loss of the data in the system, after an error in a program or a malfunction in the equipment has occurred.

rectangular coordinates, A set of axes (lines) that intersect (used for making graphs, etc.).

rectangular loop, A type of hysteresis loop that is more rectangular than S-shaped.

rectifier, A circuit that converts alternating current into direct current.

rectifiers, Convert AC to DC, make possible DC power supplies being built into AC-powered devices like radios and television sets.

recurrent transmission codes, Code in which check symbols are used to detect a burst type of error.

recursion, Basically, this is a process whereby a computer procedure or routine calls itself into operation while being executed or calls another procedure which in turn recalls the original.

recursive definition, A definition that defines something partly in terms of itself.

recursive procedure, A procedure that calls itself or calls another procedure that calls the first one again (in the computer).

reduction, The process of condensing data.

reduction, data, The process of changing raw data into an ordered, useful form. (See raw data.)

reduction, graphic data, The process of converting graphs, plotter output, engineering drawings, etc., into digital data.

reduction, on-line data, Processing data as rapidly as it is generated by the source.

redundant, Having more equipment, data, or other resources than the minimum needed; generally, overlapping or repetition.

reed contact, dry, An encapsulated switch with two wires that act as contact points for a relay.

reel, file, A magnetic tape reel known as the supply reel (feeds in for reading) by the computer.

reenterable load module, A type of load module that can be used repeatedly or concurrently by two or more jobs.

reentry system, A system in optical character recognition in which input data to be read are printed by the computer associated with the reader.

reference, cross, A notation showing that a record has been stored elsewhere.

reference, input, A reference point used to compare to. It is also a set point or desired value.

reference voltage, The voltage used as a standard of reference in an analog computer.

reference volume, The magnitude of a complex electric wave that corresponds to speech or music.

referencing, symbolic input/output, The method by which magnetic tape and disk are referred to by a computer program, i.e., symbolically instead of actual addresses.

reformatting, Changing data representation from one format to another.

refresh, CRT screen, Most often the screen is refreshed from special memory cards, a minimum of 60 times per second.

refresh rate, As regards display, the number of times per second an image on the CRT must be redrawn to keep it from flickering.

refreshing, Process of constantly reactivating or restoring information that decays or fades away when left idle, as the phosphor on a CRT screen needs to be constantly reactivated by an electron in order to remain illuminated. Cells in dynamic memory elements must be repeatedly accessed in order to avoid a fading away of their contents.

regeneration, A returning part of a signal on restoration of information that is stored.

regeneration, signal, A restoration (generating again) of a signal from another signal.

register, A row of flip-flops used to store a group of binary digits while the computer is processing them.

register attributes, A temporary storage device in a computer that is used for arithmetic, logic, and other operations.

register, buffer, A register used for temporary storage.

register, control instruction, A specific register that contains the address of the next instruction to be used.

register, half shift, Another name for a type of flip-flop used in a shift register.
(See flip-flop.)

register, instruction, A register within the central processing unit (CPU) which stores a copy of the instruction currently being executed.

register, instruction address (IAR), A computer register that contains the address of the next instruction to be executed.

register, shift, A register in which all the bits can be moved one place to the left (or the right) when a particular control signal is pulsed.

register, shifting, A computer register designed to perform shifts.

register, switch, The most basic microprocessor input device, which is simply a row of switches. Each switch corresponds to a single bit in the microprocessor data word. When the user wishes to enter information into the microprocessor, the switches are set up for a logic 1 and down for a logic 0.

registers, associative storage, Registers that are not identified by name or position but are identified by their content.

registers, external, Registers that can be referenced by a program.

registers, instruction-address, A register that contains the address of an instruction and other registers that contain the addresses of the operands of an instruction.

registration mark, A character recognition term for a preprinted indicator on the page.

regression, The rate at which an output changes relative to input changes.

regulation, voltage, A measure of voltage stability under varying load conditions.

rehashing, A process used when a hash table becomes full. By removing all entries in the original hash table, one by one, and inserting them into a new, larger table, using a new hash function, rehashing creates room for additional entries.

relational database, Advantages are that individual records can be converted to tables and can be accessed according to the meaning of the content with nested code numbers in hierarchial order.

relational operator, An operator that compares the values of two data items, for example $<$ (less than) and $>$ (greater than).

relativization, A technique which assigns relative addresses to the next written instruction address and operand address. During execution of the program, the relative address is automatically translated to an absolute address.

reliability testing, Testing the life expectancy of an element, unit, or device under certain conditions.

relocation memory, dynamic, A process that frees the user from keeping track of the exact locations of information in memory.

relocation processor, storage, A computer program routine used to relocate (put in a different place) computer programs during processing.

REM, A key word in BASIC which is used to signify the beginning of a comment.

remote computing system language, A language comprised of program statements and operator statements that permits the user to communicate with a remote computing system.

remote computing system syntactic errors, Errors such as typographical (e.g., punctuation), consistency (e.g., illegal statements), and completeness (e.g., missing parts) found in entering program coding into a remote terminal.

remote control language, See remote computing system language.

remote job entry (RJE), A situation in which a central computer accepts and processes jobs from a remote location.

remote terminal, A terminal that is at a location remote from the central processor of a computer.

reorder level, That amount of stock left when stock should be reordered.

reorder quantity, In inventory the amount of stock that is ordered when the reorder level is reached.

repair time, awaiting, The time between reporting a problem and the beginning of repair operations.

repeatability, plotter, Plotter repeatability refers to the precision with which a pen can return to a given point. Repeatability is measured in fractions of a millimeter, and it determines how well lines will meet and circles will close.

repeater station, A communications station at which a repeater is used to build up and equalize the strength of signals in a long line.

report, difference, A report showing changes (differences) from a previous computer program.

report, inventory stock, A printed report showing the current amount of each item carried in inventory that is on hand.

Report Program Generator (RPG), A programming method (language) used for relatively easy generation of reports from data file information. (See generator, report program.)

reports and feedback, factory, A system in which feedback of data is collected and analyzed to control and predict stock requirements.

representation, binary-coded decimal (BCD), A system of representation of decimal numbers in which each decimal digit is represented by four binary digits.

representation, null, A blank or empty representation.

representation, pictorial data, Representation on graphs, charts, maps, etc.

representative simulation, A model used in simulation whose parts, processes, and interactions closely relate to the system being studied.

request for repetition, automatic (ARQ), A system employing an error-correcting code and so arranged that a signal detected as being in error automatically initiates a request for retransmission.

request words, input/output, Control words in the computer used in input/output request processing.

requirements, information, The questions that may be posed to an information system.

reset, To return a condition to its original amount or state.

reset key, check, A push button on a computer used to reset some error conditions.

reset rate, The number of corrections per unit time made by a control system.

residence volume, system, The volume, i.e., disk pack, etc., that contains the operating system (software).

resident, core, A computer program or routine that remains in the main memory of the computer continuously.

resident executive, A specific computer program (in an operating system) that is a permanent resident of internal computer memory.

resistance, This measures the difficulty for electric current to flow through a component.

resistance, smudge, A characteristic of ink that resists smudging.

resistance, wear, Built-in resistance in printing ribbons to reduction of quality after use.

resistor, An electronic component with a fixed amount of resistance to the flow of electric current.

resolution, On displays, this refers to the number of pixels or addressable picture elements on the screen. Screen resolution determines the quality of the image on the screen.

resolution error, An error created by the inability of a computer (to) show very, very small changes in a variable.

resolver storage, A small part of storage on magnetic disk, drum, and tape that has a faster access than the rest of the storage.

resource, Any of the facilities of a computer system that a job or task requires.

resource allocation, Refers to the reserve computer resources for specific jobs or tasks. Resource allocation is one of the primary functions of an operating system.

resource allocation, linear programming, Using linear programming to determine the best way to allocate resources (used for managing an activity).

resource allocation priorities, The process of determining the best use of men, machine, material, money, space, and other resource in a project or to accomplish some goal. A computer program may be used to accomplish this.

resource sharing, The simultaneous or scheduled use of computer facilities by many users.

response, The expression of output as a function of input.

response, audio, Verbal reply to inquiries that may be prerecorded responses in a time-shared on-line system.

response time, The time required by the computer system to respond to the user's commands.

response, transient, Output versus time in response to a step input.

response unit, audio, A device used to provide voice response between a computer and a telephone network.

restart sorting, A point in the sort program that can be returned to if a restart is necessary.

restore, To return to an original (initial) value or condition.

retention period, The time that records are kept before they can be destroyed.

retina, A major part in a scanning device (in optical character recognition).

retrieval, The process by which a requested data item is located in a file and displayed on the terminal from which the request for the data was made.

retrieval, data, The finding of data by searching in a file, data bank, or storage device.

retrieval, fact, Recognizing, selecting, and interpreting data words, phrases, etc., and relating the data for useful results.

retrieval, information, The methods and procedures for recovering specific information from stored databases.

retrieval, information, A method used to catalog data in such a way that it is easily retrieved; or a branch of computer science

retrieval, legal, Retrieving information related to law, such as court decisions, citations, references, etc.

retrievals, false, A retrieval of unwanted data that is vaguely related to what is being looked for.

retrieve, To find and select information that is stored.

retrofit, An adjustment to a system to accommodate a change.

retrofit testing, Testing after replacing equipment or programs to assure system operation.

return, carriage, In a character printer, the operation that causes the next character to be printed at the left margin.

return instructions, Use of a return instruction permits return to a main computer program from a subroutine.

return point sorting, Same a restart sorting.

return signal, In a closed loop, the signal that is sent back to be subtracted from the input.

reusable, serially, A computer program that can be used again without reloading it into memory.

reverse read, Reading magnetic tape in an opposite direction.

reverse scan, Placing or removing punctuation or data in computer output on the way back from a forward scan. (See forward scan.)

reverse video, Function that shows dark characters on a background of light screen area.

reversible counter, A counter that can be increased or decreased according to control signals.

review, post installation, An examination of procedures and operation of a system after the original installation.

review, readiness, An examination of a site for a new computer to see that everything is ready, such as wiring, air conditioning, etc.

rewind, To return a magnetic tape to the beginning of a reel.

rewind time, The time needed to rewind a reel of tape.

rewind time sorting, The time required to rewind the magnetic tape reels during a sort.

R-F bandwidth, The frequency difference between the highest and lowest frequencies of a radio-frequency signal.

R-F bandwidth emission, The frequency difference between the highest and lowest emission frequencies of a radio-frequency signal.

RFI, An abbreviation for Radio Frequency Interference.

RGB monitor, Abbreviation for red/green/blue monitor. Generally refers to the type of CRT screen that produces color images using a trio of red, green, and blue electron guns.

RH, An abbreviation for Report Heading.

right justify applications, (1) The process of setting a right margin (that will always be lined up with characters) on a printed page, i.e., as must be done in newspaper printing. (2) In input and output data placing the data in the right-most positions of a field.

right-hand justified, When an amount in storage or in a register has no zeroes in the right-hand positions.

right-justify, In word processing, to move the contents within a register so that the least significant digit is placed in the rightmost position.

ring, file protect, A file protect ring is a plastic ring that must be in place on the back of a magnetic tape in order for data to be written on the tape. Thus, when the file protect ring is not in place, the data is protected against accidental or unauthorized writing.

ring, protecting, A plastic ring that strengthens a disk's center spindle hole. Protection rings are now built into most floppy disks to prolong disk life.

ring shift, Same as circular shift.

RJE (remote job entry), A situation in which a central computer accepts and processes jobs from a remote location.

RO, Stands for receive-only, a device that can receive messages but not transmit them.

robot, A device equipped with sensing instruments that can run itself.

robot edge detection, An algorithm by use of which a computer or robot may understand what objects it 'sees.' After the optical sensors input a picture of one or more objects, the algorithm attempts to differentiate between one object and another object, shadow, and background, by finding all of an object's edges.

robot master/slave manipulator, A robotic shoulder, arm, and hand that is guided by a human operator from some distance away.

robot microswitch, Generally refers to a type of pressure-sensing device that a robot uses to detect the presence of some obstacle by impact. The device consists of a tiny switch which is installed on a robot's arm or body. When the robot bumps into something, the switch is tripped and sends a signal to the robot's processor.

robot ribbon switch, In the science of robotics, a type of pressure transducer in the form of a long, ribbon-like wire that converts continuous pressure into electricity. Ribbon switches can be wrapped around the base of a robot for obstacle detection, or attached to its hands to detect both pressure and weight.

robotics, The field of artificial intelligence concerned with the design, production, and use of robots.

roll, A reel of tape.

ROM (read-only memory) types, (1) A blank ROM can be considered to be a mosaic of undifferentiated cells. Many types of ROMs exist. A basic type of ROM is one programmed by a mask pattern as part of the final manufacturing stage. PROMs are "programmable" ROMs. ROMs are relatively permanent although they can be erased with the aid of an ultraviolet irradiation instrument. Others can be electrically erased and are called EPROMs. (2) Information is stored permanently or semi-permanently and is read out, but not altered in operation.

ROM bootstrap, Practically every microcomputer uses at least one ROM program, the most common one being a ROM bootstrap loader that contains the programming steps to bring the computer on-line with a minimum of operator initiative.

ROM, Read-Only Memory, Generally, this is a type of computer memory which contains computer instructions that do not need to be changed, such as the instructions for calculating arithmetic functions. The computer can read instructions out of ROM, but no data can be deleted from it or added to it.

ROM voice synthesizer, Synthesizers string together words recalled from ROM programs developed by user-generated code to develop voice response.

rotational delay, The time required when accessing a disk for a selected record to pass under the read/write head.

round, To delete one or more least significant figures from a floating point number in order that it be expressed with the limited number of bits that can be represented on the computer.

route, alternative, A secondary communication path used to reach a destination if the main route is unavailable.

routine, A set of coded computer instructions used for a particular function.

routine, algorithmic, A type of program or routine that works toward solution of a problem in a distinct method as opposed to trial-and-error methods.

routine, alternate, Assignment of a secondary communications path that is used when the primary path is not available.

routine, assembly, Same as assembler.

routine, automatic, A computer program routine that will be used only when certain conditions occur.

routine, auxiliary, A special computer program routine used to assist in the operation of the computer and in debugging other routines.

routine, benchmark, A set of problems that may be computer programs that aid in judging the performance of equipment (data processing).

routine, complete, A routine that doesn't need modification before being used.

routine, control, A computer program routine that performs control functions.

routine, conversion, A computer program routine used to change data from one form to another.

routine, correction, A computer program routine used in or after a computer failure or program or operator error.

routine, dating, A computer program routine that calculates and stores dates.

routine, diagnostic, A routine used to locate a malfunction in a computer or to aid in locating mistakes in a computer program. In general, it is any routine specifically designed to aid in debugging or troubleshooting.

routine, error correction, A computer program routine used to correct a detected error while processing.

routine, fixed, A computer program routine that can't be changed during its execution.

routine, generalized, A computer program routine used to process a large range of jobs in an application area.

routine, housekeeping, The first instructions in a computer program that are only executed one time.

routine, input, A routine to control input into the computer; may be hardware or software in the machine or in a program.

routine, interpreter, A computer program routine that translates a stored program from a pseudocode into machine language.

routine, interpretive, A computer program routine that translates instructions in pseudocode to machine language and executes the instructions immediately.

routine, interrupt, A computer program routine that performs interrupt action.

routine, loading, A set of instructions used to bring data and instructions into storage.

routine maintenance time, Time devoted to maintenance on a regular schedule; includes preventative maintenance.

routine, malfunction, A routine used to locate a malfunction in a computer.

routine, message, The process of selecting a route or alternate route for a message.

routine, monitor, Same as the supervisory routine or supervisory program.

routine, patch, A computer program correction or change made at execution time.

routine, post-mortem, A computer program routine run after an operation is completed for analysis.

routine, recovery, A computer program routine used to "recover" to normal operation after an error.

routine, service, A computer program routine that performs a special function, such as diagnostic routines, dumps, etc.

routine, specific, A computer program routine using addresses that refer to explicit registers and locations.

routine, static, A computer program subroutine using no parameters except addresses of operands.

routine, supervisory, The control routine that initiates and directs all other programs and routines.

routine, trace, An executive computer program routine that is used in diagnostic tracing.

routine, translating, A computer program routine used for program translation (one language to another).

routine, translator, A computer program routine used to translate a source program into an object program (machine language).

routine, utility, Computer program routines used for housekeeping and service functions.

routine, working, A computer program routine that produces the results as contrasted with housekeeping, etc.

routing, Assignments of communications paths for message delivery.

routing indicator, In communications an identifier (label) that indicates the route and destination of a message.

row, A horizontal arrangement of characters, bits, or other expressions. Contrasts with column.

RPG, Abbreviation for Report Program Generator. A business-orientated programming language.

RS-232 interface, An interface between a modem and the associated data terminal equipment, it is standardized by EIA Standard RS-232. For voice-band modems, the interface leads are single leads with a common ground return.

RUN, A statement in BASIC which causes execution of the currently stored program to begin.

run, test, A test run is the execution of a program using test data in order to determine whether or not logical errors or syntactical errors exist in the program.

run-time error, An error that occurs during the execution of a program causing the execution to terminate abnormally.

run-time, program, The period of time a program spends actually being executed by a computer.

S

S/N, Signal to noise ratio.

S-100 bus, A power or communication line used in common by many parts of a computer, the S-100 bus is 100 such parallel common communications lines, each of which is capable of carrying one bit or signal through the entire computer.

scalar, A scalar quantity has magnitude but no direction in space. For example, temperature is scalar but velocity is not.

scan, To examine sequentially part by part.

scan, interlaced, A scanning system used for raster graphics and CRTs in which the even numbered lines are scanned alternately with the odd numbered lines, instead of sequentially.

scan, raster, The horizontal scanning pattern of the electron gun in television sets and computer monitors that use cathode ray tube display.

scatter-read, Refers to placing information from a physical record into nonadjacent locations in memory. Opposite of gather-write.

Scheduled maintenance time for equipment (done to prevent problems).

scheduling systems, sequential, A way of selecting jobs to be processed on a first-come, first-served basis.

schema, The description of the logical structure and content of a database.

schematic, A drawing that shows connections of components in a circuit.

schematic diagram, electrical, A representation (drawing) of electrical circuit elements and their relationships.

Schneider front end, A front-end train of amplifiers to interface gas chromatograph instructions to a real-time computer.

Schottky bipolar microcomputer elements, Considered to be much faster than any MOS microcomputers, smaller, less expensive, that require less energy than equivalent designs for full systems.

scientific application, A computer application of solution to scientific problems as opposed to commercial or business.

scientific notation, An expression of quantities as a fractional part and a power of ten, such as 1.37×10^3.

scientific problems, Problems solved on a computer that are not business applications. They are generally mathematical.

scientific sampling, Selecting a small group of items from the whole group of items to analyze characteristics and infer that they belong to the whole group.

scientific subroutines, Generally a set of computer program subroutines supplied by the computer company and used to perform various mathematical and statistical routines.

scientific system, A system whose emphasis is on computation in contrast to a commercial system whose emphasis is on file updating, etc.

scoring, The weakness in a place on paper so that it can be easily folded on a straight line (not perforation).

scramble time, Computer time for use by programmers who need short ''shots'' (periods of time) to test computer programs.

scratch tape, A magnetic tape available for temporary use on which data is not saved.

scratch tape (sorting), Any tapes used to hold intermediate-pass data (not permanently saved).

scratch-pad memory, An area of computer memory used for temporary storage of the intermediate states of computation. It is used in interrupt processing.

scratch-pad storage, A high-speed memory used to store information in interrupt processing.

screen, A CRT or cathode ray tube, which is a television-like device or screen.

screen, fluorescent, The coating on the inner wall of a CRT (Cathode Ray Tube) that converts electrical energy into light (CRT is a television-like computer terminal).

screen, read, A transparent part of most readers through which the document is read in optical character recognition.

screen, split, A display device screen capable of displaying part of a file on one part of the screen and another part of the same or a different file on another part of the screen.

screen splitter applications, Provide low cost horizontal, vertical, or corner insert splitting for surveillance, security, or industrial application where two video images are to be displayed simultaneously on a single video monitor.

scroll, color system, Displays may be scrolled up and down, one display line at a time, by means of corresponding instructions; some units contain a one-line erase instruction that can be used to simplify editing and updating of scrolled images.

scrolling, Generally, an operation that virtually all computer operating systems use to display data and keyboard input on the screen. Input and output appear at the bottom of the screen and travel upwards as more lines are written at the bottom. When a message reaches the top of the screen, it disappears to continue allowing more messages to be written at the bottom.

scrolling movement, Movement of text up or down, or horizontally, to show material that does not fit on the display screen in one frame.

SCR-Silicon Controlled Rectifier, SCRs and power transistors are widely used in switching direct current, and pairs of back-to-back SCRs and triacs are used to switch alternating current.

SDLC discipline, Synchronous Data Link Control, a uniform discipline for the transfer of data between stations in a point-to-point, multipoint, or loop arrangement, using synchronous data transmission techniques.

sealed circuits, Very tiny circuits that are sealed in place.

search, A systematic examination of information to find a particular item.

search, area, A term used in information retrieval to describe examination of a collection of data and selection of those items that pertain to one group, such as a class or category.

search, binary, A very efficient algorithm for searching for an item in a list of sorted data. The binary search examines the central item in the file, then the central item of the top or bottom half of the file, continually dividing the file in half until the item is found. This is one of the most efficient searches for use on a file of sorted data.

search, chaining, A method of search that leads one from one place to another until the record is found or to the end of the chain.

search, conjunctive, A type of search defined in terms of a logical product (uses the AND instruction) and contrasted with disjunctive search.

search cycle, The time required or the sequence of events used to complete a search operation.

search, dichotomizing, Same as binary search.

search, disjunctive, A type of search defined in terms of a logical sum (uses the inclusive OR instruction) as contrasted with conjunctive search.

search, Fibonacci, A technique for searching based on the number relationships of the Fibonacci series. (See Fibonacci series.)

search time, The time used to find a particular field of data in storage.

searching storage, Same as associative storage.

sec, Abbreviation for second in time measurement.

second generation computer, A computer using transistors instead of vacuum tubes that were used in first generation computers, such computers as IBM 1401, Honeywell 800, RCA 501, etc. (See third generation computer for contrast.)

second level address, An address in a computer instruction that refers to a location where the address can be found of the operand to be used.

secondary storage, Refers to external storage devices such as magnetic tape, disk, etc.

section number, The number that identifies a section of a file.

sector, Similar to a word of a computer, but also contains data bits not used by a programmer; also a sector of disk, drum, etc., a portion of a track.

security, file, Processes of keeping files unavailable to people who shouldn't have access to them (private or confidential information).

seek, (1) The process of getting records from a random access file, (2) to look for data, (3) the moving of the arm-like mechanism on a random access device to position the read/write head over the right track of data.

seek time, Generally, the measurement of the time it required for a disk drive's read/write head to find a specific track. A drive's seek time is one factor by which its overall speed is determined.

segment (noun), Refers to a record containing one or more data items. Segments are the basic divisions of data passing to and from application programs under control of database management software.

segment (verb), Refers to a procedure to divide a computer program into parts so that the program can be executed without the entire program being in internal storage at any one time.

segment mark, A special character used on magnetic tape to separate each section of a file.

segmentation, A method of dividing a computer program into parts.

segmentation and control, automatic, A method used to fit computer programs into computer memory by fitting different segments in at different times.

select, To choose from alternate or to activate the control and data channels in preparation for input/output.

select, data, A selection operation to take one of several sets of items is taken to be printed or punched.

select error, A tape-transport unit error.

selecting, Choosing certain items that need special attention from a group of data.

selection, channel, input/output, The capability of a computer to select a particular channel for use.

selection check, An automatic check to see if the correct register, input/output device, etc., was selected.

selection control, The device that selects instructions to be executed in a computer.

selection, job-request, Selection of the next job to be started based on its priority, available facilities needed for the job, etc.

selection, priority, Selection of the next job to run based on available facilities and the priority of the job.

selection, program, Switching from one job to another in the computer.

selective calling, In communications the selection of a station to receive transmission of a message.

selective dump, A dump (printout of contents) of a selected area of internal storage of a computer.

selective dump, programmed, A library subroutine that is called to be used when other computer programs are running and a dump is desired (see selective dump).

selective fading, Fading in which the different frequencies are affected differently (see fading).

selective listing, A listing of data of various sets of predetermined criteria.

selective trace, A tracing (computer) routine that traces branches or arithmetic instruction results or other reprogram activity in a selected area.

selectivity, The ability of a communications receiver to choose a carrier.

selectivity, adjacent channel, The ability to reject signals or channels adjacent to the desired signals.

selector channel, Provides a path and control between the computer and input/output devices; used with high speed devices.

selector IOP, An input/output processing unit providing data transfer between main memory and high speed input/output devices.

selector, scanner, A device used when more than one communication multiplexor is used on one input/output channel.

selectors, Various automatic switches.

self-adapting, The ability of a computer to change its performance in response to its environment.

self-checking code, A coding system used to detect errors in transfer of data (checks for loss or gain of bits).

self-checking number, A number with an extra digit on the end that is used for checking purposes as in credit card numbers.

self-demarking code, (1) A code in which symbols are arranged to avoid the generation of false combinations by two successive codes, (2) same as error-detecting code.

self-learning, The attempts made to design computers that educate themselves based on their past performance.

self-modification program, The ability with a computer program to change its own instructions prior to execution (may be done repeatedly).

self-organization, The ability of a machine to automatically organize a program into a logical sequence.

self-organizing, Those machines having the capability of self-organization (see self-organization).

self-organizing machine, See self-organization.

self-organizing system, A system designed with the capability of internal reconfiguration in response to external events.

self-repairing, An unusual characteristic of some machines that are capable of repairing themselves without human intervention.

selsyn, Same as synchro.

semanteme, An element of language that expresses a definite image for an idea.

semantic errors, Errors in meaning or intent of meaning made by a programmer in programming.

semantic matrix, A graphical procedure in semantic analysis.

semantics, The area of study of the meanings of words and symbols and the relationships of things they denote.

semantics, formal, Language aids for computer languages designed to act as a compiler and called FSL.

semantics, language theory, Meanings of words as opposed to syntax which refers to structure of a sentence.

semiautomatic message switching center, A center where an operator routes messages according to the information in them.

semiconducting material, A solid or liquid having a resistivity midway between that of an insulator and a metal.

semiconductor, A material, such as silicon or gallium arsenide, that is neither a good conductor nor a good insulator. Semiconductor devices, such as diodes, transistors, and integrated circuits are the essential parts in modern computer systems.

semiconductor circuit components, Complex circuits fabricated by suitable and selective modification of areas on and in wafers to produce patterns of interconnected passive and active elements. The circuit may be assembled from several chips and use thin-film elements or discrete components.

semiconductor IC, Semiconductors made possible very tiny circuits, shrinking finished product sizes; individual parts of circuits can be much closer together without burning up, packaged in solid lumps, in effect. Typical examples of semiconductors are: diodes, transistors, integrated circuits.

semiconductor memory, A computer memory that uses semiconductor circuits for storage.

semiconductor memory, metal-oxide (MOS), A memory using a semiconductor circuit. It is generally used in high speed buffer memory and read-only memory.

semi-fixed length record, A fixed length record that can be changed in length under certain circumstances by a programmer.

send/receive set, keyboard (KSR), In communications a combination transmitter and receiver with transmission from the keyboard only.

send-only device, A device, such as a terminal, which can send data to the computer but cannot receive data from it.

send-receive, automatic (ASR), A communications device that is a combination teletypewriter, transmitter, and receiver.

send-request circuit, A circuit in which signals are originated to select whether to send or receive data (in half-duplex service).

sense, An attempt to detect holes or marks in or on storage media.

sense switch, A switch on a computer console that the operator can turn on or off and that may be tested by a computer program.

sense types, (1) To detect signals, (2) to read holes in cards and paper and magnetic spots on tape, disk, etc., (3) to detect a switch setting, or (4) to examine data relative to a set of criteria.

sensible, machine, Has the capability of being sensed or read by a machine such as punched cards, magnetic tapes, disks, etc.

sensing element, A specific portion of a device that is directly responsive to the value of the measured quantity.

sensing, mark, The capability of reading special pencil marks from a punched card and punching the sensed data into the card.

sensitivity analysis, An analysis of the results of tests or trials of values to determine the response, interdependence, etc., of the values.

sensitivity ratio, (1) A measurement of the degree of response to change, (2) a measured ratio of change in output to the change in input.

sensor, A device designed to sense analog information concerning temperatures, flows, pressures, etc.

sensor-based, The use of sensing devices, such as transducers or sensors to monitor a physical process of condition.

sensors, dialectic, Special sensors used to read data from paper tape.

sentinel, A mark or symbol used to indicate the end of an item, field, block, etc., of data.

separation symbol, item, A control symbol that indicates the beginning of an item.

separator, A specific flag that separates items of data.

separator, file, A file that identifies logical boundaries between files. It is abbreviated FS.

separator, group, Identifies logical boundaries between groups of data. It is abbreviated GS.

separator, information, Any of several control characters used to mark logical boundaries between sets of information.

separator, record, A character used to mark logical boundaries between records.

separator, sync, The circuit that separates sync pulses from the video signal in a television receiver.

separator, unit, A specific character used to mark logical boundaries between units of data.

separator, word, A specific character used to separate words of data.

sequence, (1) To put records into a specific order (alphabetical, social security number, etc.), (2) the order the records are in.

sequence, collating, The order of a set of characters designed for a particular machine; used in comparing for high, low, equal.

sequence, control, Determining the selection of instructions for execution; generally one after another in a row until a branch may change the flow.

sequence control register, The computer register that keeps track of the location of the next instruction to be processed.

sequence error, When a record is out of sequence; may be data or instructions.

sequence number, A number assigned to an item to show its relative position in a set of items.

sequence packing, A procedure used in packing data in an accumulator (squeezing 3 words of data into the accumulator).

sequence, pseudorandom number, A sequence of numbers that is random enough for statistical purposes.

sequence queue (any), A line of items (jobs) on a computer system waiting to be processed; any sequence means they can be removed from the waiting line without regard to how they entered it.

sequence register, A computer register that controls the sequence of instructions.

sequence, sorting, The data field that determines the order of records in sorting, such as social security number, customer name, etc.

sequence-checking routine, A computer program routine that tests records as it processes them to see if they are in order; may also refer to a type of tracing routine.

sequencing by merging, A technique used in which repeating merging, splitting, and remerging results in an ordered (sequenced) set of items.

sequential control, A mode of computer operation in which instructions are executed in consecutive order (until a branch changes the flow).

sequential testing, Testing performed in a predetermined order and requiring repeated observations.

serial, (1) The handling of data sequentially as contrasted to parallel, (2) to handle digit after digit in data transfer.

serial by bit, A characteristic of data handling in equipment, handled a bit at a time, one after the other.

serial by character, Characters are sent serially as contrasted to parallel by character.

serial number, The number that is unique to a machine and identifies it (as a serial number on a car engine).

serial numbering, Numbering items with successive numbers such as paychecks, purchase orders, etc.

serial operation, An operation in a computer in which the digits are handled sequentially.

serial printer, A printing device that prints one character at a time as a typewriter does.

serial processing, Processing of one item after another, one at a time.

serial programming, The computer programming by which only one arithmetic or logical instruction can be executed at a time as contrasted with multiple programming.

serial storage, Sequential access storage as contrasted with random-access storage.

serial transfer, Transfer of data serially (one at a time, bit by bit, or element by element).

serially reusable routine, A computer program routine that is available to be used again after it's been used.

serial-parallel, (1) Using a combination of serial and parallel, e.g., serial by character, parallel by bit, (2) a type of device that converts serial input to parallel output.

serial-parallel operation, An operation used to handle bits in parallel but characters in a serial way.

service, The function of a common carrier of furnishing a set of facilities to meet a customer's communication needs (e.g., telephone service).

service area, local, In communications the area in which one can call without toll charges.

service bits, Not information bits or check bits, but other types such as indicators of conditions (see bit).

service bureau, A data processing organization that provides services to customers, i.e., they sell manpower and computer time.

service engineering, Covers the broad range of support to a customer of a computer vendor.

service, full-duplex, A service using full-duplex capabilities (see full-duplex).

service, half-duplex, Service using a half-duplex channel (see half-duplex channel).

service life, The estimated useful life of a machine after which an increase of the failure rate of advancing age makes further maintenance, overhaul, and servicing impractical.

service program, A special kind of computer program to perform a specific function such as an input program, a monitor program, etc.

service, receive only, In communications service in which a channel is capable of receiving but not sending.

service routine, A computer program routine that performs a special function, such as diagnostic routines, dumps, etc.

service routine, interrupt, A routine used for handling the condition causing an interrupt. For example, if a program was interrupted due to a lack of memory, the interrupt service routine would allocate more memory and return control back to the program.

servo, vacuum, The device that holds magnetic tape in place. It is maintained by air pressure on one side of the tape.

servomechanism, Refers to a device to monitor an operation as it proceeds and to make necessary adjustments to keep the operation under control.

servomechanism components, Devices designed to control systems using a measurable variable, a feedback control system, a closed loop system.

set, To place a storage device in a certain state (condition) or a collection of related elements.

set up diagram, A graphic representation showing necessary preparation for a computer run.

set up services, Actions performed on data messages before they encounter the processing computer program; functions performed are error checking, decoding, etc.

set up time, The time required for machine set up, i.e., the time spend getting the computer ready for a job.

several-for-one, Several actual computer instructions being generated from one instruction written by a programmer.

sexadecimal, Synonymous with hexadecimal.

shannon, A choice between two equally probable events.

share operation system, A particular translation of symbolic instructions to machine instructions, often abbreviated SOS.

SHARE organization, A computer user's group for certain IBM machine users.

shared files system, A system in which two or more users have access to a stored file but not necessarily at the same time.

shared storage, Storage that is available to two computers.

shared system, time, A system in which available computer time is shared among several jobs.

sharpness, The clarity of an image in optical character recognition.

shed, oxide, The loss of particles of oxide on magnetic tape during its use.

shield, electrostatic, A metal mesh used to screen one device from the electric field of another device.

shielding, Preventing the interaction between circuits.

shift, (1) To move characters, positions, etc., of a unit of information to the right or left, (2) a part of a 24-hour day that equipment is operated and people work.

shift charge, The amount of money charged for extra shifts of computer use beyond the base lease price charged by the computer manufacturer.

shift, logic, A non-arithmetic shift (see shift instruction).

shift, non-arithmetic, A logical shift instruction.

shift out, To shift towards one end of a register and lose the contents shifted out; zeroes fill in at the other end.

shift, phase, The time between the input and output signals in a control unit, circuit, etc.

shift, prime, The shift during which normal business takes place (such as 8 to 5 o'clock).

shift pulse, The pulse that causes a shift of characters in a register.

shift register, The computer register capable of shifting data as directed.

shifting, A technique in an internal sort in which records are moved so other records may be inserted.

shifting, field, Adjustment for the address of a field to realign an item of data.

shifting register, A computer register designed to perform shifts.

short instruction, A shorter than usual form of an instruction.

short wave, AM broadcasting in the frequency vicinity of 20 to 40 mc.

short word, A half-word in many computers.

shorted out, Made inactive by connecting a heavy wire or other low resistance path around a device or portion of a circuit.

SI (superimpose), Moving data from one place to another overlaying (superimposing on) the contents.

sideband transmission, double, In communications the sidebands not being related to each other but are related separately to two sets of modulating signals (see sideband).

sideband transmission, independent, A method using the upper and lower sidebands which are symmetrically spaced about the carrier frequency and all are transmitted.

sight check, Visual verification by a person (not a machine).

sign bit, A binary digit (0 or 1) set to represent minus or plus.

sign changing amplifier, Same as sign reversing amplifier.

sign check, A test for change in the sign (plus or minus) of a data field.

sign check indicator, A device indicating no sign or an improper sign (plus or minus) in a field after an arithmetic operation.

sign control, flip-flop, A specific flip-flop used to store the plus or minus sign of numbers (see flip-flop).

sign digit, Same as sign bit.

sign, factorial-like, An exclamation point (!), e.g., 5! (see factorial).

sign, flip-flop, Same as flip-flop sign control.

sign off, A user instruction at a terminal that ends communication with the system.

sign on, The instruction(s) the user begins with at a terminal to begin communication with the system.

sign position, The position in a field where the sign is located (plus or minus).

sign reversing amplifier, An amplifier whose output and input voltage are equal in magnitude but opposite in sign.

signal, (1) A basic term for an event, electrical quantity, etc., that conveys information, (2) an increase or decrease in an electrical force which causes a device or circuit to initiate actions.

signal, actuating, A specific pulse in the control circuitry of computers.

signal, chrominance, A combination of luminance and color signals.

signal, clock, A clock pulse used to control timing of various functions.

signal, communications, A group of waves that travel on a transmission channel to a receiver.

signal converter, A particular transducer used to convert one standard-sized signal to another.

signal, correcting, A signal sent recurrently for the correction of data (in synchronous systems).

signal, cut off, The point of degradation at which a signal becomes useless due to attenuation and/or distortion.

signal, digital, A discrete or discontinuous signal whose various states are discrete intervals apart.

signal, feedback control, The part of an output signal that is returned as an input to accomplish some effect, such as a fast response.

signal, inhibiting, A signal which may prevent a circuit form exercising its normal functions.

signal, interrupt, The control signal that demands the attention of the central computer.

signal, interrupt trigger, A signal that is generated to interrupt the normal sequence of events in the central processor of the computer.

signal, luminance, The signal that controls light values in the color CRT receiver (a television-like screen).

signal output, The signal delivered (output from) by a device or element.

signal, proceed-to-select, The signal returned in response to a calling signal that indicates that information can be transmitted.

signal, program-interrupt, Signals from external devices that interrupt the program in process.

signal, pulsing, A transmitted signal that carries information to route the call in the desired direction.

signal regeneration, A restoration (generating again) of a signal from another signal.

signal, release-guard, A signal sent in response to a clear forward signal that indicates the circuit is free at the incoming end.

signal, seizing, A signal transmitted at the beginning of a call to initiate circuit operation at the incoming end of the circuit.

signal, shaping, Same as regeneration signal.

signal, standardization, Same as regeneration signal.

signal, start (in a start-stop system), Indicates the beginning of transmission.

signal, start-dialing, A signal transmitted following the receipt of a seizing signal.

signal, stop (in a start-stop system), Indicates the end of transmission.

signal strength, A measure of the amplitude of the signal obtained from reading devices or a rise in energy level.

signal, video, An electrical signal that corresponds to lights.

signaling, binary, A mode in communications in which information is represented by presence or absence, or plus or minus variations.

signaling, closed-circuit, A type of signaling in which the signal is initiated by increasing or decreasing the current.

signaling, data rate, In data transmission, the bits per second data transmission capacity of a particular channel.

signaling, dc, A transmission method using direct current.

signaling, octonary, A type of signaling mode in which eight levels of a parameter vary to represent information.

signaling, open-circuit, A type of signaling in which there isn't any current when the circuit is in an idle condition.

signaling, quantenary, An electrical communications mode (with four levels of a medium).

signaling, quaternary, A type of signaling mode in which four levels of a parameter vary to represent information.

signaling rate, The rate that signals are transmitted.

signals, control, A wide variety of signals used to control the flow of information in computer systems.

signals, correction from, A system used to control synchronous equipment.

signals, external, Equipment failure warning signals to the operator.

signals, supervisory, Signals that indicate the operating states of circuit combinations.

signals, timing, Signals sent at regular interval to ensure synchronization.

signal-to-noise ratio, The ratio of the power in the transmitted signals to the undesirable noise present in the absence of any signal.

signal-to-noise ratio, The ratio of information signals to no information (bad) signals.

signed field, A field that has a plus or minus associated with it.

significance, (1) The number of digits of a number that have meaning, (2) the rank or order of relative magnitude assigned to a position of a number, (3) in statistics, the factors that appear and are unlikely to be only by chance.

significance, bit, A bit in an instruction that indicates that the instruction is of a certain type.

significant, An attribute of data output that has meaning for use in analysis.

significant character, least, The character in the right most position of a field or word.

significant character, most, The character in the left most position in a number or field.

significant digit, A digit of significant value to the accuracy of the number.

significant digit, least, The digit in a number contributing the smallest amount to the total quantity.

significant figures, Digits in a number that may not be rounded off without losing accuracy.

significant interval, In communications the period of time during which a given significant condition and the signal to be transmitted is (or should be) transmitted.

silicon, The main material used to make semiconductors.

silicon, components, In its pure state, it is used as a semiconductor; a non-metallic element having semiconducing properties and occurring in two allotropic forms -- dark grey crystals and a brown amorphous powder, thus used for transistors and certain crystal diodes.

silicon diode, A type of crystal diode containing crystalline silicon.

silicon solar cell, A photovoltaic cell designed to convert light energy into power for electronic and communication equipment. It consists essentially of a thin wafer of specially processed silicon.

simplex, A communications circuit capable of one-way transmission only; not commonly used anymore.

simplex channel, A communications channel capable of transmission in one direction only.

simplex mode, A mode of communications operation that goes in one direction only and that can't be reversed.

simplex system, A system not including standby equipment.

SIMSCRIPT, A general purpose digital simulation system.

simulate, Representing the functions of one system by another, e.g., using a computerized system to represent a physical system.

simulated real-time, on-line operation, The processing of data in a system along with a physical process so that the results of the data processing are useful to the physical process.

simulation, Generally, the process of representing one system by another; for instance, representing the real world by a mathematical model solved by a computer.

simulation, behavioral, Simulation of psychological and/or sociological behavior of individuals and groups.

simulation, continuous, Simulation using continuous data as opposed to discrete, such as controlling of missile flights, etc.

simulation, design and monitoring, A procedure designed for developing a model of a system using special languages.

simulation, deterministic, A simulation in which there is a fixed relation between elements as contrasted with stochastic simulation.

simulation, discrete, Simulation using discrete events such as in a queuing network. It is also called event-oriented simulation as contrasted with continuous simulation.

simulation education, Using simulation computer programs so people may be exposed to effects of environmental change, e.g., management games.

simulation manipulation, Using inputs and generating outputs analogous to those of the system being simulated.

simulation, man-machine, A simulation environment with man and the machine interacting.

simulation, mathematical, Using a model of mathematical equations. Computer elements are used to represent the subsystems.

simulation model, Using a model of a system or process and processing it on a computer, altering the variables in the process and observing the results.

simulation, operational, A simulation system incorporating processes in which people participate.

simulation, physical, Design and use of models of physical systems.

simulation, physical systems, In analog or digital computers, a development representation of physical systems, such as a chemical process.

simulation, real-time, A simulation environment in which simulated events occur at the same time they would occur in the actual system.

simulation, representative, A model used in simulation whose parts, processes, and interactions closely relate to the system being studied.

simulation, static v. dynamic, In a dynamic system the activity is time dependent; a static system is not time sensitive.

simulation, stochastic, A simulation in which random elements are the basis of calling it probabilistic or stochastic as contrasted with deterministic simulation.

simulation, supervisory program, Using a replacement program when the supervisory program isn't available in an operating system.

simulation training, Training people for a real situation by using a simulated system.

simulator, Concerns a device or a program that mathematically simulates a certain system or process in order to enable people to study it.

simulator, overload, Used to test a device by creation of an artificial condition of overload or overflow.

simulator, program, A computer program used as an interpreter to permit programs written for one computer to be run on a different kind of computer.

simulator programs, (1) A computer program or routine representing a model of a system, (2) a routine that runs on one computer and simulates another computer.

simulator, table, A computer program routine that computes values of a table as needed rather than looking them up in a stored table.

simultaneity, Events occurring at the same time, such as two input/output operations.

simultaneity, tape processing, A feature in some computers that permits data transfer from magnetic tape to occur at the same time as other central processor operations.

simultaneous, The occurrence of two or more events at the same instant.

simultaneous access, See access, parallel.

simultaneous operations, The capability of performing input/output operations at the same time that other processing is taking place.

simultaneous throughput, The central processor functioning at the same time input and output data are being transferred.

simultaneous transmission, Transmission sending and receiving going on at the same time.

sin, An abbreviation for sine.

sine, A trigonometric function (of an angle or an arc).

singing, The sound caused by unstable oscillations on a line.

single address, A method of machine instruction in which each instruction describes one operation and involves one storage location.

single chip systems, Such chips used in a minimal configuration might include a few switches for control, a ROM for implementing instructions, and a few indicators for monitoring purposes. A maximum system might include several input/output peripherals, read/write as well as read-only memory (RAM or ROM), a full-featured control systems, etc.

single circuit, A circuit capable of non-simultaneous two way communication.

single error, An error bit that has at least one correct bit in front and in back of it.

single level address, Same as first level address.

single level memory, A method of memory organization that combines fast internal memory with slower external memory and they appear to be a single memory.

single office exchange, An exchange that is served by only one central office.

single precision, The use of one word per number in arithmetic in a computer.

single sideband transmission, A method in which only one sideband is transmitted. (See sideband.)

single-address message, A message that is only deliverable to one address as contrasted with multiple-address message.

single-sheet feeding, The feeding (generally manual) of one sheet at a time rather than in a long roll or continuous form.

single-step operation, Manually operating the computer a step at a time; generally used only for debugging.

sink, data, In a data transmission system, the equipment that accepts data.

sinusoid, half, Half of a cycle of a sine wave either the positive or negative portion.

sinusoidal, A characteristic form of a sine wave.

site preparation, The activity to get the physical site ready for a computer system or other equipment to be installed.

size error, An error that occurs when the number of positions in a data field is greater than allowed by the machine or program.

skew, A degree of nonsynchronization in supposedly parallel elements.

skew character, A form of misregistration in character recognition.

skew failure, A document (in machine readable form) is not aligned properly to be read.

skew, fax, The deviation from a rectangular picture (in facsimile transmission).

skew line, A type of line misregistration (in optical character recognition) in which the line appears slanted or skewed.

skew, tape, The condition in which tape isn't being fed properly.

skip, To ignore one or more instructions in a sequence of instructions.

skip code, A code used to tell the machine to skip certain fields in memory.

skip flag, A bit set in a position in storage that causes bytes to be skipped.

skip instruction, Synonymous with no-op instruction. Many cause a skip (jump) to another location.

skip, printer, Lines are skipped on a printer as designed or as programmed.

skip, tape, An instruction to move tape forward and erase what is recorded.

skipping, printer, Advancing paper through a printer without printing (generally programmed to do this).

slab, A small group of binary digits.

slave, A device that operates under the control of another device.

slave application, A computer application in which two computers are performing the same functions at the same time; and if any malfunction occurs in one computer, the other (the slave) takes over.

slave computer, A second computer in a system used when the master computer fails (a duplicate system for backup).

slave station, In communications the station that receives data from a master station and further processes it.

slave tube, A CRT (cathode ray tube, television-like device) that is connected to an identical master tube.

slave/master, An electronic unit under control of signals from ''master'' equipment.

slew, paper, A high speed printer skip. (See printer skip.)

slice, A special type of chip architecture that permits the cascading or stacking of devices to increase word bit size.

slice of a system, A piece (part) of a system's resources.

slice, system, The part of total system resources allocated to any segment.

SLIP, Symmetric List Processor, a high-level list processing (computer) language.

slip scan, A magnetic or photoelectric device in optical character recognition equipment.

slow memory, Computer memory that has a slow access rate, relatively speaking.

slow scan television, Using a microprocessor a system permits amateur radio operators to transmit video signals in about 1/1000 the bandwidth used by commercial TV.

slow storage, A storage device that has slow access when compared to speeds of arithmetic operations in the CPU (central processing unit).

SLSI, An acronym for super large scale integration, often related to 100,000 or more transistors or associated components per chip.

SLT, An abbreviation for Solid Logic Technology.

smart terminal, Some industry people suggest a truly intelligent terminal is user programmable while a smart terminal provides built-in capability not alterable by the user.

smooth, A process of removing or decreasing fluctuations in data.

smooth contact, A contact with a smooth profile, i.e., a flush surface.

smoothing, exponential, A statistical technique.

smudge, In optical character recognition ink that is some place it doesn't belong.

smudge, ink, The overflow of ink beyond the outline of a character (in optical character recognition).

smudge resistance, A characteristic of ink (resists smudging).

SNA components, Virtual teleprocessing access method (VTAM) for the host computer, network control program (NCP) for the communications controller, and synchronous Data Link Control (SDLC) for the line discipline.

snapshot debugging, A technique of computer program debugging in which "snapshots" of contents of registers and accumulators are recorded.

snapshot dump, A dump of a computer program at various points in a machine run; a dump is a printout of storage contents.

snapshot program, A specific computer program used to trace output on certain selected instructions of another program.

SNOBOL, A language developed by Bell Laboratories; uses string manipulation and pattern recognition.

soft sector, disk, Generally a method of marking sectors or sections on a disk using information written on the disk. Generally these sector marks are used by the disk controller to locate specific areas of the disk, e.g., floppy disks typically come from the supplier with preformatted sector codes, usually written on the disk between the data portions.

software, Generally refers to all the programs, computer languages, and operations used to make a computer perform a useful function. Software contrasts with hardware which constitutes all the tangible, physical elements of a computer system such as printers and CPUs.

software applications, Refers to the type of software that performs the specific jobs to be done in a business. For example, programs that perform order entry, accounts payable, accounts receivable, and general ledger. Applications software also refers to any general purpose program for an end user. Good examples are word processing and database programs.

software, common, Computer programs and routines used in a language common to many computers and users.

software, communications, The sets of computer program routines used in interrupt processing, message queuing, error control, etc.

software, compatible, Programming language or programs that can be used on more than one computer system.

software configuration, Basically this concerns the types of, and relationships between, the system control programs installed in a computer system. These control programs include operating systems, assemblers, and compilers.

software documents, All the documents related to the computer operation such as manuals and diagrams, also compilers, library routines, etc.

software flexibility, The availability of several versions of software that runs on various computer systems.

software package, A self-contained collection of programs designed to serve some specific set of requirements. Good commercial examples would be the SPSS statistics package that is sold as a unit, as are word processing packages, but not financial single programs.

software, systems, The software which comes with the machine, from the manufacturer, and is the general name for the set of programs that make the machine run itself effectively.

software, systems and support, The wide variety of software including assemblers, compilers, subroutine libraries, operating systems, application programs, etc.

software tool, A program that is used to help solve a data-processing problem. Software tools are often used as aids in writing programs for more complicated applications, such as artificial intelligence systems.

software/hardware, All the programming systems and programs used to support a computer. The computer or equipment itself is called hardware.

software-compatible, Generally, two or more computers are software-compatible if they use the same machine language, and, therefore, can execute the same programs. For example, all Atari 800 computers are software-compatible. Similarly, all Apple II computers are software-compatible.

solar cell, Photovoltaic cell using silicon that collects photons from the sun's radiation and converts the radiant energy into electrical power with reasonable efficiency. Used first in spacecraft and for remote locations lacking power supplies, i.e., for telephone amplifiers in the desert.

solenoid, forward-break, An electromechanical device.

solid logic technology (SLT), Microelectric circuits used as basic components of the system; transistors and diodes mounted on the circuits as small as 28 thousandths of an inch square.

solid state, Usually concerns a device whose operation depends on the bulk properties of the solid materials of which it is made, as opposed to devices such as vacuum and gas tubes.

solid-state circuitry, The solid state components in computers.

solid-state component, Components such as transistors, diodes, ferrite cores, etc., in computers and other equipment.

solution, feasible, (1) A solution to constraint equations in which all variables satisfy their sign restrictions (in linear programming). (2) In a loose general sense, a possible solution that is practical.

solution, graphic, A solution to a problem obtained with graphs or other pictorial devices, contrasted with solutions obtained by number manipulation (arithmetic calculations).

solution, machine independent, A solution described in logical terms rather than related to the computer equipment that will be used to solve the problem.

solver, equation, Usually an analog device used to solve linear simultaneous nondifferential equations, etc.

SOM, Abbreviation for Start Of Message; also, Self-Organizing Machine.

sonic delay line, A delay line using a medium for acoustic delay as related to mercury delay line.

sophisticated vocabulary, An advanced and elaborate set of computer instructions that perform mathematical operations.

sort, (1) A process used to arrange records in a particular order such as alphabetical or by social security number, etc., or the computer program used to do (1).

sort (noun), Refers to a processing operation that distributes information in alphabetical, numerical, or alphanumerical groups according to a given rule.

sort (verb), To arrange a set of items in a particular order.

sort, ascending, Placing data records in order where each record has a higher (or equal) number (or letter) such as a set of data records in social security number order where each record has a higher number than the one before it.

sort, block, A method of sorting (sorting first on the most major position to separate the data into several groups to be further sorted).

sort, bubble, An algorithm which sorts a list of items into ascending or descending order. A bubble sort works by scanning the list in several passes, and in each pass 'bubbling' the highest number to the top of the list.

sort, descending, A sort in which the output records are in a descending order, the highest key being first, then each following less than the previous. (See key.)

sort, external, A sorting algorithm which sorts data contained in secondary storage, such as a magnetic tape or disk storage unit.

sort, external, The second phase of a multipass sort in which strings of data are merged.

sort, fine, An off-line sorting especially used in banks to arrange checks and deposits into customer account number order.

sort, generalized, A sort (computer) program that may be used in varying ways as specified.

sort, generated, A sort computer program produced by a sort generator.

sort generator, A computer program that generates a sort (computer) program.

sort, internal, A sorting algorithm that sorts data which is contained entirely within the computer's memory. This contrasts with an external sort which sorts data in secondary storage. Internal sorts are used on small files where all the data can be contained within memory at one time.

sort, multipass, In various sort programs many passes of the data are required to complete the process.

sort, tennis-match, A method of sorting in which sort passes are made in both directions instead of just one.

sort/merge, A procedure used to combine two or more ordered sequences into a single file.

sort/merge program, A computer program used to accomplish the sorting and merging on magnetic tape or disk, a generalized program.

sorter, magnetic character, A machine that reads magnetic ink and sorts the documents with this ink on them.

sorting, The process of arranging data records into a particular order such as alphabetical (by name) or in order by social security number, etc.

sorting (intermediate pass), The parts of a sort that aren't the first or last pass.

sorting, balanced, A technique used in sorting programs to merge strings of sequenced data.

sorting, bubble, A method of sorting achieved by exchanging pairs of elements.

sorting, collating, A sort using continuous merging until the sequence is developed.

sorting, comparison of pairs, A method in sorting in which two records are compared and exchange positions if they are out of order.

sorting, disk, Using a disk memory device for auxiliary storage during sorting. (See sorting.)

sorting, external, The sorting of data which is located in an external storage device, such as a disk unit. External sorting is used for large groups of data which will not fit completely in the computer's memory all at once.

sorting, Fibonacci series, A method of sorting using Fibonacci series concepts.

sorting, insertion method, A method of internal sorting in which records are moved so other records can be inserted.

sorting key, The field in a record that is used as the basis for a sort to sequence the records in a file.

sorting, merge, A method of sorting by merging two or more sequences of data.

sorting, multifile, The sequencing of more than one file automatically without operator intervention.

sorting, own coding, Coding provided by a computer programmer that is used in combination with the sort coding.

sorting pass, One access of each of a series of records.

sorting, phase, Sorting done in three phases, initialization, internal, and merge phases.

sorting, restart, A point in the sort program that can be returned to if a restart is necessary.

sorting, sequence, The data field that determines the order of records in sorting, such as social security number, customer name, etc.

sorting, sequencing key, The key (specific field) in a data record used for sequencing a file of records.

sorting, string, A sorting method in which several strings (sequences) of data are combined to form a sorted file.

sorting, variable length records, Sorting records in which the number of words, characters, bits, fields, etc., vary in·length.

sorting, work tape(s), Same as scratch tapes used in sorting.

sorts, tape, Sorts written to be processed on a magnetic tape, a generalized set of programs.

sound powered telephone, A telephone that derives its operating power from the speech input unit only.

source, The origin of energy.

source computer, A computer that is used to prepare input for other computers.

source data, Data that becomes computer input or data transmission equipment supplying the data.

source destination instruction, Same as functional address instruction format.

source document, The document that will be used to take data from to be converted into machine readable form.

source file, Same as input file.

source, information, An information generator.

source language, The language written by a programmer that will be translated into machine language by an assembler, compiler, etc.

source language debugging, Detecting and correcting computer program errors by looking at the source language program instead of the machine language version.

source machine, The machine (computer) used to translate a source program into an object program (machine language).

source, message, The location in a communication system where the message originates.

source module, A set of source language statements in a machine readable form.

source, noise, The origin of any unwanted signals.

source program, Any computer program that must be translated into machine language before it can be executed.

source, program library, A collection of computer programs in source language form.

space, A capacity for storing data, as on a disk, tape, or in main memory.

space attributes, (1) An impulse causing a loop to open. (2) To vertically "space up" on a printer. (3) One or more blanks.

space character, A character designed to prevent a print.

space, dead, The range of values that a signal can be altered without changing the outgoing response. It is synonymous with switching blank, dead zone and similar to neutral zone.

space, interblock, The space on magnetic tape between blocks of data on which nothing is written.

space, interword, Same as interword gap.

space key, carriage, A push button on a computer printer that spaces the paper vertically.

space suppression, In printing suppressing the automatic spacing that normally takes place before or after printing a line.

space to mark transition, Switching from a spacing impulse to a marking impulse.

space, word, The area or space required to hold a word in devices such as magnetic disk, drum, tape, etc.

space, working, A section of storage reserved for data being processed, i.e., temporary storage.

spacing, In data transmission contrasted with marking.

spacing chart, printer, A special form used to draw a layout of the printed output for a program, used in planning and documentation.

spacing pulse (teletypewriter), A signal pulse which indicates a "no current" condition.

span, The difference between the highest and lowest value of a quantity.

span, mathematical, The algebraic difference between upper and lower range values.

special character, A character other than a digit or a letter, such as $, *, +, -, #, etc.

special purpose computer, A computer designed to be used to solve a specific class of problem or small range of problems.

specific addressed location, In random access devices an address that may be directly accessed without a sequential search.

specific addressing, Same as absolute addressing.

specific code, Computer code using absolute addresses and operation codes. It is synonymous with basic code and one-level code.

specific program, A program used to solve one problem, generally used only once.

specific routine, A computer program routine using addresses that refer to explicit registers and locations.

specification, A precise definition of records, programs, concepts, hardware, etc.

specification file, Same as forms file.

specification program, A program used to design precise definitions of logic of routines and routine segments.

spectrum, frequency, The range of frequencies of electromagnetic radiation waves.

speech synthesizer, Some are hard-wired analogs of the human vocal tract that can say anything. Various portions of the circuit simulate the vocal cords, the lungs, and the variable frequency resonant acoustic cavity of the mouth, tongue, lips, and teeth.

spelling, The order of characters or symbols within words.

split, Breaking up a file into two files. It is the opposite of merge.

split catalog, A catalog with sets of entries by subject, author, and title.

spool, An acronym for simultaneous peripheral operation on line.

spooling, A technique by which data is moved from a slow input/output (I/O) device (e.g., card reader) to a fast input/output device (e.g., magnetic disk) before that data is accessed by main storage or output for the user. This helps to minimize the speed disparity between the internal speeds of the computer and the input/output devices.

spooling queuing, Technique by which output to slow devices is placed into queues on mass storage devices to await transmission allowing more efficient use of the system since programs using low-speed devices can run to completion quickly and make room for others.

sporadic fault, Same as intermittent fault.

spot, action, A spot on the face of a cathode ray tube (CRT) that stores a digit and holds a charge.

spot, carbon, A section of carbon paper on a multipart form so that only that area is reproduced on the copy (or copies).

spot, flying, A small spot of light that rapidly moves in a CRT (Cathode Ray Tube), a television-like computer terminal.

spot, reflective, A silver strip on magnetic tape at the beginning of the reel of tape.

spreadsheet, A popular type of financial modelling package of which Lotus 1, 2, 3 is an example.

sprite, A user-defined block of pixels that can be placed anywhere on the screen. Sprites are maintained directly by the hardware and simplify the programming of video games.

SPS, (1) Abbreviation for Symbolic Program System, a computer programming language. (2) Abbreviation for String Process System.

SPS (string process system), A computer programming package of subroutines used to perform operations on strings of characters.

squeal, A noise heard in magnetic tape operation caused by vibrating tape if there is friction.

squeezeout ink, Character printing in which the outline of the character is darker than the center (in optical character recognition).

SSC, An abbreviation for Station Selection Code.

stability, A characteristic of staying stable.

stability, carbon, The resistance of carbon (ribbons and forms) to deterioration (during storage on the shelf especially).

stability, computational, The reliability and validity of a computational process.

stability, light, In optical character recognition, the resistance to change of color of the image when exposed to light.

stack, A list of items with additions and deletions made to a list at one end - the top of the stack. Stacks are called Last-In-First-Out or LIFO lists.

stack pointer, The address of a location at the top of the stack.

stack, push down, Access on a last-in, first-out basis.

stack register, A special register within the central processing unit (CPU) which keeps track of return addresses for subroutine jumps. The stack is a Last-In-First-Out structure that is able to retain the correct return addresses for subroutines.

stack, storage, A group of storage elements, i.e., a stack of data.

stacked job control, The jobs (computer programs) are performed in the sequence that they enter into the system.

stacking, job, The ability of a monitor system to batch process compilations, assemblies, etc., i.e., jobs are stacked and left to run without human intervention.

stand-alone capability, The ability of a device to function independently of any other equipment part or all of the time.

stand-alone system, A microcomputer software development system or other computer components that run without connection to another computer or a time-sharing system.

standard, An accepted set of criteria for measure of performance, practice, size, etc.

standard data phones, Standard telephone company data sets used in data processing.

standard deviation, A statistical term used to compare to a normal distribution.

standard error, The standard deviation when it is considered in as a measurement of error. (See standard deviation.)

standard form, A prescribed arrangement of data elements.

standard graph, A plotted graph with an x scale and a y scale.

standard interface, A device used to connect two or more units, systems, etc., that matches a standard.

standard interrupts, Those program interrupts standard in a system. (See interrupt.)

standardization, Establishing standard procedures and methods in data processing.

standardization signal, Same as regeneration signal.

star program, A program designed by a programmer and checked so there are no mistakes, i.e., it should run the first time on the computer.

start control, analog, A push button to start a problem on an analog device.

start element, The first element in data transmission used for synchronization.

start, external device, A signal that occurs if the particular external device is not busy and the channel is not busy.

start key, A push button used to continue the operation of equipment in a stopped condition.

start of heading character, A character sent by a polled terminal that indicates the beginning of addresses of stations to receive the answering message.

start of text character, A control character used in communications to end and separate a heading and indicate beginning of message content (text).

start-stop system, A system in communications that uses a start signal to get the receiver ready and a stop signal to indicate the end of that set.

start-stop system, stepped, A start-stop system in which the start signals come at regular intervals.

start-stop time, Same as acceleration time, deceleration time.

start-stop transmission, The asynchronous transmission in a start-stop system. (see start-stop system.)

state, The condition of a unit, device, element, circuit, etc., such as on or off, 1 or 0, etc.

state, armed, The state of an interrupt level in which it can accept and "remember" an input signal.

state, disarmed, The state of an interrupt level in which it cannot accept an input signal.

state, input, The state of a channel condition, i.e., positive, negative, etc.

state, major, Generally the control state of a computer.

statement, A set of instructions that make up one unit of a computer program.

statement, declarative, An instruction in symbolic coding used to define areas, constants, and symbols, etc.

statement, execute, A job control statement that indicates execution of a job.

statement, job control, Individual statements in the job control language (JCL) that provide information to the operating system as to how the job is to be run.

statement number, A number assigned to a computer program statement to allow reference to it from other parts of the program.

static dump, A printout of the contents of computer memory at a particular time during a machine run.

static errors, Errors that are independent of time as contrasted with dynamic errors that depend on frequency.

static gain, The ratio of output to input after a steady state has been reached. (See gain.)

static printout, A printout that doesn't occur at the same time as other operations, but after.

static RAM, Data is stored in a conventional bistable flip-flop and need not be refreshed, as with the dynamic RAM.

static routine, A computer program subroutine using no parameters except addresses of operands.

static subroutine, See static routine.

static vs. dynamic simulation, In a dynamic system the activity is time dependent. A static system is not time sensitive.

staticize, A procedure or procedures used to convert serial or time dependent parallel data into static time form.

staticizer, A special storage device used for converting time sequential information into static time parallel information.

station, 1 An input or output point on a communication system; a terminal; a machine. 2 A telephone set. 3 A magnetic tape unit.

station attributes, (1) A location in a machine where a particular function is performed. (2) In communications a terminal or other device located at a particular place.

station, brush, The location in a punched card machine where reading brushes are.

station console, data, In communications a console (generally remote) that performs reading, printing, and data sending and receiving.

station, data, A remote terminal used for a broad range of communications functions.

station, display, A cathode ray tube (CRT), television-like terminal.

station, exchange, In communications a type of system in which any two customers can be interconnected by an exchange.

station extension, A telephone extension.

station, remote, Data terminal equipment used to communicate with a data processing system from a location that is spatially, temporally, or electrically distant.

station, repeater, A communications station at which a repeater is used to build up and equalize the strength of signals in a long time.

station, slave, In communications the station that receives data from a master station and further processes it.

station, subscriber, The communications service that connects a customer's location to a central office.

station, tributary, One of the many stations under control of a master station.

station, way, One of the stations on a multipoint circuit.

statistic, A numerical property of a sample (small part of a large group).

statistical analysis, A technique that uses mathematical means and computer capability to handle a wide variety of business and scientific problems when large amounts of data must be evaluated and analyzed.

statistical hypothesis, In statistical analysis, an assumption about the frequency distribution of observations.

statistical method, A technique used to gather, present, and analyze data.

statistical sample, A small set of items (out of a whole group) that is used for statistical analysis.

statistics, Study and use of the science of making predictions of characteristics using mathematical techniques.

statistics, analytical, Used to draw statistical inferences about characteristics of a "universe" of data from a sample.

statistics, Bayesian, A type of statistics that uses estimates of probability distribution in order to incorporate new data using Bayes' equation.

statistics, business, Used to evaluate risks of wrong decisions based on insufficient data being available.

status, external device, The response of its busy signal and interrupt request signal when the device recognizes its address.

status, line, The status of a communications line (e.g., receive, transmit, or control).

status maps, A table (usually) showing status of programs and input/output operations.

status table, subroutine, The computer program routine used to maintain a list of subroutines in memory and to get subroutines from a file as needed.

status word, A computer word containing information necessary to continue processing after an interruption.

status word, CANCL, The status word indicating that the remote computing system has deleted some information.

status word, communications, A special word location in storage containing status information.

status word, ERROR, The status word indicating that the remote computing system has detected an error.

status word, program (PSW), A computer word containing information used in interrupt processing.

status word, READY, The status word indicating that the remote computing system is waiting for entry from the terminal.

status words, Computer words containing various information used to control processing.

steady state, A stabilized condition in which output has reached a constant rate of change for a constant input.

step change, A change in a single increment from one value to another in negligible time.

step counter, A counter used to count steps in multiplication and division and shift operations in the arithmetic unit of a computer.

step, job, A measured unit of work from the viewpoint of the (computer) user (one or more steps to make a job).

step, program, A single operation; one computer program instruction.

step-by-step switch, A switch that is synchronized with a pulse device such as a telephone dial.

step-by-step system, A type of line switching system that uses step-by-step switches.

step-down transformer, A component whose output voltage is less than the input voltage.

stepping switch, A switching device that advances from one condition to the next when it receives an input pulse.

step-up transformer, A component whose output voltage is greater than the input voltage.

stereo microscope, A multipowered microscope used in manufacturing integrated systems.

sticking, The tendency of some bistable devices to remain in or switch back to a state (in switches and flip-flops; an undesirable condition).

stochastic variable, A statistical variable that has a probability with which it may assume each of many possible values in a set.

stock, finished, A production item that requires no further processing.

stock report, inventory, A printed report showing the current amount of each item (carried in inventory) that is on hand.

stop, automatic, An automatic stopping of computer operation when an error is detected by computer checking devices.

stop code, A code read in the reader of tape-operated equipment that stops the reader and suspends operation.

stop, coded, A stop instruction in a computer program.

stop control, analog, This control ends processing in an analog device and permits the final values to be read.

stop, dynamic, An instruction that branches to itself (in a computer program).

stop, form, On a data processing printer, a device that causes the printer to stop when it runs out of paper.

stop instruction, A computer program instruction that stops the computer.

stop key, A push button that causes a stop of processing after completion of the instruction being processed at that moment.

stop, loop, A small closed loop in computer programming used to indicate an error to the operator, etc.

stop, program, Using a computer program stop instruction to stop the computer under certain conditions.

stop signal (in a start-stop system), Indicates the end of transmission.

stop time, The time between completion of reading or writing of tape and when the tape stops moving.

stopper, The highest (has the highest address) memory location in any given computer system.

storage, A device to which data can be transferred and from which it can be obtained at a later time.

storage access, auxiliary types, Storage of relatively larger capacity and slower access than normal internal storage.

storage access, cyclic, A storage unit designed so that access to any location is possible at only specific, equally spaced times.

storage address display lights, The indicator lights on the operator's console that display the bit pattern in an address.

storage allocation, A method of reserving blocks of storage for certain information.

storage allocation, dynamic, A feature in which storage for a subroutine is assigned to the first available storage; results in storage saving.

storage, annex, Same as associative storage.

storage area, A specific location or locations used for defined purposes, such as input/output area, constant area, or an area containing a program, etc.

storage area, disk, The area(s) on magnetic disk used for work in process; not permanent or even semi-permanent.

storage area, temporary, An area of computer memory used for intermediate states of computation. It is sometimes called "scratch-pad" memory.

storage, associative, A memory device in which a location is identified by its contents rather than by names or position.

storage, associative, A storage system in which computer storage locations are identified by their contents.

storage, auxiliary, A storage device that is under the control of the computer, but not directly a part of it, e.g., disk and tape.

storage, auxiliary, The storage devices other than main storage of a computer, such as magnetic tape, magnetic disk, etc.

storage, backing, The storage devices other than main storage (same as auxiliary storage).

storage, block, A section of computer storage considered as a single element.

storage, buffer, Any of several devices that temporarily store information during transfer; storage between devices to make up for differences in speeds.

storage, bulk, Computer storage of large volume but a slower speed such as cassette and disk. It is also called external or secondary storage.

storage, byte, The type of computer storage used on the IBM System 360 (8-bit byte).

storage capacity, The maximum number of bits, bytes, characters, words, etc., that can be stored in a device at one time.

storage cells, A basic unit of storage or areas of a magnetic surface that are separately magnetized.

storage, changeable, Devices in which storage can be removed from the machine and put back later, such as disk packs, tape reels, etc.

storage circuits, Flip-flops. (See flip-flop.)

storage, circulating, Devices that store information in a pattern of pulses that are sensed, amplified, reshaped, and reinserted into the device.

storage, common, Storage that is used to hold intermediate data that can be maintained between programs.

storage compacting, Dynamic relocation of programs.

storage, computer, The storage in a data processing system that may be controlled automatically without need for human intervention.

storage, constant, Parts of storage used to store non-varying quantities (constant data).

storage, content addressed, Accessing data by the contents of storage rather than the address.

storage, coordinate, Two dimensional storage that needs two coordinates to access a location, e.g., cathode ray tube storage.

storage, core, Storage that represents data by position of magnetic cores (very tiny rings) used in internal memory of older computers.

storage cycle, The cycle (sequence of events) occurring when information is transferred to and from storage in a computer.

storage cycle time, The time required in milliseconds, microseconds, nanoseconds, etc., for a storage cycle.

storage, dedicated, Storage that is reserved and committed to some specific purpose.

storage density, The number of bits, bytes, characters, etc., per unit length, such as characters per inch, etc.

storage, destructive, Storage that needs to be regenerated to be retained, e.g., CRT, cathode ray tube storage.

storage device, A device used to receive and retain data for later use.

storage device, mass, Storage units with large capacity such as magnetic disk, drum, data cells, etc.

storage device, secondary, A device which provides additional memory for a computer system. The memory in secondary storage is usually non-volatile, in other words, is not affected if the computer is turned off or being used to execute another program. Examples of secondary storage devices are magnetic tape units and disk storage units.

storage devices, direct access, Storage devices, such as magnetic disk and ROM, that are capable of fast and direct access to storage locations.

storage, direct access, Storage devices in which the access of specific data is not dependent on the last position accessed.

storage, disk, Storage of data on surfaces of floppy or fixed disks.

storage, drum, A magnetic storage device of large capacity and with random access.

storage dump, A printout of the contents of internal storage; same as memory dump, memory printout and dump.

storage dumping, The process of transferring data from one storage device to another. (See, also, storage dump.)

storage, dynamic, The mobility of stored data in time and space.

storage, electrostatic, Storage on a dielectric surface such as the screen of a CRT, cathode ray tube, television-like device, or storage using electric charges to represent data.

storage, erasable, Reusable storage such as magnetic disk, EROM, EAROM, etc.

storage, exchange, Interchanging of contents of two storage areas; also exchange of data between storage and other elements of a system.

storage, external, Storage on devices such as magnetic tape, disk, cassette, etc., as opposed to internal storage (memory) in the CPU (central processing unit) of a computer.

storage, fast access, Computer storage with the fastest access (relative to other types of storage).

storage, file, A type of storage designed to contain a relative large file (generally direct access).

storage, fixed, Computer storage devices that store data that can't be changed by computer instructions (same as permanent storage and non-erasable storage).

storage, flip-flop, A bistable computer storage that stores binary data as states of flip-flop elements. (See flip-flop.)

storage, high-speed, Storage devices that are relatively high speed compared to the other storage devices.

storage, immediate access, Storage that has access time that is slight by comparison, i.e., very fast or real-time capabilities.

storage, inherent, Automatic storage, e.g., internal storage in the CPU, central processing unit, of a computer.

storage, input, A storage area to receive input.

storage, input/output, A storage area in the computer, used in processing input and output.

storage inquiry, direct access, Directly requesting and obtaining information from a storage device (such as from a magnetic disk file).

storage, instantaneous, Storage media with an access time that is slight compared to operation time.

storage, instruction, The area in computer storage used to store a computer program.

storage key, A set of bits associated with every word or character in a block of storage.

storage, large-capacity core (LCS), Storage in one or two million increments that can be added to some computer systems.

storage, laser emulsion, A data storage medium using a controlled laser beam to expose very small areas of a photosensitive surface.

storage light, An indicator light that turns on when there is a parity check error on a character read into storage

storage location, A storage position designated by an address (or a register).

storage locations, buffer, A set of storage locations used to temporarily hold data to compensate for differences in data rates going from one device to another.

storage, long-term, A relative term referring to data stored in internal memory for a long time.

storage, loop, A particular storage device using loops of magnetic tape as a storage medium.

storage, low-speed, A storage device with access time longer than the speed of the arithmetic operations in the central processing unit; also, slower than other peripheral units.

storage, magnetic, Various devices that use magnetic properties to store information.

storage, magnetic card, A type of storage using the magnetized surface of flexible plastic cards.

storage, magnetic disk, A storage device consisting of several circular surfaces of magnetic material upon which data is recorded and that can be used for direct access.

storage, magnetic drum, A drum-like (cylindrical) storage device with a magnetic surface upon which data is recorded; can be accessed by a computer.

storage, magnetic film, A thin film magnetic storage used for high speed internal memory.

storage, magnetic tape, A magnetic coated plastic tape on reels (like a tape recorder) that can contain data to be read and written by a computer.

storage, main, Generally the internal (fastest) storage in a computer as contrasted with auxiliary storage.

storage management, time-sharing, The relocation of computer programs, storage protection, and allocation of storage.

storage map, An aid to the programmer used to estimate the amounts of storage needed for data, etc.

storage mark, A character pointer to the left of an accumulator.

storage mark, record, A symbol used to indicate the length of a record being read.

storage, matrix, Same as coordinate storage.

storage medium, The material or device that data is recorded on such as magnetic tape, disks, RAM, etc.

storage, non destructive, Storage that doesn't need to be regenerated; such devices as cores, tapes, disks, as contrasted with destructive storage.

storage, nonvolatile, Storage media that retains information in case of power failure.

storage, off-line, Storage that isn't under control of the central processing unit of a computer.

storage, on-line mass, Mass storage devices that are available to the computer system (connected) for processing.

storage, output, Same as output area.

storage parallel, Storage in which characters or digits are processed simultaneously (in parallel).

storage, parallel search, Same as associative storage.

storage parity, Parity checking during data transfer from one storage to another storage device.

storage, permanent, A media or device capable of retaining information such as magnetic tape, punched paper tape, etc., also, non-volatile storage.

storage, photographic, Any storage using photographic processes.

storage, primary, Generally the fastest storage in a computer system, i.e., internal memory as contrasted with auxiliary storage.

storage print program, A computer program used to print the contents of storage. (See dump.)

storage, program, The internal computer storage used to store programs, routines, and subroutines.

storage protect, A computer hardware function in which sections of storage are protected against destruction, i.e., nothing can replace the information in those areas.

storage protection, Preventing sections of storage contents from being replaced.

storage, push-down, A technique used in which data enters at the top register and information is pushed down from register to register.

storage, push-up, A technique in which the next item of data to be retrieved is the oldest, i.e., been in the queue the longest.

storage, quick-access, Same as high-speed storage.

storage, random access, Storage in which the time required to access information is independent of the last location accessed, such as magnetic disk and drum.

storage, rapid access, Same as high-speed storage.

storage, recording, In communications the process that provides for preservation of signals.

storage reference count technique, A technique used to reclaim unused storage space. In this method, unused cells are reclaimed the instant they become inaccessible to the main program.

storage, regenerative, Storage such as in CRT (cathode ray tube) that needs to be regenerated to maintain the image.

storage register, A register in computer storage rather than other units of the computer; same as memory register.

storage registers, associative, Registers that are not identified by name or position but are identified by their content.

storage relocation processor, A computer program routine used to relocate (put in a different place) computer programs during processing.

storage, resolver, A small part of storage on magnetic disk, drum, and tape that has a faster access than the rest of the storage.

storage, scratch-pad, A high-speed memory used to store information in interrupt processing.

storage, secondary, External storage devices such as magnetic tape, disk, etc.

storage, sequential-access, Items are one after another in storage (e.g., on magnetic tape) as contrasted with random access storage.

storage, serial, Sequential access storage and contrasted with random access storage.

storage, shared, Storage that is available to two computers.

storage stack, A group of storage elements, i.e., a stack of data.

storage, static, Storage or information that is fixed, e.g., flip-flop, electrostatic, etc.

storage switch, Same as manual storage switch.

storage switch, manual, Sets of switches used for manual entry of data into the computer.

storage thrashing, In a virtual storage environment, thrashing refers to an excessive amount of moving pages from secondary storage to the internal storage.

storage, uniformly accessible, A type of storage in which the variation in access time is minimal.

storage unit, A general term referring to any unit capable of storing data.

storage, volatile, Storage that loses information in case of power failure.

storage, volatile dynamic, A storage medium that depends on external power to retain stored information.

storage volatility, The tendency of a storage device to lose information in case of power failure.

storage, working, Used as temporary storage for intermediate results of processing; may mean internal storage as well as disk storage.

storage, zero-access, An incorrect term implying that no time is required to access storage, although the time is very small.

store, To transmit the data from the central processing unit (CPU) or an input device to a computer memory device.

store-and-forward, A type of message switching system.

store-and-forward switching, Same as message switching.

store-and-forward switching center, A type of communications switching center in which a message is accepted when it is sent, held in store, and forwarded when the receiver is ready.

stored program, A computer program that is in storage and ready to use.

stored program computer, A general term referring to computers that have the capability of storing a computer program of instructions to the computer.

stored routine, A stored computer program routine. (See stored program.)

STR, An abbreviation for Synchronous Transmitter Receiver.

straight binary, Binary representation of binary numbers.

straight-line coding, Computer programming in which coding is repeated instead of using programmed loops.

stream, bit, Bits being transmitted over a circuit one after the other in a stream (communications). (See bit.)

strength, impact, The ability of magnetic tape to withstand sudden stress.

strength, signal, A measure of the amplitude of the signal obtained from reading devices or a rise in energy level.

strength, tear, The force necessary to tear tape or base film; a measurement of resistance to tearing.

strength, yield, The minimum force per unit cross-sectional area at which tape deforms.

string, A group of characters stored in a computer as a unit.

string, alphabetic, A sequence of letters of an alphabet; a character string.

string, bit, A one-dimensional array of bits (all in a row). (See array.)

string break, The point in a string at which no more records with higher (or lower in descending strings) belong on the string.

string, character, A sequence of characters in a row.

string, file, A string used to order or arrange records for convenient reference. (See string.)

string, flip-flop, A sequence of flip-flops in a row. (See flip-flop.)

string length, The number of records in a string (a string of data records in sorting).

string manipulation, The procedure used to manipulate (process) strings of characters, records, bits, etc.

string, null, An empty string, i.e., contains no elements.

string process system (SPS), A computer programming package of subroutines used to perform operations on strings of characters.

string, pulse, A sequence (series) of pulses in a circuit.

string sorting, A sorting method in which several strings (sequences) of data are combined to form a sorted file.

string, symbol, A one dimensional array of items ordered by reference to the relations between adjacent elements.

string types, (1) A connected sequence of characters, words, bits, etc. (2) A set of records arranged in an ascending or descending order by some criteria (their keys).

string, unit, A sequence containing only one element, related to null string having no elements.

strings, Several separate sequences of records that will be combined in the sorting process.

strip, demarcation, In communications an interface between a machine and the common carrier.

strip, encoding, On bank checks the area where magnetic ink is used to represent characters.

stripe recording, magnetic, Recording of data on magnetic stripes on a document as in magnetic-striped ledgers or on debit and credit cards.

stroke, A line segment or mark used to form characters in optical character recognition.

stroke analysis, A method of analysis used in character recognition.

stroke centerline, A line used to designate the midpoint of characters in optical character recognition.

stroke, character, A line segment or mark used to form characters in optical character recognition.

stroke edge, An imaginary line equidistant from the stroke centerline in optical character recognition.

stroke edge irregularity, Deviation of the edge of a character from its stroke edge (in optical character recognition).

structure, The arrangement of elements or parts that make up a whole.

structure, block, A technique of blocking program segments for storage purposes.

structure flowcharts, Generalized flowcharts showing input, processing, and output without indicating specific methods of processing. (See flowchart.)

structure tables, Tables representing decision logic as related to decision table.

STRUDL (STRUctural Design Language), A language used for analysis and design of structures.

stunt box, A device to perform functions such as carriage return, line feed, etc., in a teleprinter.

STX, Abbreviation for Start-of-Text. It is a control character that designates the boundary between the message heading and the text of a message to be transmitted. In ASCII, the STX character is represented by the ASCII code '002.'

style, The construction of characters (their style) in optical character recognition.

style, character, The style (construction characteristics) of a character in optical character recognition.

stylus (light pen), A pen-like instrument used as a pointer to a CRT (cathode ray tube).

stylus, electronic, A light pen used with a CRT (cathode ray tube) for inputting and changing information.

stylus printer, A printer that forms characters by pressing a set of wires against the ribbon or paper (same as wire printer).

subalphabet, A subset of an alphabet, e.g., the letters I, J, K, L, M, and N.

subchannel, In communications a channel derived from another channel.

subject program, Same as source program.

subjunction gate, Same as gate, A and not B, and gate, B and not A. (See gates.)

sublist, A typical sublist is a list within a larger list. For example, within the list (a, b, c, (aa, bb), (dd, ee, ff)) (aa, bb) and (dd, ee, ff) are both sublists.

suboptimal, Not yet optimal.

suboptimization, The process of optimizing a part of a total objective.

subprogram, A part of a computer program that is translated separately.

subprogram, loop, A segment of a program which performs a specific function. If that function is to be carried out more than once, a subprogram can help reduce the amount of programming required, as the function only needs to be programmed once and can be executed as a loop or as required during the program.

subroutine, A set of instructions given a particular name that will be executed when a main program's instructions or commands call for it.

subroutine applications, A computer program routine that is translated separately. It is generally used in several computer programs or several times in one program.

subroutine calling sequence, See calling sequence.

subroutine calls, The linkage between a subroutine and a main program.

subroutine, closed, A computer program subroutine that is stored separately and linked into various computer programs as needed.

subroutine, dating, A computer program subroutine that processes dates and times related to processing.

subroutine, direct insert, Same as in-line subroutine and open subroutine as contrasted with closed subroutine.

subroutine, division, A computer program subroutine that performs the calculations of division, reciprocals, etc.

subroutine, dynamic, A computer program subroutine that uses parameters to adjust its processing.

subroutine, editing, A computer program subroutine used with input/output operations to perform editing.

subroutine, first order, A computer program subroutine that is entered directly from the main computer program and later returned to it.

subroutine, generalized, A computer program subroutine that is general in nature and may be used by many computer programs.

subroutine, in-line, A computer program subroutine that is inserted wherever it is needed and recopied each place it is used in a program as contrasted with closed subroutine.

subroutine, inserted, A computer program subroutine that is inserted into the main computer program at each place it is used.

subroutine library, A set of computer program subroutines kept on file for use (to be incorporated into computer programs).

subroutine, linked, A computer program subroutine that is linked by special instructions to a main computer program.

subroutine, open, An in-line subroutine as contrasted with closed subroutine.

subroutine, parametric, Same as dynamic subroutine.

subroutine, relocatable, a computer program subroutine designed to be located physically and independently in computer memory as required.

subroutine, standard, A computer program subroutine designed to solve a class of problems and usable by many users.

subroutine, static, See static routine.

subroutine status table, The computer program routine used to maintain a list of subroutines in memory and to get subroutines from a file as needed.

subroutine table, A listing of computer program subroutines in main memory.

subroutine, test, A computer program subroutine used to test if the computer is functioning properly.

subroutines, I/O (input/output), Generalized computer program subroutines used to process input, output, formatting, etc.

subroutines, nest of, The situation in which one subroutine calls another and that perhaps calls another, etc., each time returning to the calling subroutine.

subroutines, scientific, Generally a set of computer program subroutines supplied by the computer company and used to perform various mathematical and statistical routines.

subroutines, violation, When a violation of subroutines occur, a violation subroutine takes over control.

subscriber line, A telephone line between a central office and some end equipment.

subscriber station, The communications service that connects a customer's location to a central office.

subscript, Generally, a symbol or number that is used to identify an element in an array.

subscript, An indexing notation, such as $X(1)$, $X(2)$, $X(3)$, etc., where 1, 2, and 3 are subscripts.

subsegment tables, Tables referring to the subsegments in each segment.

subsequence counter, A computer instruction counter used to count parts of operations (microoperations).

subsequent, A part of a program segment.

subset, (1) A set within a set of elements. (2) A contraction of the words subscribers' set. (3) A modulation/demodulation (modem) device in communications.

subsets, remote, Communications subsets at remote locations (not at the same place as the computer).

substep, A part of a step.

substitute, To replace or a replacement of an element.

substitute mode, A method of exchange buffering. (See buffer.)

subsystem, communications, Generally consists of multiplexers and parts of communications systems.

subsystem control, communication, Control by function words that activate control lines.

subsystems, A part of a system; may be sets of peripheral equipment.

subtask, A task created by a previous task.

subvoice grade channel, A channel whose bandwidth is less than that of voice grade channels.

suffix, The last part of the label name used to describe an item in a programming language.

sum, The result developed from adding two quantities.

sum check, The checking that takes place when digits are summed.

sum, check digit, A digit that reflects various combinations of summing done on a number. It is used for checking purposes.

sum, logical, The result of the inclusive OR operation (a Boolean logic operation).

sum, partial, A result obtained without carries; same as the result of an exclusive OR operation.

sum, sideways, An unordinary way of arriving at a sum for checking purposes.

summarizing, Recording data in summary form for totals and balancing.

summary, A report showing a summary of a detailed report; a condensed report not showing detail.

summer, In an analog computer a unit summing inputs to yield an output.

summing integrator, In an analog computer an amplifier used to sum voltages.

summing point, A point at which signals are added.

sunspots, Electrical disturbances that affect radio communication.

superconductivity, A physical characteristic of some materials that have zero resistance to flow of electric current at some temperatures.

superimpose (SI), To place on top of as in replacing data in storage.

superposed (superimposed) ringing, The selective ringing in party line telephones.

superscript, A numeral used in mathematical notation. One example is a power that a number is being raised to; in X squared (X2), the 2 is the superscript.

supervisor, A computer program routine that is an executive routine, a controlling routine in an operating system.

supervisor, computer, The person responsible for computer operations.

supervisor, executive, In large systems, the computer program routine that controls sequencing, setup, and execution of all runs on the computer.

supervisor interrupts, Same as supervisor-call interrupts.

supervisor mode, A mode of operation in which the supervisor program is in control.

supervisor, operating system, The part of the operating system that is the supervisor program.

supervisor, overlay, A computer program routine that is used to control the overlaying of parts of computer programs.

supervisor, program test, A supervisory computer program that is used to test other computer programs.

supervisor, system, A computer program designed to control the job flow in a system with a minimum of operator intervention.

supervisor-call interrupts, Caused by the program giving an instruction to turn over control to the supervisor (operating system).

supervisory, Those functions performed by the supervisor program.

supervisory console, A console including the operator's panel, a keyboard and typewriter, a control unit, and perhaps disk or tape input/output devices.

supervisory control signaling, Signals that automatically actuate equipment at a remote terminal.

supervisory instruction, A computer instruction unique to the supervisor used to control operation.

supervisory keyboard, In the supervisory console consisting of an operator's control panel, a keyboard and typewriter, and a control unit.

supervisory program, Computer programs used to control specific functions. (See supervisor, program test supervisor, etc.)

supervisory signals, Signals that indicate the operating states of circuit combinations.

supplementary maintenance, Machine maintenance other than normal preventative maintenance and repair.

supply pressure, That pressure at the supply port of a device.

support chips, Chips that are required to assist the CPU chip for complete operation beyond the basic processor operation, such as IOP, input/output processors, peripheral control chips, etc.

support processor, attached, One or more additional computers that are connected to increase the efficiency of processing.

support programs, Computer programs that support or aid the supervisory programs and applications programs, such as diagnostics, data generators, etc.

support systems, Systems used to develop or support other functions.

suppression, Not printing, i.e., suppression of printing.

suppression, space, In printing suppressing the automatic spacing that normally takes place before or after printing a line.

suppression, zero, The process that eliminates zeros at the left of a data field so they don't appear when the number is printed.

suppressor, echo, A device in telephone circuits to eliminate an echo sound.

surface recording, Storage of information on a surface such as the coating on magnetic tape, etc.

surface treatment, A process used to improve surface smoothness of a coating such as on magnetic tape.

suspense file, A file of information needing attention at certain times, i.e., things to be processed at particular times.

swap time, The time needed to transfer a computer program from external storage to internal storage and vice versa.

swapping, tape, Selection of alternate magnetic tape units to minimize the interruptions to processing.

sweep circuits, The circuits that guide the movement of a beam in a tube.

swing, frequency, The frequency above and below the carrier frequency.

swing, logic, The voltage difference between two logic levels 1 and 0 (one and zero).

switch, Procedure to establish a temporary interconnection between two or more stations over communications paths. Also, a short term for a line or message switcher.

switch, alteration, A switch on a computer that the operator may set ON or OFF. The switch setting may be tested while running a computer program and thus vary the execution of the program.

switch, circuit, A switching system that completes a circuit from sender to receiver.

switch, closed, A switch is closed when it is turned on, allowing current to flow through it.

switch, commutation, A device used to execute repetitive sequential switching.

switch control computer, A computer used to handle data transmission to and from remote terminals and computers.

switch, electronic, A high-speed circuit element causing a switching action.

switch, function, A circuit whose output is a function of the input.

switch, hook, The switch on a telephone (under the ear and mouth piece) that opens when one lifts the receiver.

switch insertion, A method of inputting information into the computer by means of a computer operator operating switches manually. (See input unit, manual.)

switch, interlock, An automatic circuit breaker that cuts off power.

switch, logical, An electronic device used in switching.

switch message, One of the routing points in a store-and-forward switching system.

switch, programmed, A switch that is a computer instruction or a combination of instructions that may be set and tested by the computer program.

switch, sense, A switch on a computer console that the operator can turn on or off and that may be tested by a computer program.

switch setting, branch-on, A computer program instruction that may cause a branch based on a switch condition.

switch table, priority, A specific table in computer storage that contains the status of devices operating in interrupt mode.

switch, tape feed, When turned on causes a predetermined length of blank tape to be fed.

switch, toggle, A switch in a computer that may be set manually by an operator or automatically by a computer. It has two stable states (off and on).

switch types, A device, mechanical, electronic, etc., that can be tested to select a course of action or a path to follow.

switchboard, A board containing switches for connecting and disconnecting electrical circuits.

switched message network, A communications service in which customers may communicate with each other such as TELEX and TWX.

switched message telephone network, Same as switched message network.

switched network, public, Any system that provides service to many customers such as TELEX, TWX, telephone, etc.

switches, manual address, External control switches used by an operator to select a storage address.

switching algebra, Boolean algebra which is applied to switching circuits, etc.

switching, automatic message, Automatic message handling such as reading, routing, storing of messages.

switching blank, The range of values that a signal can be altered without changing the outgoing response (synonymous with dead space, dead zone, and similar to neutral zone).

switching center, In data communications, a device which routes data from incoming circuits to the proper outgoing circuits.

switching center, automatic, A switching center where automatic message switching takes place.

switching center, automatic message, A center in which messages are automatically routed based on their content.

switching center, semi-automatic message, A center where an operator routes messages according to the information in them.

switching center, tape, The center where operators tear off punched paper tape as it comes in and manually transfer it to the proper outgoing circuit.

switching center, torn tape, Same as tape switching center.

switching, circuit, The ability to establish a direct connection between points or between two or more network ports. This can consist of either a direct electrical connection or a direct logic path through gates.

switching coefficient, A number that is the derivative of magnetizing force related to the switching time.

switching control character, A character used to control the switching of devices from on to off or vice versa.

switching, cross channel, A feature that permits program access to input/output devices through two channels.

switching, line, A technique of switching in which the connection is made between the calling party and the called party prior to the start of a communication.

switching, message (M/S), Automatic reading, storing, and dispatching of messages in communications. (See automatic message switching.)

switching network, private, A communications network operated by the customer.

switching point, That point where signals change from one position to another.

switching, push button, A switching system in which the operator can select the outgoing channel.

switching, store-and-forward, Same as message switching.

switching theory, A branch of theory related to combinational logic concerning computers, logic elements, switching networks, etc.

switching unit, communication, A unit that allows any two processors to share a group of communication lines.

switching unit, peripheral control, A unit which permits any two processors to share the same peripheral devices.

switchover, The act of changing to an alternate.

switchover, automatic, In case of a stand-by machine, the capability to switch over to it when the other machine is faulty.

syllable, A term used for groups of characters or parts of machine words, such as a byte, etc.

symbionts, Small computer program routines that run at the same time as the main program. They process information between input/output devices and magnetic media.

symbol, A representation of characteristics, relationships, or changes in ideas or things.

symbol, abstract, A symbol whose shape is not indicative of its meaning.

symbol code, A code used to identify equipment in a record inventory.

symbol dictionary, external, A list of symbols that are external (outside the current program) but defined by another.

symbol, flowchart, Symbols used to represent operations, equipment, data media, etc., in a flowchart.

symbol, item separation, A control symbol that indicates the beginning of an item.

symbol, logic, See logical symbol.

symbol, logical, A symbol used as a logical operator or a symbol used to represent a logical element.

symbol, special, A special symbol is a character that is neither a letter nor a number. For example, # and ■ are both special symbols.

symbol string, A one-dimensional array of items ordered by reference to the relations between adjacent elements.

symbol table, A table of labels used by an assembler or compiler during program translation.

symbol, terminating, a symbol indicating the end of a block of information.

symbolic address, A label assigned to identify a particular element, function, or variable. It is helpful to programmers in identifying fields of data, e.g., net pay is called NETPAY, or total cost might be TOTCST, etc.

symbolic assembler, An assembler that lets the programmer write computer instructions in a symbolic language.

symbolic assembly system, Consists of the symbolic language itself and the symbolic assembler that can translate it.

symbolic code, Computer program coding in symbolic (source) language.

symbolic coding, Used to write computer instructions in other than machine language.

symbolic editor, A computer program that permits the adding or deleting of lines in a source language program.

symbolic editor, tape, The symbolic editor program that is used to generate, edit, correct, etc., symbolic program tapes.

symbolic input/output referencing, The method by which magnetic tape and disk are referred to by a computer program, i.e., symbolically instead of actual addresses.

symbolic instruction, An instruction written in a programming language that must be translated into machine language before it can be executed.

symbolic language, Use of symbols to express formal logic.

symbolic logic, The study of formal logic, mathematical logic, and Boolean algebra.

symbolic manipulation, A technique used in list processing languages.

symbolic notation, Representation of a storage location by one or more figures.

symbolic number, A numeral used in symbolic notation. (See symbolic notation.)

symbolic programming, Using symbols to represent addresses in computer programming.

symbol-manipulating language (LISP), A powerful list processing language.

symbols, atomic, In data processing a string of letters or numbers starting with a letter.

symbols, flowchart, Symbols such as squares, diamonds, circles, rectangles, etc., that are labeled to show different functions in a flowchart. (See flowchart.)

symbols, functional, Used in a block diagram representation in functional design. (See functional design.)

symbols, standard languages, Those symbols used to represent functions and meanings that can occur in any computer program.

sync circuits, Circuits in radar and television that control the movements of the scope beam.

sync separator, The circuit that separates sync pulses from the video signal in a television receiver.

synch, A signal used to identify the beginning of a block.

synch pulse, An electrical pulse used by master equipment to operate slave equipment in synchronism with the master.

synchro, An induction machine consisting of stator and rotor elements.

synchronization, Alignment of space or time.

synchronization pulse, Pulses used to keep components in order or step relative to timing.

synchronize, To lock one element with another into step relative to timing.

synchronizer, Generally refers to a storage device used to compensate for a difference in a rate of flow of information or time of occurrence of events when transmitting information from one device to another.

synchronizer, channel, A device providing signals to control transfer of data at proper times and sequence.

synchronizer, master, The main source of timing signals; a clock-like device.

synchronizer, tape, A device that controls the exchange of data between the central processor (CPU) and tape units.

synchronizing pilot, A signal used to maintain synchronization of the oscillators of a carrier system.

synchronous, Describes a system in which events occurring in regular, timed intervals are kept continuously in step with an electronic clocking device.

synchronous clock, A clock frequency used to control the timing in a computer.

synchronous computer, A computer in which each operation is controlled by clock signals as contrasted with asynchronous computer.

synchronous data transmission, A system in which timing is derived through synchronizing characters at the beginning of each message.

synchronous gate, Usually a time gate designed so the output intervals are synchronized with an input signal.

synchronous inputs, Terminal inputs entered upon command of a clock.

synchronous machine, A machine that is timed by clock pulses.

synchronous system (communications), A system in which the sending and receiving equipment operates at the same frequency.

synchronous transmit/receive (STR), A transmission mode in communications.

syndetic, To have interconnections or connections or to cross reference in documents or catalogs.

synergic, The combination of every organ of a system, e.g., a coordinated system.

syntax, The set of rules in a programming language that specify how the language symbols can be put together to form meaningful statements. Syntax rules are similar to grammar rules.

syntax check program, A computer program that tests source statements in a programming language to detect violations of the syntax or rules of structure of that language.

syntax recognizer, A specialized computer program subroutine that recognizes the phase class in an artificial language.

syntax transducer, A computer program subroutine designed to recognize the phase class in an artificial language.

syntax-directed compiler, A compiler based on syntactic relationships of the character string.

synthesis, Combining parts to make a whole, i.e., developing a circuit, program, computer, etc., from performance requirements.

synthesis, systems, Procedural planning for problem solving.

synthetic address, An address generated by instructions in the computer program using the addresses.

synthetic language, A fabricated language, a pseudocode, or symbolic language.

SYSGEN, See system generation.

SYSIN, A contraction of system input (the input stream).

system, Generally refers to a group of interrelated devices and elements which can function together. In computer systems, the central processing unit (CPU) controls the other elements.

system, accuracy control, A system of error detection and control.

system, assembly, An assembly language and its assembler.

system, back-up, A system that uses several sophisticated error detection and correction techniques in spotting and correcting equipment and data transmission errors.

system capacity, The throughput expected of a computer system.

system catalog (SYSCTLG), In some systems, a computer file that serves as an index to all other files that the system has used or will use. The SYSCTLG shows the names, sizes, locations, and usually any other pertinent information about the files.

system chart, A flowchart of a system showing the flow of information.

system check, A performance check on a system.

system commands, Commands made by a user to the executive program, e.g., to save a program or data files.

system, communications, A computer system and associated equipment to handle on-line real-time applications.

system components, The collection of hardware and software organized to achieve operational objectives.

system concept, total, A system providing information in the right form, time, and place for decision making.

system, concurrent control, A system that permits concurrent operation of many programs.

system constants, Permanent locations containing data used by systems programs as contained in the monitor section.

system, control, A closed loop system in which a computer is used to control a process.

system, control action, That type of control action that concerns the nature of change of the output dependent on the input.

system design, The specification of the working relations between all the parts of a system in terms of their characteristic actions, functions, and/or capabilities.

system diagnosis, continuous, A system in which there is a collection of diagnostic tasks that are processed when other higher priority things are not running.

system, diagnostics, A program that detects overall system malfunctions.

system engineering, A method of engineering that considers all elements in a control system as related to industrial automation.

system, four-wire, A system in which two separate systems use several sophisticated error detection and correction techniques in spotting and correcting equipment and data transmission errors.

system capacity, The throughput expected of a computer system.

system catalog (SYSCTLG), In some systems, a computer file that serves as an index to all other files that the system has used or will use. The SYSCTLG shows the names, sizes, locations, and usually any other pertinent information about the files.

system chart, A flowchart of a system showing the flow of information.

system check, A performance check on a system.

system commands, Commands made by a user to the executive program, e.g., to save a program or data files.

system, communications, A computer system and associated equipment to handle on-line real-time applications.

system components, The collection of hardware and software organized to achieve operational objectives.

system concept, total, A system providing information in the right form, time, and place for decision making.

system, concurrent control, A system that permits concurrent operation of many programs.

system constants, Permanent locations containing data used by systems programs as contained in the monitor section.

system, control, A closed loop system in which a computer is used to control a process.

system, control action, That type of control action that concerns the nature of change of the output dependent on the input.

system design, The specification of the working relations between all the parts of a system in terms of their characteristic actions, functions, and/or capabilities.

system diagnosis, continuous, A system in which there is a collection of diagnostic tasks that are processed when other higher priority things are not running.

system, diagnostics, A program that detects overall system malfunctions.

system engineering, A method of engineering that considers all elements in a control system as related to industrial automation.

system, four-wire, A system in which two separate two-wire circuits are used for transmitting and receiving.

system generation (SYSGEN), The initial process of developing (building) an operating system in a computer system.

system improvement time, The machine "down time" used for installation of new components.

system, information, The combination of all communication methods in an organization (computers, telephones, personal contact, etc.).

system, information processing, A system that receives, processes, and delivers information.

system, information-feedback, In communications an error-control system.

system input unit, The unit used to input a job stream to a computer system.

system interface design, The engineering design of specialized input/output equipment for a computer system.

system interrupts, Programmed requests from a processing program to a control program for some action.

system librarian, A person who maintains records of files and programs in the installation.

system loader, A computer program designed to load output from compilations and assemblies into sections of computer memory.

system, macro, A computer programming system having the capability of many-for-one (or macro) instruction development.

system, on-line, A system in which the input enters a computer from the point of origin and the output goes directly to where it is used.

system, operating, A collection of integrated service routines used to control the sequencing of programs by a computer. It is synonymous with monitor system and executive system.

system output unit, The unit used by all jobs connected to the computer system.

system residence volume, The volume, i.e., disk pack, etc., that contains the operating system (software).

system, step-by-step, A type of line switching system that uses step-by-step switches.

system supervisor, A computer program designed to control the job flow in a system with a minimum of operator intervention.

system, synchronous, In communications a system in which the sending and receiving equipment operates at the (near) same frequency.

system, tandem, A variety of systems of multiplexors and master/slave arrangements. (See master/slave system.)

system, time-shared, A system in which available computer time is shared among several jobs.

system, time-sharing monitor, A collection of programs remaining in memory to provide coordination and control of the total system.

system, total, An integrated system in which all significant functions are under computer control; referred to as a total system concept.

system, total management, Various systems conceived and designed by management to control the entire organization.

system, turnaround, See re-entry system.

system utilization loggers, A computer program or a device that records statistical data about how the system is running.

system, zata coding, A system of coordinate indexing.

systematic inaccuracies, Inaccuracies caused by limitations in equipment design.

systems analysis, The study of an activity, procedure, method, or any such element to determine what should be accomplished and how.

systems analyst, A person who designs information handling systems that are implemented in parts on a computer.

systems approach, Solving a problem from the "big picture" vantage point, not solving a bunch of little problems and then trying to put them all together.

systems compatibility, The compatibility electrically, logically, and mechanically of the devices in a system.

systems consultant, The person who provides technical assistance in systems analysis.

systems design, The design of the nature and content of input, files, procedures, and output and their interrelationships.

systems generation, See system generation.

systems programmer, The person who writes operating systems and other systems programs instead of applications programs.

systems programs, The computer programs generally provided by the manufacturer to perform systems functions.

systems standards, The minimum required performance characteristics in a system.

systems test, To check a whole system against test data; also the various forms of testing parts or all of a system

T

T test, A comparison test of two data elements; used in statistics.

tab, A label, marker, or indicator; also a slang abbreviation for tabulating (equipment).

tab labels, Labels on or in a continuous form that can be processed on a computer printer then are detached and put on an envelope, etc.

table, A set of data in a (tabular) form for easy reference.

table block, A subset of a table of data or computer instructions.

table, Boolean operation, A table showing possible combination results of two variables (synonymous with truth table).

table, decision, A table of possible courses of actions, selection, alternatives. It serves a purpose such as the flowchart.

table, input/output, A plotting device used to record one variable as a function of another one.

table, look-up, A collection of data in a form easily referenced by computer programs.

table look-up, The process of searching for data that is stored in an organized fashion.

table look-up instruction, Same as look-up instruction.

table, matrix, A set of quantities in a rectangular array, mathematically arranged.

table, multiplication, An area in storage containing groups of numbers used during multiplication operations.

table of contents, volume (VTOC), An index near the beginning of a volume (of data) describing the contents.

table, program reference, A section of storage used as an index for operations, subroutines, etc.

table, random number, A table of random numbers used in statistical calculations.

table simulator, A computer program routine that computes values of a table as needed rather than looking them up in a stored table.

table, subroutine, A listing of computer program subroutines in main memory.

table, symbol, A table of labels used by an assembler or compiler during program translation.

table, transfer, A table that contains a list of transfer instructions of the computer program in memory.

table, truth, A table showing result combinations in Boolean algebra.

tables, structure, Tables representing decision logic as related to decision table.

tabular data presentation, A statistical table of data in columns and rows.

tabular language, Composed of decision tables which become the problem-oriented language used in computation.

tabulate, The process of accumulating totals by groups of data.

tachometer, A measuring instrument that indicates speeds, e.g., revolutions per minute (rpm).

tactile keyboard, Keyboard composed of sheet of mylar with a conductive pattern on its bottom side. The labeled spaces are "touched" lightly, and the action is the same to the computer terminal, calculator, or other device as pressing or hitting keys.

tag, An information unit such as a marker or label; also called a flag.

tag converting unit, A machine that automatically reproduces information from perforated or coded price tags.

tag readers, Used in thousands of stores, reads small tickets and tags with OCR-A codes, others with 18-, 25-, or 31- columns such as Dennison tickets.

takedown, The procedures following the end of equipment operating to prepare for the next set up.

takedown time, The time required for takedown after a job.

take-up reel, The reel that receives tape during processing.

talk, cross, Interference on circuits.

talker, echo, A part of a signal that is returned to the source in time to be received as interference.

talking computer, With the introduction of its "Speak and Spell" learning aid in 1978, Texas Instruments, Inc., was one of the first with low-cost talking systems using ROM-based voice response. This was followed by talking translators and talking computers of many types, most based on responses generated by voice synthesizers.

talking computer-voice synthesizer, A hard-wired analog of the human vocal tract simulating vocal cords, the lungs, and the variable frequency resonant cavity of the mouth, tongue, lips, and teeth. All information necessary to produce sounds of American English and other languages are often programmed into ROMs that reside on the synthesizer board plugged into computers.

tally, To add or subtract a 1 (one) from a quantity in counting events.

tally register, A register that holds a tally count. (See tally.)

tandem office, An office used to interconnect local end offices over tandem trunks.

tandem system, A variety of systems of multiplexors and master/slave arrangements. (See master/slave system.)

tape, Magnetic tape or paper tape used for data recording in data processing.

tape alternation, Selection of first one tape unit, then another, to allow computer operator to put on and remove tapes during processing.

tape bin, A magnetic tape storage device containing many loops off tape and having one or more movable read heads or one head for each loop.

tape bootstrap routine, In some systems used to "bootstrap" programs from magnetic tape. (See bootstrap.)

tape bound, Same as tape limited.

tape cable, A cable containing flat metallic ribbon conductors.

tape, carriage control, See tape, control carriage.

tape cassette drive system, Added storage capability for many small computers and unlimited by the number of steps that can be stored as regards programs available for near immediate use.

tape, center feed, Paper tape with feed holes in the center of the tape.

tape, certified, Magnetic tape that has been certified to have zero errors (or less than a specified number).

tape, change, A tape to be processed to update a master tape. It is synonymous with transaction tape.

tape channels, paper, Information channels, e.g., 8-channel tape has 8 channels of code position.

tape channels, punched paper, The parallel information tracks along the length of paper tape.

tape character, A character composed of bits across the longitudinal channels of a tape.

tape character check, The parity bit in a tape character code.

tape checks, magnetic, Hardware checks for faulty tapes.

tape coil, A coil of paper tape as contrasted with a reel of magnetic tape.

tape coil, paper, A roll of paper tape as coiled and ready for use.

tape comparator, A unique machine that compares two tapes that are expected to be identical. The machine stops when a discrepancy occurs.

tape compiler, BPS Fortran, A computer program that translates computer programs written in IBM System/360 Fortran.

tape, control, A paper or plastic tape used to control a printer carriage.

tape, control carriage, A paper tape used to control printer functions such as skipping.

tape, control unit, A unit (including buffering) designed to control the operation of the magnetic tape transport.

tape, core, The tape used in bobbin core. (See bobbin core.)

tape deck, The mechanism used to control the movement of tape.

tape drive, The device that moves magnetic tape past the recording heads. It is the same as tape transport.

tape dump, The transfer of the contents of tape to another storage medium (may be a printout).

tape editor, A computer program used to edit, correct, etc., symbolic program tapes.

tape erasure, Removing the information on tape (the tape is then ready for re-recording).

tape, error, A special tape used to record errors for analysis at a later time.

tape, feed, A mechanism in a magnetic or paper tape device that feeds the tape to be read or sensed.

tape feed switch, When turned on causes a predetermined length of blank tape to be fed.

tape file, (1) A file on magnetic or punched paper tape. (2) A group of magnetic tapes in a tape library.

tape, grandfather, A backup tape that was made two cycles ago, i.e., two updates were made since then.

tape input, Using paper or magnetic tape a an input medium.

tape, intermix, A feature of some computers that permits combinations of different models of tape units on one computer.

tape key, load, See tape load key.

tape label, beginning, A description of the contents of the tape located at the beginning of the tape,

tape leader, A section of tape at the beginning used for threading lead.

tape, library, A "library" of programs and routines on magnetic tape.

tape light, An indicator light that turns on when there is an error during a read or write (tape) cycle.

tape limited, The relatively low speed of the tape unit is the limiting factor in processing.

tape load key, A push button control used to initiate loading of information from tape into storage (to start processing).

tape load point, A light-reflective marker indicating the beginning of the usable portion of a magnetic tape. When a tape is rewound, it is returned to this point.

tape, mag, The slang expression for magnetic tape.

tape marker, beginning, A perforated reflective spot at the start of magnetic tape.

tape, master, A master file on magnetic tape.

tape, master instruction, A specific magnetic tape containing computer programs and routines for a run or run series that is used in a tape operating system.

tape, master program, Same as master instruction tape.

tape, Mylar, A trade name for magnetic tape made by Dupont. A polyester film with a magnetic oxide coat.

tape, numerical, A punched paper or plastic tape used in numerical control (N/C).

tape pack, The way tape is wound on a reel; a good "pack" has a uniform wind and is free of cinching and layer-to-layer adhesion.

tape, paper, A paper strip in which data is stored in the form of punched holes and other machine sensible forms.

tape parity, The parity checking feature used in magnetic and paper tape data transfer.

tape, perforated, A tape (generally paper) on which data is recorded in the form of punched holes.

tape perforating, The act of punched holes in perforated tape.

tape perforator, An off-line device used for punching holes in paper tape.

tape printing counter, A printing counter of a magnetic tape terminal that counts blocks transmitted or received.

tape, problem input, A magnetic tape or punched paper tape containing problem data to check out a computer system.

tape processing simultaneity, A feature in some computers that permits data transfer from magnetic tape to occur at the same time as other central processor operations.

tape, program, A tape containing a particular computer program required to solve a problem.

tape, punch, Synonymous with perforated tape.

tape reader, An input device that can read data from tape.

tape recording density, The bits per inch recorded on magnetic tape.

tape, red, The slang expression meaning many required operations that don't seem to directly contribute to solution of a problem.

tape relay, A method used to relay messages between transmitting and receiving stations (using perforated tape).

tape reproducer, A machine used to copy and/or edit paper tape.

tape reservoir, A length of magnetic tape used as slack for starting and stopping or change of direction of tape movement.

tape, scratch, A magnetic tape available for temporary use on which data is not saved.

tape select switch, A control switch used to select use of magnetic tape units.

tape skew, The condition in which tape isn't being fed properly.

tape skip, An instruction to move tape forward and erase what is recorded.

tape sorts, Sorts written to be processed on magnetic tape, a generalized set of programs.

tape speed, The rate at which magnetic tape moves past the read/write head during data transfer.

tape storage, See magnetic tape storage.

tape storage, magnetic, A magnetic coated plastic tape on reels (like a tape recorder) that can contain data to be read and written by a computer.

tape swapping, Selection of alternate magnetic tape units to minimize the interruptions to processing.

tape symbolic editor, The symbolic editor program that is used to generate, edit, correct, etc., symbolic program tapes.

tape synchronizer, A device that controls the exchange of data between the central processor (CPU) and tape units.

tape trailer, The end of a reel of tape containing the end of tape marker.

tape, transaction, A tape that is used to update a master tape.

tape transmitter, automatic, Same as automatic tape reader; reads, feeds, holds, etc., reels of tape.

tape transport, The mechanism that moves tape past sensing and recording devices.

tape verifier, A device used to check the accuracy of punched tape as related to a key verifier.

tape width, The physical width of magnetic tape used by a particular unit.

tape-to-printer program, A computer program that transfers data from magnetic tape to a printer.

tape-to-tape converter, A device used to convert one form of tape to another, e.g., paper tape to magnetic tape.

target, The surface in a writing tube that is struck by the electron beam.

target language, The language to which some other language is to be translated.

target phase, The running of a target program. It is called the run phase or the object phase.

target program, An intermediate or machine language program written in the target language.

tariff, Costs or rates charged in communications for common carrier services.

task, In a routine or a machine run a task is a subjob.

task dispatcher, A computer program routine that selects the next task to be processed.

task management, The set of functions in a control program that controls the use of system resources.

taxonomy, The science of classification.

TCAM-Telecommunications Access Method, A specific method for controlling the transfer of messages between the applications program and remote terminals that provides a high-level message control language.

telecommunications, Generally refers to the transmission of data over a distance, usually by electrical means. Contrasts with directly-connected equipment in close proximity.

telecommunication, To transmit or receive signals, sounds, or intelligence of any nature by wire, light beam, or any other means.

Telecommunications Access Method, See TCAM.

telecommuting, Projects for replacing physical commuting from home to the various workplaces with logical commuting, which people work at home and use a personal computer for the telecommunications channel to offices and other workplaces.

teleconference, Conference between persons who are remote from one another but linked together by various types of telecommunications systems, such as videoconferencing, AT&T's Picturephone (tm) or the various Slow Scan two-way TV systems.

telecopier unit, Facsimile units to provide long distance permanent copies on plain paper of written and graphics materials.

telemeter, A formulating and reformulating apparatus for recording the value of a measured quantity by electrical means.

telemetering, Transmission by electromagnetic means of a measurement over long distances.

telemetry, Generally, the transmission of data over great distances, especially remote control of apparatus and equipment.

telemetry, Transmission of measured magnitudes by radio, telephone, or computer with suitable coded modulation such as amplitude, frequency, phase, or pulse. A remote sensing by an instrument that converts electronic signals into data.

telephone, The telecommunications system designed for voice transmission.

telephone circuit, data, A telephone circuit capable of transmitting digital data.

telephone line, A general term used in communication practice relating to communication channels (conductors and circuit apparatus)

telephone network, private, A network (leased) operated by the customer.

telephone network, switched message, Same as switched message network.

telephone, sound powered, A telephone that derives its operating power from the speech input unit only.

teleprinter, A term used to describe telegraphic terminals; may be a typewriter-like device.

teleprocessing, The use of telecommunications systems by a computer which involves data acquisition, message switching, and computer-to-computer or computer-to-terminal communications.

teleprocessing network, A network in which data is transmitted from one point to another in the course of processing.

teleprocessing terminal, A terminal used for on-line data transmission from a remote location to a central computer.

telesynd, Remote control equipment used in telemetry.

Teletext, A generic term used to describe the broadcast of text and graphics as part of the television video signal while a similar process, Viewdata, refers to the transmission of such information on an interactive basis, usually via telephone lines.

teletype exchange (telex), An automatic teleprinter exchange service developed by Western Union.

teletypewriter equipment, See TTY.

teletypewriter switching systems, Message switching systems in which the terminals are teletypewriter equipment.

teletypewriter-exchange service, A service in which teletypewriter stations may be interconnected in the same area or in another city. Known as TWX service.

TELEX, An international communications service which uses teleprinters.

Telex (teletype exchange), An automatic teleprinter exchange service developed by Western Union.

teller consoles, bank, A device used by a bank teller to transmit and receive messages to and from the processing center.

Telpak, A trade name for a service for leasing wide band channels.

template, A plastic card with flowchart symbols cut out of it.

tensile strength, ultimate, The force per cross-sectional unit area required to break a tape.

teracycle, A million megacycles per second.

terminal, A point in a system or communication network at which data can either enter or leave; or, an input-output device capable of transmitting entries to and obtaining output from the system of which it is a part.

terminal console devices, A console-like terminal that sends and receives input and output to and from the central computer.

terminal, data, (1) A device that modulates and/or demodulates data. (2) A device for inputting or receiving output from computers.

terminal, data communication, A device used for sending and/or receiving data from a remote location (away from the central computer location).

terminal equipment, Equipment such as teletypewriters, CRTs, etc., used as terminals in communications.

terminal, full-screen, This allows the operator to type in characters anywhere on the display screen. By way of contrast, a line-at-a-time terminal allows the operator to type only at the bottom line of the display.

terminal installation, data transmissions, The installation consisting of data terminal equipment, signal conversion equipment, etc.

terminal, interactive, Terminals that are generally equipped with a display, a keyboard, and a printer. Optionally they also include a disk or other exterior storage and a microprocessor for controlling various systems and subsystems that allow such services as menu call-up selection of information needed, protected forms for a fill-in-the-blanks conversational system, and other demand, inquiry, and transaction-oriented operations.

terminal, job-oriented, (1) A specific terminal designed for a particular application. (2) A specially designed terminal to fit into the environment associated with the job.

terminal, local, A computer terminal located at the same site as the central computer. Local terminals can therefore be directly connected to the central computer.

terminal, multiplex data, A data transmission device that modulates and demodulates, encodes and decodes between two or more I/O devices and data transmission stations.

terminal, optical display, A terminal composed of an alphameric keyboard and a video screen.

terminal, remote, A terminal that is at a location remote from the central processor of a computer.

terminal room, The room associated with a telephone central office or exchange containing switchboard equipment.

terminal, teleprocessing, A terminal used for on-line data transmission from a remote location to a central computer.

terminal unit, A unit used for input or output to or from a communication channel.

terminal unit, central (CTU), A unit that supervises communications; for example, between teller consoles and the processing center.

terminal unit, multiplexor, A unit used to connect multiple terminal stations to and from the central processor of a computer.

terminals, communication line (CLTs), Input and output devices used when data is to be transmitted to or from the central processor using a communications line.

terminating symbol, A symbol indicating the end of a block of information.

termination, executive, The termination of an operating program by the executive program (in an operating system).

termination, loop, Ending the execution of a loop of instructions because of some condition.

terminator/initiator, A particular computer program that performs housekeeping tasks before and after a job.

ternary, A characteristic pertaining to selection from three choices; also relates to the number system of the base 3.

test board, Switchboard equipment with testing apparatus (telephone).

test, branch instruction, A test indicated by the computer instruction testing for greater than, negative, less than, etc., conditions.

test case, Testing a sample of data.

test, compatibility, Tests run on a system to check the acceptability of hardware and software.

test, crippled leap frog, A variation of the leap frog test.

test data, A set of data used to test a program or system.

test, destructive, A test of equipment in which part of it is destroyed or damaged.

test, diagnostic, The running of diagnostic routine or program.

test, leap frog, A computer program used to discover computer malfunctions.

test, output processor, The automated processing of output to check for errors (in a complex system).

test, parallel run, A technique for converting from one system to another in which the old system and the new system are both run for a period of time until the new system is proven and accepted. Then the old system is discontinued.

test problem, A problem used to check out a computer program.

test, program, Using a sample problem with a known answer to check out a computer program.

test, Q, A comparison test between two or more units of quantitative data.

test routine, A computer program routine used to show whether a computer is working properly.

test run, Running test data to check out a computer program.

test set, tape, A device used to locate defects in magnetic tape.

test subroutine, A computer program subroutine used to test if the computer is functioning properly.

test supervisor program, A supervisory computer program used only for testing purposes.

test, systems, To check a whole system against test data; also the various forms of testing parts or all of a system.

test tape, program, A tape that contains a program and test data to be used for diagnostic purposes.

test tone, A tone used in finding circuit troubles.

test, volume, Using a large volume of actual data to check for computer program errors.

testing, Refers to the process of running the computer program and evaluating the program results, in order to determine if any errors exist.

testing, degradation, Measuring performance of a system at extreme operating limits.

testing, loop, Checking to see if further looping is required (in computer program execution).

testing, marginal, a type of testing used in computer preventative maintenance to check the equipment. It is also called bias testing.

testing, normative, Comparing to standards of quantitative and qualitative system performance.

testing, parameter, Using a parameter to test to insure that input produces the expected output.

testing, procedural, The testing of alternative human actions in a system; distinguished from hardware or software testing.

testing, program, The processes used to check out a computer program's success.

testing, retrofit, Testing after replacing equipment or programs to assure system operation.

testing, sequential, Testing performed in a predetermined order and requiring repeated observations.

testing time, program, The machine time used for testing and debugging a computer program.

tests, procedural and exception, Tests are designed to check machine control and operation.

tetrad, Any group of four, e.g., four pulses.

tetrode, A four-electrode device.

text, The part of a message that contains the main body of information to be conveyed.

text editing, Used most often with lighted, blinking underline (cursor) that acts as a position indicator; functions occur at the cursor location on the display screen; insertions can occur by character or line; deletions may occur by character, word, line, or block, as well as by document name. Many other features can be found in software descriptions.

text editing operations, On various terminals a lighted, blinking underline (cursor) acts as a position indicator facilitating text editing functions such as insert or delete characters, lines, paragraphs, blocks, document name, etc.

text reader-processor, A device to combine usually OCR text-reading capability with a microprocessor to eliminate costly reformatting, code conversion, rekeying, verifying, and correcting of messages for transmission with programs that are usually redefinable by the user to accept new or changing input forms and output formats.

theory, automata, A theory that relates the study of application of automatic devices to various behaviorist concepts and theories.

theory, communication, A branch of mathematics dealing with the properties of transmitted messages.

theory, congestion, A mathematical theory dealing with the study of delays and losses of items in a communications systems.

theory, game, Mathematical game playing (as done on a computer).

theory, group, The theory of combining groups (a mathematical technique).

theory, information, An area of mathematical theory dealing with information rate, channels, etc., and other factors affecting information transmission.

theory, probability, A theory pertaining to the likelihood of chance occurrences of events or elements.

theory, queuing, A probability theory used in studying delays and the waiting in line of people or things.

theory, set, The study of rules for combining elements, groups, and sets.

theory, switching, A branch of theory related to combinational logic concerning computers, logic elements, switching networks, etc.

thermal, Pertaining to heat.

thermal expansion, coefficient, A measure of increase in the linear dimension of tape relative to temperature.

thermal paper, Paper coated with a few micrometers of a chemical catalyst. The coating holds two separate, colorless components - a dye-stuff and a phenol color-former; heat causes the catalyst to fuse and the two chemicals flow together; cost depends upon persistence, contrast, and print-head abrasion.

thermal printer, Often used in CRT terminals, these have few moving parts, are quiet, usually low cost but require the use of thermal paper that is expensive, sometimes difficult to read and store effectively.

thermal shock, An abrupt temperature change applied to a device.

thermistor, A special resistor whose temperature coefficient of resistance is very high.

thermoelectrics, The conversion of heat into electricity and vice versa.

thickness, coating, The thickness of tape coatings.

thickness, total, The sum of the thickness of the coating and base of magnetic tape.

thin film, Refers to an electronic component coated with molecular deposits of material in specially designed patterns.

thin film memory, A storage device of thin disks of magnetic material on a non-magnetic base.

third-generation computer, Computers with microcircuits and miniaturization of components.

thrashing, An inefficient condition that can occur in a time-sharing or multiprogramming system.

three address, A computer instruction containing three addresses of operands.

threshold element, A specific type of logic element.

throughput, The productivity of a machine per unit time.

throughput, effective, The average throughput of a data-processing device. Effective throughput is contrasted with rated throughput and provides a more accurate measurement of the efficiency of the device than its rated throughput.

throughput, rated, Rated throughput is the maximum possible throughput of a data-processing device. Rated throughput is contrasted with effective throughput.

throughput, simultaneous, The central processor functioning at the same time input and output data are being transferred.

throughput time, Generally, the time required for work to be processed by the personnel and equipment in computer operations.

throughput turnaround time, A shorter turnaround can give a unit a competitive edge. Turnaround measures the time required to reverse direction plus initialization time and measures the delay in various computer or communications systems both for throughput (initialization to completion) and turnaround of full message or document handling.

throw, paper, The distance paper moves in a printer when it is further than normal line spacing.

throw-away characters, Characters transmitted in a communications system that are used for timing purposes.

tie line, A leased line between two or more PBXs (in communications).

tie trunk, A telephone line that connects two branch exchanges.

time, acceleration, The time between the interpretation of instructions to read or write and the transfer of information to or from storage (same as start time).

time, actual, Performance of computing during the time an event is taking place.

time, add, The time needed to perform an addition in a computer. (See add-subtract time.)

time, add-subtract, The time needed to perform an addition or subtraction in a computer. It does not include the time required to get the quantities from storage and put the results back into storage.

time, answering, A communications term that represents the time that elapses between the appearance of a signal and the response made to it.

time base, A designed and controlled function of time by which some process is controlled or measured.

time base generator, A digital clock used for calculation and control.

time classifications, The classifications of time, such as serviceable, effective, down, unused, etc., related to a computer or system.

time, connect, The time between sign on and sign off that a user is connected to a time-shared system from a remote terminal.

time, current, See real-time.

time, cycle, The time used to call for and deliver information from a storage unit or device.

time division, A process in communications in which many messages time share a single transmission channel.

time division multiplex, The connection of more than one terminal to a common channel. (See time division.)

time division multiplier, Device that permits the simultaneous transmission of many independent channels of varying speeds into a single high-speed data stream.

time gate, A specific gate that gives output only at certain chosen times.

time, latency, The time interval between the read/write head of a disk drive arriving at the proper track just as the proper sector has passed by, and when the beginning of the sector passes beneath the head.

time latency, A time lag or the rotational delay time in magnetic disk or drum processing.

time, operation, Time needed by equipment to perform a particular operation.

time, operation use, The time that equipment is in actual use (not all the time it is turned on).

time out, keyboard, A feature that causes the keyboard to lock if there is more than 15 seconds between the sending of characters.

time, out of service, All time that a machine is not used due to a system failure. It doesn't include unused (scheduled) time.

time, physical system, The ratio of computer time to the problem time (in simulation).

time, preventive maintenance, Time scheduled for the maintenance of equipment (done to prevent potential problems).

time, problem, In simulation, the time interval between events in the physical system.

time, propagation, Time needed for an electrical pulse to travel from one point to another.

time, proving, Time used to insure that no faults exist in a machine (after repair).

time, real, Performing computing during the time an event is taking place in time to influence the result, e.g., necessary in missile guidance systems.

time, reference, An instant in time used for relative measurement of time.

time, reimbursed, Machine time that is loaned or rented to another organization that may be reimbursed or reciprocated.

time scale, The correspondence between time needed for a process to occur and time needed to control or analyze the process.

time, scheduled maintenance, Time used for machine repair on a regular pattern or schedule, may also include preventative maintenance time.

time, scramble, Computer time for use by programmers who need short "shots" (periods of time) to test computer programs.

time, search, The time used to find a particular field of data in storage.

time, seek, The time required to accomplish a seek. (See seek.)

time, set-up, The time required for machine set up, i.e., the time spent getting the computer, etc., ready for a job.

time share, The sharing of a device during a period of time; one user uses it, then another; several users taking turns.

time sharing, A time-sharing computer system allows several users to be connected simultaneously to the same computer.

time slice, A uniform interval of CPU time allocated for use in performing a task.

time slicing, Generally refers to the technique of breaking the CPU time into a series of brief periods, or 'slices,' each allocated to different programs in turn, to prevent the monopolization of the CPU by any one program.

time, standby, The time when equipment is not actively involved in performing its function but is available.

time, standby maintenance, Time that a maintenance person is on duty but not actively involved in maintenance and repair of equipment.

time, start-stop, Same as acceleration time, deceleration time.

time, stop, The time between completion of reading or writing of tape and when the tape stops moving.

time, swap, The time needed to transfer a computer program from external storage to internal storage and vice versa.

time switching, The time between the pulse and the response.

time, system improvement, The machine "down time" used for installation of new components.

time, takedown, The time required for takedown after a job.

time, training, The machine time used to train employees in use of the equipment.

time, transfer, The time interval used for data transfer in computer storage.

time, turnaround, (1) The time needed to reverse the transmission direction in a channel. (2) The time between submitting a job to a computer center and getting the results back.

time, unattended, The time when equipment is not in use; may be due to a breakdown.

time, unscheduled maintenance, The time between discovery of a machine failure and the return of equipment to normal operation.

time, unused, The time that is available for use but is not used for machine operation.

time, up, The time when equipment is available for productive work as contrasted with down time.

time utilization, Continued processing while records are being located for processing.

time, waiting, Waiting for a resource to become available for use.

time, word, The time needed to move a word past a particular point (or from one point to another).

time, write, The time needed to record information (output).

timer, interval, A timer (in a computer) with the ability to keep track of the time of day and to interrupt as specified. (See interrupt.)

timer, sequence, A succession of time delay circuits.

timer, watchdog, A specific timer used to prevent endless program looping in the computer.

time-shared system, A system in which available computer time is shared among several jobs.

time-sharing accounting, Keeping track of usage (time used) of the system by the various users.

time-sharing executive, The executive program that processes all the user's requests in the time-sharing system.

time-sharing, fail-soft, A graceful degradation or fail-soft in a remote computer system. (See fail-soft.)

time-sharing, HELP program, A special program designed to help the user use the system.

time-sharing, inactive mode, A user in this mode is not logged on to the system.

time-sharing languages, user oriented, Languages typically easier to use than others; more English language related.

time-sharing, master/slave modes, In time sharing, the executive program can operate in master mode and the user program operate in slave mode (under control).

time-sharing, memory protection, A feature that prevents users from getting into executive protected areas and each other's areas.

time-sharing, message switching communications, A message handling system used in large reservation systems for airlines and hotels.

time-sharing monitor system, A collection of programs remaining in memory to provide coordination and control of the total system.

time-sharing, multiple input/output channels, In a time-sharing computer serving many communications lines, multiple channels are required.

time-sharing, multiplexor channel, Provides the capability of polling and multiplexing of devices.

time-sharing, periodic dumping, A feature in which dumps (copies) of user files are placed on a backup medium to be saved.

time-sharing, random access auxiliary storage, Provision of magnetic drum and disk storage for user programs and data file.

time-sharing ready mode, A mode in which a user's task in ready status can be executed or resumed.

time-sharing, real-time, A system designed for providing data on a real-time basis with immediate response needed to continue the process.

time-sharing, running mode, A mode in which the user's program is being executed.

time-sharing, scheduling of resources, The scheduling of the processor in an optimal way to satisfy the user demands (done by the system executive in an operating system).

time-sharing, storage management, The relocation of computer programs, storage protection, and allocation of storage.

time-sharing user, The person that uses the system from a time-sharing terminal.

time-sharing, user modes, One of the following modes a user may be in: inactive, command, ready, running, waiting.

time-write interval, The amount of time required to get ready to transmit output (such as printing or writing on tape).

timing circuits, Circuits used to control time delay or duration.

timing error, An error caused by devices being "out of time" with what is expected.

timing signals, Signals sent at regular intervals to ensure synchronization.

TLU, See table look up.

toggle, (1) Pertaining to any device that has two stable states. It may be set manually or set automatically by a computer. (2) A flip-flop (synonymous with toggle switch).

toggle switch, A switch in a computer that may be set manually by an operator or automatically by a computer. It has two stable states (off and on).

token, A distinguishable unit in a sequence of characters.

toll, A charge for making a connection (telephone line) outside a boundary.

tone, The audible result of a frequency within the audio range (approximately 20 to 20,000 Hz).

tone, test, A tone used in finding circuit troubles.

tone, touch, The new push button "dialing" of a telephone number.

tones, transmission, Tones that have been converted from signals from a data set (on a telephone line).

top-down method, A technique used in compilers.

topology, In network terminology, describes the physical or logical placement of nodes (stations) in a computer network system or configurations.

torque, A force on a rigid body that causes it to rotate.

TOS (Tape Operating System), An operating system for System 360 computers used in a magnetic tape, no random access system.

total, batch, See HASH TOTAL.

total, batch, A total accumulated by adding certain quantities from each record in a batch of data records.

total, check, One of many totals used for checking calculations.

total, control, A total used to balance to; may be a significant total or a hash total.

total, gibberish, Same as hash total.

total, hash, A total that is meaningless except for verification control (e.g., a total of all customer numbers which is meaningless except to compare to that same total calculated at another time).

total system, An integrated system in which all significant functions are under computer control; referred to as total system concept.

total system concept, A system providing information in the right form, time, and place for decision making.

touch control panel, A basic element is the interfacing of glass keyboards with MOS circuitry; conductive coatings are fired onto glass panels and activate controls by touch only, no pressing or movement of a switch is involved.

touch screen terminal, A terminal that is sensitive to touch. When the screen is pressed, the pressure creates a reflected wave whose location is recorded by the computer as a coded signal.

TPI, Abbreviation for Tracks Per Inch. there are 48 TPI in some 5-1/4-inch floppy disks with 40 tracks used for actual data storage. High density floppies have 96 TPI with 80 tracks for actual storage.

TRAC, A procedure describing language for the reactive typewriter.

trace, A diagnostic technique used in program testing and debugging.

trace, macro, A program debugging aid.

trace program, interpretive, A computer program that is used to trace or check another program in an interpretive mode.

trace routine, An executive computer program routine that is used in diagnostic tracing.

trace, selective, A tracing (computer) routine that traces branches or arithmetic instruction results or other program activity in a selected area.

trace statement, A type of program statement used in debugging to trace arithmetic calculation results or logical flow of program execution (used in Fortran).

tracing, flow, A type of debugging of computer programs. (See debugging.)

tracing, logical, Tracing the paths followed after branch, jump, or transfer instructions (a debugging technique).

tracing, selective, Tracing on selected instructions or data. (See selective trace.)

track, An information recording path such as on magnetic drum, disk, or tape.

track, clock, Same as a timing track; containing pulses developing a clock signal to aid in reading data.

track density, The number of adjacent tracks per unit distance.

track, feed, The track in paper tape that contains the feed holes. (See feed holes.)

track, library, A track or tracks on magnetic disk, drum, etc., used to store reference data such as titles, key words, etc.

track, magnetic, The part of a moving magnetic medium (disk, drum, tape) that is read (or written on) by a head.

track pitch, The distance from one center to another of adjacent tracks on a magnetic medium.

track, timing, A specific track on which pulses are recorded for timing purposes (on magnetic disk, drum, etc.).

trackball, Generally, this is a device used with interactive graphics to control cursor position on the screen. Trackballs are used as cursor locators in computer-aided design and arcade games.

tracking, cross, An array of bright dots on a display device (in a cross-like form).

tracks, prerecorded, Tracks on magnetic media containing timing or permitting word and block addressability.

traffic, The information (messages) that pass through a communications system.

traffic control, A method of handling flow of something by means of a computer.

traffic control, input/output, A method in which time sharing of main memory is directed by the peripheral devices and the central processor.

trail, audit, A traceable path or record of transactions that may be used to check back through.

trailer, A distinct record at the end of a group of records.

trailer label, A tape file record, at the end of the file, containing summary information.

trailer record, A record that follows a group of records and contains data related to the group.

trailer, tape, The end of a reel of tape containing the end of tape marker.

trailing edge, The drop in voltage at the end of a pulse.

trailing end, The last end of a tape or ribbon, etc., to be processed.

train, A sequence of pieces of apparatus. (See switch train.)

training mode, A mode used for the training of terminal operators.

training, simulation, Training people for a real situation by using a simulated system.

transaction, A single action such as one sale, one record, one airline reservation.

transaction data, The data associated with a transaction, i.e., an event.

transaction file, A batch (file) of transactions ready to be processed against a master file (to update the master file).

transaction record, One record in a file to be processed against a master file.

transaction recorder, automatic, Computer routines in which information about transactions are recorded.

transaction tape, A tape that is used to update a master tape.

transaction terminal, Usually controlled by a microcomputer, in-store terminals perform front-end communications functions, provide positive control and security for store money and records. Also, often include automatic tax and change computation, automatic price and quantity extensions, programmable price look-up, and store balancing reports.

transceiver, A device that both transmits and receives data, often simultaneously.

transceiver, A terminal device that can both transmit and receive signals, usually in a common housing often designed for portable or mobile use.

transcribe, To copy data from one storage medium to another.

transcriber, Equipment used to transfer input or output data from one form to another.

transducer, Usually a sensing device used to convert energy from one form to another. For example, quartz embedded in mercury can act as a transducer and can change electric energy to sound energy.

transducer applications, An energy converter, converts one form of energy to another, such as electrical, mechanical, acoustical, etc.; the magnitude of an applied stimulus is converted into an electrical signal proportionate to the quantity of the stimulus.

transducer characteristics, Most produce a change in voltage, current, or resistance that must correspond precisely to a change in temperature, displacement, or velocity. Other key specifications are repeatability and long-term drift or stability.

transducer, syntax, A computer program subroutine designed to recognize the phase class in an artificial language.

transfer, To transfer control or to transfer data.

transfer, block, Moving a whole block of data from one place to another (in computer storage).

transfer check, Checking the accuracy of a data transfer.

transfer command, A computer instruction that changes control from one place in a program to another.

transfer, conditional, Same as conditional branch.

transfer, control, To copy, exchange, transmit, etc., data.

transfer function, A specific mathematical expression.

transfer instruction, A computer instruction such as a branch.

transfer operation, An operation that moves information from one storage area or medium to another.

transfer, peripheral, A process used to transfer data between two peripheral devices.

transfer, program control, The transfer of operational control form one computer program to another.

transfer, radial, The process of transferring data between internal memory and a peripheral device (of a computer).

transfer rate, character, The speed that data may be read or written, e.g., characters per second.

transfer rate, data, The rate at which data is read or written from or to the disk. The higher the transfer rate, the quicker the data is fed into the system and the more efficient it is.

transfer rate, maximum, The maximum number of digits per second that can be accommodated on a channel.

transfer register, A display register on the operator console showing data prior to acceptance.

transfer serial, Transfer of data serially (one-at-a-time, bit-by-bit, or element-by-element).

transfer table, A table that contains a list of transfer instructions of the computer program in memory.

transfer time, The time interval used for data transfer in computer storage.

transfer vector, A specific table that lists transfer instructions of all the programs in main memory.

transfer, word, The parallel transfer of all the bits in a computer word (at the same time).

transfluxor, A magnetic memory element related to non-destructive read-out.

transform, To change the structure or composition of information.

transformer, Electrical device that, using electromagnetic induction, transfers electric energy from one or more circuits to one or more other circuits at the same frequency, but often at a different voltage and current value.

transformer, step down, A component whose output voltage is less than the input voltage.

transformer, step up, A component whose output voltage is greater than the input voltage.

transforming, The process of changing the form (or media) of data without changing its content.

transient response, Output versus time in response to a step input.

transistor, An electronic device utilizing semiconductor properties to control the flow of currents.

transistor attributes, A device made by attaching three or more wires to a small wafer of semiconductor material (a single crystal that has been specially treated so that its properties are different at the point where each wire is attached). The three wires are usually called the emitter, base, and collector. They perform functions somewhat similar to those of the cathode grid and plate of a vacuum tube, respectively.

transistor logic families, Each has special features, advantages, and limitations and include: RTL (Resistor Transistor Logic), ECL (Emitter Coupled Logic), DCTL (Direct Coupled Transistor Logic), DTL (Diode Transistor Logic), TTL, the most common, (Transistor-Transistor Logic), and variations of these.

transistor, metal oxide, Transistors used in computer memory units.

transistor, MOS-Metal Oxide Semiconductor, An insulated-gate field-effect transistor (FET) in which the insulating layer between each gate electrode and the channel is an oxide material or an oxide and nitride material.

transistorized, Equipment or designs in which transistors (solid-state electronics) are used instead of vacuum tubes; all circuits employ transistors and not thermionic valves.

transition, A change from one circuit condition to another.

translate, To change from one language to another.

translate display, To move an image on the screen up or down or side to side.

translating program, The assembler or compiler, etc., used in computer program translation.

translating routine, A computer program routine used for program translation (one language to another).

translation, (1) The operation of reestablishing the text of a message in communications, (2) the process of converting a computer program from one language to another.

translation, algorithm, Using a specific computational method to translate one language to another.

translation, machine, The automatic translation from one representation to another.

translation, mechanical, A generic term for language translation by computers, etc.

translation, one-for-one, One machine language instruction resulting from one source language instruction.

translator, A device that converts programs written in one language into programs in another language.

translator, language, An assembler, compiler, or other routine that accepts statements in one language and produces equivalent statements in another.

translator, language, (1) A computer program used to translate a program form one language to another, (2) a program that helps translate languages such as French to English, (3) an assembler or compiler that translates "human" coding into machine language.

transliterate, A procedure used to represent characters of a language by corresponding characters of another language.

transmission, The electrical transfer of signals, messages, or other forms of intelligence from one place to another.

transmission adapter, A device that connects remote and local devices to data adapters.

transmission, analog, Sends a continuous signal range (amplitude, frequency, or phase) over a channel; filters and linear amplifiers maintain signal quality; analog voice channels are interfaced to the digital output of terminals and computers by a modem.

transmission, asynchronous, Data is transmitted at irregular intervals by placing a start bit before each character and a stop bit after each character.

transmission, bit stream, A method of transmission using a bit stream and timing intervals (see bit stream).

transmission codes, fixed ratio, Concerns various error detection codes using a fixed ratio of bits concept.

transmission codes, recurrent, Codes in which check symbols are used to detect a burst type of error.

transmission codes, spiral parity checking, A method used to detect single bit errors.

transmission control, Control units used in communications.

transmission control character, A control character used in routing messages in communications.

transmission, data, The sending of data from one place to another in a system.

transmission, double-sideband, In communications the sidebands not being related to each other but are related separately to two sets of modulating signals (see sideband).

transmission, duplex, A method of transmission whereby data can be transmitted and received simultaneously. Often referred to as full-duplex, to emphasize the difference from half-duplex.

transmission, effective speed of, The rate at which information is transmitted in average characters (or bits) per unit time.

transmission equipment, data, The communications equipment associated with the data processing equipment in a communications system.

transmission, independent sideband, A method in which the upper and lower sidebands are symmetrically spaced about the carrier frequency and all are transmitted.

transmission interface converter, A device that controls transfer of information between a channel and adapter.

transmission level, A ratio expressing transmission units.

transmission line, A communication path for (electrical) signals.

transmission modes, Simplex transmission goes only one way; half-duplex is bidirectional but in one direction at a time. Full-duplex is simultaneously bidirectional.

transmission, output, synchronous, A method of transmission of data in which timing is not critical.

transmission, packet, Short standardized packets transmitted using a network that stores and forwards messages very rapidly, containing the message and address to be forwarded.

transmission, parallel, A method of transmission in which a block of bits is sent at the same time.

transmission pulses, Electrical pulses that can be sent and received on communications lines.

transmission, serial, Data transmission of one character at a time as contrasted with parallel transmission.

transmission, simplex, Mode of transmission used for communication which is capable of transmitting data only in one direction. Simplex lines are designed such that one end contains only a transmitter and the other end contains only a receiver.

transmission, simultaneous, Transmission sending and receiving going on at the same time.

transmission, single sideband, A method in which only one sideband is transmitted (see sideband).

transmission speed, A rate expressed in bits, characters, words, etc., per second or per minute.

transmission, start-stop, The asynchronous transmission in a start-stop system (see start-stop system).

transmission, synchronous, Technique by which data is transmitted at regular, timed intervals, from one location to another.

transmission system codes, Methods used for checking character parity and block checking for errors.

transmission system, information, A system that receives and sends information without changing it.

transmission tones, Tones that have been converted form signals from a data set (on a telephone line).

transmission, vestigal sideband, A method in which one sideband, the carrier, and only a portion of the other sideband are transmitted.

transmit, To send data from one location to another.

transmittal mode, A procedure by which input and output are available to and from a program.

transmitted data circuit, A circuit that carries signals originated by the data terminal equipment; not required for receive only service.

transmitter, In telephony, a device used to convert sound to electrical energy.

transmitter, automatic tape, Same as automatic tape reader; reads, feeds, holds, etc., reels of tape.

transmitter start code, TSC.

transponder, A radio or satellite transmitter-receiver that transmits identifiable signals automatically when the proper interrogation is received, such as found on the various satellites, Westar, and others.

transport, To convey as a whole from one device to another.

transport mechanism, tape, The mechanism that controls the movement of tape.

transport, tape, The mechanism that moves tape past sensing and recording devices.

transportation, document, Moving a document to the read station in an optical character reading device.

transposition, Interchanging of two things, such as characters.

transverse check, An error control method based on present rules of character formation.

trap, A trigger causing automatic transfer of control.

trap settings, Settings that control interrupts (see interrupt).

trapped program interrupt, A system in which there is an interrupt trap associated with each type of interrupt which may be set to either respond or ignore an event when it occurs.

trapping, A feature in which an unscheduled jump is made to a predetermined location when specific conditions occur (in the computer).

traps, interrupt, A program controlled trap is provided for each type of interrupt to prevent or allow the corresponding interrupt.

travel, pen, The length of the path that a pen moves from one end of a scale to another.

traveling wave tube, An electron tube used to amplify ultra-high frequencies.

tree, Diagrams that resemble branches and trunk of a tree.

trial run, A check for accuracy by using a sample or part of actual data before the full run.

tributary station, One of the many stations under control of a master station.

tributary trunk, A trunk circuit that connects a local exchange with a toll center or office.

trigger pair, A bistable circuit.

trigonometric functions, Mathematical functions of an angle or arc, such as sine, cosine, tangent, etc.

triple precision, A procedure for retaining three times as many digits as would be normally handled.

tripler, A circuit that multiplies the frequency of an input signal by three.

trouble ticket, A small form used for reporting circuit trouble in telephone testboard work.

troubleshoot, A procedure to search for and find a malfunction in a hardware unit or a mistake in a computer program.

true complement, The complement for a given notation system, e.g., the binary true complement is the 2s complement.

truncate A procedure to drop all the digits of a number that are to the right of the decimal point.

truncate, To drop digits from a number as contrasted with rounding off.

trunk, (1) One or more conductors of an electronics station, (2) a path for transfer of data or signals.

trunk circuit, A circuit that connects two data switching centers.

trunk, communication, Refers to a circuit between two telephone exchanges or switching centers, or from an exchange to a customer's switchboard.

trunk, communications, A telephone line between two central offices.

trunk, digit transfer, A set of wires used to transfer electrical pulses (numbers) in a computer.

trunk group, A set of trunk lines in communications between two switching centers or points that use the same terminal equipment.

trunk hunting, An arrangement in which a call is switched to the next number in sequence if the first number is busy.

trunk, intercepting, A trunk where a call is connected for action by an operator (telephone) in cases of a vacant number, changed number, or line out of order.

trunk, interoffice, In communications a direct trunk between central offices in the same exchange.

trunk, intertoll, See intertoll office trunk.

trunk, LD, A long distance (LD) trunk permits connection with local, secondary, primary, and zone centers.

trunk, one-way, A trunk between central exchanges in which traffic can only begin on one end.

trunk, recording, One used for communication between operators on long distance calls.

trunk, telephone, A telephone line between two central offices used for communication between subscribers.

trunk, terminal, A trunk circuit connecting two or more terminals (telephone).

trunk, tie, A telephone line that connects two branch exchanges.

trunk, tributary, A trunk circuit that connects a local exchange with a toll center or office.

truth table, A table showing result combinations in Boolean algebra.

TSC, An abbreviation for transmitter start code.

TSO-timesharing option, Used for timeshare systems in a request/response or conversational mode type of interaction between the system and the terminals (users). It is supported by the TSO command processes and TSO applications programs.

TTL compatible signals, Because most peripheral integrated circuits are MOS devices and most peripheral devices or units are TTL-compatible, e.g., require TTL signals, additional buffering or synchronous circuitry is usually needed to mate the controllers to the devices.

TTY, An abbreviation for Teletypewriter equipment.

tube, Usually a cathode ray tube (CRT) or a television-like device.

tube, cathode ray (CRT), A television-like display device attached to a computer or used as a remote terminal.

tube, display, A cathode ray tube (CRT), a television-like device.

tube, miniature, A small glass tube used in receivers.

tube, oscilloscope, A display device used in equipment testing.

tube, slave, A CRT (cathode ray tube, television-like device) that is connected to an identical master tube.

tube storage, Cathode ray tube storage (CRT).

tube, traveling wave, An electron tube used to amplify ultra-high frequencies.

tube, writing, A special tube in which an electron beam automatically writes or scans information.

tunnel diode, An electronic device with switching speeds of fractional billionths of seconds.

Turing machine, A unique mathematical abstraction of a device providing a model for computer-like procedures.

turnaround system, See reentry system.

turnaround time, 1 The time taken to 'turn round' a processing job, i.e., the time between submission of the job and its completion. 2 The time required to reverse the echo suppressors on a switched telephone circuit. 3 The time required for a system to transfer from the receive mode to the transmit mode, or vice versa.

turnaround time attributes, (1) The time needed to reverse the transmission direction in a channel, (2) the time between submitting a job to a computer center and getting the results back.

turnkey system, Refers to a computer system sold complete and ready to use for general or specific applications; requires no additional hardware modification or planning for immediate use.

turnkey system, Agreement by a supplier to install a complete computer system so that his or her firm has total responsibility for building, installing, testing, and implementing the system including hardware and software.

tutor, electronic, A teaching machine using programmed instruction.

TV camera, scanner, An optical recognition term relating to a device that puts a character onto a sensitive photoconductive target of a camera tube.

TV terminal (TVT), Generally consists of a keyboard, electromagnetic deflection-type display. Typically this unit utilizes an ordinary or modified TV set as a display, following FCC regulations.

two state variable, A variable that can assume two states, e.g., on, off, or 0, 1, etc. It is synonymous with binary variable.

two wire channel, A channel in which transmission is only in one direction at a time.

two wire system, A system in which communication is transmitted or received over a two wire circuit.

two's complement, A value obtained by subtracting a number from the base number.

two-way communications, The user not merely accepting transmissions like passive TV viewers, but permits the user to "pull" information desired from large pools of information, providing such services as video conferencing, QUBE systems in Columbus, Ohio and Houston, Texas, and other Viewdata and Teletext-type systems.

two-wire circuit, A system in which all transmitting and receiving is performed over one pair of wires (or equivalent).

TWX, See teletypewriter exchange service.

type bar, A long narrow bar that holds the type (set of characters) used on a bar printer.

type bar, fixed, A type bar on a printer that cannot be removed by an operator.

type bar, interchangeable, A type bar on a printer that can be removed by an operator.

type, data, Refers to the various kinds of information the computer can store. For example, different data types include alphanumeric or character data, decimal numbers, and integers.

type drum, A specific device used in some printers.

type face, A character style in optical character recognition as contrasted with type font.

type font, A type face of a specific size, e.g., 12-point GOTHIC.

type font, optical, A font that can be read by both people and machines.

typewriter, console, A typewriter/keyboard device used for computer operator communication with the computer system.

typewriter console monitor, A typewriter-like console device that signals the computer operator when attention is needed; it monitors the activity of the system.

typewriter, on-line, A typewriter device connected to a computer.

U

U format, A record format that is treated as completely unknown and unpredictable (see format).

UA, An abbreviation for user area.

UART-Universal Asychronous Receiver-Transmitter, Specific device that interfaces a word parallel controller or data terminal to a bit serial communication network.

UHF-ultra-high frequency, Range of frequencies extending from 300 to 3,000 Mhz; also TV channels 14 through 83.

ultimate tensile strength, The force per cross sectional unit area required to break a tape.

ultrasonic, A frequency higher than the range that can be heard.

ultrasonics, A technology involved with sounds that are too high in frequency to be heard by the human ear.

unallowable code check, An automatic check for a non-permissable code.

unallowable instruction digit, A combination of bits (character) that is not accepted as a valid operation code.

unary, A logical operation that requires only one input value. The negation, or NOT operation, is an example of a unary operation. Unary is synonymous with monadic, and contrasted with binary or dyadic.

unbalanced, A line or network in which the impedances on opposite sides are unequal.

unbalanced error, A condition in which the average of all error values is not zero.

unblind (blind), A selective procedure to prevent some values from printing.

unblocking, A process of separating one or more records from a block of information.

unbundling, Pricing certain types of software and services separately from hardware.

uncertainty, quantization, A measure of uncertainty related to information loss.

uncommitted storage list, A list of blocks of storage that are not allocated for particular use at that moment.

unconditional, Without any conditions.

unconditional branch, A computer instruction that causes a branch to another part of the computer program (not based on a test) as contrasted with branch, conditional.

unconditional jump, Same as unconditional branch.

unconditional transfer instruction, Synonymous with unconditional branch.

underflow, The creation of a fractional quantity smaller than can be stored in a register.

undetected error rate, The ratio of the number of bits incorrectly received (but undetected or uncorrected by the equipment) to the total number of bits sent.

uniformity, As in magnetic tape, the extent to which the output is free from variations in amplitude.

uniformity, ink, The extent to which the ink has a variation in light intensity over the area of a character (in optical character recognition).

uniformly accessible storage, A type of storage in which the variation in access time is minimal.

uninterruptable power, Many semiconductor memory systems require continuous power and can be wiped clean even with the briefest power outage or "brown out." Uninterruptable power supplies or systems (UPS) represent an answer to this common problem as well as to other computer system components that require the same type power.

union catalog, A compiled list of the contents of two or more magnetic tape libraries.

union gate, Same as gate, OR (see gates).

unit, 1 A basic element. 2 A device having a special function.

unit, arithmetic, Synonymous with ALU (Arithmetic and Logic Unit).

unit element, An alphabetic signal element having a duration equal to a unit interval of time.

unit interval, In communications a unit of measure of time.

unit record equipment, Punched card machines such as sorters, collators, tabulators, etc.

unit, segregating, A unit that separates cards (such as a collator).

unit separator, A specific character used to mark logical boundaries between units of data.

uniterm, A word or symbol used to retrieve information.

uniterm indexing, A system of indexing that uses single terms (uniterms) to define a document uniquely.

unity, A set or collection considered as a single thing.

universal asychronous receiver-transmitter (UART), Transmitter converts parallel data bits into serial form for transmission over two-wire lines.

universal button box, A coined term for a set of push buttons whose functions are determined by the computer program.

universal decimal classification, An expansion of the Dewey decimal system.

universal interconnecting device, A unit that can be used with multiple systems to switch units from one system to another.

universal synchronous/asynchronous receiver/transmitter (USART), Usually an MOS/LSI device that performs all the receiving and transmitting functions associated with synchronous data communications, STR, BSC, Bi-sync., and others.

universal Turing machine, A Turing machine that can be used to simulate any other Turing machine.

universe, statistical, The whole group of things or phenomena which are similar in some way, e.g., all females between the ages of 18 and 25.

Unix, A popular machine-independent operating system expected to become a standard; developed by the American electronics giant AT&T.

unload, To remove information (such as from magnetic tape).

unpack, A process to "recover" packed data to its original form.

unscheduled maintenance time, The time between discovery of a machine failure and the return of equipment to normal operation.

unused time, The time that is available for use but is not used for machine operation.

unwind, To code, explicitly, all the operations of a cycle.

up time, The time when equipment is available for productive work as contrasted with down time.

UPC bar-code scanner, Universal Product Code (UPC) system with a photoelectronic scanner that can read print directly and cheaply in the form of bar codes of several types, transmitting that information to the computer for reaction and processing.

UPC-Universal Product Code, The symbols in the form of vertical bars of varying widths reflect light emitted by an optical scanner, the code numbers going to computers for transmission to other sources and to control printing devices to provide customer receipts after the computer responds with the identification of the product and the prices.

update, Refers to changes of the data in a file or record to incorporate new or more current information.

upload, Refers to transfers of copies of a program, file, or other information from the user's own terminal to a remote database or other computer over a communications line. Upload is synonymous with up-line loading.

uptime, The period of time during which a computer system is up, or operating correctly.

USART, See universal synchronous/asynchronous receiver/transmitter.

USASCII, An abbreviation for USA Standard Code for Information Interchange.

use time, operation, The time that equipment is in actual use (not all the time it is turned on).

μSEC, An abbreviation for microsecond, that is, one millionth of a second.

user, The person or company that uses a terminal (attached to a computer).

User Area, See UA.

user area, An area on magnetic disk storage containing user programs and subroutines, contrasted with reserved areas containing compilers, etc.

user area (UA), Area on a magnetic disk for storing semi-permanent data such as programs, subprograms, and subroutines. In contrast, reserved areas are used for storing things that may not be written into, such as compilers and track and sector information.

user modes, time-sharing, One of the following modes a user may be in: inactive, command, ready, running, waiting.

user, time-sharing, The person that uses the system from a time-sharing terminal.

user's group, An organization of people who use the same kind of equipment.

user-friendly, Generally refers to computing systems that provide for the easier use of capabilities and limitations of the operator. A user-friendly system is ready to use and easy to understand for a wide variety of people, rather than forcing the user to become expert in the technicalities of computing.

utility functions, Auxiliary operations such as file copying, file printing, and various other utility (support) functions (same as general utility functions).

utility model, A model that is studied and restudied to improve the system.

utility program, A program in general support of a computer; for example, monitoring routines, startup, READ, and others.

utility program, Computer programs, such as sorts, card-to-tape, tape-to-print, etc.

utility routine, Computer program routines used for housekeeping and service functions.

utility system, A system or set of programs that performs miscellaneous utility functions such as tape-to-disk, tape-to-print, etc.

utilization measure, data transmission, The ratio of useful data to total data.

V

V(ss), Ground for MOS circuits; voltage for substrate sources.

VAB (voice answer back), A prerecorded voice response to a telephone-type terminal that is linked to a computer.

vacuum servo, The device that holds magnetic tape in place; maintained by air pressure on one side of the tape.

vacuum tube, An electronic component consisting of electrodes placed inside an evacuated glass tube.

valence electron, An electron that is only loosely connected to its atom; hence it can be dislodged easily.

validation, Refers to data tests to determine if the system correctly adheres to a designated criterion, such as prescribed limits or specified order.

validity, The degree to which repeated processes obtain the same result.

validity check, A specific check made for the accuracy of character coding; in addition can be a reasonableness check on data.

validity, data, A measure of acceptability of data, e.g., if male was coded a 1 and a female coded a 2, a code of 3 would not be valid, or an unacceptable code pattern.

value, The numerical quantity of a data element.

value, absolute, The value of a number irrespective of its sign.

value code, A value of any of the elements in a code set.

value, desired, A hoped for or chosen value.

value, E, The difference between the radius of the outer edge of tape in a roll and the radius of the outer edge of a tape reel flange.

value, end, A value to be compared with an index, count, etc., to see if the end of that processing has been reached.

value, ideal, An expected or desired value.

value sign, absolute, The symbol, e.g., [1-4] used to indicate an absolute value number.

value-added carrier, In communications, common carriers authorized to lease raw trunks from the transmission carriers, augment these facilities with computerized switching, and provide enhanced or "value-added" services, particularly packet switching, and other services for which various charges are made.

value-added carrier class, A new class of communications services that usually relates to packet-switching services but may also relate to other computerized types of service offerings by many major new providers.

varactors, Used in spiral circuits, especially in satellite tracking.

variable, A variable is a symbolic name representing a value that changes during the program's execution.

variable address, An address that is modified before it is used each time.

variable, Boolean, A two-valued variable, such as true or false, on or off, etc.

variable connector, A flowchart symbol indicating a programmed switch capability.

variable, continuous, A variable that can assume all values on continuous scale as contrasted to discrete variable.

variable, controlled, A value or condition manipulated, regulated, or controlled by computer.

variable cycle operation, Action in which any cycle may be of different length (in a computer).

variable, dependent, A variable whose value varies by some function of another quantity.

variable, discrete, A variable that assumes only a whole number value.

variable field length, Data fields that can have varying numbers of characters from record to record.

variable, global, A variable whose name may be referred to by a main computer program and all its subroutines.

variable, independent, A variable whose value is not a direct function of another variable as contrasted with dependent variable.

variable length, A varying number of words per block (or records per block).

variable length field, A data field that may be of varying lengths as necessary.

variable, local, A data variable whose name is only defined in a subroutine or subprogram and not known to the main computer program.

variable, logic, Alterable internal logic design (electronic).

variable, manipulated, A variable that is changed to regulate a condition.

variable, measured (physical), A physical quantity such as temperature, pressure, speed, etc., that is to be measured.

variable name, The alphanumeric name assigned by a programmer to represent a variable in a computer program.

variable point, The point (such as decimal point) in a number.

variable quantity, A quantity that may assume different values.

variable range, A variable's range consists of those values the variable can assume. The range runs from the lowest possible value the variable can assume to the highest possible value it can assume. If, during the execution of a program, a variable is assigned a number not within its range, a value range error will occur.

variable, subscripted, A variable followed by one or more subscripts in parentheses, such as X(I,J), A(2), TABLE(M,N), etc.

variable, two state, A variable which can assume two states, e.g., on, off, or 0, 1, etc. (synonymous with binary variable).

variable, two valued, Same as two state variable and binary variable.

variable word, Varying numbers of characters in a unit (word) of data.

variable-length record, A data record whose length is not fixed to any constant value. The actual length of a particular record is attached to the front of the record's data so that the program can recognize a record's length.

variable-length record file, A file containing data records that vary in length (the number of characters vary in each record).

variance analysis, A statistical estimate of probabilities (by comparing variances).

variations, calculus of, A calculus (mathematical) relating to maxima/minima theory of definite integrals.

variolosser, A variable attenuator or a device whose loss is controlled by voltage or current.

varioplex, An electronic device used in a time-sharing multiplex system.

variplotter, A high-accuracy graphic recording device.

varistor, A passive resistor whose resistance is a function of current or voltage.

VCA, An abbreviation for valve control amplifier.

VDT-Visual Display Terminal, Generally includes all devices that permit input to a computer by a user, not a computer operator, specifically, through a keyboard and/or some other manual input method (light pen, cursor control, function buttons, etc.) and whose primary output method is visual, either alphabetic, graphic, color, or combinations.

vector, Vector quantities have both magnitude and direction in space. For example, velocity is a vector while temperature is not.

vector, column, The elements of a single column of a matrix are the components of a vector.

vector line, A line denoting magnitude and direction, contrasted with scalar denoting magnitude only.

vector quantity, A quantity that has both magnitude and direction.

vector, transfer, A specific table that lists transfer instructions of all the programs in memory.

vectored interrupt, When an interrupt occurs, the processor jumps (vectors) to a specific location that contains the instructions on how to service the interrupt.

vector-mode display, A mode in which straight lines between two points can be displayed.

veeder counter, A device that counts punched cards in peripheral equipment.

velocity limit, A limit that the rate of change of a variable cannot exceed.

Venn diagram, A diagram showing set relationships; shows overlapping relationships.

verb, computer, Refers to an instruction in a programming language that causes action. For example, ENTER, WRITE, and PRINT are all verbs.

verbs, processor, Verbs used by a language processor that do not cause action at object time.

verbs, program, Verbs that generate machine instructions in an object program as contrasted with processor verbs.

verification, The act of comparing data to the original source data.

verification, design, The tests used to determine that a design meets the required specifications.

verification, program, The task of proving that a given program works correctly.

vertical display, The height in inches of the display screen (CRT).

vertical format, Arrangement of data up and down on a page or paper as contrasted with format, horizontal.

vertical output stage, In a CRT (cathode ray tube), the power amplifier stage in a vertical sync circuit.

vertical raster count, The number of addressable positions across the height of a cathode ray tube.

vertical redundance, In a parity checking system, an even number of bits in odd parity system or vice versa.

vertical redundancy check (VRC), An error-checking method whereby parity bits are used for each character.

Very Low Frequency, See VLF.

VHF-Very High Frequency, The range of frequencies extending from 30 to 300 MHz, also TV channels 2 through 13.

VHSIC-Very High-Speed Integrated Circuit, The American Department of Defense (DOD) attempt to develop superspeed integrated circuits.

vibrating-sample magnetometer (VSM), A device used to determine the magnetic properties of magnetic material.

video digitizer, A typical video image analyzer digitizes and stores video from a TV camera or image source, enters it into the host computer for display on a TV monitor.

video display units, data transmission, Any input or output equipment capable of displaying information on a screen, usually a CRT (see CRT).

video picture composition, Composed of thin horizontal lines that glow with varying intensity and change quickly. In the U.S., there are 525 lines in a standard video picture, created every 1/30th second by the electronic beam that zigzags across the screen, top to bottom.

video, reverse, Dark characters displayed on a light background of a screen. Reverse video is analogous to books, where black-inked characters are printed on white pages.

video signal, composite, The signal that consists of picture signal, blanking pulses, and sync pulses in a CRT (cathode ray tube).

video terminal, A small computer or specific device for entering information into and receiving information from a computer system and displaying it on a screen. A typewriter-like keyboard is used to enter information.

video-data interrogators, In communications a device comprised of a keyboard and separable associated display.

videodisc, A laser-read direct access device used for storing audio and visual information to be replayed on a television screen. Videodiscs are similar to compact disks (CD-ROM) for computers.

videodisc computer system, Players of about 35 pounds or more and appearing much like a phonograph provide both sound and pictures, but the disc itself is searchable for specific tracks containing bits of information in high density. On some systems 54,000 frames, each numbered, can provide massive database storage and very rapid retrieval. Recording on the disc is simple, fast, and provides one of the most efficient information retrieval tools known.

videodisc pits, optical, Means that the pickup system involves a low-power laser beam so that nothing actually touches the tracks (pits) on the disc. Tracks on the disc are actually a series of pits of information as coded and read from a coated reflective metallic surface.

videograph, A high-speed cathode ray printer.

videotex, Refers to the various systems which make computer-based information available through VDUs and modified TV sets to people at home and at work.

Viewdata, A generic term for the use of ordinary television sets and adapters (decoders) to provide two-way communication with very large and varied databases through the use of telephone-computer connections. Began in England in 1978 as a commercial venture, this type system has spread around the world with such other names as Antiope, Videotext, and others.

Viewdata-type systems, A service developed by the British Post Office that has been licensed by many companies in other lands, this system conveys information over telephone lines to the consumer's or business person's TV set, as selected and ordered individually from large computer databases. It is controlled in an interactive manner and compatible with Teletext-type systems that use the TV set specially encoded or with an encoder but without the telephone lines, using the blanking spaces on the screen without interfering with normal reception.

violation subroutines, When a violation of subroutines occurs, a violation subroutine takes over control.

VIP, An abbreviation for Variable Information Processing.

virgin coil, A paper or plastic tape with no punches in it.

virgin medium, A storage medium with no data recorded in it.

virtual, Apparent, as contrasted with actual or absolute.

virtual address, The immediate address or specific real-time address.

virtual address, effective, The address developed after indirect addressing and/or indexing have taken place.

virtual memory, (1) Using disk storage as an extension of main computer memory, (2) a type of memory in which paging or segmenting is used to simulate larger memory.

virtual storage, A technique designed to maximize and optimize the storage available in a computer by using areas on secondary storage devices as extensions of internal storage. Pages of data are swapped back and forth from disk and main memory.

virtual storage, paging, In a virtual storage system, paging refers to the swapping of data and programs back and forth from real storage to virtual storage.

VisiCalc, A software package used for financial planning and budgeting. VisiCalc led to a number of similar products being launched, such as spreadsheets.

visual display console, A CRT, cathode ray tube, television-like device that permits visual display of computer contents.

visual display terminal (VDT), Includes all devices that permit input to a computer by a user and usually with a keyboard, light pen, or special function keys, with a visual output; also called TVT, for TV terminal by amateurs or computerists.

visual display unit, Same as display unit.

visual display unit (VDU), A computer device that displays information on a television-like screen. One type of visual display unit is a CRT (Cathode Ray Tube). Visual display units usually have an attached keyboard used for entering data.

visual scanner, Devices that scan optically.

vital records, Records that are essential for legal and/or financial purposes in a company.

vital records center, A place used to house records classified as vital to the organization.

vital records code, A coding system used for reference to vital records.

VLF, An abbreviation for Very Low Frequency.

VLSI-Very Large Scale Integration, Usually means chips with more than 10,000 transistors but can range up to 100,000 or more components.

VMOS, Offers very tight geometries for chips increasing densities and speed-power product over and above that would be achieved with NMOS; air within the V-groove of the chip provides isolation.

vocabulary, (1) A list of operating codes or instructions for a specific computer, (2) a unit of information treated as an entity.

vocabulary, sophisticated, An advanced and elaborate set of computer instructions (that perform mathematical operations).

Voice Answer Back (VAB), Audio response devices can link computer systems to telephone networks. They provide voice responses to inquiries made from telephone-type terminals.

voice frequency, A frequency within the range used for transmission of speech as in telephone lines.

voice grade channel, This type channel permits transmission of speech and accommodates frequencies from 300 to 3000 Hz. It is also suitable for the transmission of digital or analog data.

voice recognition, Refers to a technology in which human voice patterns are analyzed by a machine to determine words spoken. Recognized words and commands are sent to a computer system that converts them into physical functions.

voice terminals, Voice input and voice output terminals are most popular, voice answer back (VAB) systems were the earliest used. Voice input systems followed and voice synthesizers have become available for thousands of applications; voice logging, voice inquiry are some of the types.

voice unit (VU), A measure of the volume of electrical speech.

void, An undesired absence of ink on a document.

volatile, A characteristic of data that can be lost during power failure.

volatile dynamic storage, A storage medium that depends on external power to retain stored information.

volatile file, A rapidly changing file (very active file).

volatile memory, A storage medium that depends on power to retain stored information.

volatile storage, Storage that loses information in case of power failure.

volatility, The loss or alteration of electrical energy in computer storage.

volt, Unit of measure of electric potential.

voltage, Electrical pressure, i.e., the force that causes current to flow through an electrical conductor; the difference of potential between any two conductors.

voltage, reference, The voltage used as a standard of reference in an analog computer.

voltage regulation, A measure of voltage stability under varying load conditions.

volume, A unit of external storage that can be read or written by a single access mechanism or I/O device.

volume control, automatic (AVC), An electronic system in radio receivers.

volume, reference, The magnitude of a complex electric wave that corresponds to speech or music.

volume statistics, Groups of facts related to the nature and level of an operation.

volume table of contents (VTOC), A file containing the names, sizes, locations, and other pertinent information about all the files contained on a large, fixed disk. On small floppy disks, the VTOC is usually called the directory.

volume test, Using a large volume of actual data to check for computer program errors.

volume unit, A unit of measurement for electrical speech power in communication work.

voting processors, With one instruction stream being executed, but with 3 or more separate processors to execute these instructions, voting proceeds by comparison. If any result differs, the erring CPU is "voted" out of the configuration. The remaining machines then continue to operate until the faulty CPU is repaired; often a fourth processor is kept on standby to replace an erring processor.

VRAM-Video Read-Only Memory, VRAM provides a direct link between microcomputers and the video input of a television or CRT.

VTAM-Virtual Telecommunications Access Method, Access method or line that gives users at remote terminals access to applications programs.

VTOC (volume table of contents), An index near the beginning of a volume (of data) describing the contents.

VTR-Video Tape Recorder; also VCR-Video Cassette Recorder, Open reel and cassette tape systems for recording and playing video programs, graphics, and data programs.

VU (voice unit), A measure of the volume of electrical speech.

W

WACK-Wait Before Transmitting Positive Acknowledgement, A binary synchronous communications sequence sent by a receiving station to indicate that it is temporarily not ready to receive.

WADS (Wide Area Data Service), Much like WATS (Wide Area Telephone Service).

wafer, The silicon ingot that is cut into thin slices on which all the chips are fabricated; classes are 3-inch, 4-inch, and larger; slices as well as ingots are known as wafers.

wait, A condition in time-sharing or real-time in which a time delay occurs before getting information.

wait condition, A circumstance in which transition into the ready state depends on occurrence of events.

waiting list, A list of programs waiting to be processed (synonymous with queue).

waiting state, The state of an interrupt that has not yet become active (but is armed).

waiting time, Waiting for a resource to become available for use.

wand bar code readers, Using various optical wand scanners, data can be quickly entered by "reading" shelf labels, UPC codes, and other codes directly to the computer, the wand being low-cost, simple, portable, and often shaped like a ballpoint pen.

wand, terminal, Refers to a specific input device used to read optical bar code labels by sensing the optical pattern of the light and dark areas.

warmstart, On most systems, a specific way of resetting a computer without erasing the contents of memory. The program in memory is preserved, and only elements of the operating system are reset.

warm-up period, The time needed after energizing a device, before its rated output is reached.

warm-up time, The time needed for a device to get energized.

warning marker, destination (DWM), A reflective spot on magnetic tape that is sensed photoelectrically to indicate the end of the tape is coming.

watchdog timer, A specific timer used to prevent endless program looping in the computer.

WATS (wide-area telephone service), A service that provides the customer with the ability to call within a certain zone for a flat monthly rate (no charges per call).

watt, A unit of electric power required to do work at the rate of 1 joule per second; power experience when 1 ampere of direct current flows through a resistance of 1 ohm.

wave, Physical activity that rises and falls, or advances and retreats, periodically as it travels through a medium; a propagated disturbance usually periodic, such as a radio wave, a sound wave, or a carrier wave for transmitting data signals.

wave, carrier, The frequency of a signal with no intelligence until it is modulated by another signal of intelligence.

wave form, The specific shape of a wave.

wave, short, AM broadcasting in the frequency vicinity of 20 to 40 mc.

wave, sky, A wave that travels through the air rather than along the ground.

waveguides, Metal tubes used to interconnect points in uhf equipment.

waveshape, Same as wave form.

way station, One of the stations on a multipoint circuit.

way-operated circuit, A circuit shared by three or more stations (party line).

WDPC (Western Data Processing Center), One of the largest university computer centers, oriented to business applications (at UCLA).

wear product, Material that is detached from tape during use, such as oxide particles.

wear resistance, Built-in resistance in printing ribbons to reduction of quality after use.

weighted area masks, A set of characters (in character recognition) which theoretically render all input specimens unique, regardless of size or style.

weighted average, An average in which some values were valued more heavily than others.

Western Data Processing Center (WDPC), One of the largest university computer centers, oriented to business applications (at UCLA).

what if studies, With relevant data usually from databases, analysts and executives can investigate the implications of a question, such as "what if we had increased price 6 months ago, what would total profit be" and other similar projection or exploratory problems to aid planning decisions.

wheel printer, A printer that has type face mounted on wheels or discs.

Wide Area Data Service (WADS), Much like WATS (Wide Area Telephone Service).

wideband data sets, Data sets that permit rates of 72,000 bits per second.

width control, A hand control on a CRT (television-like device) that controls the width of the picture.

width, stroke, A distance measurement of a stroke (see stroke).

width, tape, The physical width of magnetic tape used by a particular unit.

willful intercept, Intercepting messages when there is station equipment or line trouble.

Winchester disk, A popular type of fixed disk used with microcomputer systems. A type of 'hard' disk in contrast to 'floppy' disks.

Winchester technology disk drive, Hard disks that have non-removable media, disk surface and heads permanently sealed in a contamination free chamber, large capacities, fast access, long operating life, operator proof due to its non-interference technology, and protection features.

wind (magnetic tape), The way in which tape is would on a reel (uniform or uneven, etc.).

winding, A conductive path of wire.

winding, drive, That pulse of current in a winding (wire).

window, display, Generally refers to a rectangular region of the screen which can display specific graphics images independent of the rest of the screen's display.

wing panel, A panel that is added on sides of existing panels.

wire board, A plug board, control panel, etc.

wire, magnetic, A wire made of or coated with magnetic material.

wire network, private, A network (telephone or telegraph) reserved for use by one customer.

wire, open, A conductor above the surface of the ground, i.e., on insulators.

wire, order, An auxiliary wire circuit used by maintenance people in communications installations.

wire printer, A type of printer that forms characters by forcing a set of wires against the ribbon or paper.

wire, storage, A wire coated with magnetic material and used for magnetic recording.

wire wrap, A method of electrical connection made by wrapping wires around specially designed terminals.

wired program computer, A computer controlled by a device such as a plugboard (wired sequence of operations).

wiring board, Same as a control panel.

word, (1) A set of characters, (2) a unit of data, and (3) a unit of storage.

word, alphabetic, Consists only of letters.

word, banner, The first word in a data file record.

word, call, The word that identifies a computer program subroutine.

word, CANCL status, The status word indicating that the remote computing system has deleted some information.

word capacity, The number of characters in a computer word.

word, communications status, A special word location in storage, containing status information.

word, computer, Generally concerns a string of bits which can occupy a single addressable location. A word (of 4, 8, 16, 32, or 64 bits) is interpreted by different processors of the computer as different items, such as instructions, quantities, and alphanumeric characters.

word, computer, A set of 1s and 0s that is a unit of data or instructions in a computer.

word, double, Multiple adjacent bytes beginning on a double work boundary that can be handled as a single unit.

word, effective, The word actually accessed in a computer operation on a single word.

word, error status, The status word indicating that the remote computing system has detected an error.

word, fixed, A computer characteristic of a constant number (fixed number) of characters per word (see fixed-length word).

word, fixed-length, A computer word with a fixed number of characters (with no variation from one word to another in that computer).

word, half, Equivalent to half a computer word (two bytes in many computers) (see byte).

word index, (1) A computer storage word or register used to modify addresses in instructions, (2) an index based on the selection of words used in a document.

word, information, A computer word that isn't an instruction (data as opposed to instructions).

word, instruction, A word of computer storage containing an instruction (or will be treated as an instruction).

word length, Various processors use various numbers of bits to make up a word. The word length may either be a fixed or a variable number of bits. The 16- and 32-bit word systems are most popular.

word location, effective, The actual storage location (indicated in an address in a word addressing instruction).

word, long, The longest element a computer can process in computer words, such as double word, full word, etc.

word, machine, An information unit of a particular computer.

word mark, An indicator used to denote the beginning (or end) of a word.

word, numeric, A word containing only numeric characters.

word oriented, A type of memory system used in computers.

word, parameter, A word in a computer program subroutine used to specify certain data and conditions.

word, partial, Using part of a word.

word period, The amount of time (interval) between signals representing digits.

word processing, Interactive information-retrieval systems, management information systems, text editing, translation, and typesetting systems controlled by small computers.

word processing (WP) communications, Communicate in a dial-up mode, can establish a network allowing a draft to be routed for review and comment before transmission, often connected to copier-printers for mass printing, distribution of specific product changes, etc.

word processing, automatic document generation, Can assemble documents automatically from previously stored sentences, paragraphs, or pages with automatic insertion of variable data; can compile letters, conditionally - one letter to specific customers as personalized for prospects, etc.

word processing/data processing, The convergence of data and word processing is progressing rapidly due to popularity of distributed processing, drop in microcomputer prices, gains in communications and microform technology, ink jet printing, and advances in software support for distributed and decentralized systems.

word processor, This type of software package generally allows the user to input text to the system which can then be edited or reformatted at will before being printed out.

word, READY status, The status word indicating that the remote computing system is waiting for entry from the terminal.

word separator, A specific character used to separate words of data.

word, short, A half word in many computers.

word space, The area or space required to hold a word in devices such as magnetic disk, drum, tape, etc.

word, status, A computer word containing information necessary to continue processing after an interruption.

word time, The time needed to move a word past a particular point (or from one point to another).

word time comparator, The circuitry used to compare the word time counter to a specified word time.

word transfer, The parallel transfer of all the bits in a computer word (at the same time).

word variable, Varying numbers of characters in a unit (word) of data.

word wrap, A procedure to reformat text in a word processing system after insertions or deletions. It prevents a user from spending more time reformatting than inserting and deleting. In automatic word wrap, a program reformats a paragraph each time editing extends or shortens a line, so that text always appears neatly positioned.

words, constant, Descriptive data that is fixed (constant)

words, input-output request, Control words (in the computer) used in input/output request processing.

words masks, Words of particular bit patterns used in logical operations.

words per minute, See WPM.

words, reserved, Special Cobol programming language words that cannot be used for data names.

work cycle, A sequence of memory elements needed to perform a task, job, or execution to yield production.

work distribution chart, A listing of duties and responsibilities of personnel related to the job under study.

work in process queue, Items that have been partially processed and are "queued" (waiting in line) to be completed.

work load, An amount of work to be accomplished in a given period of time.

work measurement, A set of rules used to establish relationships between the quantity of work performed and the man and/or machine power used.

work process schedule, The schedule of electronic data processing activity to most effectively use equipment.

work queue, input, The line of jobs to be submitted for processing.

work queue, output, Output from computer jobs that are in line to be printed or transmitted into final form.

work tape(s) sorting, Same as scratch tapes used in sorting.

workfile, Often this refers to a temporary working copy of the program currently being edited.

working data files, Non-permanent files (temporary usage).

working equipment, That set of equipment that is operating while standby equipment is not operating.

working memory, The memory that stores information for processing and releases it after it is used.

working routine, A computer program routine that produces the results, as contrasted with housekeeping, etc.

working space, A section of storage reserved for data being processed, i.e., temporary storage.

working standard, A system in communications used to compare the transmission quality of other telephone systems or parts of systems.

working storage, Used as temporary storage for intermediate results of processing; may refer to internal storage as well as disk storage.

worst case, The set of circumstances in which the maximum stress is placed on a system.

worst case design, A circuit design (or other) designed to function with all the worst possible conditions occurring at the same time.

wow and flutter, Terms used to describe changes in output frequency caused by tape speed variations at low and high rates, respectively.

WPM, An abbreviation for words per minute.

WP-Word Processing boilerplate applications, Operator merges previously-recorded text segments to create a new document; accepted and often used procedures for storing and indexing segments so that they may be combined into new documents quickly and with minimum operator activity.

wrap around storage, Returning to the lowest numbered storage location after the highest numbered one.

wrap, wire, A method of electrical connection made by wrapping wires around specially designed terminals.

writable control store, Usually a RAM, a name given to read/write memory used in the control portion of a system enabling the system designer to change the external characteristics of the system.

write, A command for the process of transferring data from a computer to an output device.

write, gather, An operation that "gathers" non-consecutive locations in computer memory to form an output record.

write head, Generally refers to a magnetic device used to write data on a storage medium, such as a magnetic tape or disk.

write key, Concerns a code in the program status double word that may be tested to determine whether or not a program may write into specific storage locations.

write lockout, A situation in time-sharing that prevents programs from writing at that time.

write, memory lock, A write protection field in the memory of some computers.

write operation, scatter, Getting data from one place but transferring parts of it to several output areas.

write time, The time needed to record information (output).

write-protect disable, A specific system that overrides the physical write-protect tab on a disk, letting a software manufacturer write software to write-protected disks without inserting or removing tabs.

writer, output, A service program that moves data from the output queue to an output device.

WRU-Who Are You?, Transmission control character used for switching on an answerback unit in the station with which the connection has been set up, for initiating a response including station ID of persons, equipment, or station status.

WS, An abbreviation for working storage.

XYZ

xerographic printer, Usually a page printer in which the character pattern is set for a full page before printing using the principle of xerography, the technique used in copies.

xerography, A patented dry copying process.

X-mas tree sorting, A method used in the internal part of a sort program.

XMT, Abbreviation for transmit.

XMTR, Abbreviation for transmitter.

XY plotter, Devices used with a computer to plot graphs.

XY recorder, A recorder that makes a record of one voltage with respect to another.

yield strength, The minimum force per unit cross-sectional area at which tape deforms.

yoke, A group of heads in magnetic recording that are fastened together.

yoke, deflection, The ring around the neck of a writing tube that contains the deflection coils.

zap, To erase.

zata coding indexing, A unique library system of indexing documents.

zata coding system, A system of coordinate indexing.

zener, A semiconductor diode capable of conducting heavy currents.

zener diode coupling, Circuit modules that use zener diodes for coupling circuits.

zero, Nothing, the digit "0" used for place holding in numbers.

zero binary, One of the two binary digits (0 and 1) that represents the lack of magnitude (the off condition of on/off).

zero center, A special telephone trunk switching center serving a group of primary centers.

zero complement, A complementing method.

zero compression, A procedure to eliminate the storage of insignificant leading zeros, and these are to the left of the most significant digits.

zero condition, The state of a magnetic cell when it represents zero.

zero, count interrupt, An interrupt triggered when a count pulse interrupt has produced a zero in a clock counter.

zero elimination, A process used to eliminate leftmost zeros before printing a number.

zero fill, A procedure to fill or pad in which the unused portion of a field, record, or fixed-length data block is padded with zeros. For example, if a numeric field is 8 digits long, and the number 714 is inserted into it, the zero fill routine would pad the leading portion with zeros, after which it would read 00000714.

zero kill, A special feature in some card sorters.

zero match gate, Same as agree, OR (see gates).

zero output, The output from a magnetic cell in the zero condition.

zero proof, The procedure of adding plus and minus values (to get a zero result) in verifying accuracies of totals.

zero punch, A punch in the third row from the top of a punched card.

zero suppress, Procedure to eliminate zeros or other insignificant characters from a computer printout.

zero suppression, A procedure to convert computable numerals into human-readable format.

zero suppression, The process that eliminates zero at the left of a data field so they don't appear when the number is printed.

zero-access, The ability to obtain data in a relatively short period of time.

zero-access addition, Adding a number to another number in a computer where the resulting sum ends up in place of the second number.

zero-access storage, An incorrect term implying that no time is required to access storage, although the time is very small.

zero-address instruction, A computer instruction with no addresses.

zeroize, To fill storage space with zeros (in a computer).

zero-level address, A computer instruction address that is used as data by the instruction of which it is a part (synonymous with immediate address).

zeros, leading, Zeros appearing to the left of a number in a storage location. For example, the number '00843' has 2 leading zeros, and the number '000943' has 3 leading zeros.

zone, The 12, 11, or 0 punches in a punched card; also, the portion of character coding that is needed to represent non-numerical data.

zone, dead, The range of values that a signal can be altered without changing the outgoing response (synonymous with switching blank, dead space, and similar to neutral zone).

zone, minus, The part of a code that represents a minus sign in a number.

zone, neutral, The range of values of parameters in a control system in which no control action occurs.

zone, plus, The part of a code that represents a plus sign of a number.

zone punch, The punch (11, 12, 0) in a punched card that when combined with numeric punches creates non-numeric characters.

zoned format, A format used in binary-coded decimal representation in computer storage (see format).

ZOOM, An assembler or compiler which is part of GAP (General Assembly Program).

NOTES

<u>NOTES</u>

NOTES

<u>NOTES</u>

NOTES

NOTES